THE PASSAGE TO EUROPE

Luuk van Middelaar

THE PASSAGE TO EUROPE

HOW A CONTINENT BECAME A UNION

Translated by Liz Waters

YALE UNIVERSITY PRESS
NEW HAVEN AND LONDON

Published with the support of the Dutch Foundation for Literature.

Originally published in Dutch by Historische Uitgeverij as *De passage naar Europa*
– geschiedenis van een begin © Luuk van Middelaar 2009

For information about this and other Yale University Press publications please contact:
US Office: sales.press@yale.edu   yalebooks.com
Europe Office: sales@yaleup.co.uk   www.yalebooks.co.uk

Set in Minion Pro by IDSUK (DataConnection) Ltd
Printed in Great Britain by TJ International Ltd, Padstow, Cornwall

Library of Congress Cataloging-in-Publication Data

Middelaar, Luuk van, 1973–
[Passage naar Europa. English]
    The passage to Europe : how a continent became a union / Luuk van Middelaar.
        pages cm
    Translation of: De passage naar Europa.
    Includes bibliographical references and index.
    ISBN 978-0-300-18112-8 (alk. paper)
1. European Union—History.   2. Europe—Politics and government—20th century.
    I. Title.
    JN30.M53513 2013
    341.242'209–dc23

                                                                    2013001315

A catalogue record for this book is available from the British Library.

10 9 8 7 6 5 4 3 2 1

'But shan't we have to accept battle?' remarked Prince Andrew.

'We shall if everybody wants it; it can't be helped. But believe me, my dear boy, there is nothing stronger than those two: patience and time, they will do it all.'

Leo Tolstoy, *War and Peace*

Contents

Preface

Deciding on a date proved as difficult as deciding what to say. The prime minister's political address on Europe that, by sheer anticipation, grew into 'The Speech', had already been postponed several times when Number 10 discovered that the chosen day would now coincide with the fiftieth anniversary of the Treaty of Franco-German Friendship, on Tuesday 22 January 2013. A sacrosanct affair, gate-crashing it might just prove one diplomatic affront too many. Bringing the event forward by a day would mean jostling for the limelight with the second inauguration of the American president, who that very week had warned the British prime minister that cutting links with Brussels would only reduce London's clout in Washington. Opting for the apparently safe date of Friday 19 January and a venue in the Netherlands (preferring its capital Amsterdam over government seat The Hague, since that would allow his good friend the Dutch prime minister politely to keep his distance), he was forced by an escalating terrorist crisis in North Africa to re-postpone to the 23rd – at which point he decided that a packed room at the London office of an American news agency would do just as well. Thus, even before its leader had spoken, one thing had already become clear to the British public: an attempt to redefine the country's relationship with the rest of Europe would not be without its constraints.

This is merely the most recent episode in a long, continent-wide story that is set to continue for many years to come, but nowhere do the key questions and contradictions in the European Union stand in such sharp relief as they do in the British debate. What is Europe for? It seems we are faced with a choice between two visions: either it is just a market, a service provider, a means to an end, something you can be practical about, or it is a political project, a dream, a promise, in some sense an end in itself, an emotional matter. Or is this the wrong way of looking at it?

What drives the Union and why is it moving at all? Some would point to a Brussels bureaucratic conspiracy, others to pragmatic readjustment in a fast-changing world, yet others to clueless collective drift. Then there is the ever-more fraught relationship between the Union and the peoples of Europe. Political leaders sometimes seem to vacillate between involving voters and avoiding any risk of public defiance. Some commentators suggest that decisions on the size and shape of cucumbers or on sardine quotas can be made without the whole democratic jamboree, but in that case how do such things come to spark fierce nationwide debates about sovereignty and democracy, about keeping control and having a say?

The eurozone crisis, still with us as this book goes to press, has exacerbated all these tensions, as well as making a better understanding of the stakes and probable outcomes more urgent than ever. Bankers and investors in the United States and China, trading partners across the globe, a British prime minister betting his future on new treaty negotiations – the whole world wants to know how Europe will get through this test.

The binary logic of op-ed pages would have us choose between a 'United States of Europe' and 'Eurocalypse Now'. Either the turmoil is forcing member states to make the 'federal leap' so passionately wished for by a few – so the argument goes – or else all this intense activity aimed at ending the crisis merely marks the beginning of the end, a last firework before night comes down on the old continent. The account that follows suggests that neither fate awaits us: not a revolution, since Europe is patient; nor a break-up, since Europe is tough. The adventure of turning a continent into a Union, although spurred on by crises and dramas, is a slow affair, often taking paths that nobody had foreseen. Perhaps this should not surprise us. Even America has seen countless twists, turns, reverses, crises and fresh starts on its journey from 1776 to the present.

Recent experience will inevitably leave its mark, all the more so for being painful. From now on nobody in the eurozone can ignore the fact that Greek mendacity, Spanish exuberance or Irish recklessness may affect their own job prospects, retirement or savings. This is not just to say that economies are interdependent. In 2011, a vote on the euro in the Slovak parliament made headlines all over Europe, as did an election result in Finland, the announcement of a referendum in Greece and, a year later, a ruling by Germany's Constitutional Court and a decision by the European Central Bank. In 2013, national elections in Italy, with high stakes and a formidable cast, as well as those of the Union's powerhouse Germany, will be followed with intense interest across the continent. The discovery that all euro countries share a destiny certainly creates tensions, but the political will of both leaders and peoples to stay together has proven stronger than many predicted – or are able to explain.

As the past sixty years have amply shown, the Union disposes of a unique political glue. The adhesive may be invisible, but it works, and underestimating it can come at a cost (in real money for those traders who bet on the break-up of the euro in 2012 and lost hundreds of millions of dollars). By making both the Union's cohesive force and its inner contradictions more palpable, recent events help us to approach the future, first of all by resolving misunderstandings and recasting the terms of the debate. Two elements stand out: Europe's driving forces, and the need for public consent. The two are linked: nothing has fuelled people's suspicion of Europe more than the niggling sense that change is being forced upon them as part of a Brussels plot.

To anyone who regularly reads their country's newspapers, national politics appears as a constant stream of surprises, setbacks and scandals, often with utterly unanticipated outcomes. It is clear to all that, in a democratic setting, far less ever goes according to plan than they might fear or hope. Europe, a club of volatile democracies, is no different.

Momentum originates in an unpredictable series of decisions, often by national leaders grappling with events both at home and abroad and forced to deal with them jointly, sometimes with obvious reluctance. This political interplay offers a more plausible explanation than either the pseudo-logic of integration theory and federalist teleology or the Eurosceptic worldview of evil conspiracies and Brussels-led schemes to impose foreign rule. Since the Greek maelstrom became evident in early 2010, certainties have evaporated and taboos have been violated, red lines crossed and rules rewritten. Dragged along by necessity, prodded by conflicts of interest and clashes between political cultures in which no one has been able to claim authorship of an overall plan or a common vision, the Union is dealing with the shock in ways that are deeply instructive.

Pulling the 'emergency brake' sometimes works, but the pressure of events can be such that it is simply impossible – as a famously inflexible British prime minister discovered. After the fall of the Berlin Wall she fought for a year against the forces of continental change ('No, no, no!'), only to meet her downfall as a result. It seems cleverer, as her successor has recognised after seeing how ineffective his veto was at an ill-tempered summit in December 2011, to make the most of evolutions and try to get something out of them.

In this particular case, London endorsed change and even encouraged its partners to pursue further eurozone integration, yet remained irritated by the amount of diplomatic energy being spent on preventing a 'dangerous monetary experiment' from ending in catastrophe, rather than on the business of jointly delivering prosperity. While its partners struggled, London repeatedly insisted that the single market must remain 'at the heart' of the Union, but the reality is that with the single currency the Union has acquired a 'second heart', and most other governments consider it vital to keep both of them beating, even if they do not agree on exactly how to achieve this.

To the majority of member countries it seems natural for Europe to evolve over time, a view embodied in the infamous words 'ever closer union', present from the start. In contesting this vision, the one European country without a written constitution often invokes the letter of the Treaty, whereas for many on the continent it is the spirit that counts – a spirit best summarised as 'advancing together'. But when it comes to 'doing stuff together', this vaguely-defined togetherness can at crucial moments become more important than the stuff itself. So when British politicians complain that their partners are 'changing the rules of the club', they miss the point: Europe was – and is – always destined to be a club with ever-changing rules.

There is a good reason for this. No project, no treaty can anticipate the creativity of history, let alone prepare an adequate response. The founding states' idea of anchoring Europe in a system of rules, which they hoped would provide some civility and predictability to relations between them, was a visionary plan after the long, double world war of 1914–45. This strategy reveals its limitations each time new challenges arise and the member states feel the need to confront them jointly. That is the source of the tension, throughout the past six decades, between the desire for certainty and the need to face up to change. It explains why Europe is a club that loves rules and keeps changing its own.

Even the briefest glance at the Union's past shows how improbable it is that we have ended up where we are today – an observation that has huge implications for how we approach its future. Today we are not in a period of flux after which things will settle down (as some seem to hope). Global economic and technological change, shifts in the geopolitical landscape, the march of neighbouring peoples towards democratic equality – all these slow trends can have sudden repercussions. Events will continue to produce surprises, and will need to be dealt with one way or another.

This brings us to the second issue about which the terms of the debate need to be recast: the need for public support. In The Speech, the British prime minister asked for Europe 'both to deliver prosperity and to retain the support of its peoples', which immediately makes clear that in his mind, even if the Union were merely a market, political choices would still be involved and democratic accountability needed. This rather casts doubt upon the usefulness of the distinction between Europe as a means and as an end.

Roughly speaking, for the past sixty years there have been three main goals of European cooperation: peace, prosperity and power. All member states subscribe to each of these three ends, albeit with varying degrees of intensity. There are variations that occur over time – it is no secret that the peace motif, decisive at the post-1945 founding, has worn thin in Western Europe, whereas the globalisation challenge of acting jointly in the world has gained in importance – but variations also occur between states: some countries have emphasised economic motives, concentrating on growth and prosperity, while others seemed more attracted by the political goals of continental stability, entrenched democracy and global influence. It is not always possible to distinguish precisely between the two, another point confirmed during the eurozone crisis: Berlin's decision to avoid a Greek euro exit was motivated by both financial and political concerns. Moreover, even the economic goal of prosperity requires very political means to achieve it, including the art of convincing the public.

The advantage of portraying Europe as a practical means, a tool for achieving results, is obvious: everything becomes technocratic, so we should all be able to agree. The politics of it is masked. The single market – cherished by the British, but also by the Dutch and the Scandinavians – is the cornerstone of this pragmatic approach. At first sight a market resembles such inoffensive things as a customs union or a free trade area. The fact, however, is that building a market, unlike creating a free trade area, continually requires new legislation which, even if mostly technical, at times involves deeply political choices. In Europe's Internet economy, who decides the rules on consumer privacy? If a British family moves to France to set up a bed and breakfast, will the parents and children be able to access local hospitals and schools? What about their Polish and Lithuanian fellow-travellers back in the UK? If there is a European market for financial services, who will pick up the tab when a bank goes belly-up? These political implications were precisely why the British walked out of the first market negotiations, back in 1955. A market is not a factory delivering results ('press the growth button'); rather, it is a playing field for economic interests, its shape defined by political decisions and choices that often result from fierce negotiations and conflicts.

This is where the trouble starts: how to muster public support for market legislation when a government can be *outvoted* by its partners? After all, in the Union, political battles take place both within countries (between industry and trade unions, for instance) and between countries (as when some advocate protectionism and others prioritise cheaper imports). Even if most European decisions are packaged as compromises, there may be situations in which a country clearly ends up on the losing side. How to explain that at home?

Compare this to national politics. Every day any national government – in Poland, say – takes decisions that can be contested to varying degrees by opposition parties, be disliked by voters, even trigger protests or strikes. As a general rule, however, even the protesters accept the legitimacy of the Polish government itself. They might want the Polish prime minister to leave office tomorrow, but they would still consider him 'our (infuriating) prime minister' and speak of 'our (disappointing) parliament' and 'our (bad) laws'. Political identity trumps the outcome of the political process. This is clearly the weak spot in Europe's case. Few people, and not only in Britain, consider European decisions to be 'our' decisions or European politicians 'our representatives'. (Tellingly, in most countries 'our commissioner' refers only to the one national among the European commissioners, while members of the European Parliament are often seen as representatives of 'Brussels' rather than as speaking for 'us' out there.) Yet this feeling of ownership – incredibly difficult to grasp, let alone to create – is exactly what is needed to confer legitimacy on joint decisions. Results are important, but they can never do the trick on their own, both because bad times may follow good and because outcomes are often the product of a political battle. This is one reason why the absence of a national veto increases the challenge.

In recasting the terms of the debate, an indispensable first step is to acknowledge that the European game is not taking place primarily on Brussels terrain. European politics is played out between the governments, parliaments, jurisdictions and populations of all the member states. Ultimately, the circle of members comes before the Union. Europe cannot be reduced to a square mile of buildings in Brussels, Luxembourg and Strasbourg.

This is an updated version of a book that appeared in Dutch in 2009. The storm that has raged since then might have suggested that it would need to be rewritten from scratch, but the way Europe has responded to events and major shocks is precisely the book's central concern. The euro crisis has been in that sense a 'live-fire test', making more visible the politics within the Union that it aims to describe.

In telling the story I have tried to avoid taking sides. In my view the best political philosophy is the kind practiced by Machiavelli, Locke, Montesquieu and de Tocqueville: not normative thought with universal pretensions but a reflection on politics based on experience, often personal, of the era.

I happen to be witnessing the latest episodes from a privileged vantage point. In January 2010 I relinquished the status of independent author to become speechwriter to the first permanent president of the European Council. I watched the Greek rollercoaster from the start, followed by leadership changes in Dublin, Rome and Paris, nightly negotiations between European leaders and bankers to see who would blink first in paying for Greece (the bankers lost), the saga of Dominique Strauss-Kahn's arrest as he was about to head for Berlin for euro talks with the German chancellor, grey central bankers waking up to find the press had turned them into superheroes, and (as the British deputy prime minister put it) 'an acronym winning the Nobel Prize': these have been eventful years. As this preface is written, more lies ahead, with the threat of a Greek euro-exit subsiding and that of a British exit from the Union making its entrance.

My first stay in Brussels ten years ago furthered my political education. The implicit codes, the double or triple meanings behind everything that was said or done, the institutional rivalries, the battles to secure a chair at a particular negotiating table, the leaks to the press, the playing with time and delays – in order to grasp the importance of all these things, you had to be there on the ground.

It struck me that the Commission, in its brochures and information campaigns, was speaking to an imaginary public of 'European citizens' without expecting any response. The 2005 French and Dutch referendums on the constitutional treaty allowed me to gauge the effects of this offhand treatment of the public from a different perspective. By then I was working as a political advisor in the Dutch parliament. In The Hague I noticed the prevailing tendency of Dutch parliamentarians to see the European Union as an occupying power, which strengthened my conviction that in any account of European politics, the battle for the public should be placed centre-stage.

The way people write and talk about Europe is at least partly responsible for a lack of interest in the subject, which is why I decided to avoid all jargon. Specialist language not only allows people to hide behind empty words (which is bad enough), it often serves as a smokescreen, concealing rather than explaining political moves and power plays. The reader will therefore not find, apart from in a few quotations and the endnotes, those confusing acronyms that are the hallmark of manuals of law and politics. Instead of writing EU, I will talk of the Union, and so on.

The decision to avoid jargon comes not just from a preference for plain speaking. It is part of an attempt to escape the grip of existing concepts and develop new tools. When I began writing I had an intuitive sense that the available narratives and analyses of Europe were overlooking something essential. Its political life somehow seemed to be missing. But how was I to introduce that life without falling into the trap of thinking along the usual lines? To discover anything new you need to set aside what you already know. A frontal attack on existing concepts would probably only reinforce their grip. American philosopher Richard Rorty once wrote that interesting philosophy is usually 'a contest between an entrenched vocabulary which has become a nuisance and a half-formed new vocabulary which vaguely promises great things'. What he says next perfectly sums up what drove me: 'I am not going to offer arguments against the vocabulary I want to replace. Instead, I am going to try to make the vocabulary I favour look attractive by showing how it may be used to describe a variety of topics.'

In escaping the prison of existing language, the key lies in experience. I have therefore looked back to those who founded and worked in political Europe: national leaders, ministers, diplomats, parliamentarians, civil servants and judges. Their experiences emerge from speeches and debates, from their memoirs and from incidents related by journalists and historians. I have also drawn on my own observations and on invaluable conversations with many of the participants. At the age of eighty-nine, former German Chancellor Adenauer recognised that 'experience guides thought and action; nothing can replace it, not even innate intelligence, least of all in politics'. Politics is the means by which societies try to gain a grip on the endless course of history. It cannot, therefore, be understood outside of time or the experience of time – the pressure of events, the simultaneity of conflicting demands, moments of crisis, the temptation to postpone. The term 'passage' in the book's title helps to avoid well-worn terms such as 'integration' and 'construction', but it also serves to introduce a temporal dimension: it evokes movement through time and in a certain direction, and it stresses an analogy between the metamorphoses of political Europe and 'rites of passage', the ceremonial practices that ensure symbolic continuity through moments of transition in an individual's life (birth, baptism, marriage, coronation. . .). Hence the focus here on such intermediate forms as the threshold, the door, the bridge, on names and renaming, and on the importance of distinguishing between a step and a leap.

Many current theoretical debates in the literature on the subject fall into a language trap, which is why this book prefers to start from the classic question: 'What is politics?' It examines three forms of politics: decision-making and law-enforcement (Part I), the capacity to act in the contingency of time (Part II) and the attempt to link rulers and people (Part III). Europe is taken as a case in point. There is little room here for voguish issues such as the opposition between 'hard power' and 'soft power', the finesses of 'multi-level governance' or the depth of the 'democratic deficit'. I pay more attention to classic categories like foundation, change, representation, legitimacy, responsibility, events and freedom. Even when it obviously draws upon the treaty and the institutions, this is not the work of a lawyer or a political scientist but a book by a political philosopher and historian, convinced that the essence of politics lies in its relationship with time.*

A hare looking at us from a taxidermist's shelf cannot explain how it found food, evaded a fox or bounded through the forest. For anyone attempting to understand the development and functioning of a political system, the graphs and diagrams valid at a specific moment will not prove any more loquacious. Certainly, we can say 'here is the snout and here are the paws', or indeed 'here are the voters and here is the Court', but that would be to overlook the motivations that make life so captivating, the endless succession of events and encounters that prompt action.

Forest, 21 February 2013

---

* The book ends with an extended bibliographical essay that highlights its most important sources and further defines its position in relation to existing studies.

Prologue

Discourse is no mere verbalisation of conflicts or systems of domination but the very thing for which and with which one fights, the power one is aiming to seize.

Michel Foucault (1971)[1]

THREE EUROPEAN DISCOURSES

Pub banter about Brussels regulations, lectures on competition law, shop-talk from Euro-experts, blogs by political commentators – even the most fleeting remarks about Europe are political weapons. The talk is not innocent. As Foucault said: discourse is not just the articulation of conflict, but the territory to be won.

There are no neutral, scientific terms for political developments. Are the Belgians a nation? Is Russia a democracy? Are London and Ankara in Europe? Questions like these cannot be settled among academics. But that is not to say that you can avoid being an ideologue only by remaining silent.

Time can sometimes bring resolution. Take the Franco-Algerian conflict of 1954–62. To the Algerians it was a 'war of independence'; to Paris, a 'civil war' – two clearly incompatible positions. History decided who was right: the French now accept that it was a war fought for national independence. The conflict between the northern and southern states of America in 1861–65 ended in victory for the central authorities. It therefore remains a civil war.

The subject of this book has no final outcome. The relationship between Europe and the member states (Part I), the outside world (Part II) and the people (Part III) is as yet fluid. But we must not therefore suspend judgment. There are two ways forward. We can explore what has already happened, the events of the past sixty-five years, bearing in mind the unpredictability of the future. That is the main purpose of this study. The other option is to chart the political discourses deployed, to examine their usage and contexts, their weaknesses and strengths – an approach outlined in this prologue to arm us against the naïve notion that political terms refer to a reality beyond themselves.

States, citizens, offices

In the torrent of words devoted to European politics, it is possible to distinguish three basic discourses. We might label them 'the Europe of States', 'the Europe of Citizens' and 'the Europe of Offices'. More traditionally they are known as confederalism, federalism and functionalism. Each has its favoured European institutions, its characteristic political style and prescriptions, its university home bases. Each treats history in its own way.

Those who speak of a Europe of States believe that European politics has most to gain from cooperation between national governments. Nations retain their sovereignty, but in matters of mutual interest they may sometimes take joint decisions. Only states have sufficient authority and operational capacity to buttress European unity. Supporters of this approach have little desire for central institutions, preferring to rely on meetings between ministers or national leaders at diplomatic conferences along the lines of Vienna 1814–15. They seek peace between as many European states as possible and prosperity for their peoples. Some advocates of European confederation have their sights set on a glorious leadership role for their own home nation.

The words and concepts employed by the Europe of Citizens are quite different. Here the idea is to detach certain powers from national executive, legislative and judicial authorities and transfer them to a European government, parliament and court, paving the way for federation. As in the American republic, these central bodies would exercise power over citizens directly, bypassing the constituent states, their legitimacy resting on a European electorate. This approach therefore invests high hopes in a European parliament and Europe-wide public opinion. Just as the advocates of a Europe of States are not actually the states, so representatives of this discourse are not today's (national) citizens, but mainly writers and intellectuals who feel qualified to speak on behalf of a new European citizen, unconcerned that most citizens of flesh and blood are barely even aware that such capacity exists. The federalists' ultimate goal is a democratic society that thinks of itself as a single political – even cultural – entity.

The Europe of Offices talks of transferring specific governmental functions to a European bureaucracy. Aims and guidelines would be set down beforehand by the states, with the central bureaucracy then left to act autonomously within those parameters. Political life is seen as overrated and superficial: more fundamental than the interplay between governments, parliaments and electorates are the broad economic and social forces that shape everyday life; European unity can arise from gradual changes to the habits and concerns of millions of individuals; a rational bureaucracy is sufficient to steer the process. Such functionalists believe there is no need for any visionary goal.

Each of these discourses originates in an environment of its own: state power, civic spirit, administrative rule. The States approach goes back as far as the European states system itself. In the fifteenth century, King Podiebrad of Bohemia, shocked by the Turkish military advance, wrote to his fellow Christian princes, describing in detail his plans for a council in which they would all take a seat. In the midst of the devastating Thirty Years' War, Cardinal Richelieu, advisor to the French king, Louis XIII, proposed something similar (though without success). After the peace of 1648, the European states did not take up the idea of a confederal alliance, but relied instead on a balance of power. This worked more or less to the satisfaction of monarchs and national leaders for centuries. Not until the end of the tragic period of 1914–45 (referred to by one of those leaders as 'a thirty years' war')[2] was a Europe of States again advocated by such statesmen as Churchill and de Gaulle.

A Europe of Citizens became conceivable only after the French Revolution. The rupture of 1789 made writers and thinkers more aware of a common history. Novalis, Burke and later Guizot equated Europe with, respectively, Christendom, freedom and civilisation. In 1814, the philosopher Saint-Simon produced a plan for a European parliamentary system, and in 1849, a year after a fresh series of democratic revolutions, writer Victor Hugo came up with the term 'United States of Europe', the federalist slogan to this day. After the First World War, Austrian Count Coudenhove-Kalergi captured imaginations with his Pan-Europa, an organisation that would unite 'people, not states'. Intellectuals including Einstein, Apollinaire and Thomas Mann rallied round, as did the French statesman Aristide Briand and Konrad Adenauer, mayor of Cologne. It was not until the Second World War that their approach gained momentum. A 'European Movement' grew out of the anti-Nazi resistance, bringing together people in Italy, Belgium, France, Switzerland, the Netherlands, Norway, Yugoslavia and indeed Germany.

The concept of a Europe of Offices emerged after 1945. Its spokesmen were senior civil servants, by far the most influential among them a Frenchman called Jean Monnet who had helped to set up allied agencies for transport and resupply between American, British and French forces during the two world wars, and who had worked for the League of Nations in Geneva in the early 1920s. Other prominent functionalists included Dutch banker Johan Willem Beyen and French economist Robert Marjolin. In 1944 Beyen had helped lay the foundations for the international monetary system, and a decade later, as a non-party foreign minister, he was one of the major forces behind moves to create a European common market. In 1948 Marjolin became the top civil servant in the organisation used by seventeen Western European countries to distribute Marshall Aid. He later spent many years as vice-president of the Commission in Brussels.

At the end of the Second World War, numerous conferences were held on the subject of the 'European idea' and the place of states and citizens within it. The Europe of Offices turned out to offer the most practical plan. It was first launched in 1950 in the mining and steel industries. Twelve years later, when it was fully operational, Commission President Walter Hallstein put the Offices thinking into words: 'The very nature of this world necessitates a redefinition of what we ordinarily mean by words like "politics" and "economics", and a redrawing, perhaps even the elimination, of the semantic frontier between the two.'[3]

The political battle between the Europe of States, of Citizens and of Offices regularly results in new power relationships, new ideological constellations and new terms. Take the concept of an 'institutional triangle'. It refers to a balance, which must be preserved, between the Commission, the Council of Ministers and the European Parliament – the three European institutions into which the three currents of Offices, States and Citizens had meanwhile flowed. The term 'triangle', introduced shortly after the first direct elections to the European Parliament in 1979, is rhetorically brilliant. It reconciles the conflicting positions by prescribing an equilibrium, offering a mathematical justification for political choices.

In time, three hybrids developed, and these determine how we think today: supranationalism (Offices and Citizens), intergovernmentalism (Offices and States) and constitutionalism (States and Citizens). The first two are the oldest and they dominated the debate for decades. In Brussels and in certain academic circles, every institutional change in Europe is still set against a scale running from 'supranational' (or 'community') at one end to 'intergovernmental' at the other. In many ways it is an empty distinction. Constitutionalism arose in the 1990s out of an awareness of the inadequacies of both. It instead proposes reading the situation as a matter of public concern that involves all citizens and all member states.

Disciplinary constraints

Language harbours unexpected constraints, even at the level of single words. Take the subject of this book. What to call it? Terms in circulation include European 'integration', 'construction', 'unification' and 'cooperation'. Although apparently descriptive, each has its own resonance and means of duress. Integration suggests a quasi-chemical process that leads to amalgamation; construction evokes a building project on a vacant site; unification might take place either voluntarily or by force; while cooperation emphasises the continuing independence of member states. It is intriguing, for example, that after a resounding 'no' vote in the 2005 referendum on a constitution, the Dutch government, for years an advocate of 'European integration', switched to using the term 'European cooperation' in communicating with the public, whereas the French government, also faced with a '*non*' that year, went on talking of 'European construction'.

Each of these Europes – of States, of Citizens and of Offices – was born of a desire for a Europe with one particular appearance (rather than another), so all three approaches had a normative vocation. But at the same time each has a cosy relationship with specific areas of academia, which naturally all like to think of themselves as analytical rather than prescriptive. This is food for thought. Is there an inadvertent political partiality within every branch of academic endeavour that turns its attention to Europe? If so, what are these inclinations?

The three terms 'integration', 'cooperation' and 'construction' provide a starting point. Each has an affinity with one of the three European discourses and the hybrids derived from them. Each is in vogue in certain academic disciplines, offering a yardstick by which to measure the current state of play and a framework for organising knowledge and expertise.

The Europe of Offices has the support of scholars of integration. Functionalism was the brainchild of economists (who coined the term 'integration'), sociologists and political scientists, all of whom have traditionally felt at home with the worldview and procedures of offices. Since the 1950s, they have measured and gauged and sounded out everything the central bureaucracy hoped to stimulate: trade flows, consumer trends, public opinion, travel patterns, manufacturing standards and administrative practices. Expertise on integration requires measurable results, so in this particular linguistic arena administrative policy is more popular than capricious politics.

The Europe of States draws upon academics who prefer talk of cooperation. Here the experts are historians, or scholars of international relations, who think in terms of states and peoples. Their enthusiasms lie with the study of war and peace, power and self-interest, flags and elections. They rely on facts and their own common sense. Their profession requires them to set the stage, then pick characters and plots and construct a narrative. They tend to present a dark, uncivilised world – the distant past or the geopolitical jungle – with their hero, the State, striding forth to impose its will. To many historians, loyal to their discipline's links with the nineteenth-century nation state, political Europe is a farce. They dismiss as propaganda any narrative in which, instead of France, Germany or England, this strange thing called 'Europe' steps out from the shadow of the centuries to take a leading role. Among them are to be found the intellectual purveyors of Euroscepticism, supported by their colleagues in departments of international relations where European institutions are taken rather more seriously – if mainly in an effort to show that they dance to the tune of their sovereign masters, the states.

The Europe of Citizens lacks strong ties to an academic community. Since the European citizen is not yet a reality, this way of speaking draws on the concept of construction. Writers and intellectuals aside, it is mainly the language of lawyers, familiar as they are with the creative power of rules. While knowledge of economics and social science exists by dint of concrete results, and historians and political analysts talk of the emergence and exercise of a public will, the discourse of legal scholars revolves around the moulding of unfamiliar or uncontrolled situations into a specific form. What until 1952 was true of the offices of the Community was true of the European citizen forty years later: he existed only as an idea. By giving him legal status in 1992, constitutional law (said the critics of the time) created an empty shell. But in legal thinking we quite often come upon empty shells that are gradually given content, which explains why the Europe of Citizens, although also supported by philosophers and writers, owes its biggest debt to the scholars and practitioners of the law. Only a legal rule can turn a concept into an institutional fact.

Of course the success of the discourses of Offices, States and Citizens has fluctuated over time. Changing fortunes in European politics after 1950 helped to determine which story held the greatest appeal. At any given moment, one discipline will see things (fact) or produce arguments (norm) that are invisible or unthinkable in other disciplines.

The most erratic destiny was reserved for the Europe of Offices. In his *The Uniting of Europe* (1958), American political scientist Ernst Haas, a key proponent of this line of thinking, looked at how the young Community had changed political behaviour in the member states. He compared the attitudes of parties, unions and industrialists towards the Coal and Steel Community in 1952 with their positions in 1957 and concluded that European unification was all about economic interests. Ideology was irrelevant. As a self-confessed Offices thinker, his verdict was: 'The economic technician, the planner, the innovating industrialist, and trade unionist advanced the movement – not the politician, the scholar, the poet, or the writer.'[4]

Haas' analytical categories ('policy brokers'; 'expansive logic of sector integration') were at first eagerly adopted by the offices in Brussels, where the decline of the nation state was studied with an intensity that suggests gleeful anticipation. A turbulent decade later, the mood had changed. Haas was forced to acknowledge that his theory underestimated the impact on integration of the geopolitical situation and of autonomous socio-economic change. He had failed to appreciate the potency of longstanding political loyalties and charismatic national leadership. In a word: 'De Gaulle has proved us wrong.'[5]

Not until the mid-1980s did the Offices discourse find favour again, when a new generation of political scientists put forward the concept of 'governance'. This fashionable term meant that experts, once they had listened to sectoral or functional interested parties, could take decisions outside classic territorial or democratic frameworks. Such theories of governance – think of *Regulating Europe* (1996) by political scientist Giandomenico Majone or *Governing in Europe* (1999) by Fritz Scharpf – were gratefully adopted by the central bureaucracy. Brussels lobbyists, to their own surprise, were suddenly seen as respectable representatives of a European civil society.

Meanwhile, States thinking, with its wait-and-see attitude, took great intellectual pleasure in refuting the unrealistic expectations of both its rivals. In the behaviour of de Gaulle in the 1960s – so shocking to Offices ideologues – adherents of the States discourse saw their intuition confirmed. American specialist in international relations Stanley Hoffmann wrote: 'Politics is a matter of will . . . Either Europeans must develop more effectively the will to surmount their present divergences and build a common structure, or things will go on as they always have, with European states acting separately, rather than acting as a *faisceau*, as a more or less unified cluster of states.'[6] He was not at all persuaded that the European nation states were about to vanish. Anything a state was unable to accomplish on its own in economic or military fields could surely be achieved by 'means far less drastic than hara-kiri'.

More recent representatives of the Europe of States are likewise keen to take issue with the claims of Offices thinkers. British historian Alan Milward argues that the founding of the Community meant not the end of the nation state but its rescue. He presents statistics for coal production, trade and agricultural prices from the early years of the Community and concludes:

'Integration was not the supersession of the nation-state by another form of governance as the nation-state became incapable, but was the creation of the European nation-states themselves for their own purposes, an act of national will.'[7] American political scientist Andrew Moravcsik concurs: 'The integration process did not supersede or circumvent the political will of national leaders; it *reflected* their will.'[8]

In Citizens thinking, by contrast, the European order was seen as an entity above and beyond the constituent states. With this new constitutional tack, the study of political Europe departed its native soil of international relations for the previously unexplored territories of law and political theory.

Constitutionalism found its initial foothold in the facts and norms of the law. American academic Joseph Weiler pointed out that ever since the 1960s, while its political system was acquiring intergovernmental traits, Europe's legal system had adopted a federal form by accepting a number of groundbreaking rulings from the European Court. Responses to these two developments were formulated in separate circles, so the Europe of the political scientists bore little resemblance to the Europe of lawyers. Weiler was a go-between who showed that within legal forms lurked political power-grabs, which one discipline glossed over and the other preferred to contest.

Then the notion of a European constitutional order started to draw attention to its standard building-block – the citizen. This turned the spotlight on the European Parliament and invited talk of European democracy, public life and identity. German philosopher Jürgen Habermas pointed out the presumptions contained in this line of thinking. In 1995 he wrote that European democracy cannot be made a reality 'unless a European-wide public sphere develops in the ambit of a common political culture: a civil society with interest associations, non-governmental organisations, citizens' movements, etc.; and naturally a party system appropriate to a European arena'.[9] Adherents of the Citizens discourse believe such preconditions can eventually be fulfilled.

Not all theoreticians of citizens' representation placed their bets solely on the European Parliament, incidentally. Political philosopher Larry Siedentop, for example, in his *Democracy in Europe* (2000), advocates a European senate, with authoritative national parliamentarians serving as senators. In the spirit of Montesquieu, he regards the dispersal of power as the best way to avoid creating a Union dominated by bureaucrats. Active citizenship and constitutional consciousness can act as a brake on centralisation. To Siedentop's dismay, the European elite has failed to see that 'the *form* of the state' is decisive for the quality of public life.[10] He attributes this failure to the subordination of political ideas to economic thought. Consider, for instance, how Margaret Thatcher, with business interests in mind, agreed to a far-reaching change to the European treaty in 1985, in order to help bring about an internal market by 1992, but deeply regretted it later, when she saw the political implications.

In May 2000, contemplation of the form that Europe should take moved beyond the academic world to return to politics. In a speech marking the fiftieth anniversary of the Brussels offices, German Foreign Minister Joschka Fischer violated a taboo by speaking about Europe's ultimate goal. His speech sparked a diplomatic and constitutional debate, and eventually gave rise to a constitutional treaty, a concept that lay halfway between the Europe of States and the Europe of Citizens.

Across sixty years, claims to knowledge crystallised around the procedures of offices, the power-play of states and the representation of citizens – or, put another way, around policy, politics and polity. The accompanying academic disciplines provide three pairs of spectacles, each with its own way of sharpening perceptions. All three can exist happily side by side. At the same time, it turns out that Foucault was right: the choice of reading glasses is a political one. Each comes into play, like it or not, in the battle between and within national and European institutions. Each of the three academic discourses formulates a truth – about the disappearance of politics, the resilience of the nation state or the current condition of democracy – that hints at the fears and desires underlying its quest for truth.

How can we escape these ideological constraints? Or must we abandon the attempt, relinquishing a disappointed claim to objectivity in order to settle for lazy relativism?

The tribunal of events

Politics is a game that creates a connection in the present between an open future and a closed past. Its historicity helps to explain how the three discourses can be both right and wrong. To define the term 'ideologies' more precisely, we might speak (as does Raymond Aron) of 'expectations that await the verdict of time'.[11] Given that the future is by definition open – this openness finding its democratic expression in the plurality of ideologies and the existence of a political opposition – one particular vision *may* become a reality. In that sense, ideological discourses are right and have the right to exist. However, once this open future is drawn through the needle of the present and woven into the permanent fabric of the past, these ideologies will be judged. It then becomes possible to measure the gap between word and action, between promises and facts. This is where ideologies are wrong.

Hence their need to renew themselves constantly and hence the pejorative connotation of the word 'ideology', especially since the tension between a vision of the future and actual reality was cranked up to the point of absurdity in the 'really existing Socialism' of the Soviet Union.

The three discourses on the European order are ideological insofar as they make a legitimate appeal to the future, while remaining subject to the judgment of history. No surprise, then, that the three basic lines of thought – States, Citizens, Offices – appeared at their most ideological in the immediate post-war years, when there was mainly a future and little, if any, 'really existing Europe'. Since the beginning of Europe's foundation, in 1950, new facts and events have put all three to the test. The normative discourses have been forced to adjust their aspirations, the accompanying academic disciplines their depictions of reality. In the years since, none of the three has retained its analytical cogency. Academics now use the label 'sui generis', jargon for 'a case apart'. We are told, apologetically, that the Union is an 'enigmatic organisation', seemingly 'fathomable only to legal scholars or eccentric Europe experts'.[12]

Instead why not learn from historical vulnerability? The lesson is this: the essential historicity of politics must not be bracketed, not dismissed as a matter of sadly unavoidable chance ('exogenous factor') or as an adjudicator deciding the outcome afterwards. It must be given a central place in our understanding of Europe. We need to pay attention to events, to unexpected impacts on the course of things. In reality, events are central to the business of politics. Apt in this regard is John Pocock's definition of government as 'a series of devices for dealing with contingent time'.[13] Politics is the form in which a society deals with the unknown.

It is therefore worth taking seriously the experience of politicians, the best of whom know they are at the mercy of the vicissitudes of time. British Prime Minister Harold Macmillan demonstrated this awareness when, after a long dinner, he famously answered a question from a young journalist about what he feared most for his government: 'Events, dear boy, events.'

Each of the three discourses encourages an illusion that can blind its supporters to the historicity of politics. Among Offices ideologists this was particularly striking: they stopped time completely to dwell in a depoliticised now. To them, Europe was a 'living laboratory' (Haas), politics an activity that – in static circumstances – achieves results and provides technical solutions to concrete problems. Citizens ideologists longed for a radically different future. They dreamed of a federal Europe, which would clearly serve peace and democracy, and they expected people to ally themselves to that idea as a matter of course. Their appeal to the unknown made them vulnerable to the reproach that they were mere believers. States ideologists, meanwhile, derived their certainty from the past. To them, Europe was a continuation, perhaps by new means, of a centuries-old national will. They wore their scepticism with pride.

To be able to withstand the vagaries of fate, it is important to comprehend the link between past, present and future. The great French historian Marc Bloch spoke of 'solidarity of the ages'. This, he said, was so effective that 'the lines of connection work both ways. Misunderstanding of the present is the inevitable consequence of ignorance of the past. But a man may wear himself out just as fruitlessly in seeking to understand the past, if he is totally ignorant of the present.'[14] Events and developments taking place before our eyes change history.

THREE EUROPEAN SPHERES

In November 1876, Bismarck scribbled in the margin of a letter he had received '*Qui parle Europe a tort. Notion géographique*' ('Whoever speaks for Europe is wrong. Geographical expression'). It was a lesson learned at the negotiating table: 'I always came upon the word "Europe" in the mouths of politicians who wanted something from other powers that they did not dare ask for on their own behalf.'[15] Although the term was meaningful, both geographically and culturally, no one could claim to speak on behalf of Europe. The continent as a whole had no parliament, no court, no currency, no bank, no bureaucracy, no flag, no government, no law, no real sense of itself as a people.

Nowadays countless political players take decisions on behalf of 'Europe'. They are listened to, and generally their policies or rules are implemented or obeyed. There is obvious rivalry between them, however. The assembled heads of government, the president of the Commission, the Court, the Parliament, the duo that is the French president and the German chancellor, the trio of Paris, Berlin and London, the countries of the eurozone – they and many others speak in Europe's name; but very often they fail to offer a satisfactory rebuttal to Bismarck. When pressed, member states are still divided, as we saw at the time of America's invasion of Iraq and again with the financial crisis. Europe was powerless when war broke out on the continent for the first time since 1945 and Yugoslavia fell apart. Most people have no idea what goes on in Brussels. There are still European states outside the Union. In view of all this, European politics remains a hollow concept.

The simple question of whether Europe exists as a political entity turns out to be extremely tricky to answer. We are faced with a dizzying array of geographical boundaries, legally binding treaties, historical events, political pretensions, cultural traditions and social customs. Even within any one frame of thought, no obvious answer presents itself. Conceptual clarity is lacking. At the very least a number of categories need to be brought together.

The search for a new paradigm might begin with a distinction between the spheres in which European states have organised their dealings. There are three of them and they encompass each other like concentric globes. Each sphere has its own principles of dynamism and order, each its own rules and etiquette, ranging from top to bottom on the scale of violence – from war and threats of armed force to the veto and qualified majority voting. Each is distinguished by its self-image, by the specific psychology of its players, and by its public.

The outermost sphere derives its rather blurred delineation from geography and history. It embraces what has come to be called 'wider Europe': all the sovereign states on the continent, known for many years as the Concert of Europe. Dynamism here is derived from the pursuit of self-interest by the states, order mainly from a balance of power and from territorial borders.

Then there is the innermost sphere, created by a founding treaty signed in 1951. Calling itself a Community, it covers a legally demarcated but ever-expanding economic realm within the participating states. Dynamism here originates from an idea of the future: the 'European project'. Order and a firm footing are provided by a pact signed by the states: the founding treaty.

The third is the intermediate sphere. It arose between the other two unexpectedly, and with immediate effect, the moment the Community was founded. This in-between world went unnoticed for years and cannot be fully captured in legal terms. Perhaps for that reason, it has not been given a name. Yet it is crucial. This is the sphere of Europe's member states. As in the outer sphere, dynamism arises from the pursuit by each country of its own national interests, but also – and this is the surprise – from a growing awareness of common interests. Its most powerful ordering principle is membership, but both the law and the balance of power are important as well. This sphere is intermediate in character, sometimes overlapping with the outermost sphere, sometimes with the innermost. It is intermediate in its functions as well: to bind, to establish relationships, to absorb events, to make transitions.

It was precisely in those transitions that the member states discovered the unique nature of their intermediate world, which is sometimes neither outer nor inner. When the members act together, as a single entity, they are the motor of 'Europe'.

The outer and inner spheres

The outer sphere, the arena of a wider Europe, invites power politics by its very nature. This is a world of sovereign states, once ruled by kings and princes, now by more-or-less democratic governments, each of which pursues power and national interests on behalf of its population. There is no European entity here, no whole that embraces or transcends the states.

The Concert of Europe had existed since the sixteenth century. Political relationships between states, visible in shifting national boundaries and changing alliances, were shaped by a balance of power. That was the unwritten rule that sustained the system. The balance was upset by every war or threat of war, and was recovered through negotiations, concessions and compromises at the next peace conference. The Peace of Westphalia (1648) and the Congress of Vienna (1814–15), after the Thirty Years' War and the Napoleonic Wars respectively, brought about a drastic reordering of borders and alliances. The Paris conference that resulted in the Treaty of Versailles (1919) after the First World War is a more recent example.

It is worth noting that this system of congresses followed a period in which the states had come together at papal councils. The last great council was called by Pope Pius II after the fall of Constantinople (1453) – a kind of European crisis summit, held in Mantua in 1459. The transition from council to congress signifies a gradual transformation from European Christendom, under the vertical, politico-theological authority of Rome, to a continent of sovereign states caught up in a secular, horizontal interplay of alliance and rivalry. Theologians ceded power to diplomats and lawyers. No longer did 'the thunderclaps of papal excommunications and interdicts' keep everyone in line, but instead the 'art of persuasion, interpretation and negotiation'.[16] Modern European diplomacy was born.

Relationships between European states were framed in early international law, which regulated matters such as diplomatic immunity for ambassadors, the neutrality of certain countries and territories, and the rights of foreign subjects within national jurisdictions. No attention was paid to such rules in dealing with the non-European world, as the populations of Europe's colonies would discover. From the eighteenth century onwards, there was talk of 'European public law', a shared set of mainly unwritten rules, unenforceable but nonetheless recognised. At the Congress of Vienna, Talleyrand made several emphatic appeals to 'the public law of Europe' in his efforts to defend French interests – to the annoyance of the Russian tsar and other participants.[17]

In the outer sphere of European politics – embodied by figures like Richelieu, Metternich and Bismarck – boundaries are of decisive importance, especially the borders between states. The lines on the map are an expression of the modern state, sovereign in its territory, a single entity as seen both from within and without. In contrast to religious and civil wars, rampant and unchecked, international conflict was at least confined to a time and a place. Territorial borders therefore had a pacifying effect. As a general rule, the more secure its external borders, the more freedom a state could give its citizens inside them.

As well as shared borders, there is the border with the non-European outside world, which has never been clearly defined. True, there has long been a sense of a shared European historical and cultural space, but it did not have an unambiguous geographical boundary in 2000 any more than it did in 1700. Belonging to Europe was a matter of will and permission, interest and co-option. Borderline territories have always existed at the edge of the continent. In 1648 all European princes and heads of state sent representatives to the Congress of Westphalia, 'except the English king, the Muscovite tsar and the Ottoman sultan'.[18] A century and a half later, in Vienna in 1814–15, England and Russia came to the table and played leading roles. Turkey has been a dubious case for centuries. From the eighteenth century onwards, the Ottoman Empire was keen to join the European club, and it implemented internal legal reforms for that purpose. At last, in 1856, in return for its services during the Crimean War and with the support of Paris and London, it gained the coveted status of 'European state'.[19] So the boundary between Europe and non-Europe is not geographically arbitrary (Germany, France and Italy have never been asked to prove themselves European), but borderline cases are decided by politics.

The failings of the outer sphere formed the historical backdrop against which European initiatives after 1945 were launched. The system had proved incapable of preventing its own self-destruction over the preceding thirty years. Furthermore, for decades the smaller countries had grown increasingly weary of their defencelessness amid the brutal power-play of domineering larger states. They were now eager to seize the opportunity – presented, in part, by the supremacy of America – to reform European relationships.

Beyond its role as historical backdrop, the external sphere is an ever-present reality. In March 1969, when French President Charles de Gaulle was asked in the privacy of his study how Paris intended to prevent Germany dominating the continent in future, he answered gruffly, 'by war'.[20] When, in early 2008, the Serb province of Kosovo broke away unilaterally and was recognised as an independent state by, among others, Paris, London and Berlin, a Russian ambassador threatened the use of force. When, later that year, Croatia tried to take a step towards accession, it was blocked by its neighbour Slovenia, already a member state, which insisted that an eighteen-year-old boundary dispute between the two countries over a short stretch of Adriatic coast must be resolved first. It is also interesting to note that, just as the informal Concert of Europe did in years gone by, nowadays the European Union confers the prized title of 'European state' on the continent's countries. Thus in 2008, Ukraine, a former Soviet republic and independent since 1991, was recognised by the Twenty-Seven as a European *country*, still one step short of being acknowledged as a European *state* (and potential member of the club).

The borders between European states remain fundamental as a political ordering principle. Today's member states have learned from experience that border conflicts between members and candidate members have to be resolved before accession. There is no mechanism in place for doing so. Think of the complications presented by a divided Cyprus during the current negotiations between the Union and Turkey; or the longstanding difficulties in relations between Britain and Spain because of Gibraltar; or, even further back, disputes between Bonn and Paris over the status of the Saar region (an issue that, far from coincidentally, had to be resolved between the sealing of the two European founding treaties of 1951 and 1957, starting with an exchange of letters by Schuman and Adenauer about the Saar on the very day the Treaty of Paris was signed).

So even now, and even within the Union, relationships between states on the European continent are played out to some extent in this purely political environment of power balances, wars and border disputes. Here the law is international law, not least the rules of war and peace. No one can speak 'in Europe's name' without being put in his place by a contemporary Bismarck.

The inner sphere, the Europe of the Community, is governed by a treaty. It presents a stark contrast to the outer sphere. The main goal of founders like Robert Schuman and Paul-Henri Spaak was a radical break with power politics, a complete transformation of international relations on the continent. Above all, they were thinking of France and Germany, traditional enemies that had fought three devastating wars in the space of one human lifetime. So the concept of durable peace in Europe was wedded to efforts to curtail diplomacy. Of the thirty European states in existence at the time, six took part in the first such scheme, the Coal and Steel Community, which applied all these ideas to a small but crucial field of activity.

Its founding treaty (1951) differed from traditional pacts, in that it provided not only for the usual reciprocal obligations, but also for two institutions staffed by people who did not represent their national governments or parliaments. These were the High Authority (later the Commission), which would take decisions in the name of shared European interests, and the Court, set up to oversee compliance with the treaty. Here lay the break with the past. Stressing the intended contrast with old-style diplomacy, founder Robert Schuman wrote at the time of signing:

> From now on the treaties must create not just obligations but institutions, which is to say supranational organs with their own independent authority. Such organs will not be councils of ministers, or councils composed of representatives of the governments involved. Within these organs there will be no confrontations between national interests that need arbitration or reconciliation; these organs are at the service of a supranational community with objectives and interests that are distinct from those of each of the participating nations. The individual interests of those nations merge into the common interest.[21]

In the original vision of the inner sphere, Europe was never going to emerge out of a clash of national interests. Such conflicts were plainly too intense, the wounds of the last war too fresh. Instead it must exist as far as possible outside the domain of the nation states. Member states would agree to comply with formal decisions taken by the High Authority. The Community was made a legal entity, represented both inwardly and outwardly by the Authority. It may seem a mere formality to give a newly established body 'legal personality', but that status created scope for further innovations, as we shall see.

The term 'community' had been introduced by a lawyer belonging to the German delegation. He was drawing upon the classic sociological distinction between *Gemeinschaft*, a solid and durable association that confers an identity, and *Gesellschaft*, an engagement that is looser and more open. This distinction is part of the standard repertoire of the German intelligentsia, and the choice of *Gemeinschaft* shows just how high aspirations were. To its originators, the Community was a means to an end – their real goal was European unification. The term also indicates how they regarded the states: they were all equal under law. Inequalities of power were swept aside, as were the balance of power and the whole diplomatic box of tricks. The treaty regime was an invitation to a common struggle, sustained by an *esprit communautaire*, a 'community spirit'.

The inner sphere derives its order and footing from the pact. To this day, the Commission and the Court can operate independently only when able to invoke an article of the treaty, a 'legal basis' or a formal competency. This is both a blessing and a curse. A blessing, because the treaty offers solid ground – the Commission can develop initiatives in the name of the treaty; the Court can pass judgment in the name of the treaty. A curse, because many representatives of the inner sphere, especially in the Commission and Parliament, would like to break out through the cracks in the pact. Are there not, after all, countless areas that the treaty omits to mention and where 'Europe' nevertheless urgently needs to set to work?

Change in the inner sphere is guided by a vision of the future: the 'European project'. At foundation, this project ceased to be a utopian mission and became a practical construction site, a workplace of six states. They were an advanced guard, starting work on a project that would eventually embrace the entire continent. In a sense, the Europe of the inner sphere is living on credit. The construction project confers a dual mission, one part of which is to extend policy areas where work is already taking place – such as mining, agriculture and trade policy in the early years – into neighbouring fields. This is known as the ongoing 'construction' of Europe, or the 'communitisation' of policy. The inner sphere's other mission is to broaden itself geographically, to persuade more states to participate, perhaps until it coincides with all the sovereign states on the continent. Seen in this light, the current members are, as Monnet stated, merely the 'pioneers of a wider Europe, whose boundaries are determined purely by those who have not yet joined'.[22] It proves tempting to pursue the first mission by stealth, which sometimes works. For any far-reaching changes, however, the inner sphere has to await a new treaty.

In the inner and outer spheres, dynamism and order follow comparable patterns. In the latter, movement originates with the states, sometimes leading to wars and border disputes, after which peace and a balance of power are restored by confirmation or adjustment of the borders. In the former, it is the internal dynamism of the European project that produces a great range of initiatives. They fall either within or across the boundaries of the treaty and are sometimes endorsed after the fact by a treaty change. These are endless cycles. But whereas in the case of a border adjustment laid down at a peace conference people will often glumly acknowledge years later that the seeds of the next war were contained within it (textbook case: Versailles 1919), the European founding treaties of the post-war years deliberately included an invitation to their own revision.

This is thoroughly original. The principle that motivated the European project is expressed in general terms in the treaty text. The preamble to the founding treaty of 1951 speaks of an 'organised and vital Europe' that must be 'built' and of the 'foundation of a broad and independent community among peoples'.[23] In other words: 'to be continued'. Consequently, changes to the inner sphere, which would normally amount to an infringement of order, can be seen as reaffirming its spirit. This makes the founding treaties 'Paris 1951' or 'Maastricht 1992' substantially different from the peace treaties 'Westphalia 1648' through to 'Versailles 1919'. The inner sphere is defined by the link between dynamism and order, between project and treaty. Life there is lived between mission and law.

The intermediate sphere of the member states, and its table

The 1950s dream of the founders remained a dream. Much was achieved on the construction site of the European project, but not unification. This fact ought long ago to have focused attention on the intermediate sphere, which emerged unnoticed along with the Community. But everyone was looking the other way. While States ideologists ascertained to their satisfaction that everything had remained as it was, and while in Community circles there was keen anticipation of the day when the Commission in Brussels and the Parliament in Strasbourg would become a European government and legislature, political progress was taking place elsewhere – neither in the inner sphere nor in the outer sphere but in between, in the sphere of the member states. This unexpected bonus of the founding act was overlooked because it did not fit with the dominant language and frames of thought, yet the intermediate world has turned out to be the principal source and vehicle of European politics. It therefore has a central place in this book.

Even at their earliest meetings, from September 1952 onwards, the ministers of the six founding states discovered that they shared more than just a treaty, simply by virtue of the fact that they were sitting at the same table. This was officially the table of the Council of the Community, and someone from the High Authority was also present, the intention being that the ministers would talk about coal and steel. But they noticed that they could bring more to the table than the treaty prescribed. In the late 1950s, for example, the thought occurred: Well now, since all six of us are sitting here, couldn't we quickly run through current affairs in the world as well?

This question led to protracted controversies. The governments of the Community persuasion (led by the Netherlands, along with Belgium) said: No, we can't do that, we can act like a club only so long as we follow the script of our marvellous treaty; just getting together around the table means reverting to diplomacy, and we all know where that led in 1914 and 1939. The governments of the States persuasion (led by Gaullist Paris) said: Sitting round a table exchanging thoughts on world affairs is fine, but then those people from the community institutions have to leave; they've no business discussing foreign policy. Both sides considered the other's view unacceptable; mutual distrust led to an impasse.

It was 1970 before the Six found a way out, presented to them by a 'circle-squaring' francophone Belgian diplomat.[24] In future, the ministers of foreign affairs would discuss the state of the world – America, the Middle East, Russia – twice a year, while a supporting committee of senior diplomats, with no central office, would meet four times annually. This was called 'European Political Cooperation'. A fascinating intermediate forum had been invented. Unlike ordinary meetings of the Council, for which ministers gathered every month in Brussels or Luxembourg, these conferences took place in the capital of whichever country held the rotating presidency of the Community.

Sometimes ministers scrupulously separated the two conference tables. In 1973, for instance, they gathered to discuss foreign policy in Copenhagen in the morning, before coming together as a Council of Ministers to discuss community affairs in Brussels in the afternoon. The Danish government provided an aircraft to get them from 'A' to 'B'. Such extravagances – a gift to cartoonists – are concrete examples of the way in which the sphere of the member states and the inner sphere move independently of each other.

There were further frictions of this kind. The pre-history of the euro, the period of monetary cooperation between member states, includes an illustrative episode. It began in 1969. German Chancellor Willy Brandt – by his own account 'encouraged by Jean Monnet and urged to great caution by the governmental departments responsible'[25] – proposed to his fellow leaders a future European monetary union, complemented by a European monetary fund. The fund would eventually require a pooling of the member states' monetary reserves, which in turn would provide a policy instrument as a counterpart to monetary union. Various circumstances (and pressure from France) meant that the fund was created long before a European currency was in prospect, but (owing to German counter-pressure) in an extremely stripped-down form. It was a typical compromise.

The Bundesbank, the most powerful central bank of the Six, was unhappy with Brandt's undertaking, fearing that interference from the Brussels offices would endanger its independence (the more so since the Commission's monetary affairs portfolio had traditionally been in French hands). As a result, the European Monetary Cooperation Fund was set up in 1972 outside the Community Treaty, based on an agreement between the six central banks. One of the bankers involved recalls:

This bothered the Commission and it insisted that the Fund be established by Council regulation. The central banks – perhaps regarding this insistence as no more than a reflection of bureaucratic instincts never entirely absent in Brussels – in the end acquiesced that, parallel to their own agreements, there should be a Council regulation establishing the Fund. Once it was issued, however, the services of the Commission informed the surprised central banks that as a result the Fund now was no longer based on Central Bank agreements but had become part of Community legislation. This meant that any change in what was basically an arrangement between central banks now depended on Council decisions made on the proposal of the Commission, with central banks merely in an advisory role.[26]

It was a salutary experience. The central bankers realised that they did not want to follow the script of the European project and reacted by giving the fund purely administrative tasks, using a different table for their real discussions. They preferred to meet as a free circle of central bankers, rather than under the treaty regime – but they did meet.

In the way it refers to the membership, European parlance provides an excellent means of expressing the unique nature of the intermediate sphere. From the moment the Community was founded, there was talk of 'the Europe of the Six', or simply 'the Six'. Later, when new members joined, this became 'the Nine', 'the Ten', 'the Twelve' – currently 'the Twenty-Seven' and about to become 'the Twenty-Eight'. Grammar aids interpretation: numerals used autonomously, although themselves singular, require a plural form of the verb. Thus: 'The Six *have* decided . . .' This is not the same as 'the Community *has* decided . . .', since the member states as a whole can make decisions of which the Community is the object. Here ordinary linguistic usage offers access to the invisible sphere of the states. Rule of thumb: if a construction in which 'the Six' (or 'the member states', 'the capitals', 'the heads of government') cannot be replaced by 'the Community', that indicates that the action concerned takes place in the inter-mediate sphere rather than in the inner sphere. For example: 'the Six open talks with London' or 'the Twelve reach an accord on a new Commission'.

Dynamism in the intermediate sphere arises primarily from the fact that each member state pursues its own interests. That is, after all, what every electorate demands of a democratic government. The Six now belonged to a Community, but they were still part of a wider Europe. France, Germany, Italy, the Netherlands, Belgium and Luxembourg did not disappear from the map in 1952. They held on to their positions on the continent and in the world (four of the six had colonies). They had their own constitutional laws and political cultures, their own languages and customs, socio-economic systems and histories. They had not transformed themselves into federal states of a new political entity. True, on limited economic terrain they inter-wove their interests, but in all other respects they remained fundamentally themselves. Even on the new European construction sites of agriculture and trade they were determined not to sell themselves short.

In the face of these national interests – a many-headed source of disquiet – three organising principles operate in the sphere of member states. Initially the situation resembled that of the old European concert of states, with dynamism arising from conflicts of interest, order from a balance of power. Whenever national interests cropped up, Community ideologues were suitably disappointed. According to the treaty, the states were technically equal; yet it was soon clear that what Paris could demand at the negotiating table, the Netherlands or Belgium could not. (Bonn could, perhaps, but the Germans tended to be accommodating, particularly towards the French.) The balance of power was impossible to ignore.

It was unexpectedly tempered, however, by two other organising principles. First, the political fact of membership turned out to be funda-mental. All member states had an interest in seeing their Community function properly. The Community did not stand outside them, even though they sometimes imagined that it did; rather it brought about an increasingly tight interweaving of their economic and other interests. To a limited degree the states drew closer. During a profound crisis in 1965–66, the members discovered that in actual fact they could not walk away from the table. One powerful member state, France, tried it but returned after seven months to sit in its 'empty chair'. In some sense, the member states were stuck with each other. (Their governments have, to this day, proved unable to convey this uncomfortable discovery to their populations.)

Then there was the law. Old international law, which continued to have a moderating effect on relations between states in the outer sphere, was joined in the intermediate sphere by the new community law. This strange phenomenon had not been foreseen. A German lawyer who analysed it in 1965 discovered that the governments of the Six had already taken dozens of decisions because of the treaty, but formally outside it. These included the appointment of European commissioners and judges, the establishment of subsidiary bodies, 'speed-up decisions' and agreements with other countries – in other words, business that the governments dealt with as members of the Community, but externally to it, as a 'circle of member states'. He claimed that these decisions were located halfway between community law and international law, and described them as 'legal hybrids', 'without logic and consistency', which both bound the states and were a source of community law.[27] These hybrids, which are still with us, point to the fact that in between classic diplomacy and the life of the Community, a sphere with its own rules was developing.

We would be ill-advised to dismiss these observations as sophistry. Generally speaking, legal and diplomatic forms serve to express political relationships, offering access to invisible powers. An absence of legal logic should not be argued away out of hand as a systemic error. In reality, history is not logical. We would be wiser to interpret formal incongruity as an indication that conflicting forces are at work. Take the term 'constitutional treaty', rejected by many as internally contradictory or even a 'juridical monster'.[28] Legal orthodoxy sees international treaty law and domestic constitutional law as impossible to combine, certainly; but anyone who, after lengthy and combative negotiations between twenty-five states, finds himself confronted with a 'constitutional treaty' (2004) should not attribute this to constitutional illiteracy among politicians. Such an intriguing legal fact can more sensibly be seen as a repercussion of a political compromise, or indeed as an invitation to investigate exactly what forces are in collision.

Dynamism arising from each nation's pursuit of self-interest; order through membership, law and a balance of power: these suffice to describe the momentum specific to the intermediate sphere, except on one decisive point. Membership of the club not only has a mitigating effect on reciprocal relationships (order), but also motivates joint action towards the outside world (dynamism). The member states discovered as time went on that, as well as their own separate interests, they had shared interests that flowed from membership. In fact there were more and more of them. Up to a point, these mutual interests concerned the functioning of their Community – the inner sphere could not propel itself and sometimes needed a nudge from outside; but there were also times when the member states wanted to act as a closed circle, or indeed needed to, as for instance in negotiations with Washington or Tokyo on trade tariffs, or in talks with London about British accession. The outside world or the specific situation sometimes demanded a single point of contact. In trade relations, for example, the Commission represented the Six, in close consultation with the Council of Ministers – an arrangement that flowed from the Community's common external tariff. But some member states decidedly did not want the Commission to speak for all members on foreign policy. They would therefore need to organise something for themselves.

The breakthrough came in 1974, with the establishment of the European Council, a periodic gathering of the leaders of member states. In the early years, eight summits were held, where the national leaders met to overcome sticking points by consensus, to spur on the Community, or to exchange views on international relations. This was classic diplomacy in a new form, a contemporary 'Vienna 1814–15', but for members only. France repeatedly took the initiative, usually in consultation with Germany. The smaller countries feared that through these summits unpredictable power politics would enter community life, at the expense of legal certainty.

At the summit held in December 1974, French President Valéry Giscard d'Estaing managed to give the table a permanent shape and a regular schedule. Neither the treaty nor the public had asked for this forum. It was a political coup. The nine heads of government would henceforth come together three times a year, twice in the country of the rotating presidency and once at Community headquarters in Brussels or Luxembourg (note the inexhaustible creativity of the European compromise factory). Within ten years, the European Council had grown to become the Community's highest decision-making body. Only there could disputes between member states over the common budget, expansion onto new construction sites, or the accession of new members be settled.

The European Council stood outside the Community. In the inner sphere there was a nagging fear that this forum was a source of 'intergovernmental contagion' – indeed that it would reveal itself to be a 'cuckoo in the Community nest'.[29] Such metaphors demonstrate how impregnable the boundary between spheres was taken to be. From the Community side came the reassurance that heads of government could take no formal 'decisions'; their political agreements were given legally binding force only afterwards, at the level of the Council of Ministers. Community lawyers repeated year after year that the European Council, unlike the ordinary Council, was 'not an institution' and would not be allowed to become one. They were fooling themselves. The table of the national leaders placed itself at the top of a Brussels pyramid that had developed over the years. At the bottom were countless national committees of civil servants; above them came the weekly meetings between ambassadors of the member states and their deputies, the monthly gatherings of foreign ministers, and the meetings of sectoral ministers (economic affairs, agriculture and so on); all this was topped off every few months by summits of heads of state or government. The circle of member states had organised itself, with the European Council as its most highly evolved institutional expression.

It was a body that appeared to operate halfway between the outer and inner spheres. In the early 1980s, an astute observer wrote that, with the creation of the European Council, the member states of the Community 'had acquired a machinery that could, if rightly used, transform it into a real Concert of Europe'. They found themselves facing a practical reality:

It was the Community's misfortune, however, that the latter-day successors of Castlereagh and Metternich were obliged for one reason or another to devote a substantial portion of their time to haggling over the price of cheese, or the levels of German and British contributions to the Community's minuscule and lopsided budget or the problems of French pig farmers rather than to the high political questions with which they might have been expected to concern themselves.[30]

Nonetheless, halfway between the spheres of the Concert of Europe and the European project, its agenda wavering between Cold War and goat's cheese, stood the table of the assembled member states. It would turn out to be a formidable vehicle.

Transitions between the spheres

The three spheres of European politics engage in all kinds of relationships. The two points of transition are between member states and the continental outer sphere and between member states and the institutional inner sphere. To use the customary legal terms, at stake are *accession* to the club and *amendment* of the treaty. For these fundamental decisions, the member states operate formally as a collective. The governments take a joint decision, which their populations each have to ratify. The procedures are practically identical in all other ways, too. In the founding treaty, incidentally, the articles covering accession and amendment are adjacent.[31]

In their prologue to the founding treaty of 1957, the Six cordially invited 'the other peoples of Europe who share their ideal' to join them. And in the main text: 'Any European State may apply to become a member of the Community.'[32] This provision produced something lacking in other relationships with the outside world: a difference in treatment between European and non-European states (although who is and who is not European has never been decided). It suggests a profound consciousness of a shared geographical and historical space, the legacy of the Concert of Europe. The consequences were immense. The entrance ticket to the Community became a coveted prize in the game of European power politics. This was obvious in 1961–73, the period of British overtures, a repeated French veto on British membership, squabbles between Paris and the other Five, and finally an accord between the Six and London. Since the fall of the Berlin Wall in 1989, accession has once more become the member states' favoured instrument for dealing with their European surroundings.

For changes to the treaty, too, member states act jointly. Over the past twenty years, Europe has stumbled from treaty to treaty – from 'Maastricht

1992' to 'Lisbon 2007', and who knows what beyond that. This political quest for a form that will fit the historical situation has been particularly laborious, because the inner sphere cannot simply renew itself. It relies on the assent of all the governments and all the populations. The member states combined, fully decked out with their governments and peoples, are Europe's constituent power. The fact that everything can be blocked by a 'no' from one electorate – Denmark in 1992, Ireland in 2001 and 2008, France and the Netherlands in 2005 – demonstrates the weakness of the club vis-à-vis its members. The fact that a solution is found time and again demonstrates its strength.

Some may like to note that there is also a subtle difference between the two procedures. Whereas the governments negotiate treaty changes at intergovernmental conferences (which is to say in a format derived from classic diplomacy), they negotiate with prospective new members as a Council (in other words, as a Community institution). The difference is telling. After all, if the member states were to sit around the table with an interested newcomer at an intergovernmental conference, the formal distinction between members and candidate would disappear. Everyone would be sitting there on his or her own behalf, in the umpteenth replay of 'Westphalia 1648', and no one would be able to speak for the organisation that had been established in the meantime. With a treaty change, the problem is precisely the opposite: the club of member states would lose its freedom of manoeuvre if it operated according to the treaty script, as a Council of Ministers in the midst of the Community and its institutions. This pleasingly illustrates how the circle of members occupies and marks out a sphere of its own. In dealing with the most fundamental matters, it behaves towards the institutional inner sphere as if it were from the outer sphere whereas it behaves towards the continental outer sphere as if it were from the inner sphere.

The member states jointly control the shape Europe takes – something none of them have the power to do individually. Often the circle of members is invisible and inaudible, but whenever the situation requires it to speak unanimously, the inner sphere obeys and the outer sphere listens.

'On Europe's behalf'

The emergence of two new spheres of European politics raises fresh questions about representation. Are there now in fact people or institutions that can speak 'on behalf of Europe'?

In the continental outer sphere nothing has changed. No one is any better able than in Bismarck's day to 'speak for' Europe and sound credible. But what about the inner sphere and the intermediate sphere of the member states? Why are so many national leaders, judges, parliamentarians, ministers and commissioners happy to announce that Europe is doing something or believes something when they are often unable to convince the public, and occasionally even question each other's right to speak?

Political institutions are by nature invisible. No one has ever seen the Roman Empire or the Kingdom of Spain. What we see are buildings where power is wielded, fortifications in a field, lines on a map, flags flying. Based on such visible representations, we assume the existence of whatever it is they represent. When soldiers go to war 'on behalf of Rome' or ministers sign a treaty 'on behalf of Spain', we are prepared to accept that these invisible entities can speak and act. There is no reason why it should be any different with Europe.

Political philosopher Thomas Hobbes threw light on this mechanism of representation. In *Leviathan* (1651) he conceives of the state as something artificial, a body politic, a 'person' – an audacious departure from the idea of the state as divinely ordained. According to Hobbes, the state is an 'artificial person', who speaks and acts on behalf of a multiplicity of people. It is crucial that this speaking and acting happens in a public arena, on the world stage. Hobbes points out that the Latin *persona*, which originally meant 'guise' or 'external appearance', began its advance into everyday parlance via the derived theatrical meaning of 'mask'. The first 'persons' were actors, players; later the term was used for other acting or speaking representatives, such as a defence advocate in a court of law. All the world's a stage. As he pursues his argument, Hobbes loses sight of this theatrical origin, but it remains of essential importance for the 'political person' who claims to speak for a multitude. The play must convince; the representation must succeed.

Now we can turn the whole thing on its head and see politics as a battle for an 'on behalf of'. What matters is whether a claim to representation is accepted in reality, and by whom. There is no scientific or legal arbiter. Ultimately, the public decides. So the best way to find out whether 'Europe' exists as a political body is to investigate whether there are 'natural persons' who can plausibly claim to speak and act in Europe's name.

Whose claim to speak on behalf of Europe is recognised, and by what kind of audience? Back with this question to the three spheres of action in European politics. Having dismissed any such claim by the geopolitical outer sphere, we are left with the inner sphere of the institutions and the intermediate sphere of the member states that unexpectedly accompanies it. The two claims are rather different. The inner sphere is eager to speak in the name of the European treaty, the European project or European citizens. The intermediate sphere, by nature less assertive, claims to speak on behalf of the assembled European member states and their peoples.

First, the inner sphere. It's claim appears promising. The 'persons' who populate the Community's institutions, released from their national trappings, can in a sense speak on Europe's behalf. This was a tremendous breakthrough, experienced as a liberation. The moment was celebrated symbolically by the first chairman of the High Authority of the European Coal and Steel Community, Jean Monnet. In that role he was offered the first European *laissez-passer*, in 1953. These were to be given to each of the members of the Authority and their staff. (In those days, travelling from Luxembourg to Germany involved obtaining a visa from the occupying authorities.) The specially designed document was presented to him ceremonially. In front of his astonished civil servants, Monnet asked an aide to hand him his French diplomatic passport, saying: 'We're going to burn this now.'[33] He had become a European.

It is this 'on Europe's behalf' that lends the Commission (successor to the Authority) and the Court and Parliament their right to exist. Yet a contemporary Bismarck might ask: 'On whose behalf are you speaking, actually?' The response is not always convincing.

The European Court of Justice is perhaps in the strongest position. It speaks on behalf of the European treaty – in the name, as it were, of the material from which the inner sphere has been built. On that basis, it can speak with authority to the member states, to their citizens and to other institutions. Its word is law. Moreover, the Court, owing to a remarkable judicial coup, has succeeded in becoming the official interpreter of the founding treaty. Since that coup, it has spoken on behalf not only of the letter of the treaty, but also of its spirit – in other words, on behalf of Europe's founding moment. In the inner sphere, this moment has the status of a quasi-divine *fiat Europa*, with the treaty as quasi-Scripture. So by making such a claim, the Court acquired a sacerdotal authority – useful when performing its primary task of making the law felt by means of words and gowns (rather than swords).

The Commission appeals to a dual 'on behalf of'. In supervising compliance with the rules, it speaks on behalf of the European treaty; in making proposals it speaks on behalf of the European project. It finds the latter more exciting. Its political vocation – as distinct from its administrative tasks – is contained in the project. In legal terms, this vocation expresses itself as an exclusive right to take the initiative in policy proposals. The Commission is deeply attached to its monopoly on the opening move. The Europe on behalf of which it speaks politically is a vision of the future.

The judges, of course, pass judgment without interference from, or consultation with, political powers in the member states. The Commission likewise derives its neutrality from a 'separation of powers' of this sort. Commissioners are explicitly forbidden to take instructions from any member state.[34] This does not prevent them from giving due consideration to the interests of member states, as indeed they must, since their task is to make proposals that are balanced and acceptable to all members, sometimes even to mediate between them. It does mean, however, that they cannot and must not speak on behalf of any one member state. A customary detail illustrates this. A commissioner who wants to bring up a matter concerning his own country in a meeting will refer to it with a smile as 'the country I know best' – at which point his colleagues will also smile briefly, to signal that the danger has been recognised and avoided. Such codes place the Commission as a whole in a position to speak 'in Europe's name'.

A treaty and a project – but where do the people come in? They enter via the Parliament. In its very essence a parliament is a representative body. The Strasbourg Assembly speaks not on behalf of the treaty or the project but on behalf of Europe's citizens. For over thirty years it has been directly elected by them. It has the potential to become an extremely powerful political entity, permeating the entire inner sphere. The Commission and the Court are also reinforced by the existence of European citizens. The outward effects are increasing. For example, the Parliament offers a platform to prominent figures who wish to speak to European citizens, be they European heads of government, foreign heads of state or world-famous champions of noble causes (in which category Nelson Mandela, the Dalai Lama and Aung San Suu Kyi have been guests of Strasbourg in recent years).

Yet the figure of the citizen harbours a weakness. In reality, the European citizens on whose behalf the Parliament – right from the start – wanted to speak did not yet exist as such. This put the institution at a disadvantage compared to the Court and the Commission. Whereas it is possible to invoke the words of the treaty or the ideas of the project without fear of contradiction by the abstraction thereby represented, people of flesh and blood are a different matter. There can be no parliamentary representation without an active role for an electorate, the chance to participate and to object. There is heavy traffic between the Parliament and all kinds of organisations that speak on behalf of citizens' interests, but the general public has only limited access to the Assembly. A person who speaks 'on behalf of the voters' without those voters knowing they are being represented is not in a strong position. Because of this vulnerability, the concept of European citizenship became, of necessity, part of the European project.

In the sphere of the member states, the 'on behalf of' works very differently, since they cannot speak in the name of European treaties, projects or citizens. No one is neutral. Each speaker is tied to his or her own national origins. This may seem a curse, but there is a reverse side here, too. While the potential power of the inner sphere conceals an actual weakness, the weakness of the intermediate sphere conceals a strength. Its 'on behalf of Europe' is the strongest – when it speaks at all.

In the Council of Ministers, everyone speaks on behalf of a member state. At the table of the ambassadors, instructions from nation states are not forbidden, as they are in the Commission; in fact they are what such gatherings are all about. Although the Council is formally a community institution on a par with others, those others regard it with suspicion. Are these 'real' Europeans round the table (so the ideologues of the inner sphere ask themselves), or does naked national interest predominate? Can we be sure no diplomatic practices are sneaking in through the back door? The solution proposed in the treaty was that the Council would increasingly take decisions based on a majority among ministers, thereby reducing the risk of national blockades and encouraging European opinion-forming. In reality, the ministers departed from this script. They preferred to avoid outvoting each other. Here we see the mores and powers of the member-states sphere at work, making the Council a maverick among community institutions. The inner world of the treaty and the project overlaps with the intermediate world of the circle of members, both visibly and tangibly.

Precisely because of that overlap, the Council of Ministers has been able to give birth to a powerful European spokesmanship. The secret lies in the form in which it organises itself: the conference table. The most important figure is the host, the head of the table, the president. Such a figure was, of course, required from the start to call the meeting or to chair it, but also – and in this connection more importantly – to speak to other Community institutions, the Assembly in particular. It was impossible for six ministers to address a parliament simultaneously. The Council also had to be able to send the Commission, for example, a letter signed by a single individual (even though the Commission has a representative at the Council table in most cases, and at all levels).

Inevitably, every president of the Council came from one of the member states and thus lacked Europe-wide legitimacy. The member states sought a solution in a rotating presidency. Every six months the gavel moved on one place, around the circle, originally in alphabetical order. As long as there were six, nine or ten governments, a country's turn would come around every five years at most. The presidency conferred prestige, but it was no simple undertaking. Many leaders knew from experience how difficult it was to speak on behalf of the entire table. Anyone who was still unaware of this would see the gavel moving towards them.

The Council of Ministers could speak on behalf of the national governments. Everyone at the table was 'authorised to commit the government of that Member State'.[35] Different configurations soon evolved, such as the agriculture council for agriculture ministers, or the transport council for transport ministers, each of them speaking for an aggregate of sectoral interests. For more general business, there were sessions on general affairs, attended by the foreign ministers. They, too, committed their governments. The treaty did not, however, provide for a body able to claim commitment from all member states at the highest political level.

The heads of state or government, meeting at summits that from 1974 onwards were formalised as the European Council, stopped that gap. Their 'on behalf of Europe' is strong. Of all the bodies representing the circle of member states, the European Council alone both measures up to the political jungle outside and has authority over the community world within. Its position is based not on formal competencies but on a powerful bond with the public and a capacity to influence events. It acquired the latter partly because of its small but crucial overlap with the inner sphere (made visible at the table by the presence of the Commission president), which enables it to channel inwards the force of external impacts.

The national leaders are expected to be able to commit not only their governments, but also their parliaments to European Council decisions, and in that sense they speak on behalf of their populations. (It is no accident that this power is greatest for each leader shortly after an election victory.) So the European Council can, in theory, speak in the name of the total population of member states. Here, too, the role of spokesman was until recently held by a rotating presidency. If everyone at the table reached an accord, the president could speak to the outside world on behalf of all. But speaking to the populations of the member states proved more difficult: even the president was at the table on behalf of one population. To reach the public in another member state, he or she needed, so to speak, to go over the head of a colleague. European Council presidents who came from the larger member states proved the most successful at addressing the European public as a whole (Kohl, Mitterrand, Blair, Merkel, Sarkozy).

An important reform, implemented in 2010, was the introduction of a 'permanent' president of the European Council. This individual, selected from among former or incumbent heads of government, holds the presidency for a maximum of five years without playing any other national political role. In theory, as the most senior figure in the intermediate sphere, he speaks both to the outside world and to the public on behalf of all the national populations combined, not just on behalf of his own. This gives the president of the European Council (potentially at least) a more powerful voice than either the Commission president (who speaks on behalf of the treaty, the project and the citizens) or the president of the European Parliament (who speaks on behalf of the citizens). It creates an 'on behalf of Europe' stripped of national connotations, no longer arising from the inner sphere alone, but also from the intermediate sphere of the assembled member states. It marks off the circle of members more clearly from the outer sphere.

As Thomas Hobbes put it: 'A multitude of men are made *one* person when they are by one man, or one person, represented.'[36] Whether this political embodiment of Europe will succeed and endure, only time will tell. Everything depends on the people chosen – the first of them, the Belgian Herman Van Rompuy, and his successors – as well as on events, and on the interplay with the public. In view of what the sphere of member states represents and what historical reality it has replaced, it seems particularly fitting that, of all the public addresses this first president has given while in office, the most convincing and moving came in Oslo in late 2012, when he accepted the Nobel Peace Prize on behalf of the Union.

The birth of purgatory

It seems that – for even the best writers on European affairs – it is tempting to contrast the outer sphere of the continent with the inner sphere of the treaty: to put 'Europe' on one side and 'EUrope' on the other.[37] Why do people forget about the circle of European member states in between the continent and the project? Why have the actions, power and organisation of the political in-between world not been properly recognised?

One possible explanation lies in the power of the dominant frames of thought. Since 1950, a dichotomy – supranational (or community) on one side, intergovernmental on the other – has pervaded thinking about European politics. The intellectual sympathies of the two sides lie, roughly speaking, with the self-image of the inner sphere and the power struggle and clash of interests in the outer sphere. Whereas intergovernmentalism tends to limit itself to supercilious irony, to the feigned nonchalance of 'Europe has seen nothing new since Bismarck', supranationalism produces a great deal of paper and prose all the time. The inner sphere is a word-factory. This is true not just of the treaty itself, with its regulations and guidelines and countless legal commentaries, but of all the interpretations and justifications of the methods and aims of the European project that buzz inexhaustibly around it. Many in the academic world have been seduced by this Brussels buzz (and the funding that accompanies it), sparking predictable (but not entirely unjustified) sarcasm on the rival, intergovernmentalist side.[38]

Amid this tit for tat, the intermediate sphere – which was always able to overlap with either of the others and gained its independence only with time – struggled to gain a solid foothold. Supranational thinking was quick to place the sphere of the member states in the same category as the outer sphere; intergovernmental thinking accepted the gift with gratitude and gave it the kiss of death (*nihil novum*).

Yet this explanation is not quite adequate. The intermediate sphere has not simply been, as it were, shouted down. The fact that it has remained unnoticed and unnamed cannot be blamed on the force of the competing discourses alone; it arises in part from its own essentially political nature: ungraspable as quicksilver, weighty yet agile. The intermediate sphere has found its autonomy in transitions between the spheres, in mediation between outer and inner. Joint control of the entrance proved decisive. It was there that the member states experienced themselves as a club. As such, they neither fall under the regime of the treaty nor belong in the each-to-his-own outer sphere. It is precisely its special place in time that makes the circle of members so intangible. It brightens when necessary, when an uncertain future demands a joint response.

This accounts for the fact that the intermediate sphere of European politics has mainly been recognised, the opportunity it offers mainly seized, by national politicians whose goal it was to merge the historical forces of the outside world with the qualities of the inner – French and German leaders foremost among them. It is they who have expected the in-between world to provide, on balance, freedom rather than coercion. For the many other national leaders who have given shape to the intermediate sphere and populated it, the advantages have been less obvious. Whether they like it or not, they are handed two hats: one national and one European. The national hat comes first; it is their political *raison d'être*, a trophy coveted often for years, presented to them by their own electorates. The European hat is a bonus, an extra – compulsory and demanding. This second hat offers access to a more spacious environment, a larger political game. At the same time, it reminds them of the coercion of the European negotiating table, which seems unmentionable back home.

Perhaps an analogy might clarify the thinking that underlies this book. Europe is experienced in inserting an intermediate element between two poles, an element that liberates both thought and action – a third estate between warriors and priests, a parliament between ruler and people, synthesis derived from thesis and antithesis. Perhaps the best example of all is purgatory, which in the Middle Ages nestled in between heaven and hell. It created space for redeemable sins, for punishment containing the prospect of redemption, and it was therefore hugely liberating for life on earth, which endlessly hovers somewhere between good and evil.

In his remarkable book about the 'birth of purgatory', *La Naissance du Purgatoire*, Jacques Le Goff shows how twelfth-century theologians made this intermediate space conceivable step by step. To break through the antithesis between hell and paradise, between the eternally damned and the saved, involved nothing short of a conceptual revolution. The importance of the hereafter in medieval life meant that it touched upon all facets of existence, including the experience of time and space. Such a revolution could not be achieved in a single step. Purgatory acquired its conceptual coherence only with time, in theological commentaries, such as that of Brother Pierre Le Chantre, or in prayers. Eventually it carved out a place for itself in the minds of the faithful. Dante's *Commedia*, with its circles of hell, purgatory and heaven, is the most beautiful of all testimonials to it.

To some extent, the three spheres of European politics resemble these three circles. So for fun (and only for fun), try reading the following extract from Le Goff's book and imagine Christian souls to be the European states, hell to be the geopolitical outer sphere of war and violence, heaven to be the promise-laden inner sphere, and purgatory to be that unexpected product of European politics, the intermediate sphere of the member states:

> Purgatory is situated in a position that is intermediate in more than one sense. In respect of time it falls between the death of the individual and the Last Judgment. But before settling in this location, as it were, Purgatory had first to pass through a period of uncertainty ... Whether the time of Purgatory was earthly time or eschatological time long remained a matter of controversy ... Spatially, Purgatory is also in an in-between position, between Hell and Paradise. Yet for a long time it tended to be confused with one or the other pole. Before it could begin to exist in its own right, Purgatory had to supersede both ... Above all it had to detach itself from Hell, of which it long remained a relatively undistinguished department, a sort of upper Gehenna. This wrangling between Hell and Paradise suggests that to Christians Purgatory was no minor issue ... The soil had to be prepared by long and arduous effort. Purgatory was not ultimately a true intermediary. Reserved for the purification of the future elect, it stood closer to Heaven than to Hell. No longer in the center, Purgatory was situated above rather than below the true middle.[39]

PART I

THE SECRET OF THE TABLE

The law of majority-voting itself rests on an agreement, and implies that there has been on at least one occasion unanimity.
Jean-Jacques Rousseau[1]

The Transition to Majority

How does a state originate? Contemporary political philosophy has neglected the mystery of beginning. Rather than examining how states are founded, it focuses on rights and representation within existing states; rather than the creation of power and authority, it discusses the separation of powers and the limits to be placed on authority. This conceptual neglect amounts to a major deficiency. The Americans who invaded Iraq in 2003 and blithely removed the local tyrant had clearly failed to pay sufficient attention to the issue of foundation. The country descended into anarchy and civil war. Apparently we need to be faced with the ruins of a state before we can see how hard it is to fabricate a political order and how impressive, therefore, is its mere existence, how mysterious its birth.

Once the miracle has occurred and a political body exists, it will strive to become an indubitable fact. The best approach is to come up with a good birth story (Romulus and Remus fed by a she-wolf; the Magna Carta compiled; the Bastille stormed). A good story somehow makes us forget the scars left by the historical breach. Like a fig leaf, it covers up naked contingency, making us think: Yes, that's right, that's how our society came about; that's where it started and it went on from there step by step. So a founding myth, however improbable, reinforces the sense of inevitability, without which no political order can function; whereas a factual history of a nation's beginnings, involving coincidence, a rift, a foolish act, perhaps violence, will only undermine it.

From the sixteenth century through to the eighteenth, Europe's greatest political thinkers did in fact rack their brains over the conundrum of foundation. Bloody religious and civil wars had destabilised the established order. Philosophers, including Hobbes, Locke and Rousseau, urgently needed to know how it was that people could arrive at a point where they were willing to give up some of their freedom as individuals in return for greater security or power as a group. This led to the hypothesis of the state of nature, the lawless and violent condition in which humanity was thought to have existed originally, and to the conclusion that people had left their old, natural existence by means of a social contract binding them collectively to a king or a state that maintained order. So the mystery of foundation was solved by placing it outside time, before history began.

Today's geopolitical jungle of sovereign states might be compared to that hypothetical state of nature in which individuals wandered the earth before nations came into being. For nations, the question now is whether – and if so, how – they can increase their security and power by relinquishing some independence. How would European states make that joint leap out of the state of nature? Or, as Locke would put it, under what conditions is it possible to say of an alliance between princes or states that it creates a single body politic encompassing them all?

For Hobbes, Locke or Rousseau, the answer to this crucial question lay in the transition from decision-making by unanimity to decision-making by majority, since at that point the whole became greater than the sum of its parts, the singular replaced the multiple, the constituent powers gave way to the constituted power.

John Locke in particular, in his *Second Treatise of Government* (1690), devotes several paragraphs to the connection between foundation and majority decision-making. If a majority of votes cannot bind a political body in its entirety, then it immediately falls apart. Any founding contract that leaves a veto in place is worthless. Without majority decision-making there can be no political order. A return to the veto represents a reversion to the state of nature.

In *Leviathan* (1651), Thomas Hobbes describes the transition from many to one as resulting from representation. Political representation works when one individual or legal entity is able to speak on behalf of many. If the entity in question is composed of individuals, like a parliament or a jury, the majority must prevail. Otherwise there is a danger that 'by the diversity of opinions and interests of men' it will remain 'mute' – particularly unhelpful in wartime.[2] The European Union discovered this at the start of the Iraq War, in the spring of 2003. 'Warmongers' London and Madrid were irreconcilable with 'cowards' Paris and Berlin. Hobbes would have been able to explain precisely why Javier Solana, Europe's foreign policy chief, was speechless for weeks.

In the leap to majority, Jean-Jacques Rousseau distinguished between the founding moment with its fundamental rules on the one hand, and day-to-day politics on the other. The act of foundation, which he wrote about in *Du contrat social* (1762), requires unanimity. Everyone has to agree that, from a certain point onwards, a majority decision will be valid. After all, 'What right have the hundred who want to have a master to vote on behalf of the ten who do not?' Rousseau's exemplary conclusion, as given above, was: 'The law of majority-voting itself rests on an agreement, and implies that there has been on at least one occasion unanimity.'[3] At the same time, he understands how unlikely it is that all concerned will recognise the advantages of having laws in common before they have been transformed into a society by those laws. A people presumes a state and a state presumes a people. Here Rousseau encounters the vicious circle that lies at the heart of every attempt to found a state. He believes the only way to break this circle, other than by violence, is by appealing to a higher, divine power.

Once a state exists, the situation is quite different. Urgent or trivial matters can then be decided by majority. In his *Considérations sur le gouvernement de Pologne* (1771), Rousseau discusses the notorious veto held at the time by every representative in the Polish diet, the Sejm. He is convinced that a veto is sensible when it comes to changing fundamental laws that determine the form of the state, but not for executive decision-making. Initially a way of safeguarding a people's freedom, it had become an instrument for undermining order. He writes that, although the veto was 'good when the body politic was being formed, or remained in full perfection, it becomes absurd and disastrous as soon as change becomes necessary. And change will always be necessary, above all in a large state surrounded by powerful and ambitious neighbours.'[4]

This warning was of little use to Poland. In the real-life unrest of the time, the veto brought the country to ruin. In 1772, a year after Rousseau made his recommendations, Poland's three powerful neighbours Austria, Russia and Prussia took to dividing up its territory between them. After this happened for the third time, in 1795, the country disappeared from the map for more than a century. Ever since, the example of the Polish diet has served as a dire warning.

Rousseau would say that so long as each of the European states has a veto, they do not comprise a single political body. Discord and impotence lurk in wait. The shortest route to Europe's foundation corresponds to the transition from unanimity to majority. Before that transition, each state is sovereign and any one of them can block anything at any moment. After it, the Union is sovereign and all member states risk being outvoted at any time. The invitation to the states is: Go on, jump! Or is it rather less simple than that?

European parlance is full of references to the veto. To Offices and Citizens thinkers it represents an obstacle; to States thinkers, a weapon in negotiations. When reference is made in debates to an 'extension of qualified majority voting', a new 'formula for a double majority' or the importance of majority voting for 'increasing the decision-making capacity of the Union', the existential question is sometimes passed over. We all too easily forget what is truly at stake (perhaps that is the purpose of the jargon). Hobbes, Locke and Rousseau come to our aid here, reminding us that the transition to majority decision-making is inseparable from questions about the foundation or unification of Europe.

How is that transition going? The notion of a simple leap from 'before' to 'after', from the jungle of the national veto to a united Europe, is misleading. The conundrum of foundation is not so easily resolved. Europe has undoubtedly developed over the past sixty years partly in line with the majority theory, but nevertheless the member states have held out against it, with surprising results.

Four observations to begin with. First, there is an important distinction to be made between the European Union and international organisations like the International Monetary Fund, the United Nations or the World Trade Organization, where binding majority decisions are not unusual (although the majority principle is sometimes offset by a veto for important members, as it is in the United Nations Security Council). States that belong to these organisations do not worry that membership will jeopardise their independent political lives. These are institutions and agencies that function as tools wielded by the states, whereas the European Union addresses itself, with its rights and duties and with a story about the political future, not just to the member states but to their populations. Unlike an instrumental organisation, the Union competes to some degree with the states. Whereas ordinary international organisations exist outside the states, as service providers to them, the European Union seems increasingly to want to embrace its members. Some European leaders have expressed a fear that their country will 'dissolve in Europe like a lump of sugar in a cup of coffee' (Czech premier, Václav Klaus), or that membership will mean 'the end of a thousand years of history' (British opposition leader Hugh Gaitskell, in 1962).[5] No one has ever suggested this as a possible outcome of their country's joining, say, the World Health Organization. The difference in experience explains why, in the Union, majority decision-making is a pressing, existential issue, far more so than for other international organisations.

A second observation: in Europe the issue of unanimity versus majority is not a black-and-white one. The system of voting differs from topic to topic, and there are many exceptions, argued over for decades. In this respect, the Union finds itself between two extremes – half in a state of nature and half out, as it were. True, movement (insofar as there is any) happens in one direction only: a veto may sometimes be abolished; it is never reintroduced. But the transition is not a leap – it clearly takes time. As we shall see, the interim is not wasteful delay; it is essential to what will follow.

The fact that it takes time raises, thirdly, the question of where to start. Note that Europe's foundation is being achieved in the reverse of a logical sequence. In political logic we can distinguish between two levels: that of a founding treaty and its revisions, and that of everyday decisions within its framework. As Rousseau observed, the normal order would be to begin with a definitive act of foundation for an independent political body and then to move on to legislation by majority. In Europe, the order has been reversed. So this book looks first at the transition to majority voting for ordinary decision-making (Chapter 1) and only then at the creation and revision of the founding treaty (Chapters 2 and 3).

This apparently illogical sequence has one serious side-effect: it impedes good story-telling. The fact that Europe's foundation does not happen at a specific moment, but instead takes time, is not an inherent drawback. The metaphor of a path might suggest itself – a route from unanimity to majority that stretches ahead of the newly formed Union. It implies an epic in which the hero overcomes all obstacles along the route one by one, constantly facing mortal danger in the form of the 'guillotine of unanimity' (Bettino Craxi).[6] The Union as Hercules. Alternatively, we might consider the psychological plot of a *Bildungsroman*, with an emphasis on the growing insightfulness of the member states, who in due course divest themselves of their 'national egotisms' (Paul-Henri Spaak).[7] The member states as a gathering of Wilhelm Meisters. In either genre we would find ourselves on a simple, historical timeline, able to accommodate the idea that the truly existential choices, decisions about war and peace for example, lie at the end of the road. But these linear narratives are undermined by the contradictory sequence and by a simultaneity of developments. It proves impossible to make a convincing story out of it all. At best, this is a novel with flashbacks and switches in narrative perspective. The resulting complexity undoubtedly contributes to public confusion about Europe, and to the mediocre quality of performances by story-telling politicians.

Fourth, and most importantly, we will discover that majority decision-making has indeed had a decisive impact on unification, acting as a catalyst, a threat and an ideological litmus test. We will also gradually discover that it is neither a necessary nor a sufficient condition for the emergence of a European political body. Not a necessary condition, since to this day most decisions – and certainly the more important – are taken on the basis of consensus between the member states. Not a sufficient condition, because a majority decision rejected by an outvoted government and its people would either be unenforceable or amount to foreign domination. Both outcomes have led the member states to realise that, if they want to function as 'Europe', it may not be necessary (or even desirable) to transfer all activities to the institutional inner sphere. It turns out to be possible for member states to join together and use means other than formal majority voting to put pressure on individual members. In short, the ideological battles and political crises surrounding the veto have both strengthened the cohesion of the institutional inner sphere and taught Europe to recognise itself as a circle of member states.

1

The Step Across

Unanimity ... has been the means of reaching decisions that generally preceded rules on majority decision-making ... And when fossilized into a procedural rule, it can lead to the power of one over all. But this occurs only at the terminal phase, or the phase of decline ... Before then and elsewhere, the need to achieve consensus still creates a bond and is the opposite of the veto; people want and need to reach an understanding.

A.J.P. Tammes (1951)[8]

On 18 April 1951, the Coal and Steel Treaty was signed by the founding states in the Salon de l'Horloge at the Ministry of Foreign Affairs in Paris. It was a remarkable gathering. The French host was Foreign Minister Robert Schuman, a former premier, whose career had begun before the Great War in Lorraine, then still part of Germany. From Bonn came Chancellor Konrad Adenauer, aged seventy-five, acting as his own minister of foreign affairs at the first international conference since 1932 to include a member of a democratic German government. Representing Italy was eighty-year-old Count Carlo Sforza, a descendant of the family that had ruled over Milan and the surrounding region during the Renaissance. Others present were the Belgian Paul van Zeeland, twice prime minister before the war, Joseph Bech, a Luxembourger who had stridden the world stage uninterruptedly for a quarter of a century, and Dutchman Dirk Stikker, brewer and liberal politician. Over the previous few days they had negotiated robustly on a number of unresolved issues. There were so many last-minute changes that by the *moment suprême* no official treaty text had yet been prepared. The solution was simple. The six ministers, beginning with Adenauer for Allemagne, signed a blank sheet of paper. The spirit of the accord stood surety for the letter. Europe began as an unwritten page.

A leap to majority for ordinary decision-making was embedded in the founding treaty. All the signatories agreed to it. For certain decisions – the coal price, say, or a mine closure – it was sufficient in principle for a majority of the Six to give their consent. All were then committed. In such cases, the whole took precedence over the parts: the club assumed its shape independently of the member states. In that sense, Europe, conceived in the Schuman Plan of 9 May 1950, was born with the signing of the Treaty of Paris.

Much remained unclear in April 1951. What would the new entity look like? Who would speak on its behalf? What was its relationship with the founding states? Expectations varied. The answers did not lie in the texts of the treaties, but were produced over time by chance and by combat. All the same, even in the months between Europe's conception and its birth, there were clues to the way things were going, and there were more clues to come during the 'relaunch' of 1955–57. In two strides, the national governments placed themselves at the centre, around the table. Then two events, taken together, gave an unforeseen but decisive twist to Europe's shape. These were moments of passage: a silent judicial revolution begun in 1963 and an unprecedented crisis in 1965–66, with effects that lasted for many years to come. In both cases, everything turned on the relationship between the whole and the parts.

At the table

First, back to 9 May 1950. Jean Monnet, whose idea the Coal and Steel Community had been, wanted the European offices to be as independent as possible. Power to decide on coal and steel matters would lie with a 'supranational' High Authority, to which the national governments relinquished part of their sovereignty. Within the framework of the treaty, the Authority would act as a kind of federal government. A counterweight could be provided, if necessary, by institutions of appeal, such as a Court. This practical plan served a higher goal. Sharing sovereignty over one economic sector represented, according to Schuman and Monnet, 'a first step in the federation of Europe'.[9]

The goal was clear, but the outcome was rather different. During negotiations in Paris in the summer of 1950, the French blueprint won the full support of the Germans. In London, by contrast, such ideas were taboo. Prime Minister Clement Attlee publicly branded the proposed High Authority 'an irresponsible body appointed by no one and responsible to no one'.[10] The British therefore stayed at home. The representatives of the Benelux countries, especially the Dutch, feared that Monnet's Authority might bring 'a true dictatorship' to bear on the mining industry,[11] but they came to the negotiating table, and by doing so accepted the principle of supranational decision-making.

The conflict came to a head around the matter of national governments. In Monnet's vision, they would draft the rules and then leave implementation to the Authority. But Dutch negotiator Dirk Spierenburg regarded application of the rules by independent civil servants without governmental consultation to be unwise, all the more so since developments in the mining industry affected economic life as a whole, for which governments bore responsibility. Monnet backed down, on condition that the ministers acted 'in concert'. 'You're right,' he said to Spierenburg, 'we need to get them involved in this.'[12] So, on 12 July 1950, a new European institution suddenly appeared: the Council of Ministers. It was assigned advisory powers and its approval was needed for some of the Authority's decisions. This gave national ministers a firm grip, but they were also stuck with each other because of the condition imposed by Monnet.

The mechanics of Europe had now adopted its initial configuration: a supranational authority, a council of ministers, plus parliamentary and judicial control. It remained to be seen just what kind of animal this Europe was. The original goal, Schuman's 'federation', had been omitted from the treaty text. Instead the founders aspired to make their peoples into 'a broader and deeper community'.[13]

In September 1952, the offices in Luxembourg opened. Members of the Authority and the national governments had their own conference tables. Monnet and Spierenburg's invention was working. 'In practice the ministers showed themselves to be fully engaged with it,' one witness said, 'and they were soon acting as "a club", outside of their institutionally very limited powers.'[14] Right at the founding moment, unexpectedly and independently of the treaty, the intermediate sphere of the member states appeared.

In fact its emergence can be traced back to the very first meeting of the Council, in September 1952. As a participant observed: 'Despite his small stature, Monnet, the president of the High Authority, exuded the authority appropriate to his position. The ceremonial, the festivities, the dinners, it was all ... almost breathtaking.'[15] In this ambience, the six foreign ministers, anticipating ratification of a treaty establishing a European army (a quite different text that happened to have the same signatories), decided to have a draft statute drawn up for a 'European political community'. They took this highly political decision, which had little to do with coal or steel, as a gathering of the Six. So the Council of Ministers, created as a Community institution, immediately became the favoured consultative body of the circle of members.

Another telling event took place a year later. Faced with the first post-war slump in the Western European economy, the ministers in the Council agreed

on the need for joint economic analyses and a joint assessment of the repercussions of the crisis for the coal and steel industries. There was nothing
about this in the treaty, so the Council had no authorisation; but the Belgian
minister, Jean Duvieusart, saw a way forward: 'Let's do it as "representatives of
the governments united in the Council"'.[16] So it was that research into
consumer purchasing power began, and the High Authority's statistical office
came to busy itself with far more than just mining statistics. The formula
proved productive, leading within a decade to dozens of decisions by the Six
that fell outside the treaty. (These were the '*Mischformen*' or 'hybrids' of international and community law that an astute German lawyer would talk of later,
and which typify the intermediate sphere.)[17]

A few years after signing their founding treaty, the same six states sat around
the table again. The mood was more cautious. In the intervening period, their
ambitious plan for a European army had run into the sand – exit Monnet.
Between 1955–57, the Six drew up a treaty on a European common market.
In its content it went further than the previous pact. The agreements, no
longer limited to a particular sector, had the potential to affect all of national
economic life, especially industry and agriculture. The form the treaty took,
however, was relatively modest: it concentrated solely on economic concerns.
Higher political aims were kept out of the preamble, aside from the deliberately vague phrase 'an ever closer union among the peoples'.[18]

The institutional mechanics looked more modest in 1957 as well. The
institutions remained the same, but the distribution of power was different.
There was to be no High Authority, but instead a Commission. That sounded
more innocuous. Its main tasks were to monitor adherence to the rules and to
make proposals. The Council of Ministers would decide what was to become
of those proposals. In many areas, such as agriculture, only agreements in
principle were made; the actual rules had yet to be formulated. There was no
kite-flying this time about the Authority/Commission merely needing to
apply the rules set down in the treaty. Lengthy (if not permanent) negotiations
between the states lay ahead. This, too, demonstrated the need for the Council
to have the power to take decisions. The governments' conference table had
moved to the centre of decision-making.

Conversations around the ministers' table formally followed a set script,
known as the 'community method'. The Commission had the exclusive right
to initiate proposals for Council decisions that would benefit the European
market. The Council could decide by majority, so long as the outcome did not
deviate from the Commission's initiative. The member states could change a
proposal received from the Commission only if they did so unanimously. This

form of majority voting at the ministers' table was due to come into force for quite a few policy areas after four, eight or more years. The smaller nations, in particular, were content to accept the majority principle. They felt that certain legislation would turn out to be indispensable for the market, engendering a common interest that justified being able to bypass the veto. The entire set-up was an institutional balancing act.

Majority voting, built in for the near future, is an element that stands out. Its consequences would be anything but trivial. According to one of those present, during negotiations in the Château de Val-Duchesse in Brussels nobody ever used the word 'supranational'.[19] The central place allocated to the governments meant there was no reason to do so. Majority voting did potentially give the circle of member states a supranational character, but at the same time the built-in delay meant that a fundamental conflict, inherent in the treaty, over the relationship between the whole and the parts remained hidden. For this reason among others, one French negotiator called the Rome pact 'a meticulously ambiguous treaty'.[20]

So, in the seven years between the Schuman Declaration and the signing of the Treaty of Rome, the national governments installed themselves at the centre of European politics. Although the originator of the Coal and Steel Community at first wanted to keep them out, they were given advisory and endorsement powers (1951), and later decision-making powers (1957). From that point on, the ministers met as a Council at least once a month, instead of every three months as before.

The position occupied by the ambassadors of the Six was significant as well. They met every week, along with a representative of the Commission, to discuss matters as they arose and to prepare for Council meetings. Having started out in 1953 as a small group of shuttle diplomats, in 1958 the ambassadors formed themselves into the Committee of Permanent Representatives of the Member States, based in Brussels. This forum proved to be a crucial point of connectivity in community life: the ambassadors represented national interests in Brussels and, conversely, community interests in their capitals. Because the Committee had come into being outside the treaty, one of the ambassadors jokingly called its members 'les enfants naturels de la Communauté' – 'the Community's bastard children'.[21] (Not until 1965 was it given treaty status.)

The power of the assembled ambassadors, on the boundary between diplomacy and politics, soon became legendary. In their Committee, countless conflicts between member states were ironed out or settled by negotiation, and economic interests were weighed, bartered and interlinked. There was considerable pressure to produce results. So many joint decisions needed to be made by the Six that only the most important unresolved business could be passed on to the ministers (who had enough to do at home). In Community circles, some at first feared that the ambassadors would erode the power of the Commission, whose job it was to present proposals to the Council; but there was a growing realisation that their forum was an essential link between the capitals and 'Brussels'. All those involved testify to the extraordinary atmosphere that prevailed among the ambassadors. Fierce debaters became fond of each other, and even though they sometimes spent all day arguing, a remarkable *esprit de corps* developed. After eleven years at this table, the proud Gaullist Jean-Marc Boegner said on leaving:

> I have loved that Committee just as we all love it. I would say that I have loved it as a sailor loves his ship, as a peasant loves his field or his vineyard . . . Indeed, it seems to me that what characterises the group that we form is that it allows us to be entirely ourselves within it, . . . that we feel that we are all equal within it.[22]

This 'circle of equals' – scoffed at by the pure-in-doctrine as 'the devil's work'[23] – was one of the earliest forms in which the unforeseen intermediate world of the member states manifested itself. It was the place where trust between the members slowly grew.

The ongoing conversation between ministers (monthly) and between ambassadors (weekly) boosted club feeling enormously. Crucially, the governments sat round the table together. This made the emerging European political body more viable than it would have been in the rarefied, federal atmosphere of Monnet's original vision. It was able to live up to its responsibility towards the national populations.

The Treaty of Rome had created a new basis for Europe, and now two questions arose in a heightened form. First, how much weight would be given to the wishes of an individual government when a joint decision was made? How strong was your case if you were against something that four or five others favoured? This is the constitutional question of majority. Second, what was the relationship between a joint decision, once taken, and everyone's individual decisions? Could you agree to 'A' as a minister in the Council in Brussels, and then at home, with your own government in Paris, Rome or The Hague, opt after all for 'B'? This is the judicial question of precedence. The two issues are fought out in separate domains, yet at stake in both cases is the degree of collective coercion, the relationship between the complete circle and the individual members. From 1958 onwards, the precedence and majority questions formed the battleground where the nature of the relationship between member states and their club was thrashed out.

According to the generally accepted ideological dichotomy, there were only two possible paths for the Six: majority with precedence (supranationalism) and unanimity without precedence (intergovernmentalism). Looked at objectively, two further combinations were conceivable: majority without precedence and unanimity with precedence. Here were four alternative ways of filling the unwritten page from the Salon de l'Horloge.

The actual course of events was different from anything the ideological templates could have helped to predict. As it turned out, the member states did not take the supranational path for one issue and the intergovernmental path for another. (This puts in its proper place the brainteaser of an antithesis often found in specialist literature.) Instead they twice did the same thing. Twice the states chose the option with the most robust form of collective coercion. The outcome: precedence for the club and consensus among the members.

Both choices were made in Luxembourg, the first in a ruling by the Court on 5 February 1963, the second in a political accord of 29 January 1966. They determined the path taken during those three decisive years, eliminating the other three possible options. Europe is still living with the unexpected result.

THE SPIRIT

The six founding states had not agreed in advance how to settle any conflict that might arise between a European regulation and a national one. What if the national ministers took a joint decision that was not complied with, or was even undermined, by one of their number back home? Such things happened. It might be a one-off incident, a moment of weakness. In that case, the others – or the Commission, which acted as a watchdog – could go to the Court and the problem would be resolved. But the conflict might be more fundamental. What if a member state were to justify the violation of a European rule by referring to laws already adopted by its national parliament, or even to its constitution? Then it would be law against law. Which would have precedence?

In international law, a state will usually decide for itself how to meet its international obligations. If it breaches them, it can be made answerable to international forums. In the case of the Community in 1960, the other member states and the Commission could institute legal proceedings at the European Court in Luxembourg against a member state that was failing to comply with community regulations. The Court would find in favour of the plaintiffs and the accused would then have to adjust its national legislation.

It was questionable, though, whether this classic resolution mechanism would suffice for the Community. It would place an excessive burden on the Commission and would be extremely time-consuming, with lengthy disruptions to the common market as a result.

The dilemma soon landed on a national judge's desk. In the early 1960s, the haulage firm Van Gend & Loos, which had transported several tonnes of a particular type of plastic from West Germany to the Netherlands, found itself faced with an increased import duty and lodged a complaint with Dutch customs, appealing to the Treaty of Rome. The tax authorities claimed, based on other national decisions, that there had been no unjustified increase in the duty. The Dutch judge hesitated and first asked the opinion of the European Court in Luxembourg about an underlying issue: did the European treaty, written with the member states in mind, also grant enforceable rights to individuals? The anticipated answer was 'no', which would have settled the case. But that was not the outcome.

The ruling of the European Court of Justice in the *Van Gend & Loos* case is regarded as a milestone in the history of European law. Many a legal handbook has remarked on how 'far-sighted', 'audacious' or 'innovative' the judges in Luxembourg were, while at the same time stressing that they did nothing more than draw conclusions from the treaty. This is puzzling. How can the mere application of a rule denote a fundamental revision? The paradox goes to the heart of the case. The ruling of 5 February 1963 is a European moment of passage that relied for its success on self-abnegation. Although there is little to add to the standard account, it is useful to take a look at the court case and its outcome, in order to appreciate *Van Gend & Loos* not as the famous stepping-stone of legal doctrine, but as a breakthrough in the political relationship between member states and the club.

Not only the parties to the case, but also the Belgian, German and Dutch governments and the Commission made their opinions known to the Court. No, the three governments objected in chorus, the treaty is binding for member states only in the context of international law. If we breach the terms of the treaty, we can be reported to the Luxembourg Court by another member state or by the Commission, but not under any circumstances by our own citizens in a national court. We'll stay the boss in our own homes, thank you very much. The Commission, however, like Van Gend & Loos, believed private citizens should be able to protect themselves against violations of the fundamental rules of the European Community.

On 5 February 1963, the seven-headed European Court of Justice reached a surprising verdict. First of all, the Court declared itself qualified, in the face of procedural objections from governments, to answer a question posed by a judge in a national court. It thereby safeguarded its right to speak. The Court then argued that the answer to the question lay not just in the explicit provisions of the pact, but also in (note the sequence) 'the spirit, the general scheme and the wording' of the treaty. It thereby ensured itself space in which to speak. Of the three manifestations of the Treaty of Rome to which the Court was appealing, it was the spirit that did the creative work, to judge by the ruling's spectacular key findings:

> The objective of the EEC Treaty, which is to establish a common market, the functioning of which is of direct concern to interested parties in the Community, implies that this Treaty is more than an agreement which merely creates mutual obligations between the contracting states. This view is confirmed by the preamble to the Treaty which refers not only to governments but to peoples ... [The] nationals of the States brought together in the Community are called upon to cooperate in the functioning of this Community through the intermediary of the European Parliament ...
>
> The conclusion to be drawn from this is that the Community constitutes a new legal order of international law for the benefit of which the States have limited their sovereign rights, albeit within limited fields, and the subjects of which comprise not only Member States but also their nationals.[24]

The Court, starting out with merely an 'objective', had produced in a few sentences nothing less than 'a new legal order'. Access to community law for individual citizens did not mean that the Court was opening its doors to them, but that national courts must guarantee compliance with European regulations. Faced with an increased import duty for Van Gend & Loos, Dutch courts dealing with customs duties would have to reach a verdict compatible with the treaty.

What makes this ruling by the Court so revolutionary? Lawyers discern in it the birth of, as the jargon goes, 'direct effect' – the principle that individuals can, under certain circumstances, appeal to the treaty over the heads of the states. There is nothing trivial about this. To a quite remarkable degree, it ties together European and national legal systems, and the consequences of this for the relationship between individuals and Europe are considerable. In a single strategic move, the Court had bound two further groups, each of which had tasks and interests of its own, to the workings of community law. First, every national judge was henceforth also a European judge. He or she had a duty to apply European regulations, not through the Court in Luxembourg, but within any court of justice or tribunal, no matter how high or low or in which domain of law. Second, from this point on, any participant in economic life – manufacturer, wholesaler, employee, consumer – could force a member state to adhere to those rules. This, too, was a deliberate move on the part of the European Court, as demonstrated by the remark in *Van Gend & Loos* that 'the vigilance of individuals concerned to protect their rights' would be a useful addition to monitoring by the Commission and the member states. One of the seven judges would later put it even more strongly: 'When a private individual turns to a judge for recognition of a right that he derives from the treaty, he is not merely acting out of self-interest but becomes thereby a kind of assistant to the Community.'[25] At a stroke, hundreds of courts and millions of potential plaintiffs were made available to serve Europe. From a judicio-sociological point of view alone, *Van Gend & Loos* was a masterful move.

Yet this is not the principal significance of the ruling. Something fundamental preceded the new judicial maxim, something occasionally forgotten by legal experts. An essential precondition for the successful proclamation of a direct connection in law between individuals and Europe was that the states allowed themselves to be set aside. In the audacious way in which the Court bypassed them lies the genius of the judgment. Against the will of the founding states (of which three had, in fact, objected during the sitting), the Court put the spirit of the pact before the letter of the treaty. The Court was bluffing. That goes without saying. After all, who can know the spirit of a pact? And who can decide that the judges, rather than the founders, are qualified to speak on behalf of that spirit? If the founding states had been asked in advance to accept that the objective of the Community 'implies that this Treaty is more than an agreement which merely creates mutual obligations between the contracting states', they might perhaps have recoiled. In that sense, the Court was playing for high stakes in *Van Gend & Loos*. As it turned out, all the members accepted the ruling, and only then – not before – did the Community become 'a new legal order'. The European Court had calmly appointed itself the supreme spokesman for the founding spirit.

The political success of *Van Gend & Loos* can therefore be attributed to a clever game with time. The Court staged a coup on 5 February 1963 in the name of a new, autonomous legal order, while claiming that – although no one had been aware of it – this order was as old as the treaty itself. So its infringement of the status quo was concealed. Or, more accurately, the break with the founding moment was located in the past. The judges, as it were, said encouragingly to the states: It's all right, this isn't a leap; you crossed that bridge a long time ago.

As soon as the states believed they had crossed the bridge, as soon as the six founding governments recognised the Court as spokesman for their pact, they were judicially tamed. From that moment on, by appealing to its own fictitious origin ('1957'), the Court was easily able to formulate legal principles that would strengthen the position of the European club. This is where lawyers (their mouths watering) set to work. But when regarded from our chosen perspective – that of Europe's foundation – all these things derive from that first moment of passage on 5 February 1963.

One subsequent step is of relevance here. As we have seen, the Court plucked the first fruit of the new situation from *Van Gend & Loos*, namely the 'direct effect' of European law. (We now know that the tree was actually planted only when the states left the Court undisturbed to pluck that first fruit.) In its ruling, the Court did not immediately pronounce upon that other important principle, the precedence of European over national law. In slightly different circumstances, it might have harvested this tempting fruit straight away; but there was no need, since the Dutch constitution stated that international treaties took precedence over national legislation. Such a move might have proven one immodest gesture too far, and the Court decided to wait for a more auspicious moment.

The opportunity soon came, arising from a conflict between an Italian consumer and Italy's national electricity board. Again it was a low-ranking judge in an administrative court who, because of potential incompatibility between a national decision and the European pact, wanted to know whether certain provisions of the treaty had 'direct effect'. Again a national government vigorously contested the legitimacy of an individual request, and again the outcome was a legendary Court ruling, *Costa/ENEL* of 15 June 1964. Building on *Van Gend & Loos*, the seven judges ruled:

> By contrast with ordinary international treaties, the EEC Treaty has created its own legal system . . .
>
> By creating a Community of unlimited duration, having its own institutions, its own personality, its own legal capacity and capacity of representation on the international plane and, more particularly, real powers stemming from a limitation of sovereignty or a transfer of powers from the States to the Community, the Member States have limited their sovereign rights, albeit within limited fields, and have thus created a body of law which binds both their nationals and themselves.
>
> The integration into the laws of each Member State of provisions which derive from the Community and more generally the terms and the spirit of the Treaty, make it impossible for the States, as a corollary, to accord precedence to a unilateral and subsequent measure over a legal system accepted by them on a basis of reciprocity. Such a measure cannot therefore be inconsistent with that legal system . . .

The precedence of Community law is confirmed by Article 189 . . .

It follows . . . that the law stemming from the Treaty, an independent source of law, could not, because of its special and original nature, be overridden by domestic legal provisions, however framed, without being deprived of its character as Community law and without the legal basis of the Community itself being called into question.[26]

Although less spectacular in its summing up, this was a handsomely constructed self-affirmation. In the first of the findings cited here, the Court corrects itself: European law, as a legal system, does not, on further reflection, fall under 'ordinary' international law, but is autonomous. In the second of its grounds, the Court avails itself of new elements of the founding treaty, or at least elements unused in *Van Gend & Loos*, to reinforce that autonomous legal order. Only then is it ready to invoke the spirit of the pact in order to deploy the principle of precedence, which it formulates first negatively (no national precedence) and then positively (European precedence), before reaching its confident conclusion. In short, the Court sets the tree rather more firmly in the ground before plucking, in the name of the spirit of the treaty, the coveted fruit. The European legal system had placed itself above the national legal systems.

So did the states again fall for a bluff? Not all of them, or not immediately. Another decade passed before the six founders formally recognised at the highest judicial level the precedence of community regulations, as announced in *Costa/ENEL*. By doing so, they gave their blessing to the Court's coup, since – unlike the founding states, which suddenly heard in 1963–64 what they had supposedly agreed to in 1957 – all the states that subsequently joined knew exactly what they were doing. On the occasion of their entry into the European order, all the accession states – from the British, Irish and Danes in 1973 to the Croatians in 2013 – have had to sign up to the Luxembourg jurisprudence. They were not pushed into it after the event, in the name of the spirit of the treaty. They jumped.

Although there were further skirmishes, the battle between courts over ordinary decision-making had now been settled in favour of the European legal system. When Germany introduced a road tax for foreigners in 1990, for instance, its right to do so was disputed in the European Court. A German minister came in person, in his court robes, to plead for the retention of the *Strassenbenützungsgebühr*. The Court ruled unambiguously that this road tax was in conflict with competition regulations. Bonn accepted the verdict. Joint decisions, once made, are binding and enforceable.

Now, lastly, to an address by a former president of the Court, a judge at the time of *Van Gend & Loos* and *Costa/ENEL*. This is an unparalleled piece of Court rhetoric from 1976, in which both the spirit of the founding treaty and the realities of the Community structure are used to buoy up the 'self-evident' principle of precedence:

> Compiling such a large number of treaties and regulations, developing at great expense so many institutions shared between Brussels, Luxembourg and Strasbourg, then allowing a member state blithely to prevent with one stroke of the pen the thereby promulgated joint regulations from being applied on its own territory – that would be a well-nigh insane undertaking, which we could not possibly assume to have been wished for by those who framed the treaties ... ! This at least was the assessment of the high courts and law courts of the majority of our states, when they implicitly or explicitly judged that it was in the nature of things that Community law must be common to all and must therefore prevail over the law of each member state. But that which goes without saying becomes even clearer when it is said, especially when the principle has in fact been contested from time to time.[27]

THE EMPTY CHAIR

In 1965, storms swept across the Europe of the Six. France stayed away from Brussels for months and threatened to withdraw from the treaty. Two national elections – German in September and French in December – contributed decisively to the outcome of the conflict, which reached its final stage in January 1966. In the end, none of the Six got everything it wanted, yet all could claim victory. The one obvious loser was the seventh party at the table.

A latent tension between two visions of the European order erupted into what can be seen as Europe's first constitutional crisis. The unprecedented turbulence of these events and the return to the table are signs that it was a vital moment of passage for Europe. To avoid simply falling into the usual patterns of thought, it is worth examining events as they happened.

The outcome, the 'Luxembourg Compromise' of 29 January 1966, is generally seen as causing a blockage in European politics. The Six did indeed put the script of the treaty aside for a long time, but they also became aware that one could not step away from the European table at will, into the free outer sphere. One member state (France) tried it, but returned to its 'empty chair' after seven months. Between the inner sphere of the treaty and the outer world of diplomacy, they had unexpectedly come upon an in-between world, with its own rules and its own forms of duress. For this intermediate sphere of the member states, the Compromise of January 1966 represented a 'coming-out' – recognition by the Six of a joint existence outside the treaty. In the decades that followed, it would transpire that Europe, based on this somewhat ungraciously vilified accord, was able to develop into a political body – not as the Brussels inner sphere, but as an increasingly tight-knit grouping of member states.

Crisis and compromise

The issue at the heart of the crisis was the transition to majority decision-making, planned for 1 January 1966. The date was laid down in the Treaty of Rome. The states had given themselves (in principle) twelve years to establish a common market, starting in 1958. This period was divided into three four-year stages. Whereas the step from the first to the second stage, at the start of 1962, had been governed by a hard-fought transition decision, the step from the second stage to the third was to take place automatically. From that moment on, the Council of Ministers would decide by majority on vital matters such as grain prices, trade agreements and the movement of capital. Clearly this would drastically alter the relationship between the member states and their club. But how?

In Brussels, hopes were high for the anticipated breakthrough to majority. Once liberated from the threat of national vetoes, only the Commission could speak on behalf of Europe. That at least was the belief of Commission President Walter Hallstein. In April 1962, this former professor of constitutional law explained the new Brussels orthodoxy to an audience of American academics: 'The principle of majority voting is employed by the Community for its regular proceedings; the rule of unanimity, which was one of the stumbling blocks of previous experiences, is here reserved for exceptional cases ... Moreover, majority voting becomes more and more the norm for Council decisions as the treaty's transition period progresses.'[28] He regarded decision-making by unanimity among the states as a final spasm of the founding phase, which was nearing completion. Moreover, Hallstein was convinced that European economic integration went beyond economics. It created a new '*zôon politikon*',[29] a political animal. Within the young Community, his own institution was the equivalent of, if not a head, then at least an engine. This line of reasoning brought the Commission president close to claiming to represent a 'government of Europe'. By using the technical word 'executive', he stopped just short of that taboo term.

In Paris, too, there was an awareness that 1 January 1966 was now very close. General de Gaulle had been in power since 1958. Against expectations, the old war hero had fully complied with the European treaty, and, especially where French agricultural interests were at stake, he also ensured that the other member states complied with it. As he made clear at his celebrated press conferences, this was not for love of things supranational. Referring to one expression that had been incorrectly attributed to him – '*l'Europe des patries*' (the Europe of the fatherlands) – de Gaulle told the press on 15 May 1962: 'The fatherland is a human, sentimental element, whereas Europe can be constructed only on active, authoritative, responsible elements. What elements? *Eh bien*, the states! . . . I have already said and I repeat that at present no other Europe is possible than that of the states, aside of course from that of myths, fictions, parades.' And on majority decision-making: 'At the present time there is no way to have recalcitrant nations constrained by a foreign majority.'[30]

The General indulged in more than just rhetoric. Back in 1960, at his request, a French minister had investigated how the 'federal virtualities' in the Treaty of Rome, especially majority decision-making, could be 'inactivated'. Carelessness on the part of a secretary resulted in his confidential memorandum finding its way into a newspaper. French plans for a European 'political union' dating from 1961 and 1962 were likewise perceived as a barely concealed attempt to undermine the community institutions (and had for that reason been rejected). So both sides were in a position to know each other's standpoints and intentions in advance.

In the spring of 1965, the affair gained momentum. In mid-March, Commission President Walter Hallstein went on an official visit to America. He spoke with President Johnson in the White House and with the secretary of state for defence at the Pentagon. This latter step, entry into the inner sanctum of national security, was without precedent. Remarkable, too, was the fact that Hallstein stayed in Blair House, usually reserved for visiting heads of state. In the corridors, it was rumoured that, when asked by an American journalist what exactly his function was, Hallstein had replied, 'a kind of Prime Minister of Europe'.[31] The pretensions of its president exposed agitation in the Commission as a whole. According to a French commissioner, himself a sceptic, the majority of his colleagues were of the opinion that the hour of glory was approaching. They were dreaming of a 'Tennis Court Oath' *à la* 1789.[32] (A little over six months later, a constitutional oath would indeed be sworn, but of a very different kind.)

On 22 March, the Commission voted in favour of an ambitious package of proposals, which, if accepted by the member states, would amount to the longed-for political leap. The driving forces behind it were Hallstein and the Dutch commissioner, Sicco Mansholt. It cleverly linked three issues: the financing of agriculture, the Community budget and parliamentary competencies. In brief, farmers would in due course be paid entirely out of a European agriculture fund, and to that end import duties on agricultural and industrial products would flow directly into a European treasury, while Europarliamentarians in Strasbourg were to be given a decisive say on how the money was spent. The first point was, in theory, quite uncontroversial. The striking thing about the second was that, from a certain time onwards, revenues would greatly exceed expenditure, and the Commission had a monopoly on proposals for spending the money. The third point meant that members of the European Assembly would be able to change the budget against the wishes of as many as four member states. In a breach of protocol, Hallstein revealed the plans two days later, at a sitting of the Strasbourg Assembly – which in those days still consisted of delegates from national parliaments – before they had been sent to the member states. The Commission was addressing national parliaments and public opinion directly, over the heads of the governments. To their displeasure, the ministers had lost some of their freedom of manoeuvre. France, which held the presidency, felt particularly aggrieved.

The decisive debate in the Council of Ministers took place on 28–30 June 1965, at the Palais des Congrès in Brussels. The conflict came to a head around the question of whether the three pionts needed to be considered as a whole (the view held by Italy, Germany and the Netherlands) or whether the Council could limit itself to an accord on the first (France). The French, whose interests lay in an agreement on agricultural financial regulation, did not want to be drawn by the bait of that first point into the political trap the Commission had set with the second and third, but the Italian, German and Dutch delegations insisted on including Community resources and the European Assembly's budgetary powers in the package. All three governments were under pressure from their own parliaments, which took the perfectly reasonable view that they ought to have the influence they had lost at a national level returned to them at a European level. The Italians had a specific problem, in that the previous agricultural regulations had worked to their disadvantage. For the Dutch, an anti-French attitude in European affairs had been a constant for years, if not centuries. New was the West German position. Since the resignation of Chancellor Adenauer in the autumn of 1963, Franco-German relations had cooled. The Belgians and Luxembourgers sought a compromise. In this complex field, little progress was made on the Monday (28 June) beyond technical deliberations on the financial settlement.

It was not until the afternoon of the Wednesday that discussions resumed. Many expected a marathon session, with the president, as was customary, stopping the clock at midnight so that they could continue negotiating until agreement was reached. The Italian Amintore Fanfani reiterated Rome's wish to give Europarliamentarians the right to approve the budget. German Secretary of State Rolf Lahr backed him up. Maurice Couve de Murville then solemnly warned on behalf of France that if the commitment to a new financial settlement for agriculture was not acted upon, there would be 'no Community' any longer.[33] As chairman, he proposed limiting discussion to the apportionment of financial burdens. Only the Belgian, Paul-Henri Spaak, supported Couve de Murville. Commission President Walter Hallstein fiercely defended his plans. Then the German minister, Gerhard Schröder, spoke for the first and last time. He insisted on including the Commission's entire three-point package, and informed his colleagues that the Bundestag had unanimously adopted a resolution that afternoon calling on his government to support the Strasbourg parliament. As far as the financial settlement went, no one advocated any unseemly delay, but Schröder saw no reason for sticking pettily to 1 July. It was an arbitrary date and 'not the year thousand'.[34] After this decisive intervention it was time for the dinner.

When they resumed at half past ten in the evening, there was only an hour and a half left. The French tried in vain to overcome Italian objections to the financial settlement (an offer from Finance Minister Valéry Giscard d'Estaing was rejected by his Italian counterpart). At two minutes past twelve the lights went out in the Palais des Congrès. It was now 1 July. At half past midnight, Couve de Murville summed up all the positions. No one had anything to add. The seven delegation leaders withdrew behind closed doors for another hour. Then it was over. At two in the morning, Couve de Murville, as chairman of the Council, held the customary closing press conference, saying that a serious crisis had broken out. Later that morning, from the Elysée Palace, came a declaration that France had decided to 'draw the legal, economic and political consequences' from the fiasco.[35]

This was no bluff. On 6 July, Charles de Gaulle withdrew practically his entire Council delegation to Paris until further notice. Thus began the French boycott of the Community, soon dubbed the 'politics of the empty chair'. No one had reckoned with this step. According to the agriculture commissioner, de Gaulle's violation of the European pact risked 'the greatest disaster since Hitler'.[36] The melodramatic comparison is a measure of the uncertainty about what would happen next.

The last day of June 1965 marked the start of an entirely new phase in the constitutional crisis. The departure of France meant that something else altogether was at stake. The Commission's set of proposals was no longer on the table. Hallstein had overplayed his hand. It was now a matter of the survival of the Community. The conflict lay where de Gaulle had wanted it from the start: between the states. What contemporaries suspected is now beyond doubt: the French president was bent on a rift. The crisis surrounding the financial settlement (about which Paris was right in a formal sense) was for him an 'unexpected pretext'.[37] The unspoken aim of the operation was to block the transition to majority decision-making. Couve de Murville later stated that he had discussed with de Gaulle a month earlier how they could benefit from the approaching clash: 'Confident of his blessing, I went back to Brussels and I burned the bridges.'[38]

The question now was how the other states would react. The Belgians' initial reflex was to fall back on bilateral diplomatic consultation. Spaak, seeing his life's work under threat, was willing to mediate. He was prevented from doing so by his German and Dutch counterparts, at the margins of a Nato meeting. Chancellor Ludwig Erhard was facing Bundestag elections in September and did not want to negotiate with de Gaulle before then. During a state visit to Rome on 7 July, Erhard implored the Italians, who had taken over the six-month presidency, to 'face the General as a Community'.[39] The previous day, France had formally asked for the forthcoming Council session to be cancelled. Rome ignored this request and the meetings planned for July went ahead. Despite misgivings on the part of Belgium and Luxembourg, the Five – as they would be called from this point on – gathered as a Council on 13 July. They declared their meeting valid: it was France that was failing to meet its obligations by staying away. This procedural counterstroke was of symbolic importance. Europe continued to exist even in the absence of one of its founders. At the same time, it was a gesture that put paid to de Gaulle's strategy of imposing a new *modus vivendi* by engaging in bilateral diplomacy.

The Five were still failing to present a united front; but with his 9 September press conference marking the start of the French political season, the General drove them together. He laid into supranational Europe mercilessly, referring to the Commission as 'some technocratic, stateless and irresponsible Areopagus', its proposals of the past year 'usurpatory' in character. De Gaulle also provided his own interpretation of the crisis: 'What happened in Brussels on 30 June with regard to the agricultural financial regulation has brought to light not only the persistent reserves of most of our partners toward the inclusion of agriculture in the Common Market, but also certain basic errors or ambiguities that appear in the treaties on the economic union of the Six. That is why, sooner or later, the crisis was inevitable.'[40]

The French president outlined the risk posed to his country by majority decision-making. Everything Paris had gained, in agricultural matters, for example, might be taken away at any moment by majority. The Community, he said, could resume its work 'only after a delay whose extent cannot be foreseen'.[41] It was de Gaulle's minister of foreign affairs who drew the operational conclusion. A settlement on agricultural financing would no longer be sufficient, said Couve de Murville on 20 October in the Assemblée Nationale: France wanted a 'complete revision' of the founding treaty.[42]

Meanwhile there was intense diplomatic traffic between the Five, centred on Bonn. The German elections of 19 September had resulted in victory for the Christian Democrat Erhard. From now on, the German government could afford to be tenacious. The first opportunity to demonstrate this was at a Council meeting on 25 October, where the Italian chair urged the Five to reply to the French. In a respectful but firm public declaration, they reiterated their attachment to the founding treaty: 'The Governments consider that the solution of the problems confronting the Communities must be found within the framework of the Treaties and of their Institutions.'[43] They invited France to a special meeting of the Council that no one from the Commission would attend, an eventuality provided for in the treaty. This was a major concession to the French, given their criticism of that institution, although it was made easier by the fact that – for the Five, too – Hallstein had become 'a burdensome presence'.[44] Even more remarkably, the Five negotiated a secret accord, unmentioned in the Council's conclusions, which they showed to the French. It was a solemn declaration that the founding treaty must not be altered. The document was signed by the five ministers, each of whom kept a copy. From that point onwards, the Five operated as one in the crisis, as sworn allies. This was no 'Tennis Court Oath' of 1789, but it was certainly a constitutional vow.

Now it was a matter of waiting for the French presidential elections in December. De Gaulle declared himself a candidate only one month beforehand. In a pompous statement on television, he asked the electorate for 'mass support', convinced he would win an absolute majority in the first round. It was a miscalculation. The way in which the European crisis affected this national election was totally unexpected. In late October, the most important farmers' federation – with 5 million members – called on the French to vote against de Gaulle. The farming population, estimated to make up 20 per cent of the electorate, feared that, along with the Community, agricultural financing was at stake. The business world made known its view that a quick solution to the crisis was of huge economic importance. The five other French presidential candidates all capitalised on these European concerns. The relatively unknown centrist Jean Lecanuet had the most supranational message – he even received an endorsement from *père fondateur* Jean Monnet. In the first round, Lecanuet, from a standing start, won 15 per cent of the vote. To his own disappointment, de Gaulle managed only 44 per cent, and his entourage briefly feared he might withdraw. In the second round, the General faced the Socialist François Mitterrand (whose Vichy past he knew about but did not exploit), who had joined the fray as 'the European candidate'. The president won, with more than 55 per cent; but victory did not expunge the humiliating lesson of the first round. De Gaulle now knew that a majority of the French would not support his policy on Europe.

The end-game could begin. In between the two rounds of elections, de Gaulle had let it be known through his prime minister that France was about to accept the invitation issued by the Five. Again a question of diplomatic form arose. The Five wanted to gather as a Council, the French as simply six governments. The compromise was a conference in Luxembourg on 17–18 January 1966, which met the French demand for a meeting outside Brussels. To the Five, the duchy had European connotations, and to underline the connection the Luxembourgers chose as a location the conference hall at the Hôtel de Ville, where Monnet had opened the first meeting of the High Authority in 1952. The presence of the secretary-general of the Council confirmed the community character of the gathering. As agreed, the Commission was not represented.

On behalf of Paris, Couve de Murville placed two issues on the table. The first had to do with the way the Commission operated. The French had put together a list of behavioural rules for the institution, ranging from how to receive ambassadors of third countries (only in the presence of the Council) to how to announce proposals (first to the member states and only then to the Parliament and the public). Taken as a whole, his list revealed the depth of French annoyance at the red-carpet pretensions of the Brussels bureaucrats. Although the Five thought some of the complaints ridiculous, the ambassadors, deputising for the six ministers, fairly easily reached agreement on milder terms that could be taken up with the Commission.

The second issue was more fundamental and led to a head-on collision: France demanded a veto and the Five refused to grant one. Couve de Murville was concerned about situations in which weighty national interests were at stake. The easiest solution would be to remove majority decision-making from the founding treaty, the Frenchman said. But it seemed that parliamentary ratification for such a revision would be difficult to obtain in Rome or The Hague. He needed to come up with an alternative solution. The Five, for their part, refused to accept any text that involved a departure from the Treaty of Rome. Italian Emilio Colombo was vociferously indignant, German Gerhard Schröder and Dutchman Joseph Luns testily dug in their heels. Luns insisted on expressing his view that a veto would amount to the 'paralysis' of the Community.[45] The Belgian, Spaak, conciliatory, stressed the shared belief that in the case of differences of opinion an accord must be sought 'in all wisdom'.[46] He proposed a system with several rounds of discussion. Again a sticking point was reached when it came to the possibility of resorting to a vote *in extremis*. For France that remained anathema; for the Five it was essential. At this point the decision was made to adjourn.

On 28–29 January, the Five resumed their deliberations in Luxembourg. The atmosphere was more relaxed, almost 'springlike'.[47] Couve de Murville negotiated with a smile, Schröder showed less irritation than ten days earlier, and even Dutch Foreign Minister Luns was constructive. The only remaining dispute concerned veto versus majority. The impasse was the same. Legally speaking, the positions were incompatible, as became clear all over again after a day and a half. At the same time, there was a political desire to reach an accord. They could either paper over the point at issue or look the conflict in the face. It was Spaak who advocated the latter option. Heated debate followed. In the end, the ministers of the Six agreed on a joint declaration, which the chairman, Pierre Werner, made public shortly after midnight. The text is known as the Luxembourg Compromise and it runs as follows:

Majority voting procedure

I. Where, in the case of decisions which may be taken by majority vote on a proposal of the Commission, very important interests of one or more partners are at stake, the Members of the Council will endeavour, within a reasonable time, to reach solutions which can be adopted by all the Members of the Council while respecting their mutual interests and those of the Community, in accordance with Article 2 of the Treaty.

II. With regard to the preceding paragraph, the French delegation considers that where very important interests are at stake the discussion must be continued until unanimous agreement is reached.

III. The six delegations note that there is a divergence of views on what should be done in the event of a failure to reach complete agreement.

IV. The six delegations nevertheless consider that this divergence does not prevent the Community's work being resumed in accordance with the normal procedure.[48]

This was the accord that persuaded the French to return to their seat in the Council. The ministers of the Five proudly announced to their parliaments that the treaty remained intact – although Luns in The Hague described the outcome as a 'tie'.[49] In Paris, de Gaulle contentedly informed his government: 'The supranationality has gone. France will remain sovereign.'[50] They were sitting around the table as the Six once more.

Passage

The constitutional crisis of 1965–66 represents a decisive transitional moment. The standard account focuses on the price that France exacted on 29 January 1966 for returning to the table: namely the veto (point II of the accord), which is said to have hindered decision-making for at least the next twenty years. More fundamental, however, is the fact that the Six decided to go forward together (point IV) and agreed how.

What had happened? Outside the sphere of the treaty, the Six had laid down a fundamental rule. This was an ultimate safeguard for the member states, protecting them against majority decision-making, and it allowed the Community to continue to exist. Just as, on further consideration, the Bill of Rights (1791) was added to the American Constitution as a series of amendments designed to protect individual citizens against the federal state and the will of a majority of voters, so in Europe the individual countries protected themselves, on further consideration, against the will of a majority of states. This fact alone is enough to make the Luxembourg accord a crucial constitutional moment. It is the European version of the Bill of Rights.

But that was not all. Tellingly, the accord was reached between a reluctant Five, who wanted an untainted Community, and a reluctant Paris, which would have preferred to stick to the old way of doing business between states. Out of an unprecedented clash between the rules of the inner sphere and those of the outer sphere, space for European politics emerged. That space had been available before, but it was now expanded and, for the first time, formally recognised. The Luxembourg Compromise can therefore be regarded as formal confirmation of the existence of the intermediate sphere. It could also be argued that for each member state it represented a compromise between membership and treaty.

That is not how it was seen. According to the standard account, 1966 marked the start of a habit of using the veto that paralysed European decision-making until the mid-1980s. In the dominant, pro-Community view, this situation was both undesirable and unjust. There was an eagerness to reason the Compromise away. A former president of the European Court astutely commented that he knew nothing of a crisis, 'because the law took its course'.[51] One of his successors called the Compromise 'a spurious element of Community law, bound to fade out gradually'.[52] 'There is nothing in the Accords of Luxembourg', the secretary-general of the Commission stated baldly in 1967.[53] In the European inner sphere, the accord was spoken of as an unpleasant aberration, a temporary diversion, a myth. By contrast, the Gaullist belief, found here and there in the reference books, was that the Compromise meant a resumption of normal interaction between the European states, a 'realistic and durable arrangement'.[54] According to this interpretation, the political veto exacted by the accord restored complete freedom of action to each state.

In a sense, this fruitless dispute was a continuation of the head-to-head argument between the Five and Paris in the months before 29 January 1966. Both sides still deny that anything fundamental happened or changed that day. Neither interpretation can explain the considerable impact of the Compromise on the European order; however, its curious effects did make possible the current situation, in which voting by the member states is fairly routine (incomprehensible for States ideologues) but at the same time the 'Luxembourg veto' still hovers like a ghost above the conference table (inconceivable for Citizens and Offices ideologues). This extraordinary situation makes sense if we take into account the distinction between spheres of action. Between the treaty-bound inner sphere and the geopolitical outer sphere, a third had squeezed in: the intermediate sphere of the members – misunderstood, ambivalent and productive.

The transition to majority voting was the catalyst. The Six had promised to give up their vetoes on much legislation as of 1 January 1966. Five states wanted to try it, one did not. That one could not be forced and a rift was in prospect. The genius of the Compromise is that the Six could carry on delaying the existential (political) decision, yet as a Community they could still cross the (legal) threshold of 1 January. Ever since 30 January 1966, Europe has had one foot on either bank of the foundational river – a position that makes it stronger, not weaker.

The new relationship between the circle as a whole and the individual members that the Compromise created is easier to understand in the light of a chain of prior events that were captured in the text before being borne out by subsequent events. We will deal with each of these three phases in turn.

Prior events

Even before the decisive conference in Luxembourg, the status of the club was clarified on two points: an uncertainty about its spokesmanship was resolved and its foundations were underpinned.

The spokesmanship question was brought to a head by the approaching majority leap on 1 January 1966. Who would speak and act 'on behalf of Europe' after the abolition of the veto? Events provided an answer that no one had foreseen. In the spring of 1965, Hallstein clearly had the Commission in mind for this role, but the crisis left that assumption in tatters. De Gaulle, by contrast, believed that, so long as France stayed away from Brussels (an absence that in the end lasted for seven months), no one could speak on Europe's behalf. He, too, must have been forced to think again as reality unfolded. Both men were proved wrong. Europe's mouthpiece was the aggregate of member states, united in the Council.

The Commission was unquestionably the loser in the empty-chair crisis. The springtime bluff by Hallstein and his colleagues proved hopeless; their political aspirations were rumbled and the Commission played barely any role at all in the sequel. It was not even asked to mediate in a conflict over the fundamentals of the Community, as its absence from the decisive meetings in Luxembourg demonstrates. Technical expertise proved of little value when the Six were faced with a political crisis. In fact, the Commission president was the one and only victim of these events: at France's request, his mandate was not renewed. The Commission was forced back into the position of a subservient bureaucracy. It would be many years – not until the arrival of Jacques Delors in 1985, in fact – before it regained its self-confidence.

De Gaulle read the situation differently. As he saw it, the Community ceased to exist politically simply as a result of the departure of France from the Council. 'Our chair will remain empty; every meeting will be invalid', he said on 1 July.[55] According to the General, Europe was now dormant and these were simply six states gathered together, as they had been before 1950. This consistently maintained standpoint did not, however, tally with what actually happened.

From 13 July onwards, it was the Council that manifested itself as the focus of the life of the club. Given the absence of France, this was remarkable. Yet at the same time, here lay the secret. During the crisis, the Council fulfilled two functions. First, the monthly ministerial conferences and weekly meetings of the ambassadors provided the Five with an institutional discussion forum. They understood that they could win the war of nerves with Paris only if they continually aligned their positions and did not allow themselves to be played off against one another. At the ambassadorial level especially, this sense of solidarity proved a powerful force. Second, the Five acted in the Council as if they were the Six. True, in the empty-chair period only minor decisions were taken, with the absent party giving its assent in writing, but nevertheless the Five kept the European machinery ticking over. Paris cooperated at a bureaucratic level while remaining an observer at a political level, grinding its teeth. (In November, Couve de Murville spoke derisively of a 'pseudo-Council', presumably as illegitimate as a pseudo-Tsar.)[56] Yet from the perspective of the Five, who regarded the French as violators of the treaty, the Council was symbolically strengthened. In the absence of one of their number they came to realise that the club existed independently of its members. The empty chair made the autonomous existence of the table all the more apparent.

As for underpinning the foundations, it turned out that Paris wanted to amend the founding treaty, whereas the Five reaffirmed their allegiance to it. Events prior to Luxembourg once again clarify the relationship between the member states and their club.

General de Gaulle was able to say precisely which parts of the Treaty of Rome did not suit him, but he was less specific about alternatives. In mid-October, he told the Dutch ambassador in Paris that it was of little concern to him, so long as the procedure was set down in writing. In private, he expressed a preference for a joint declaration by the governments 'without signatures, ratifications and the whole shebang'.[57] Evidently the Elysée had in mind an accord between the governments that would amend the founding treaty, bypassing the formal amendment rules.

To the Five, this became the main stumbling block. A few days after Couve de Murville's appeal for a 'general revision' of the European order, the Five swore their secret oath: the Treaty of Rome was to remain intact. The effect of this constitutional vow was to anchor the Community more firmly in the political lives of the member states. The laborious amendment procedure, in later years often seen as a brake on joint developments, served in these circumstances as protection. The club derives self-assurance from the requirement of dual unanimity: signatory governments plus ratifying parliaments and/or populations. Thanks to the Five, it need have no fear of being dismantled by the governments on a whim. Europe had protected itself against a deleting stroke of the pen.

The founding treaty was buttressed by the national electorates as well. The role of parliaments and populations during the crisis is striking. It was pressure from the Italian, German and Dutch parliaments on their governments that made the clash of 30 June unavoidable, just as it was the election result of 5 December that limited de Gaulle's freedom of action and forced Paris to reach an agreement. From the perspective of the European order, the French presidential elections of 1965 were a resounding reaffirmation of the verdict of the Court in *Van Gend & Loos* that the Treaty of Rome 'refers not only to governments but to peoples'. In short, while the governments of the Five swore allegiance to the letter of the founding pact, the peoples of the Six endorsed its spirit.

The outcome of both battles, over spokesmanship and over the founding treaty, took the European body politic in one specific direction. It gained sufficient independence from its member states between July and December 1965 to enable it to survive the divisive deadline of 1 January 1966. In the absence of the government of one founding member, the club retained a voice and strengthened its foundations. It was on this basis that the Compromise took effect.

The text

To what extent does the text of the Luxembourg Compromise support the interpretation that this was a decisive moment of passage for the European order as a whole, moving it beyond the veto?

The first provision makes clear that all six delegations were convinced that, should an issue be extremely sensitive for one of them, they would have to carry on negotiating until it became possible to reach unanimity. None of the governments felt that, as soon as the treaty allowed for it, there must – there and then – be a vote. Each knew that the sword of majority might strike them tomorrow. The debate was over how long it would be necessary to go on negotiating in such a case. They did not succeed in drawing up firm rules on the matter. Spaak had proposed a maximum of three rounds of negotiations, but Couve de Murville rejected that idea. In the end, they agreed on the open formulation 'within a reasonable time'. This allowed for a breathing space, without introducing the possibility that talks could stretch on interminably.

The conflict contained in the Compromise rests in provisions II and III. The parties failed to agree on what should happen if no consensus was reached, even after a delay. France believed there could then be no decision. Its interpretation was that all member states therefore had a veto on sensitive issues. The other member states seemed to disagree. This difference of opinion was expressed in the Compromise but not resolved. The text makes no mention of a right to a veto, only of a unilateral announcement that a veto is being deployed. As a Dutch senior civil servant summed it up afterwards: 'Five partners ascertained that the sixth was going to be in breach of the treaty.'[58] Yet as a senior French civil servant remarked: 'What could the other five countries do? Take decisions by majority after 1 January, determine that France was refusing to implement them, then drag it in front of the European Court of Justice for violating the treaty? That was conceivable but absurd. The Community would have split apart.'[59] The negotiators in Luxembourg wisely left it to future practice to resolve the conflict – although they all knew what the outcome would be.

To get ahead of ourselves for a moment, this veto did indeed work. Later in 1966, when France first appealed to a vital interest to block a European majority decision, its veto was honoured. In reality, it was only then that the use of a veto, as announced in the text, became, after all, the right to a veto. Did only France have this right? No. Although the Five had promised each other beforehand that they would not invoke the accord, in practice such noble abstinence proved beyond them: the Five started to play the trump card as well. Their appeals to it were respected. The 'Luxembourg veto' was therefore not a privilege accorded to one member, but a right accorded to all.

The concluding fourth provision is one of agreement, and it brought an end to the crisis of the empty chair. It is fundamental. The coercion of the table was irresistible. The Community continued to exist, and the Six remained together as six.

The designation 'Compromise' is an accurate one, applied to the text as a whole. Nonetheless, in the literature it is *bon ton* to remark scornfully that in Luxembourg the Six did not really reach a compromise, but at best an 'agreement to disagree'. It seems that many authors regard this as an inferior category of decision. Any such disdain is both superficial and misplaced.

The text takes the form of a political accord, and one of historical importance. After seven months of uncertainty, it brought France back to the European table. More importantly, it made a repeat of the crisis unlikely. To threaten to withdraw would, in future, be implausible because superfluous, as even Paris realised. Now that every member had a potential veto, their circle would not quickly be blown apart again.

In its content, the text represents the convergence of two incompatible beliefs about the European order – no mean achievement. The French recognised the legal reality of the founding treaty, which they had been unable to change. The Five recognised the political reality of weighty national interests, which could not be set aside in the name of Europe. The Compromise forced those two worlds to relate to each other within the European intermediate sphere of the Six. It was a political compromise both fruitful and essential, creating a shared reality. It therefore provided the space required – both conceptual and constitutional – to keep the Six together as table companions.

Any disdain for the Luxembourg Compromise needs to be challenged still further. As a matter of fact, the put-down that it is 'merely an agreement to disagree' makes no sense, since that is the fundamental tenet of any political body, the basic understanding between its members, allowing room for conflicts to come to a head without tearing the community apart. Since Ancient Greece, it has been called 'politics'. An agreement to disagree is a kind of stripped-down constitution that enables parties and opinion-holders to thrash out their disagreements in public; the barest minimum of form required for any fight over content. Now we can see the deeper meaning of the term 'constitutional crisis' when applied to the events of 1965–66. The clash, in which one side had long wished for a European government and parliament, while the other wanted nothing to do with any entity above the level of the state, ended up with the constitutional minimum for a political community: the recognition of a space for irresolvable conflict, not between citizens but between member states.

At this point, the Six, as a political body, broke out of the straitjacket of the treaty and of legal rectitude (which leaves as little room for compromise as religious rectitude) and opened themselves up to politics. To that degree, the Luxembourg Compromise resembles those historical accords in which opposing parties escape from a sometimes bloody, intractable impasse by setting their most profound convictions aside, thereby creating the preconditions for political coexistence. In this sense, the Compromise deserves almost the same status in the history of the European body politic as the Pacification of 1917 in Dutch history or the Edict of Nantes (1598) in the history of France.

This claim raises questions of its own. If the Luxembourg Compromise opened up a space for European politics, what kind of politics was it? A kind that did not previously exist? Renewal did not take place within the states individually. In their dealings with one another, they naturally continued to pursue power and interests after the accord, just as they had done before. It was for the member states jointly that a new era arrived. The young Community, represented by the Commission, had systematically turned away from the uncertain world of politics, both doctrinally and by inclination, seeking support for its decisions in the letter of the treaty, speaking to the states in the language of obligation, law and competencies. Furthermore, it had refashioned its pen-pushing effeteness into a promise by Offices ideologues that an era had dawned all over the world in which the boundary between bureaucracy and politics would become blurred. The Luxembourg Compromise made the first inroads into this rigid world by demanding a place in the life of the club for three previously undervalued concepts: interests, time and authority.

The open and elastic term 'interests' is the first of the three to appear in the text. The shared starting point in the accord is the question of what to do if 'very important interests' are at stake for one or more of the 'partners'. Given that the word 'partners' refers to the member states, what is meant here (although the terms are avoided) are national interest and the general interest. In the European political tradition, the general interest is not a recognised fact, but is rather the object and outcome of an ongoing political struggle. It is therefore hardly surprising that the six governments in Luxembourg failed to frame criteria that would define which interests were 'very important' and which were not. Set criteria would have closed up the gap through which political judgment had just entered. (In a sense, the ministers would have reduced themselves to civil servants.) Yet the notion of 'very important interests' is not entirely arbitrary, as future events would show. It is also striking that the Five took the opportunity to ascribe 'interests' to the Community itself (see the final part of provision I). This was a gift to the club of a kind with which the founding treaty had been extremely parsimonious.

Closely linked to these separate and shared interests, the Compromise, secondly, introduces time, specifically the 'reasonable time' within which a solution to any conflict of interest would have to be found. This is time that must be gained – time, therefore, in the form of delay. In the Compromise, the member states said to each other: Better an agreement tomorrow than one of us outvoted today. The aim was to create an opportunity for negotiations. After all, if on the one hand majority voting is rejected (a blow dealt to the promises of the inner sphere) and on the other hand violence and war are renounced (a blow dealt to the habits of the outer sphere), then the only remaining means of breaking through a barrier between equal partners is by negotiation.

In the Community as conceived by Monnet or Hallstein, traditional diplomacy was emphatically resisted. Problems were expected to be technocratic and the partners imbued with the community spirit. Every question had in some sense an answer that was 'correct', both technically and morally, and that answer would be formulated by the Commission. In such logic there was no place for negotiations, and a request for postponement was a sign of ill will. In practice, this proved a delusion. Even in the very early years of the Community, the Council of Ministers – along with its important gateway, the gatherings of ambassadors – broke through many an impasse between the member states by making 'package deals'. In its haggling over agricultural prices, financial burdens and political posts, the Council showed itself to be a successor to the early modern peace conferences, at which European princes exchanged territories, shifted boundaries, arranged marriages and made alliances until a 'balance of power' was achieved. Actual practice also demonstrated that the equality of all member states, as laid down in the treaty, was a fiction. Not everyone at the table had the same amount of say.

In the accord, the Five, albeit reluctantly, recognised this '*irréductible diplomatique*'[60] as a fact of community life. Since the Compromise, it has been impossible to imagine European politics without requests for delay or for extra time in which all interests can be woven together. In one sense, though, things have moved on radically from the traditional mechanisms of diplomacy: the minority is brought to heel in a relatively civilised manner. No longer are threats backed up by military arsenals. Instead, the sword dangling over the conference table takes the form of a vote.

The third element, authority, does not appear explicitly in the text of the Compromise. Yet it was presumably a major factor in the silent acquiescence of the Five to the French demand for an ultimate veto. Governments know that the promulgation of a resolution is no guarantee that their people will accept it. To ensure compliance, a national government can ultimately resort to the use of force against its citizens. This might lead to a perilous situation, however, if people were to protest against a European decision in which their own state had been outvoted. Minister Couve de Murville asked a French parliamentarian who grumbled about agricultural prices, saying they could have been determined by majority vote, 'whether he really believed it was possible to decide against Germany, say, on the price of wheat. Who would then take responsibility for the revolt by German farmers that might result, the Commission or the member states?'[61]

The Community did not have the means to enforce compliance with a collective decision against the will of one of the governments. The experience of the Coal and Steel Community had shown that authority could not be conferred on an institution simply by calling it a 'High Authority'. In the Luxembourg Compromise, the Five, under pressure from de Gaulle, recognised that the authority of a European resolution resides with the states.

This realisation introduced a political dimension into the Community that the founding treaty had breezily passed over. A hundred years earlier, British political analyst Walter Bagehot had explained the problem succinctly: 'There are two great objects which every constitution must attain to be successful . . . Every constitution must first gain authority, and then use authority; it must first win the loyalty and confidence of mankind, and then employ that homage in the work of government.'[62] First authority, then government. In 1965–66, the Five (and the Commission) discovered that those in favour of establishing a European government will always find themselves unable to reverse this sequence. Seen through Bagehot's eyes, the Treaty of Rome was little more than a decision-making framework, a set of administrative rules without any firm lines of authority. Not until the Compromise did the Six close the gap and weld government and authority together. By doing so, they furnished themselves with their first rudimentary 'constitution'.

These three political elements of the Luxembourg Compromise – interests, time and authority – have interwoven and strengthened the structures of Europe and its member states. The governments are the link. Theirs is a dual role. The Compromise gives them a guarantee in advance that no joint decision will go against very important national interests. During negotiations, it confers on them not just a right but a duty to take the time to reach a joint decision. Afterwards, the existence of the 'Luxembourg veto' as an option that they have decided not to deploy forces them to take responsibility vis-à-vis their own electorates for the decision reached.

It is the psychological certainty of being able to block a resolution if you truly oppose it that makes consensus possible. The need to achieve consensus therefore operates not just as a veto but as a bond: people want and need to reach an understanding.

Subsequent events

In the image used earlier, because of the Luxembourg Compromise the member states, not having the power to leap collectively across into majority decision-making, found themselves with one foot on either bank of the European foundational river. The straddling of the river prevented a rift. From 30 January 1966, whether the states shifted their weight onto the foot of power politics (veto) or that of the treaty (majority) depended on their political appraisal.

In light of this, having examined the prior events and the text, we can now look at subsequent events. The Community's standard account takes the detrimental effects of the Compromise after 1966 as a starting point, and then describes its inevitable overthrow before reaching the happy ending of a return to treaty-based purity in 1987. This is the version that will be told first. The fact is, however, that the political reality introduced into Europe by the Compromise did not disappear. There are two ways of demonstrating this. On the one hand, we will see that the Compromise functions to this day as an invisible weapon of negotiation between member states. On the other hand, it will become clear that the elements it introduced – interests, time and authority – have gradually embedded themselves in the treaty. Anyone neglecting either of these two continuities misses something essential, namely the way the Compromise made possible the passage from legal system to political body.

Dominance, overthrow, happy ending? – 1966–87

From 1966 onwards, a veto culture prevailed in the Council of Ministers. Practically all decisions were taken unanimously, even when no 'very important interests' could be discerned. Although the Compromise was invoked perhaps only ten times in fifteen years, it hung over the table at every meeting. As soon as one partner objected, the debate was quickly terminated. Hundreds of Commission proposals failed to reach the finishing line. One unforeseen side-effect of the veto was that these proposals could not be voted out either, so dossiers remained on the table for years, contributing to the impression of work piling up. Whatever Community lawyers might contend, the Compromise was part of the life of the club.

This is certainly how it seemed from Britain's point of view. When the United Kingdom became a member of the Community in 1973, its government was of the opinion that the Luxembourg Compromise formed part of the jurisprudence it would have to – and in this case was eager to – endorse. In contrast to continental Europe, no one in London objected to the existence of a rule outside the treaty. The British constitution itself, after all, is a set of unwritten rules, conventions and customs. From a British perspective, the Compromise was a 'constitutional convention', in the sense of an unwritten rule that supports a political order.[63]

There were several attempts to confine the use of the veto within the boundaries intended for it in Luxembourg, to ensure that it was a weapon for use in emergencies, not a card casually played. After a declaration suggesting as much by the national leaders in 1974, there was a slight increase in the number of majority decisions. There were also suggestions that the motive for using the veto should always be put in writing, so that the government deploying it could be forced to take public responsibility for any impasse. Slowly the atmosphere was changing.

A crucial incident occurred on 18 May 1982. For the first time, the Council held a vote against the wishes of a member state. It was the annual decision on agricultural prices. The British wanted to use their veto to block the process because of a row over the budget – a different dossier. This was seen as unacceptable. A majority of the Council believed that the 'very important interests' in the Luxembourg accord must concern the point at issue. The Belgian chair pushed the vote through and London was outvoted. The British claimed they were the victims of the first ever breach of the Compromise. One former minister warned that the fate of 'a fallen oak' awaited the Community if the Ten did not understand that respect for the Luxembourg Compromise was essential for its operations, and indeed its survival.[64] Remarkably, Paris sided with the old Five. The French agriculture minister was quite specific afterwards: the Compromise had not been abandoned by her government, but 'its goal has never been and can never be to permit a member state to paralyse the functioning of the Community'.[65]

This gave an important steer to the effect of the Compromise. On the one hand, there was a need to convince partners in the Council that the national interest invoked was both serious and relevant – it was no good just casting about for a pretext. On the other hand, the interests of the Community as a whole carried weight in the process of forming a judgment. The minor concession the Five had carefully worked into the text in 1966 (in the closing part of provision one) had borne fruit. For the first time, the political notion of 'interest' worked against the veto and in favour of the club.

Four political facts contributed to the changed mood. First, since 1979 the European Parliament had been directly elected. It quickly discovered that majority decision-making in the Council was a precondition of its independent political existence. It therefore began to rebel, which had an impact on the parliament-sensitive German and Italian governments. Second, in 1979 Margaret Thatcher had come to power in Britain. She irritated her partners with her habit of unashamedly throwing up obstacles. Third, Greece had joined the Community in 1981 as its tenth member, and Spain and Portugal were in the waiting room to become its eleventh and twelfth. This increase in the membership strengthened the argument that the veto was becoming unworkable. Fourth, in May 1981 the French, by electing François Mitterrand, had chosen a president who could rule without the Gaullists (who had been part of the French government ever since the General himself was last in power). This final point was decisive.

Mitterrand's conversion was not immediate. Only after the fiasco of his Socialist experiment (the watershed moment coming in 1983, when he had to admit to being unable to exit the European Monetary System without damaging the French economy) did he seek in Europe a new projection screen for hope and statesmanship. Three weeks before the European elections of June 1984, the French president addressed the Strasbourg Parliament, interrupted several times by applause:

> How can the complex, diversified unit that the Community has become be governed by the rules of the Diet of the old Kingdom of Poland, where every member could block the decisions? We all know where that led. It is time we returned to a more normal and more promising way of doing things. The French Government, which was behind this compromise, has already proposed that it be used only in specific cases. The more frequent practice of voting on important questions heralds a return to the Treaties.[66]

This solemn speech, almost a European creed, sealed the fate of the Gaullist doctrine: the route to majority decision-making lay open. The use of a slogan popular in Brussels circles at the time is striking: 'a return to the Treaties'. It is a brilliant lie. This was a return to a place where Europe had never been. The journey to terra incognita that de Gaulle had refused to undertake on 1 January 1966 was sold by Mitterrand eighteen years later as a return to a home port.

Here lies the genius of the Luxembourg Compromise. The political leap to majority voting could be disguised as a repair to a juridical slip that had preceded it. The straddling of the foundational river in 1966 meant that, almost invisibly, each member state was able to shift its weight from one foot to the other. Europe founded itself backwards.

From here things moved quickly. In June 1984, the leaders, gathered in Fontainebleau, set an institutional committee to work, and in Milan a year later they decided that a formal change to the treaty was needed. The aim was to create an internal market by 1992. The British plan of limiting the neces-sary amendment to an unwritten 'constitutional convention', an agreement external to the treaty after the example of the Luxembourg accord, met with incomprehension. (Thatcher's foreign minister, Geoffrey Howe, said after-wards: 'Many times I explained this informal "British" approach to groups of bewildered continental parliamentarians for whom charters, declarations, solemn acts, single acts, constitutions even, were their real *raison d'être*.'[67]) In the new treaty, called the Single European Act, all members agreed to introduce majority decision-making for five treaty articles.

These new agreements had repercussions for the relationship between the members and their club. Along with its content, Europe's form promptly changed. This became obvious on 20 July 1987, at the first gathering of the Council after the new treaty came into effect. The ministers decided on new rules for their meetings. What the president of the Council had formerly done on his own initiative now became mandatory whenever a majority of the ministers asked for it – namely, to hold a vote. A determined majority would be able to make things extremely difficult for a minority.

A ghost over the table – 1987 to today

Did the Luxembourg Compromise continue to exist after 1987? This is a bone of contention of almost theological proportions.

In community circles, there was a sense of deliverance at last from a thorn in the side, a view supported by the fact that, in practice, decision-making accelerated. In 1985, a state successfully appealed to the 'Luxembourg veto' for the last time. The principle of majority voting was no longer contentious, and in the Council votes took place fairly regularly.

Then again, in a ratification debate in the House of Commons in April 1986, British Foreign Secretary Geoffrey Howe claimed that 'as a last resort, the Luxembourg Compromise remains in place untouched and unaffected . . . It is not a provision of the Treaty; it is a component of political reality in the Community . . . and is in no way affected one way or the other by the Single

European Act'.[68] During ratification of the subsequent treaty, in 1992, both Douglas Hurd (Howe's successor in London) and French Premier Pierre Bérégovoy made similar noises. They said the Compromise existed, therefore it existed.

The belief that the Compromise has disappeared and the notion that it still hovers over the table like a ghost are not entirely incompatible. The changed practice in the Council, on the one hand, and the explanations given by national politicians, on the other, indicate that there has been a return to the French position of 1966 – to the claim that the Compromise provided for a blocking move *in extremis* and that it was a safeguard against threats to life and limb, a Bill of Rights.

Yet the situation had changed radically in those two decades. The interests of the member states had been pushed in the direction of their common interests to such an extent between 1966 and 1987 that the veto had become difficult to use. In 1992–93, the British considered deploying their veto to block the introduction of directives on parental leave and working hours, but they abandoned the idea 'on the grounds that the exercise might backfire'.[69] They chose instead to contest the resolution via the European Court. You could still threaten to shoot, but even Paris and London were beginning to fear that actually opening fire would do most damage to their own positions. The transition made possible by the Compromise had begun. In reality, the member states were increasingly leaning their weight on their institutional foot, but they kept the other foot on the ground in case of emergency – which was a story they could tell the public at home.

Although the route to majority decision-making now lies open, consensus remains the norm. After 1987, consensus was no longer reached 'under the shadow of the veto' but instead 'under the shadow of the vote'.[70] Every minister knows it is more useful to rake in a few concessions in the give-and-take of the negotiating table than to remain the outsider and end up with a lonely 'no'. Even member states that find themselves in the majority prefer to bring as many malcontents on board as possible, for the sake of solidarity and to avoid future problems of compliance. The threat of majority produces consensus. Although there has been no actual leap to majority voting, the pressure of the club on its members has substantially increased.

In this community of consensus, the Luxembourg Compromise is still occasionally invoked. It works as a negotiating tactic by which a minister can make clear that the objections of his or her member state to a proposal are exceptionally serious. The watchword is 'vital interests' or 'very important interests'. These concealed references are generally sufficient to bring about an agreement, whether by means of a special provision, a transition period or some other legal device.

There are still member states that want to keep the Luxembourg Compromise alive. Forty years after the Compromise came into being, on 20 February 2006, Poland had certain objections to the reform of the sugar beet market, which required the assent of agriculture ministers. Warsaw was demanding compensation of 50 million euro for its sugar farmers. Although his partners grumbled that 'you don't go pulling the emergency cord for such a trivial sum', the Polish minister announced in a letter beforehand that he was going to invoke the Luxembourg Compromise. The delegation from Hungary, a member state for less than two years, had to ask the lawyers at the table what on earth that meant. Paris and London understood the situation all too well. Both the French and the British agriculture ministers had been asked by their leaders to support the Polish veto for reasons of principle, even though, as sectoral ministers, they were actually in favour of the beet plan.

In the Agriculture Council, general confusion arose. The Polish minister proudly made his appeal to his country's 'very important interests'. Yet he was outvoted. The plan was accepted with opposing votes from only Poland, Greece and Latvia. What had happened? The Polish–French interpreter, apparently unfamiliar with the Compromise, did not recognise the watchword and translated the Polish for 'very important' by using some feeble word like 'significant'. This meant that the French and British ministers could ignore the instructions from their capitals with a clear conscience and simply vote in favour. The poor Polish minister, who did not protest at the meeting, must have thought his veto card had somehow failed to work. Had the minister been more experienced, he would have made a fuss until the matter was referred to the European Council.

The successors – 1974 to today

Even those who believe the Compromise is dead and not even lingering on as a ghost floating over the conference table would have to admit that successors have emerged. Since 1966, the notions of interests, time and authority for which the Compromise demanded a place have gradually been made more formal, in defiance of Brussels orthodoxy. The association has been politicised.

The central role lay with the European Council of heads of state or government. Its establishment in December 1974 was intended, among other things, to clear the blockages caused by the 'Luxembourg veto'. If the ministers in the various Council constellations – agriculture, transport, trade – were unable to come up with a solution, the European Council was a final organ of decision-making where the Gordian knot could be cut. Passing a decision up to the national leaders was a way of gaining time, and it also afforded a chance to weave together yet more national interests into a universally acceptable agreement. Summits are the ultimate negotiating forum, in which the member states as a whole speak to the member states individually.

From the moment the sectoral ministers started taking their decisions 'under the shadow of the vote', a fascinating interplay began between the Council of Ministers and the European Council. A minister in danger of being outvoted on a specific matter of interest will sometimes take emergency diplomatic measures to stave off the decision, bearing in mind that his boss may be able to extract concessions at the next summit. This often happens informally, perhaps through the blocking of some other dossier that requires unanimity until the point on which the minister risks being outvoted is off the table. One example is the threat by the Bulgarian government in October 2007 to refuse to sign a particular accord with Montenegro unless the European Central Bank approved the inclusion of the Cyrillic spelling of 'euro'. The problem was resolved at the next European Council meeting – in Sofia's favour.

A drastic version of this tactic has been tried. When, in March 1996, the 'mad cow' crisis broke out in Britain and the panic spread to the continent, a European committee of experts recommended a temporary ban on exports of British beef to the rest of the world. London was incensed. Scientific evidence that mad cow disease might be a public health risk was tenuous, and anyhow there was no reason to discriminate against British beef alone. The Commission recognised this in May, but under pressure from worried consumers, a minority of member states blocked attempts to relax the ban. A furious John Major announced to the House of Commons a policy of total obstruction. He ordered all decision-making that required unanimity to be blocked until a solution was found. The aim was to have the subject of beef placed at the top of the agenda at the next meeting of the European Council. It was a successful move and the meeting in Florence became a 'mad cow summit'. The British got their way and Major ended his tactic of obstruction. In his memoirs, the British prime minister justified his blockade – a paper variant of de Gaulle's empty chair – with a rather striking claim: 'I had played by the club rules and the club had changed them.'[71] Ignoring the code of conduct laid down in the Compromise amounted to a betrayal of club feeling, on which the intermediate sphere depends.

The option of appealing to the European Council was formalised in the case of European foreign policy. General policy decisions on international affairs are taken by consensus, but some implementation orders can be passed by majority (at least according to the treaty). It is interesting to note how the

Treaty of Amsterdam (1997) articulates an exception: 'If a member of the Council declares that, for important and stated reasons of national policy, it intends to oppose the adoption of a decision to be taken by qualified majority, a vote shall not be taken. The Council may, acting by a qualified majority, request that the matter be referred to the European Council for decision by unanimity.'[72] This provision, known as the 'emergency brake', can be read as the first treaty-based successor to the Luxembourg Compromise. The elements are the same: considerations of national interest produce a right to delay, specifically until the next summit, where a decision will be taken by consensus. In the Treaty of Lisbon (2007) this emergency brake is retained, but its articulation has been sharpened to read 'vital and stated reasons of national policy' – a choice of words redolent of the Compromise.[73] The treaty includes similar emergency brakes in the fields of family law and criminal law.

The third neglected political concept that the Compromise introduced into the European order, 'authority', has asserted itself differently from the other two (interests and time). The member states recognised in 1966 that European decisions rely upon the authority of the states. The Gaullist lesson that no decision can in the end be enforced against the will of a national government, remains incontrovertible. The European institutions still lack the authority to quash a revolt. Still, we now know that this situation has not hindered the transition to majority decision-making (something de Gaulle would find discomfiting). Nor has that transition resulted in European decisions henceforth resting on the authority of the institutions (something Hallstein would regret). Events took a different course. Instead of depending on the states severally, European decisions now rest with the states jointly. Consequently there is now a greater willingness on the part of national governments to accept responsibility for such decisions, even those on which they have been outvoted.

Taking responsibility in this way means defending decisions as European decisions in the face of your own parliament and public opinion. When it comes to majority decisions, national governments – like it or not – are obliged to act as representatives of a European authority. The constitutional consequences are considerable. The difficulties that governments encounter in acting on behalf of Europe are, to a great degree, what drives their half-hearted search for a Europe-wide public (see Part III).

***

The two fundamental constitutional questions that the founding treaty left open – or answered all too brashly – have crystallised over the course of three decades. First, in the twelve years that followed the *Van Gend & Loos* judgment of 1963, all the founding states recognised that their joint jurisdiction takes precedence over their individual jurisdictions. This meant the states were judicially tamed. Europe became a legal order, with the Court as its judicial mouthpiece. Second, all member states have gradually come to accept that they are part of a political body in which they can be outvoted. At the same time, all can rest assured that if they truly oppose something and manage to present a clear and credible case, a solution will be found. They acquired this assurance in 1966, during the most serious crisis in the history of the Community. Although the accord in question has virtually disappeared from view, the fundamental norm it expressed remains in force. All compliance with European decisions originates in the will of the member states. Consensus is the norm. This is also why Europe's political mouthpiece became not the Commission, which many saw as preordained for the role, but the Council of Ministers and later the European Council of heads of state or government.

So on the one hand the treaty has tamed the states individually, and on the other the states have jointly taken firm control of the helm. As a result of the straddling of the foundational river made possible by the Luxembourg accord, Europe was able to develop not merely into a legal order but into a political body. This is a reality that would be familiar neither to de Gaulle nor to Hallstein, but it is today's reality.

That, then, is the secret of the table, the shared conference table where the bond of the treaty is more important than formal rules on decision-making. Finding a solution to every problem is a joint responsibility, which means that as soon as a rule exists, whatever it may be, about how to reach a decision, that rule will promote decision-making. Under pressure, consensus can always be achieved.

Exactly how it is done – the pushing and pulling, the open cards, the cards kept close to the chest, the duplicate cards, the proposals on the back of envelopes, the calculations scribbled on menus, the deals made in the corridors during adjournments or cooked up beforehand in the capitals – all that is another story. But every one of these little secrets contributes to the success of the European table, to its Secret with a capital S.

2

The Leap

Consider then duly before you leap, for after the Rubicon is once passed, there is no retreat.

Centinel (1787)[74]

A European treaty can come into force only after manoeuvring its way through two gates of unanimity. It requires signature by heads of government or by governmental representatives of all the participating states, followed by assent from the populations by referendum or vote in parliament. Between the first gate and the second lies a period of uncertainty, since one question arises repeatedly: What will have to be done if, despite their initial endorsement at governmental level, not all the states ratify in the end?

One such period began with the signing of the Treaty of Lisbon on 13 December 2007. The collision came six months later: the Irish people voted 'no'. Ratification was brought to a standstill. What next?

In essence, there are always three possibilities: legal continuity (a single 'no' vote brings down the treaty, so everything remains as it was); constitutional breach (the 'yes' voters – but how many as a minimum? – go forward with a smaller Union, leaving the 'no' voters behind); or political coercion (the 'ayes' put pressure on the 'nays' to go along after all, or to accept a new joint solution).

Which variant bobs to the surface depends on the specific configuration, the balance of power between 'yes' and 'no'. Relatively small and peripheral Denmark and Ireland could be forced to hold a second referendum after their 'no' votes in 1992 and 2001, respectively, but not France after its *'non'* in 2005. This discrepancy alone is sufficient to demonstrate that ratification is more than merely a legal matter. The motives for amending the treaty do not go away for the lack of one signature. Although there is a formal requirement of unanimity, a majority does exert pressure.

What would a transition to qualified majority voting at the ratification stage involve? What would it look like? Or is this not even a meaningful way of talking?

A MAGIC SPELL

In the final quarter of the eighteenth century, thirteen small states in North America faced this same question. Independent from their motherland, Britain, since 1776, they were unsure whether it would be best to stride the world stage as thirteen or as one. They made the leap, with a gusto that even in those days astonished the diplomats of the old continent. This fascinating history holds up a mirror to the foundation of Europe. I am recounting it here not for the sake of a blanket comparison between American nation-building and European unification, but purely to offer an analysis of the political and legal founding leap from unanimity to majority that was made in America between 1787 and 1791.

Anyone hoping to see anything in that mirror should bear in mind that the American founding moment has been mythologised in retrospect. It is the story of a summer in Philadelphia during which, under George Washington's chairmanship, brilliant minds like James Madison, Alexander Hamilton and Benjamin Franklin put together a constitution that is still in force – the ideal starting point for growth into a world power, or so American schoolchildren are taught. Europeans are fond of explaining why American unification was so easy. The thirteen states spoke the same language and had recently joined forces to throw off the British yoke, so what could be more natural than to become one country? We forget that the outcome was not at all self-evident at the time. It is therefore useful to remind ourselves of the contingencies, trivialities and masterstrokes of the birth of America.

The American Constitution was written between May and September 1787 by representatives of twelve of the thirteen American states, at a convention in Philadelphia. Only little Rhode Island refused to send anyone. The intention had been to revise the Articles of Confederation – the 1781 treaty by which the Thirteen, after gaining their independence in 1776, entered into a relatively loose collaboration. Their central authority was soon discovered to be politically and financially rather weak, hence the idea of improving the treaty of confederation. In the course of that summer, however, the Convention put together an entirely new constitution. Executive, legislative and legal powers; tax, slavery and press freedom – little remained off the table. There was some hard bargaining, too, between large and small states, for example, and concerning the economic interests of merchants, planters, shippers and financiers. Yet in essence what was at stake was not the shape to be given to a national government, but whether there should even be one. Later historians have erased that fundamental point (perhaps to avoid invalidating the founding myth), but there was no foregone conclusion.

The coup represented by the American Constitution lies in the seventh and final article: 'The Ratification of the Conventions of nine States shall be sufficient for the Establishment of this Constitution between the States so ratifying the Same.' This majority provision was the magic spell that made possible the passage from the old order to the new, clearing the way for a non-violent transition from many to one, from a union of states to a federation.

Virtually no one understood this at the time, as is clear from the debate. The provision was briefly discussed on 29 August 1787. At issue was the threshold, or the minimum number of ratifications needed for the new constitution to take effect. Pennsylvania favoured a simple majority, the signatures of seven of the thirteen states. Virginia opted for two-thirds (nine states). Connecticut wanted three-quarters (ten states). Only the representative from Maryland contended that all thirteen states must agree. Otherwise, he said, the Articles of Confederation currently in force could not be annulled.

How was the issue settled? By a vote! On 31 August, the threshold was set at nine states. This vote did not require unanimity. In politics, great revolutions can sometimes be traced to tiny procedural nooks. Hardly anyone returned to the subject, either in the Convention or in the ratification debates in the thirteen states. Yet this clause signified an existential break with the established order.

Representative Daniel Carroll from Maryland had a point, after all. By signing the Articles of Confederation, the states had only recently established an 'eternal Union', according to which every one of them retained its 'sovereignty, freedom and independence'. Each of the thirteen states, through its parliament, held a veto on changes to the treaty of confederation.

So the men who wrote the constitution in Philadelphia did more than merely extend their mandate a little. They broke with their shared politico-legal order. Article VII amounts to a double move to that end. First move: the transition to majority. The old Union can be disbanded without unanimous assent, so long as nine of the thirteen states accept the new Union – not a word about the fate of any non-ratifying states. Second move: the invocation of peoples in the plural. The Convention asks the thirteen parliaments to step aside and present the constitution to thirteen constitutional conventions, specially elected by their peoples for that purpose. In other words, it appeals to the underlying constituent power of the thirteen populations, bypassing their parliaments, the natural, legitimate defenders of the established order.

To round off this constitutional coup, on 12 September 1787 the Philadelphia Convention arrogated the voice of the people – a people in the singular this time – by beginning the preamble to the constitution with the famous words 'We, the People of the United States'. Behold the precise moment when the people created the state and the state the people.

Now there was a text, but without ratification it meant little. The ratification process, with its hovering between thirteen and one, its propaganda, its fierce debates, its haggling and its two 'no' votes, formally lasted from 17 September 1787, the final day of the Convention, until 21 June 1788, with ratification by the ninth state, New Hampshire. Nine out of thirteen: the threshold had been reached. But at that point, the two most important states of New York and Virginia had yet to join. Their absence would have carved the territory of the Nine into three pieces and, given their significance, the result would have been akin to a united Europe without France and Germany.

Virginia made the first move. The rich plantation-owners' state gathered on 2–27 June for a convention in Richmond. It was a fight to the finish. In his opening speech, anti-federalist Patrick Henry wondered what all this was about – a constitution being written in Philadelphia in the name of a single American people: 'Who authorized them to speak the language of We, the people instead of We, the States? ... The people gave them no power to use their name.'[75] Three talented federalists – James Madison, John Marshall and Edmund Randolph – took a stand against Henry, but he gave heroic orations and almost snatched victory until, exhausted, he let go of the bone and lost the vote (by eighty-nine to seventy-nine). So now there were ten states. Meanwhile, 400 miles to the north, the New York convention opened in Poughkeepsie, under the chairmanship of one George Clinton. The majority leaned towards 'no', but a sharp-witted Alexander Hamilton argued and threatened and on 26 July unexpectedly won the battle (thirty to twenty-seven). That made eleven, and the two major states were on board.

Four months earlier, Rhode Island, which had not only declined to send anyone to Philadelphia, but also refused to organise a convention, had voted 'no' in a referendum by a large majority. And in early August, at the last state convention, North Carolina also voted against. So the final result was eleven out of thirteen. In April 1789, America's first federal government was resolutely inaugurated for eleven states.

The two stragglers scratched their heads. In late 1789, a second convention in North Carolina, acutely aware of the direction in which events were moving, voted in favour of the constitution after all. Convention member James Iredell had tried to raise this point fifteen months earlier, during his state's first attempt at ratification: 'A gentleman has said that we ought to determine in the same manner as if no state had adopted the Constitution. The general principle is right, but we ought to consider our peculiar situation. We cannot exist by ourselves.'[76] They could not divorce themselves from the concrete historical situation, as his compatriots now understood. Finally, in May 1790, recalcitrant Rhode Island faced up to reality: it made the transition and entered the Union.

These outcomes endorsed the principle of majority ratification in Article VII. There were countless points at which the debate could have become bogged down. But it did not. The anti-federalists accepted defeat and the old Congress of the confederacy dissolved itself. A new, federal Congress replaced it and a president took office. By these acts, the public and the politicians accepted that two principles superseded the treaty of confederation: first, the constituent power of the peoples in the states; second, the primacy of the whole over the parts. Everyone acted as if the Articles of Confederation had already been annulled.

It is curious that the revolutionary Article VII was so little disputed. James Madison, hugely influential in Philadelphia and fully aware of the constitutional breach, was surprised. Under a pseudonym, he acknowledged in the New York press in early 1788 that the Convention had deviated from its task on one point: 'Instead of reporting a plan requiring the confirmation *of all the States*, they have reported a plan which is to be reported and may be carried into effect by *nine States only*. It is worthy of remark that this objection, though the most plausible, has been the least urged in the publications which have swarmed against the convention.'[77]

Few had even noticed. Nevertheless, Madison laid the objection aside. He called it an 'absurdity' to make the fate of twelve states dependent on the perverse whims of a thirteenth, especially when, like the intractable Rhode Island, it represented only a sixtieth of the people of America. Elsewhere he argued: 'To have required a unanimous ratification of the thirteen States would have subjected the essential interests of *the whole* to the caprice of corruption of a *single member*.'[78] Madison cleverly switches the burden of proof and turns the desired outcome, the whole, into a pretext for isolating one part. Challenged to say how an unconstitutional, non-unanimous dissolution of the confederacy can be justified, Madison invokes powerful defenders by 'recurring to the absolute necessity of the case; to the great principle of self-preservation; to the transcendent law of nature and of nature's God . . .'[79] It is as if he knows it is wrong and is shouting to drown out the transgression.

The anti-federalists clearly had the law on their side, yet they barely brought this argument centre-stage at all. Only in Maryland – which at the Philadelphia Convention had been the most persistent supporter of the proposal for unanimous ratification that was ultimately voted down – was there any sense of having been steam-rollered by Article VII. Flamboyant convention member Luther Martin – he had a reputation for rarely being sober and frequently holding forth for hours on points to which he objected – afterwards told the parliament of Maryland what a perfect argument their representatives had produced in Philadelphia against ratification by majority. They had said that although the majority principle was indeed valid as soon as there was a constitution, when entering into or dissolving a constitution precisely the opposite applied. It could not go ahead without 'the consent of every individual who was party to the original agreement'.[80] It was a scandal, he said, that in the leap from thirteen to one, via nine, four states had simply been shown the door. This consistent (if somewhat agitated) representative was ignored. On 26 April 1788, by sixty-three votes to eleven, his beloved Maryland threw itself into 'those chains which are forged for it'[81] – the Union.

Why were so few people impressed by the old order? No one reading the speeches and debates of the time will come away convinced that what removed the obstacle was an acute awareness of the constituent power of the people. Nor would anyone claim that the people allowed themselves to be caught unawares by a federalist plot. It seems there was a diffuse sense of crisis, of a need for change, of a moment that had to be grasped. 'Every man says that something must be done', said anti-federalist Henry during the Virginia Convention.[82] This was apparently one of those 'Machiavellian moments' in which, according to John Pocock, a people becomes conscious of a state's mortality and takes hold of its fate by turning to face the future. In other words, the ratification of the new pact was achieved as a result not of constitutional pretensions or political carelessness, but of historical consciousness.

It says a great deal that the transition was experienced as a leap. Just jump, to save yourselves, some urged. Take care, warned others, including one anti-federalist pamphleteer: 'Consider then duly before you leap, for after the Rubicon is once passed, there is no retreat.'[83] The American people saw the Rubicon and jumped. On 4 July 1788 public rejoicing broke out in several places after ratification by the ninth and tenth states. In Philadelphia, around a thousand men paraded through the streets, bearing aloft a Greek temple with thirteen pillars; solemn speeches were delivered and cannon fire sounded from the harbour.

All thirteen states came into the new Union within a period of a little over thirty months – after much negotiation, but without civil war, without partition, without intervention by foreign powers. This was indeed quick, but it was not an instant passage. For their transition from many to one, even the Americans needed time.

THE HOST ON THE STEPS

This foreign precedent makes clear how a transition to majority at foundation would go. First condition: just as the convention members in Philadelphia in August 1787 opted for the bluff of Article VII rather than the rules of the confederation already in force, so European politicians would have to decide at some point, in violation of existing treaties, that to reshape their Union non-unanimous ratification would suffice. Second condition: just as, between September 1787 and May 1790, the thirteen-fold American public, under pressure from the historical situation, accepted majority decision-making (as is apparent from their actions), so the multiple European publics would have to acknowledge the facts of a foundational leap.

Since 1945, many in Europe have longed for a 'Philadelphia moment'. A great deal of thought has been given to the first condition. Some politicians have gone in search of a magic formula along the lines of Article VII, as a way to get majority ratification pushed through for the Community or for the Union. Their use of dry legal prose in doing so should by this stage fool no one: it serves to create a gateway to an existential political question. To this day their search has proven fruitless, which is why they have never needed to give much thought to the second condition. No visible foundational moment has yet arrived. Surprisingly, the member states have turned out to be capable of jointly making the foundational urge tangible to individual nay-sayers even without any leap to majority. Time and again, all the states climb back on board.

One distinction deserves emphasis. There are two possible opportunities for a foundational leap to majority decision-making: a vote on a new treaty now, or an agreement to decide by majority on any future change to a new treaty. In both cases, the component parts relinquish their constituent power for the benefit of the whole, and in constitutional logic it becomes possible to talk of foundation. But the difference is important. The second case allows for a process that is legally sound, since the parties determine now by unanimity that the treaty can be amended in the future by a majority. (This was how Rousseau and, later, Maryland's Luther Martin thought it should go.) With a vote on a new treaty now, the founding act does not disguise itself: it resides in the violation of the old rules on revision. (This was the trick in Philadelphia.) Advocates of this shorter passage seem motivated by the thought: Why agree to do tomorrow what can be accomplished today? – 'Hic Rhodus, hic saltus.'[84]

All the European treaties that came into force from 1951 onwards were agreed upon unanimously. The need for consensus is contained in a treaty article. There are always two moments of unanimity: the governments come together to compose an amendment; then they ask each separate parliament or population to ratify it. Both moments have their own situational coercion, which determines the likelihood of a breakthrough to majority.

First there is the formulation of treaties by European governments, sitting at a shared negotiating table. The coercion they feel differs according to whether a founding treaty is being considered (in the practical sense of a text that founds a new organisation) or a treaty of amendment. Any government lacking the appetite for a founding treaty can – indeed sometimes must – stay away. This became clear during the founding of the Coal and Steel Community in 1950. The British were happy to accept the invitation from the French foreign minister, Robert Schuman, to join the talks, but they refused to commit themselves in advance to the principle of a supranational authority. They wanted to come to the table, but retain the right to walk away. Although Schuman was prepared to permit London to be an exception, his advisor, Jean Monnet, convinced him that this would fatally damage the plan: 'Soon there will be no community rules left at all', he said, but only another intergovernmental organisation.[85] Thus Paris fended off the British. At the outset of a venture, the party taking the initiative is the strongest. The veto has no place here: the reluctant either stay away or are kept away from the table; only the willing remain.

A treaty of amendment is different. A government can, if it so wishes, block every change (up to a certain level) by using its veto. It has a seat at the negotiating table and the existing rules of amendment are on its side. Usually the advocates of change will threaten to press on with a smaller group of countries in pursuit of their aims. During the ratification crisis of 2005–07, the Belgian and Italian premiers publicly advocated the founding of a 'core Europe' (as it is known in the self-congratulatory jargon). In such a scenario, no foundation by majority is forced through, but instead a new, smaller Union is founded by unanimity. In view of the legal complexities – dissolution of the old Union also requires the assent of all – this threat functions mainly as a way of putting pressure on the obstructionists. The threat may, however, be carried out when the blockage concerns the reinforcement of certain policies, rather than their complete revision. In December 2011, for example, the eurozone countries were so determined to strengthen budgetary discipline that they bypassed the British veto by setting up new mechanisms outside the treaty. After this move, Britain angrily objected to the other twenty-six using the Union's buildings for their undertaking, suggesting it could even seize the Court of Justice, although the mood improved some days later. The usual result of threats to move on with a smaller group is that negotiations among governments continue until there is an accord that all can sign.

Now to the period of ratification by European parliaments and peoples. They are not sitting round a table. Unlike the governments, they decide neither jointly nor simultaneously. They therefore feel less situational pressure. Several governments have signed a European treaty only to see their parliaments or populations decline to ratify it. Formally speaking, the agreements made must then be abandoned for lack of ratification by all the signatory states. Yet it is here, at the stage of ratification by parliaments and peoples, that the opportunity to create a European founding moment has been sought.

Tampering with the founding veto was therefore initially seen as a matter of introducing a rule governing how treaties come into force: one legal ruse and you would have the dreamed-of political leap. With just a couple of words (so those in favour argued), everything could be arranged. Such plans have been worked out in detail, mainly by representatives of the institutional inner sphere, who are already, in a sense, living 'after the leap'. They see the veto held by the founding states as bondage, and majority as longed-for emancipation.

In 1984, five years after it was first directly elected, the Parliament proposed a majority provision. It was part of a full draft treaty, put together at the urging of the Italian Europarliamentarian Altiero Spinelli, a former resistance hero and a federalist from day one. The idea was that this draft treaty could come into effect based on ratification by a simple majority of member states, so long as they represented two-thirds of their total populations. As things stood in 1984, this meant ratification by six of the ten member states, provided they included three of the four largest. The formula seemed to have been developed with an eye to a potential rift between those states that wanted to go 'forward' and one or more others that were lagging behind – everyone was thinking of London, which was not shy of using its veto in the Thatcher years. Although the draft garnered praise all the way to the German Bundestag, the governments never seriously examined the clause about ratification.

Eighteen years later, some were of the opinion that a Philadelphia moment had come closer because of the establishment, for the purpose of drawing up a constitution, of a European Convention in which not only the governments were represented, but also the national parliaments and the European institutions. Here the ratification issue was bound to arise. The unanimity rule did not fit with the foundational ambitions of convention members from the inner sphere. Moreover, coming together to do months of work that could be nullified by a single 'no' vote was not an attractive prospect for anyone. Candidate member state Malta quickly came to serve as the spectre of an absurdly small potential obstructionist – the European equivalent of Rhode Island. In this atmosphere, several convention members drew up detailed constitutions that involved a leap to majority.

The most original proposal came from French Senator Robert Badinter: 'The Constitution shall enter into force on the first day of the twenty-fifth month following the deposit of the fifteenth instrument of ratification by a signatory State having taken that step.'[86] At the time, in 2002, the Union had fifteen members, with another ten states on the point of accession. The provision could therefore be interpreted as an exhortation: Let's get our institutional affairs in order before we enlarge the Union. Although European treaties generally come into force shortly after ratification by the last member state, Badinter's proposal meant another two years would have to pass after the threshold had been reached. This may have been intended as a period in which hesitant states could still join, rather in the way that North Carolina and Rhode Island sailed into the harbour of the Union.

That same year, the boss of the inner sphere, Commission President Romano Prodi, produced his own 'courageous' proposal for a constitutional breach. The idea was that the governments would sign, along with the constitution, a separate treaty about how it was to come into force, in which they agreed that the constitution would be valid as soon as three-quarters of the states had ratified it and that they would withdraw if they could not convince their populations.[87] This was legally ingenious, but aimed too much at finding a magic formula *à la* Article VII (first condition) without paying due attention to public acceptance of the promise to withdraw (second condition).

Suggestions and incentives arising from the inner sphere are fascinating, but in the end it is the member states that need to take the leap. The risk is theirs. They have to weigh the chances of an initiative being blocked by one obstructionist against the likelihood that they will at some point be the only nay-sayer themselves. The stakes could not be higher.

One other aspect is relevant here. Panicky stories about the absurdity of the veto had no basis in fact in 2002. Four times in less than twenty years, the member states had wriggled through the double gate of unanimity into a new treaty: the treaties signed in 1986 (Single European Act), 1992 ('Maastricht'), 1997 ('Amsterdam') and 2001 ('Nice') were all ratified according to the formal requirements.

Along the way, there had in fact been two individual 'no' votes, and on both occasions the blockage was removed. Obstructionists Denmark and Ireland did not hold the Union to ransom. Under pressure from their partners, Copenhagen and Dublin decided to request the support of their populations a second time for exactly the same treaty. They added a few clarifications for the benefit of their own peoples, without any legal consequences for the other member states; Denmark was allowed to withdraw unilaterally from several agreements. Both governments won their second-chance referendums. Such experiences were a source of confidence that the circle of members would always be able to persuade any laggards. They also taught that the obstacle of unanimity was less absolute politically than it seemed legally – an alarming thought for individual members, perhaps, but reassuring for the club.

At the Brussels Convention of 2002–03, representatives of the member states debated publicly for the first time with representatives of the inner sphere about how a new treaty would come into force. The proposals for majority ratification came nowhere near to being passed, but the configuration did produce another constitutional moment of transition, namely formalisation of the responsibility of the totality of member states.

This innovation was contained in the final provisions of the initial draft. The text was drawn up behind closed doors by a secretariat and a twelve-headed Praesidium in early April 2003 and sent to convention members. The existing article on ratification was adopted *mutatis mutandis* as 'Article G':

> 1. The Constitutional Treaty shall be ratified by the High Contracting Parties in accordance with their respective constitutional requirements. The instruments of ratification shall be deposited with the Government of the Italian Republic.
> 2. The Constitutional Treaty shall enter into force on ___, provided that all the instruments of ratification have been deposited, or, failing that, on the

first day of the month following the deposit of the instrument of ratification by the last signatory State to take this step.

Next, however, comes a surprising innovation in the form of a new, third clause:

> 3. If, two years after the signature of the Constitutional Treaty, four fifths of the Member States have ratified it and one or more Member States have encountered difficulties in proceeding with ratification, the matter shall be referred to the European Council.[88]

This is a subtle but important turn of phrase, which rests on the distinction between the legal and political consequences of a failure of ratification. The formula does not dispute that a 'no' vote hinders the coming into force of the new treaty. Legally, everything remains as it was: unanimity is required, as ever. The innovation lies in the recognition that a shared political responsibility for the situation arises. Two elements make this clear. First, the clause specifically states where responsibility lies: not just with ratifying or non-ratifying states, but with the highest political expression of the intermediate sphere, the European Council. Second, a threshold is attached to the creation of that shared responsibility: four-fifths of the member states. Everyone's veto remains formally in place, but a political shadow falls over it. In truth, this is a transition to majority as far as foundational responsibility is concerned.

In that one sentence, the member states gave themselves, as it were, a host on the steps. He receives latecomers, hears their excuses, but will not refuse anyone entry. He may even decide, if the latecomers do not want to cross the threshold but their presence seems necessary, to call the guests waiting indoors back out again, so that the festivities can continue informally outside.

Ahead of the plenary debate on the final provisions, convention members were permitted to submit amendments. The political purport of revision and implementation had not escaped any of them. It was a paper debate that particularly enthralled Europarliamentarians and the national parliamentarians of the smaller member states. The former organised themselves by party allegiance (Christian Democrats, Socialists, Liberals), the latter mostly by state (Finland, the Netherlands, Austria, Portugal), sometimes supported by governmental representatives (Belgium, Luxembourg). The larger countries, and especially their governments, kept remarkably quiet.

For anyone seeking change, Article G offered three points of departure. First there was the mode of pronouncement by the populations. The idea arose of making a referendum compulsory. The most ardently federalist and the most anti-federalist members of the Convention would have preferred this: both wanted member states whose constitutions did not provide for binding referendums to hold advisory ones. The federalists stressed the Union-wide character of such consultation. Europarliamentarian Olivier Duhamel already had a date: the day of the European elections in June 2004. His colleague Johannes Voggenhuber suggested that the votes should be counted not only per member state but for the Union as a whole, with the president of the European Parliament announcing the overall result. Neither spelled out what the status of this 'European result' would be. The Union-wide referendum was an obvious attempt to make constituent power reside with the citizens of Europe as a whole, thereby giving greater legitimacy to any attempt to overturn one or more negative national referendums. It was a cautious variation on the American 'We, the people', the audacious opening line that in Philadelphia had been a corollary to the leap to majority contained in Article VII. Everyone at the Brussels Convention recoiled before this declamatory bluff – a restraint that makes all the more sympathetic the idea of a European people encountering itself in a result.

The federalist wish to see the people decide met with complete agreement from a handful of anti-federalists, including a Danish, a French and a British Europarliamentarian, a British member of parliament and a Czech deputy. To them it was nevertheless a matter of referendums. They consistently emphasised the need for unanimous ratification. Twenty-five referendums meant twenty-five chances of a 'no'. The Dane Jens-Peter Bonde, doyen of the Eurosceptics, had sufficient confidence to pick up the gauntlet of the idea of a simultaneous referendum. As if negotiating terms for a duel, in response to Duhamel he named an 'even more European' date: 9 May 2004, the anniversary of the Schuman Declaration. So the outer flanks of the debate were eager for a constitutional shoot-out. The weapons were unevenly matched: the 'no' camp gave itself twenty-five bullets, the 'yes' camp, one.

The Convention's mainstream steered well clear of these democratic cowboy antics. Many sought a breakthrough via ratification by a majority of the states. One Christian Democrat Europarliamentarian collected almost thirty signatures in favour of an amendment by which the constitutional treaty would come into force after ratification by four-fifths of the states. Two Liberals garnered twenty signatures for a similar proposal, involving a majority of five-sixths of the states. The supporters of this radical idea were not the most prominent members of the Convention. The one government that signed up to the plan was Luxembourg's, represented by a former Commission president, Jacques Santer.

The third focus of the amendment debate was the innovation proposed by the Praesidium concerning the role of the European Council. It was to take the matter in hand two years after signature, if four-fifths of the members had ratified and one or more had not. This left some members of the Convention baffled. The representative of the Lithuanian parliament remarked: 'Part 3 of Article G highlights the potential problem, but fails to offer a solution.'[89] So scrap it. That was also the suggestion of the governments of Luxembourg, the Netherlands and Austria. The Dutch government made absolutely clear that it saw the provision as a threat: 'The possibility that the Treaty can come into force without ratification by the Kingdom of the Netherlands is unaccept-able.'[90]* For Luxembourg, the only member state to support majority ratifica-tion, the problem lay elsewhere: the provision might lead to the European Council having to wait two years before it could act.

The plenary debate in the Convention chanced to take place only a week after the signing in Athens of the Treaty of Accession which approved ten new member states. The notion that no single member should be allowed to obstruct the entire club might gain credibility with the prospect of a Maltese, Cypriot or Lithuanian veto. The British governmental representative spotted the danger and planted a red flag early in the debate: 'It is tempting to say that a Union of 25 cannot be held up by one Member State, but . . . amending these provisions would be a mistake and a challenge to our democratic legitimacy.' He added: 'Political credibility comes from unani-mous decisions on major steps forward.'[91] The advocates of ratification by majority were unable to wrench this flag out of the ground. On further reflection, the national parliamentarians were less enthusiastic about the idea of such a break with existing rules, and among governments there was even less eagerness.

Ratification by majority had so little support in the Convention that the Praesidium was able to dismiss the idea immediately after the debate ended. The dispute over shared responsibility for foundation was fought out behind the scenes. The vice-president of the Convention, former Belgian Premier Jean-Luc Dehaene, wanted to keep the new third clause; Secretary-General Sir John Kerr, a senior British diplomat, wanted to scrap it. Dehaene won. The sentence was removed from Article G, however, and made part

---

* Two years later, after a 'no' from his own people, the Dutch prime minister acted in the spirit of his country's suggested amendment by immediately declaring the treaty dead, on the evening the result was announced, thereby repudiating the joint European responsibil-ity for the situation that the provision was intended to express.

of a separate political declaration. This was necessary, since, as a French senator had remarked during the debate, 'If a problem emerges with ratification of the Constitutional Treaty, it cannot be settled by the treaty itself since that, by definition, will not have come into force'.[92] So by the time Convention Chairman Giscard d'Estaing handed the draft treaty to the governments in July 2003, the sentence had become a 'Declaration annexed to the final act'. Not a magic spell, but an exhortation to look for a solution together.

At the intergovernmental conference that concluded in 2004 under Irish chairmanship, the clause was controversial. The Irish, who did not have fond memories of the pressure put on them after their 'no' vote in 2001, would have liked to get rid of it altogether. Shortly before the final accord, Dublin put the sentence into indirect speech. After some squabbling, it ended up in the officially published treaty as 'Declaration 30', which runs:

> The Conference notes that if, two years after the signature of the Treaty establishing a Constitution for Europe, four fifths of the Member States have ratified it and one or more Member States have encountered difficulties in proceeding with ratification, the matter will be referred to the European Council.[93]

Here ended, for the time being, the European quest for a transition to majority at the commencement of a new treaty. The idea of a break with the existing legal order turned out to be unacceptable to almost all member states, to the disappointment of the inner sphere. Whereas in Philadelphia in 1787 only one state defended unanimity (Maryland), in Europe in 2004 only one state advocated majority (Luxembourg). The states retain their position, underpinning the European order.

The recognition by the member states of shared political responsibility for a new pact is striking. The declaration added to the treaty represents the first fruit of the European quest for a majority transition. It poses no fundamental challenge to the individual member states, but the club is slightly reinforced in relation to them. No foundational leap here, but a consolidation of the constitutional experience gained.

When the constitutional treaty with this sentence attached was rejected by the French electorate on 29 May 2005, and three days later by the Dutch, the leaders did not wait two years before discussing the matter. The shock was too great. At the June 2005 summit a period for reflection was introduced. Several of the states put the ratification process on hold.

At a summit in June 2007, the member states decided to give in to the nay-sayers and delayers by replacing the ambitious constitutional treaty with a treaty of amendment. Although they arranged that 'the Declarations as agreed by the 2004 IGC will be taken over by the present IGC',[94] the Council's legal department decided that Declaration 30 was no longer relevant. No one asked either for the sentence to be restored, or why it had not been included. The Treaty of Lisbon (2007) does without a host on the steps.

3

The Bridge

A state without the means of some change is without the means of its conservation.

Edmund Burke (1790)[95]

MASTER OF THE TREATY

A political body's rules for change are not trivial; they reveal its essence.

The first question is whether such rules exist. The Ten Commandments that Moses brought down from the mountain contain no amendment rules, unlike the constitutions of most modern states. The former were intended for all eternity, whereas the latter acknowledge historical contingency. Revision rules allow for the assimilation of new events, but also for the repudiation of identity. At stake here is the place of a political body in time.

Next comes the question of how easily change can be brought about. Is the political order cast in stone or is it a plaything of the public mood? One of the defining characteristics of constitutions is that the ordinary legislature cannot alter them. In the classic formulation by American Chief Justice John Marshall (1803), the Constitution is the 'supreme law of the land' because it is 'unchangeable by ordinary means'.[96] Seen in this way, the hierarchical distinction between fundamental rules and ordinary rules rests not in their content but in their degree of resistance to change. A change to fundamental rules is called a revision, and a change to ordinary rules, legislation. The ease with which rules can be altered also determines the relationship between revision and founding. In looking at fundamental rules, we can distinguish between those that are changeable and those that are sacrosanct. For example, no matter what changes may be made to its constitution, France remains a

Republic.[97] Anyone wanting a return to a monarchy must stage a coup. In a pact that makes no distinction between fixed and changeable elements, any revision will formally represent a refounding.

Third, the question arises as to who decides on change to a political body. There is an essential distinction between the original founder (for example, a nation or a group of states) and the institutions called into being at its foundation (such as a parliament). The founding treaty itself, according to Emmanuel-Joseph Sieyès, who in 1789 became the first to articulate this distinction, 'is the work not of the *pouvoir constitué* but of the *pouvoir constituant*'.[98] In the case of amendment, however, this does not always apply. Some political bodies are indeed unable to implement any revision without referring back to the original founder or founders (for instance by referendum) or by gaining the assent of all territorial components. Others, however, entrust amendment to the constituted powers (for example, to the parliament in a specific mode). Only in this latter case can we talk of self-renewal, of a political body that stands on its own two feet, emancipated from its founders. The 'by whom' question determines the degree of independent political life.

How does Europe deal with these three political questions, the 'whether', the 'how' and the 'by whom' of treaty renewal? The 'whether' question is of relevance here because, although all European treaties from 1951 onwards included a revision procedure, the first occasion on which it was seriously invoked sparked fierce controversy. Only after the gate was unbarred in 1985 did the 'how' and the 'by whom' come into play.

Once again, the possibility of transition from unanimity to majority functions both as an exhortation and as a threat; once again, the main result is not a formal coronation of the inner sphere but a strengthening of the intermediate sphere of the members. This subtle difference reveals a great deal about the nature of the Union. The member states do not allow themselves to be pushed aside, but they do discover ways to move forward together as Europe.

Before looking at two key moments in the battle over revision rules, it is worth casting a glance at the legal starting point. In the founding treaty of 1957, the Six defined the rules for change thus:

> The Government of any Member State or the Commission may submit to the Council proposals for the amendment of this Treaty.
>
> If the Council, after consulting the Assembly and, where appropriate, the Commission, delivers an opinion in favour of calling a conference of representatives of the Governments of the Member States, the conference shall be

convened by the President of the Council for the purpose of determining by common accord the amendments to be made to this Treaty.

The amendments shall enter into force after being ratified by all the Member States in accordance with their respective constitutional requirements.[99]

The three questions posed above – 'whether', 'how' and 'by whom' – were answered unambiguously in the treaty. First, yes, the pact can be amended. Europe is empowered to react to what the founding states had earlier called 'unforeseen difficulties which are brought out by experience'.[100] Second, the procedure is indeed a good deal more demanding than it would be for ordinary decisions, and Europe therefore formally recognises a distinction between revision and legislation (though not between foundation and revision). Third, revision is governed by subtle role-playing, in a prelude and three acts. Prelude: the initiative lies both with individual members and with the Commission. Act I: the decision as to whether revision will be discussed lies with the Council (an institution). Act II: the decision as to what revision will be introduced lies with the assembled governments of the member states (the founders). Act III: the decision that a change will actually go through lies with, as implied in the final sentence, the national governments (separately), parliaments and peoples. The Prelude throws the ball in the air, Act I leads off, Act II negotiates, Act III ratifies. On the face of it, the second and third acts seem decisive, which would mean no self-renewal for the Union, but at most renewal by the founding states. Europe, therefore, does not stand on its own two feet.

In any debate about the nature of the European order, this point is of great importance. The central question concerns whether the Union is a 'normal' international organisation or 'more' than that. Roughly speaking, supporters of the Offices and Citizens discourses place their bets on the *pouvoirs constitués* (institutions); those of the States discourse on the *pouvoirs constituants* (member states). The former contend that the Union is a special entity because of the unique function given to the Court, Commission and Parliament, whereas the latter claim it is a perfectly normal association of cooperating sovereign states, as demonstrated by the revision procedure. It is understandable that States ideologists present this particular argument as their trump card. The power of the members to change the treaty is fundamental, and the power of the institutions is derived from it. In theory, the states could one day decide to shut down the Commission or the Court, or even the entire edifice. Because of their monopoly on revision, the German Constitutional Court described the member states in 1993 as the 'masters of the treaty'.[101]

Yet this is not the last word on the matter. The commitment to joint renewal included in the revision rules is in no sense self-evident. The paradox is that the founding treaties of most 'ordinary' international organisations – the Charter of the United Nations, for example, or the Articles of Agreement of the International Monetary Fund – can be altered by their member states by majority (sometimes with a veto for the most important members). This cuts across the ideological categories of Brussels, in which those who say that the Union is not an ordinary organisation advocate majority decision-making, and those who say that it is swear by unanimity. Something else seems to be going on with Europe – something that has escaped the attention of both sides.

The duress of joint renewal took shape in two moments of passage. In 1985, the amendment rules were applied for the first time (the 'whether') and in 2002–04 they were changed (the 'how' and the 'by whom'). On both occasions, the club was strengthened vis-à-vis its individual members, even though they did not relinquish their positions. As a result, the label attached by the German Constitutional Court requires just one small correction: the member states as a whole are a single 'master of the treaty'.

Coup in Milan

On 28 and 29 June 1985, a summit of the presidents and prime ministers of the Ten took place at the impressive Castello Sforzesco in Milan. In the castle from which the Renaissance dukes of Milan ruled over the surrounding region, the Italian premier, Bettino Craxi, fulfilled his role as chairman splendidly. Other major players were British Prime Minister Margaret Thatcher, German Chancellor Helmut Kohl and Greek Prime Minister Andreas Papandreou; but the Frenchman, the Belgian, the Dutchman, the Irishman, the Dane and the Luxembourger all made their voices heard. The Spanish and Portuguese premiers, their countries on the point of accession as members eleven and twelve, attended as observers. All were accompanied by their foreign ministers. The new Commission president, Jacques Delors, and his number two completed the line-up: twenty-five men and one woman in the Sforzas' castle. A kilometre away, in front of the gothic cathedral in the heart of Milan, almost a hundred thousand people gathered on the second day for a demonstration in favour of a 'European Union' – waving green-and-white flags with the letter E, addressed by the president of the European Parliament and stirred by Italian military bands playing Beethoven's 'Ode to Joy'.

The purpose of the Milan summit was to decide whether the Community's founding treaty should be amended. Since 1958, the member states had lived according to the rules they imposed on themselves in Rome. Circumstances had changed since then, and the Six had become the Nine and, more recently, the Ten. For some fifteen years, the heads of state or government had repeatedly announced that they wanted to give the Community a 'political' footing, for which the French had introduced the term 'European Union'. Yet none of this had ever gone beyond fine words.

In the spring of 1984 things started to move. The Strasbourg Parliament had adopted a draft federalist treaty in February, drawn up by the Italian Altiero Spinelli. The German Bundestag voted almost unanimously in favour of this blueprint, and the parliaments of Italy and the Benelux countries were enthusiastic as well. The question was whether the governments would do anything with it. Here the initiative was taken by Paris, holder of the rotating Council presidency. On 24 May, President François Mitterrand announced to the European Parliament his country's 'willingness' to 'examine and defend' the Spinelli draft, saying there would have to be talks about treaty change.[102] More important was the breakthrough during the 25–26 June summit in Fontainebleau. In a former imperial and royal hunting palace, the leaders reached an accord on the problem of the British budget contribution, which had been dragging on for five years. Everyone was enormously relieved. Now they could turn their attention to the future once more.

Still in Fontainebleau, they agreed to establish a committee to look at institutional reform. Mitterrand chose Maurice Faure as his personal representative, the man who had signed the Treaty of Rome in 1957 on behalf of France – it seemed the French president was serious about refoundation. In March 1985, the committee advocated a 'qualitative leap': the will of the member states as a whole must be expressed through a 'genuine political entity . . . i.e. a European Union'.[103] Its two most important recommendations were for more qualified majority voting in the Council of Ministers and the convening of an intergovernmental conference to negotiate on a Union.

On the first issue, relaxing the hold of the veto, all member states agreed in principle. Even London could live with more majority decision-making, at least insofar as it facilitated plans for the European internal market that Thatcher was so keen to see. The dispute was over whether this would necessitate changes to the treaty. The British maintained that a gentlemen's agreement in the European Council would suffice. The Commission argued that an internal market would remain a pipe dream so long as 90 per cent of the required legislation had to be agreed unanimously. Several articles would need to be amended to permit the introduction of the 300 or so legislative measures required by 1 January 1993. The second issue – whether Europe should become a political union – was a separate matter, but both items ultimately raised the question of whether there would have to be an intergovernmental conference on treaty change. This was the focus of the Milan summit.

The outcome was extremely uncertain. Two camps emerged in advance. In favour of change were the Benelux countries, Ireland and, in particular, the host, Italy. Craxi had made the success of Rome's Council presidency contingent upon an agreement in principle on a Union. Furthermore, he, a Socialist, was caught up in a tug-of-war with his Christian Democrat foreign minister, Giulio Andreotti, over who was doing most for European unification, which was fervently advocated by the entire Italian parliament. (All Italian political parties, except the neo-Fascists, were to take part in the huge federalist demonstration on the square in front of the cathedral that Saturday, 29 June.) Opposed were Britain, Denmark and Greece. Thatcher thought treaty change not just unnecessary but undesirable, fearing that too much high-flown lyricism would find its way into binding articles. The Danish government was barred by its parliament from ceding any power to 'Brussels'. Athens was hoping to use its veto to extract financial advantages. The positions of France and Germany were unknown.

Where did they stand? In secret, Paris and Bonn were working on a European treaty of their own. Only the Italians, chairing the summit, knew of it. The French wanted to improve coordination of the foreign policy of the Ten by means of a General Secretariat of the European Union, which would also steer the Commission. The Germans were after a reduction in veto rights and more power for the European Parliament, although in the text itself there was little trace of either. (Backstage rumours suggested that Bonn had agreed to the plans because German Foreign Minister Hans-Dietrich Genscher was after the new post of secretary-general to the Union.) The Franco-German strategy – to keep the document secret until the summit, where the Italians could launch it as a basis for negotiations – failed dismally. Shortly before he left for Milan, Chancellor Kohl slipped up in a debate in the Bundestag: under attack by the opposition for not doing enough for the European cause, he bragged about the forthcoming initiative. To avoid embarrassing Kohl, Paris had to confirm the existence of the draft treaty. This meant that Rome, in the chair, had little choice but to condemn the scheme out of hand – inducing *Schadenfreude* in the smaller nations and the Commission, which were delighted by the failure of an attempt to undermine their cherished community method by introducing an intergovernmental secretariat. What had been intended as a Franco-German surprise manoeuvre ended as a spectacular flop that featured prominently in the media the following day.

So when they all gathered in the Sforzesco Castle on the morning of Friday, 28 June, no one could tell what the day would bring. Thatcher thought she had convinced the chairman, Craxi, in an early-morning tête-à-tête, that an intergovernmental conference was unnecessary. She repeated this at the meeting: better to do business straight away in Milan, among ourselves, than to sit round the same table several months hence, saddled with a commitment to ten parliamentary ratifications, or even referendums. In view of British behaviour in the recent past, this offer of a gentlemen's agreement was greeted with some scepticism by her partners. Andreotti expounded upon their senti-ments, sounding off about good European behaviour. Thatcher snarled at him: 'Stop that awful rhetoric, will you!'[104] With greater restraint, but no less resolve, the three Benelux prime ministers argued for legally binding accords and a 'strengthening of the Community institutions'. Kohl placed the emphasis on a stronger European Parliament. Mitterrand tried to repair the damage caused the previous evening without abandoning the idea of a political secre-tariat. He seemed to agree with Thatcher that the first priority was to comply with the existing voting provisions of the Treaty of Rome. Commission President Delors advocated amendments to just three treaty articles, with an eye to the internal market. He made no reference to a 'Union'. From the chair, Craxi surveyed the battlefield and insisted that they must find a way to reach agreement in Milan on certain points, and then they could discuss the rest at an intergovernmental conference. The leaders thereupon left it to their ministers – Andreotti, Howe, Genscher, Dumas and the rest – to come up with a way out of the impasse. As evening fell, the British and French press judged that London had succeeded in its aim of avoiding a formal amendment to the treaty.

Here the myth-making begins. By his own account, German Foreign Minister Genscher could not get to sleep that night and scribbled something in a notebook. In the haste of his morning ablutions, he dictated his thoughts to an aide as he shaved, the bathroom door ajar. This *Badezimmerpapier* ('bathroom paper') would be at the root of the summit's final conclusions. According to Delors, his people, too, worked through the night, and it was they who gave Craxi the decisive nudge.

On the morning of the second day, as the Piazza del Duomo filled up with Euro-federalist demonstrators, Mitterrand and Kohl held their usual working breakfast. Many decisive deals have been done over a croissant and a soft-boiled egg, but not this time. The president could not understand why the Italians wanted to delay everything. The chancellor muttered that the inter-governmental conference must be over and done with by December. When the leaders resumed their meeting, the paper prepared by their ministers was on the table. The first sentence ran: 'The European Union begins; the member states will conclude a treaty about the form this Union will take.'[105] It was rejected immediately. No progress at all had been made. The pragmatic British wanted to avoid ambitious words like 'Union' and limit the discussion to the decision-making process; that way the Community would at least move forward. The mood deteriorated. Several adjournments followed. Denmark and Greece remained opposed to any amendment to the treaty. It gradually became clear that only the proposal by Sir Geoffrey Howe could lead to consensus. It was not far-reaching and made no mention of a 'Union', but it did improve decision-making. After a late lunch, Paris and Bonn almost succumbed to the charms of London's pragmatic minimalism.

The Italians were alerted to this rapprochement, which would scupper their plans. At the end of the Saturday afternoon, after a further adjournment, came Bettino Craxi's masterstroke. For the first time in the ten-year history of the European Council of heads of state or government, the chairman asked for a vote. He explained that the convening of an intergovernmental conference was a simple procedural decision, which could be taken by majority.

For a second there was silence, then all hell broke loose. The Danish prime minister, Poul Schlüter, spoke of 'rape'.[106] Papandreou protested that the item was not on the agenda and cried 'coup'.[107] The Greek was so angry with Craxi that he threatened to walk out. Thatcher was astonished and furious. (Her spokesman was to say afterwards: 'It is not irritation to the Prime Minister. It is total volcanic eruption. Krakatoa has nothing on it.'[108]) In the confusion, there was a fleeting chance of a compromise that would include both the British package with informal relaxation of unanimity *and* an intergovernmental conference. Then the enraged Papandreou said it was one or the other or he really would leave. It was a moment before everyone understood what this meant. Craxi was faced with a choice: less-burdensome legislation now or a chance of political renewal. He chose renewal, perhaps thinking of his Christian Democrat rival and the demonstrators outside. Meanwhile the British had discovered that the article invoked by the Italian premier spoke of prior consultation with the European Parliament, and as sudden friends of the Strasbourg Assembly they accused him of a procedural breach. Craxi rebutted the objection – the formal decision would follow later – and called for a vote. In favour of holding an intergovernmental conference: Belgium, Germany, Italy, Luxembourg, the Netherlands . . . then Ireland . . . and then, after some hesitation, France. Opposed: Denmark, Greece, Britain. Seven against three. The club had decided by majority to take the path of renewal.

While festive fireworks coloured the night sky above the Castello Sforzesco in the green and white of the federalists, speculation began over the significance of Craxi's coup. European schism, fresh start or dead end? The first conclusion seemed far from fanciful. Kohl and Mitterrand both described the summit as a salutary moment of truth that made clear where everyone stood. Old Spinelli's entourage could also see how this might herald a constitutional rift between two groups of states. Belgian Premier Wilfried Martens spoke optimistically of a turning point in the history of the Community. Luxembourger Jacques Santer was more cautious: as incoming chairman of the Council, he would have to put the pieces back together as of Monday, 1 July. Thatcher, meanwhile, was venting her spleen on the radio: 'If we can't decide here, why should another conference be able to decide any better?'[109] Yet she moderated her tone and made it known that she would send a representative to the conference 'to express [our] point of view'. Papandreou agreed to do the same. Dissenter Schlüter was alone in being unable to commit until he could gain the assent of the Danish parliament. Many believed the conference might fail to achieve anything (the general consensus in the British newspapers on Monday morning). Then again, seasoned diplomats were convinced by the Saturday evening that all the obstacles would be removed. One anonymous minister of foreign affairs said of Thatcher: 'If we can actually get her to the trough, she will drink.'[110]

That was indeed how it went. The British prime minister, home from Milan, weighed up the options. For the British economy, there was a great deal to be gained by the creation of European markets for financial services and transport, for example. In return, Thatcher was prepared to pay the price of a strengthening of the Commission and Parliament and more qualified majority voting in the Council (preferably in areas where the veto favoured the more protectionist economies). Greece and Denmark also came to the table; Spain and Portugal, still in the waiting room, were allowed to participate.

The intergovernmental conference went well and the tensions of Milan were quickly forgotten. There was no more talk of a rift between the states. On 2–3 December 1985, the twelve heads of government, at a meeting in Luxembourg, reached a political accord on a new treaty.

To the disappointment of the French and Italians, the result was given the hard-to-sell name of the 'Single European Act'. The notion of a 'Union' had been abandoned. Delors had pushed hard to get it removed. His 'nightmare' was that Europe would be sliced in two: on one side the economy, based on the Treaty of Rome; on the other the formalisation of cooperation on foreign policy.[111] The title *Acte unique* or 'Single Act' was intended to reassure the

Commission and the Benelux countries that everything would be put into effect within a 'single' Community framework. The term 'Union' was hidden away in the preamble. The British, with their aversion to rhetoric, were content with this solution.

There were tensions still to come during the signature phase. The Danish minority government failed to secure a negotiating mandate from its parliament, so it decided to ask the population for one by referendum. In Italy, under Spinelli's influence, disappointment prevailed about the limited expansion of powers for the European Parliament and the further postponement of a 'Union'. The parliament in Rome would allow the Craxi government to sign only after the treaty had been approved by the Strasbourg Assembly (which was thereby given a veto on treaty change that it formally lacked). The Greeks went furthest of all: they were unwilling to sign until they could be certain the other eleven would. To keep up the pressure, the Council – now chaired by the Dutch – decided on an unusual procedure: a two-stage signature. The Single Act was signed by nine member states in a sober ceremony in Luxembourg on 17 February 1986. After a supportive resolution from the European Parliament and a positive Danish referendum, the last three member states put their names to the Act on 28 February 1986 in The Hague. All the governments were on board.

During the ratification period, one more unexpected obstacle arose. At the very last moment, the Irish Supreme Court ruled that the Irish government ought to have organised a referendum and was still obliged to do so. The Irish people gave their assent, enabling the European Single Act to come into force on 1 July 1987. Two years after the starting-gun in Milan, the club had renewed itself.

How could something that in May 1985 had seemed impossible – for example, that London and Copenhagen would ever accept a revision of the treaty – become a political reality so quickly? And how is it that Europe has managed to navigate its way through this demanding cycle of renewal several times since?

Something extraordinary happened on the afternoon of Saturday, 29 June 1985. One of those present remembers the vote as an 'historic moment of vacillation', as the 'transposition of a profound political reality into a framework you would never have thought would allow it'.[112] Although three member states protested vehemently, the Ten were carried along by a momentum for reform that persists to this day. The key lies in a procedural nook, in a forgotten majority provision of the treaty. This piece of legal detail had historic consequences for European politics, as the Greek Papandreou

realised there and then – hence his furious cry of 'coup'. After decades of stagnation came unremitting change; after firm anchorage in the treaty came the
opportunity to capitalise jointly on the flow of time. It is a magnificent
moment of passage.

So what exactly happened in the forum of the leaders when Bettino Craxi
unexpectedly forced a majority decision? The scene is often recounted as an
anecdote in the history of the European Council, or as a colourful incident
in a series of treaty changes; but it is far more than that. It creates an essential
link between those two lines of development. In short, Craxi exposed the dual
capacities of the European heads of government and pulled those two capacities apart in time. By doing so, he opened the way to Europe's permanent
renewal, and also endowed the Community with a robust supreme authority.

The dual capacities of the heads of government are these: they are representatives both of the constituent powers (severally) and of the constituted
power (jointly). Margaret Thatcher seems not to have understood this
even after Milan, to judge by her remark, 'Why should another conference be
able to decide any better?' The point is that it would not be just 'another
conference'. In Milan, the heads of government had come together as a
European institution, whereas at the intergovernmental conference in
Luxembourg they would be sitting round the table as representatives of
the sovereign founders.

Ever since the European Council was set up in 1974, this distinction had
been present in a dormant form, but it had never previously been awoken. The
most powerful European *pouvoir constitué* had remained concealed within the
pouvoir constituant of the states. Thatcher was doubtless not alone in regarding
Milan as a contemporary version of the Congress of Vienna of 1814–15, a place
where national leaders negotiated, exchanged points of view, took decisions by
consensus – but could never be outvoted. That was indeed how summits of
heads of government had functioned in the early years of the Community. The
European Council continued this practice and retained the epithet 'summit',
which made the innovation virtually invisible. Yet at the same time it was an
institution in the midst of others. The European Council was obliged to respect
community law, counted the Commission president among its members and
provided a report of every meeting to the European Parliament. Furthermore,
at its founding an agreement was made that the heads of government could,
when appropriate, sit in their ministers' seats, thereby formally constituting a
'Council' at the highest level, a Community body. In fact, therefore, for ten
years consultation between heads of government had been standing on the
threshold between two worlds, with one foot in the (uninstituted) in-between
world of the member states and the other in the (instituted) inner sphere. In

Milan, this duality was suddenly exposed to the full light of day. By getting the heads of government to vote – and by gaining their assent to do so – Craxi pushed the European Council in over the threshold. Suddenly it manifested itself unmistakably as an institution.

Just a few weeks before Milan there had been a G7 summit in Bonn, again with leading roles for Kohl, Thatcher, Craxi and Mitterrand. The Frenchman, as it turned out, was alone in resisting the proposal that they should start trade negotiations as soon as possible – something the American side was keen to see. In Bonn, Mitterrand had threatened: 'If these summit meetings don't revert to their original form, France will no longer come. Finding ourselves in a minority in an institution is something we can handle. But this is not an institution; we're here to get to know each other better and to harmonise our policies. That's all.'[113] Compare this with Milan. Thatcher could have repeated there word for word what Mitterrand had said. Instead, she allowed herself to be persuaded by her own legal team to resign herself to a vote. In doing so, she was recognising the European Council as an institution.

We may wonder what this body added to the 'ordinary' Council, where the same governments sat round the table. The difference in function is essential. In that Council, national ministers made decisions about specific interests and specific problems – agricultural prices, product safety standards, fishing quotas. In practice, it transpired that, if these issues expanded and overlapped, the sectoral ministers were unable to resolve them. This led to stagnation, unless the heads of government stepped in, which they did from time to time. With the establishment of the European Council, the involvement of national leaders was systematised. Ever since, Europe has operated on the principle that if the leaders cannot find a solution, no one can. Presidents and premiers are also expected to be able to commit their populations to agreements made at summits. Only collectively, therefore, do they have sufficient authority to take European decisions that go beyond policymaking at a technical level and make deep inroads into national or shared political life.

The first political revision of the European order involved an almost existential decision. After all, whatever its content, the very fact of a first amendment transforms the nature of the association. Having been static and fastened to its origins ('Rome'), it becomes active, historical. It opens itself up to development through time. In other words: the club becomes more political.

Everyone realised that the leaders would have to take this step themselves: the future of your nation in Europe cannot be left to sectoral ministers. Shortly before leaving for Milan, Chancellor Kohl spoke in the German Bundestag about the historic importance of the 'Union' for his country and for Europe. The previous day, Irish Prime Minister Garret FitzGerald had discharged that same task in Dublin. In the week after the summit, both men reported back to their parliaments, as did most of their fellow leaders. But in the meantime something had happened, and the premiers now stood before their home electorates in a different role. Ten national leaders climbed to the summit in Milan and, despite all the grumbling, they came back down as a single entity. Suddenly they were speaking on behalf of Europe.

Here lies the brilliance of Craxi's bluff. The vote in Milan forged a link between European self-renewal and the forum of the leaders. Having started out as a picnic on a mountain, conferring no obligations, the summit became an encounter from which the leaders descended with politically binding tablets of stone. Moreover, this transformation took place in response to an existential question about the identity of the European order over the course of time. The vote that unbarred the gate to revision also accredited the European Council as an institution uniquely placed to take responsibility, on behalf of the club, vis-à-vis the separate national electorates.

This fascinating political transformation relied on a legal mechanism in which every cog – every little word – counted. It is useful at this point to re-examine the revision procedure contained in the founding treaty. The decision on reform had to take place in three acts, each with a specific set of players: first *whether* change would happen (Council), then *what* change (governments) and finally *that* it would go ahead (populations). All Craxi did was to have the 'whether' question settled by majority among the leaders. In Act II and Act III the national governments and populations retained their veto; there was no tampering with this source of self-assurance for the member states. Yet the entire mechanism leapt forwards. Here is how renewal unfolded.

Act I, Scene I: breakthrough (Milan, 29 June 1985)

By a majority decision, Craxi pushes the European Council in over the threshold, disguising it as a normal Council. The most fundamental question for a political body – to move or not to move – rests, from this moment on, with the constituted power. The joint leaders never again let go of this question. *Secret:* coup disguised as procedural decision.

Act I, Scene II: commitment (London, Copenhagen and Athens, July 1985)

On their return from Milan, the British, Danish and Greek heads of government do *not* say to their own parliaments: Last Saturday in Milan we were outvoted, but we'll get our own back in six months' time with a veto during that damned intergovernmental conference in Luxembourg. No, Thatcher, Schlüter and Papandreou feel forced to ask for support for the European Council's decision. (Only Schlüter fails to get it and has to go to the intergovernmental conference without a mandate.)

Secret: those outvoted nevertheless have to take responsibility for the decision. As soon as your European partners start talks about the future of the club, you had better take your place at the table. Otherwise you run the risk that they will think up all sorts of things in your absence, presenting you with an unpleasant choice between going along and getting out altogether. You need to be there, and at home you will have to say why.

Act II: negotiation (Luxembourg, September–December 1985)

The unanimity requirement turns out not to block an accord. At the negotiating table, the veto loses its edge. Refusing to speak is not difficult; continuing to refuse to assent to anything whatsoever once discussions have started is almost impossible. As soon as all the governments are round the table, a game of give and take begins, in which a compromise will always be found. True, this is often accompanied by odd exemptions, protocols, unilateral declarations and other trimmings, but these merely serve to allow everyone to assent in the end for reasons of their own. As a result, the compromise text will be described by federalists and legal experts as 'inadequate' and 'lopsided'. This is no catastrophe. The political force keeping everyone on board is simply stronger than legal logic.

Secret: once the 'whether' of revision has been answered in the affirmative, a 'what' will always flow from it. As soon as everything is potentially in motion, with everyone chasing after his or her own little plans, it becomes politically impossible to cancel the show and matters of substance will have to be discussed. Worse, the prestige of those present means that at some point, on pain of derision from press and public gathered nearby, a 'result' will have to be announced. Pressure from the outside world does its bit to help bring the table to a decision.

Act III: ratification (Brussels, Copenhagen, Bonn, Athens, Madrid, Paris, Dublin, Rome, Luxembourg, The Hague, Lisbon, 1986–87)

The heads of government, who fired the starting pistol on behalf of the complete circle in Act I and reached an accord with each other on behalf of their member states in Act II, appear on behalf of both in the final act to face their parliaments and/or populations. Hence the refrain at press conferences after a summit: '*Bon pour la France et bon pour l'Europe*'; 'Good for Britain and good for Europe'; '*Goed voor Nederland en goed voor Europa*'. Wearing two hats enables them on the one hand (as heads of state or government) to defend a revision, if necessary, based purely on national interest, while on the other hand it increases the pressure on them (as members of the European Council) actually to secure a majority in favour of the proposed change. After all, national leaders who have to return to the European Council after a 'no' vote from their own parliaments or populations will have lost authority with their colleagues. A scathing group verdict awaits: 'He didn't deliver his voters.' This interplay between the two roles generally proves sufficient. Of the 103 times since Milan that a European leader has asked a parliament or population to ratify a new treaty, assent has been given at the first opportunity on 97 occasions.

Secret: no matter what type of revision is decided upon, it can, by definition, be recommended at home as 'good for Europe and good for our country'. In reality, only this dual message is both sellable and credible. Anyone who appeals to the common interest alone ('Historic day for Europe') will almost immediately be told by press and opposition that he or she has bartered away the national interest, seduced by pats on the back from other leaders. Anyone who presents the outcome purely as a national victory forgoes the chance of a credible defence of the messy compromise that a summit always produces. ('Game, set and match', crowed the British premier, John Major, on his return from Maastricht. He came within a whisker of losing the vote on the treaty.)

As a result of these four secrets taken together, Craxi's 1985 coup meant that after almost three decades of constitutional stasis, the gate was unbarred. From the moment the political question as to *whether* revision was necessary was pulled inside and answered by majority, Europe has been in a permanent state of renewal. In the second and third acts it is the constituent powers whose governments decide, always unanimously, *what* amendments will be introduced; their populations then need to agree *that* they can go through. In this sense, the member states remain the master of the treaty. But they do not have the luxury of standing still. Strictly speaking, 1985 did not see the introduction of anything resembling European self-renewal; but it did mark the start of what looks very much like self-propulsion.

COLLISIONS AND SHORTCUTS

The growth of the club into a political body with a certain amount of revisory power brought new players onto the European stage: the highest national constitutional courts. With every treaty revision, constitutional judges – such as the British Lords, the German *Bundesverfassungsgericht* and the French *Conseil constitutionnel* – investigate the relationship between the amended European pact and their national legal systems. An important issue for them is whether their own government has handed over more competencies to the club than the national constitution allows.

The question that accompanies all such revisions is: What if European foundations are laid that are incompatible with a member state's constitution? Which will take precedence? This resembles an earlier point that arose in the 1960s concerning legislation. Then the dilemma was: What if a European regulation clashes with a national one? The European treaty has priority, was the answer, as enforced by the European Court. Yet this solution cannot work in the case of a revision. The distinction is essential to the way the circle of member states operates.

First back to 1963–64 and the Court's coup in determining that European regulations had precedence over national legislation. A clash at that level became impossible. If two laws were on a collision path, the traffic from Brussels or Luxembourg had the right of way. Within twelve years, all member states had accepted this principle. For legislation, the European Court was set above the highest national courts.

There was one squabble en route, a harbinger of what was to follow. In a famous judgment of 1974, the German Constitutional Court (alone among the national courts) attached conditions to the rule of precedence: European law could take precedence over ordinary German law, but not automatically over clauses in the German constitution or the protections it offered. The *Bundesverfassungsgericht* was acting as protector of the fundamental rights of the German people – an extremely weighty role, given German post-war taboos surrounding, for example, euthanasia and abortion. Rules that flowed from a transfer of powers to community level could not trump German constitutional protection, argued the judges in Karlsruhe – certainly so long as there was no alternative to that protection at a European level. The German Constitutional Court was therefore at odds with a European tendency to pre-empt the future. It drew a line and said: so long as the protection of fundamental rights is not guaranteed, we reserve the right to declare a European regulation inapplicable in Germany 'because and in so far as it collides with one of the fundamental rights enshrined in the Constitution'.[114]

This verdict – known as the *Solange* ('so long as') judgment – shocked Luxembourg and Brussels. There was now a hitch in the propitiously developing 'autonomous' European legal order. The German Constitutional Court had no reason to assume that the treaty itself posed a threat to the fundamental rights of the German people. 'Karlsruhe' dealt mainly with the consequences of the upcoming transfer of powers to (or creation of powers at) a European level, based on the treaty, without the national parliaments being required to pronounce on them first. If these new regulations touched upon fundamental rights, then the court would stand in the way.

It sounded more of a threat than it was. In the end, the two camps grew closer, and with time the danger of a clash was averted. 'Luxembourg' called into being a form of protection that was given the benefit of the doubt by 'Karlsruhe'. In 1986, in a second *Solange* judgment, the German Court ruled that so long as the protection of fundamental rights by Europe was equal to that available in Germany, the stipulation would be waived. The German Court did keep peering over the fence, however, to check that the protection was still in place.

The next step came in 2000. On the initiative of the German government – the decision being taken during the European Council meeting in Cologne in 1999 – all members agreed to have a European catalogue of fundamental rights compiled. A special convention of governmental representatives, national parliamentarians and Europarliamentarians, plus a European commissioner, was charged with the task, under the chairmanship of Roman Herzog, a former German president who had once been president of the German Constitutional Court. His appointment meant that the highest German political and legal authority was deployed to guarantee fundamental rights at a European level that were equal to Germany's. In 2000, the Fifteen formally adopted a 'Charter of Fundamental Rights of the European Union', which has since gained in status. At the intersection between legislation and fundamental rights, the danger of a collision seems to have abated.

But there was more. European law could collide with the German constitution in other ways, too.

Beginning in 1972, a remarkable development had taken place almost unnoticed. The Community had drastically extended its powers without any formal change to the treaty. This was 'revision-lite'. The heads of government set the mechanism in train at the Paris summit in 1972. They agreed to expand the European construction site by adding policies on energy, the environment and the regions, and they invited the Commission to come up with proposals. Narrowly interpreted, the treaty had nothing to say on these subjects. The solution was to resort to a legal shortcut known as the 'flexibility clause'.[115] This provision could be invoked if action seemed necessary because of the market, but the treaty did not provide for it, so long as all the governments were in agreement. In that case, no treaty change was required. The governments found this useful, because it meant they did not need to turn to their parliaments or populations for ratification. The Commission, too, was happy to expand its field of activity – here a higher European vocation and a bureaucratic tendency went hand in hand. So national governments and the Commission joined forces to sideline the national parliaments.

Karel Van Miert, who was summoned to Commission President Delors' office immediately after his appointment as transport commissioner in early 1989, has explained how it worked:

> He had a map of Europe in front of him on which he had drawn the major transport arteries with a felt-tipped pen – large infrastructure projects to make possible, for example, the High Speed Train. I pointed out to him that the European Community had no authority over large infrastructure projects. Transport by air, by road, by rail and by water . . . all fine, but infrastructure policy was still firmly anchored in the national competencies. 'Don't worry about that', said Delors. 'Just try to find out what the Commission can do to integrate networks better in that area, too.'

According to Van Miert: 'He didn't need to tell me twice.'[116]

Via this shortcut, which was interpreted extremely broadly, countless European powers came into being, even in areas that had nothing at all to do with the market, such as emergency aid to non-member states. The authoritative American law professor J.H.H. Weiler therefore claims, with reference to the shortcut, that after the Paris summit of 1972, 'no core activity of state function could be seen any longer as still constitutionally immune from Community action' and 'no sphere of the material competence could be excluded from the Community acting under Article 235'.[117]

This development caused particular concern in Germany because of that country's federal structure. The German constitution sets out, at least broadly, the powers of the federal government and those of the Länder. This results in a consciousness – greater than in most other European countries – of the importance of the power to create powers or to assign them, a meta-power known as Kompetenz-Kompetenz. As European renewal progressed, the Länder realised that their powers could disappear down a shortcut via Bonn to Brussels. They believed this meant that the Community was arrogating to itself a meta-power, which was surely not what the members had all signed up for. Both the Bundesrat, in which the Länder are represented, and the German Constitutional Court were worried.

From 1987 onwards, conflict loomed large. After the Milan summit, the circle of member states had unexpectedly acquired the power of self-propulsion. As well as a back door for the expansion of its content, there was now a front door available for changes to its form. Did Europe have fully-fledged revision powers?

The German Constitutional Court did not sound the alarm at the first opportunity, the introduction of the Single European Act, but it did at the second. Plaintiff Manfred Brunner turned to 'Karlsruhe' in response to the Treaty of Maastricht (1992). He believed his rights as a German citizen had been violated by Bonn's signing of the new pact. Because of the expansion of European powers, 'state authority in Germany is no longer actually exercised by the elected representatives of the entire German people'.[118] The Union seemed to have arrogated to itself this meta-power, given that the treaty said: 'The Union shall provide itself with the means necessary to attain its objectives and carry through its policies.'[119] Well, argued the plaintiff, that said it all: this was no longer a shortcut but a public highway. The crux of his grievance was that the value of German suffrage and citizenship was being undermined. The parliamentarians in the Bundestag and the Bundesrat ought not to have voted in favour of 'Maastricht' without first going back to the people by holding a referendum.

In October 1993, the German Constitutional Court issued an elaborate response known as the 'Maastricht ruling'. Just as it had in 1974, the Court announced: We're still here. True, the Court found against the plaintiff (meaning Germany was able to ratify, the fifteenth and last member state to do so), but that was not the end of the matter. Karlsruhe judged that a viable national democracy needed to be preserved. Brunner's complaint was declared admissible. German judges ruled it had been conceivable that, without any warning, 'the protection of the competencies of the German Bundestag will be transferred to an institution of the European Union or the European Community, constructed by the governments, to such an extent that the . . . indispensable minimum requirement of democratic legitimacy of the state power that citizens face will no longer be adequately met'. The Court determined that this was 'not yet' the case.[120] The Union was still an organisation based on a treaty – a league of nations. The German state was one of the 'masters of the treaty' and could always withdraw from the Union. The plaintiff's concern was therefore misplaced, for the time being at least; but in response to a future change to the treaty, such a complaint might be declared valid. Karlsruhe was issuing a warning, although it took no action. On this matter, German constitutional judges did not dare to cause an acute political crisis.

'A new *Solange*?' was the question in the specialist press after the Maastricht ruling.[121] But the 1993 verdict was about an issue of principle – the future of German democracy as such – rather than merely about the protection of citizens' fundamental rights within that democracy. Furthermore, the Maastricht ruling placed a heavier burden on the future. The formula in 1974 had been 'so long as A does not guarantee certain rights, there is a danger of collision'. In time the danger was averted. That 'so long as A does not guarantee certain rights' had contained the prospect of 'once it does'; but the formula in 1993 was 'so long as B, there is *not yet* any danger of collision'. Given the inbuilt direction of movement of the Union, this danger would undoubtedly increase. In the battle over revision powers, a clash on a matter of principle had appeared on the horizon.

In 2009, the moment of truth seemed to have arrived. This time Karlsruhe was to rule on the constitutionality of the Treaty of Lisbon, signed by the German government two years earlier. Again its ruling sounded more severe than it turned out to be in practice. The judges approved the treaty's ratification, on condition that the German parliament strengthened its supervision of the government's European tasks. It also set limits on the Union's future development by stating that every member state must retain the ability to determine its own economic, social and cultural shape. Although some Brussels observers reacted with surprise and shock, the Karlsruhe Court was building on previous verdicts: there cannot be a single European political body; the member states must remain masters of the treaty; national democratic life must be preserved. One striking element was its explicit questioning of the democratic pretensions of the European Parliament, along with its exhortation to the German parliament to assume its European responsibilities. The 'Lisbon ruling' therefore contains an internal tension. It attempts both to protect national political life and to involve national politicians more closely in European affairs. It puts the brakes on Europe's development, while at the same time requesting participation in any discussions about treaty change. In 2009, Karlsruhe thereby added acknowledgment of Europe's intermediate sphere to an existing distrust of its inner sphere.

This tension over the power to change the treaty will not go away. The solution sketched out by 'Luxembourg' in 1963–64 with regard to legislation – the European treaty takes precedence – was neither possible nor desirable in the case of revision.

In terms of *pouvoirs constituants* and *pouvoirs constitués*, the member states are the 'masters of the treaty', as the Court in Karlsruhe had declared in 1993. They have *Kompetenz-Kompetenz*, or meta-precedence. Applied to the relationship between national constitutional courts (or bodies with a comparable function) and the European Court, such reasoning gives precedence to the national courts. It has been argued, conversely, that the European Court has meta-precedence based on the 'autonomy of European law'. But the Court exists because of the founding treaty. If the pact is changed by the member states, how can the Court appeal to the terms of the treaty as a way of opposing that change?

The position of the German judges is unsatisfactory as well, however. Their conclusion that, in the case of a constitutional clash, national interpretations take precedence over European interpretations raises a question: which Europe are they talking about? The shared foundation is not formed by the European institutions but by the member states as a whole, outside the treaty. So Karlsruhe did not clash with 'Luxembourg' but with the assembled governments, including Bonn. The battle over the power of amendment is not fought purely between the inner sphere and the member states, but within the intermediate sphere as well, in the world of dual roles – founder-state Germany and Germany the member of the European club, for example.

A conflict over revision powers, which is ultimately fought out between the member states jointly and the member states severally, is built into Europe's foundations. This need not lead to difficulties. Tensions, including legal tensions, must be absorbed and addressed. Judicial conflict needs to be solved by political dialogue – between courts, between European institutions and member states, and between member states.

When constitutional clashes cannot be prevented by reasoned argument, ingenuity or delay, two resources remain: international law, which the states encounter in their relationships outside the treaty, and the political fact of membership. European law rests, in the end, on the latter. Ultimately a member state has the freedom to avoid the next European intersection by turning back. If any doubt about this remained, it was removed by the most recent Union treaty (2007), which states: 'Any Member State may decide to withdraw from the Union in accordance with its own constitutional requirements.'[122]

FOOTBRIDGE

After the gate was unbarred in Milan in 1985, four revisions of the European order followed in increasingly quick succession: 1986, 1992, 1997 and 2001. The fundamental question of whether renewal was needed was no longer asked. Each treaty set down, in advance, the terms for a discussion about its own amendment. In a metaphor with echoes of the hours of discussion at the table, there was talk of 'leftovers'. The leftovers from Maastricht (1992) were discussed in Amsterdam (1997); the leftovers from there in Nice (2001). Even then the plate was not empty and the leaders realised that they needed to find a different way, which was how movement arose on those other fundamental questions: the 'by whom' and the 'how'.

The heads of government started the process with an experiment. Gathered in the palace of the Belgian king in Laken in late 2001, they decided to set up a convention. This political conference was given a year to contemplate a new European treaty. The national governments and parliaments were represented within it, as were the Commission and the Parliament. The *pouvoirs constituants* and the *pouvoirs constitués* were jumbled together, with all the representatives seated alphabetically.

Beforehand, most governments regarded the Convention as an innocuous advisory body. They did not try to block its establishment, since they would be taking the real decisions themselves, at an intergovernmental conference planned for 2003–04. But the Belgians and the Germans, both having pressed for the Convention to be set up, saw it as a serious player. Its unclear status was a source of tension. Suddenly conflict over the issue of who would give shape to renewal, now and in the future, was built into the mechanism. This in turn opened up a debate about that other fundamental question: how easily does the European political body permit change?

Most of the revision rules developed by the Convention were adopted by the governments and ended up in the Lisbon Treaty. Did it manage to build in a transition to amendment by majority? No. But by unforeseen routes the political pressure exerted by the member states as a whole on the member states individually nevertheless acquired legal forms.

Naturally, the 'who' question was the catalyst for these changes. The national leaders in Laken who asked a hundred politicians to think about Europe's future ought to have predicted that those hundred would soon claim to be speaking on behalf of Europe.

From day one, the Convention transformed itself from a think-tank into a constituent assembly. It made this metamorphosis explicit early on by renaming itself. The 'Convention on the Future of Europe' became the 'European Convention': a small change of wording but a different world. Chairman Valéry Giscard d'Estaing strove to give the body the historic authority of a European constituent assembly. He flirted with the illustrious American precedent of Philadelphia 1787, encouraged the extension of the Convention's mandate, and in mid-2003 was able to deliver to the national leaders a complete draft constitution. Yet from the start this constitutional bluff ran into trouble. Just as George Washington had requested Congress in 1787 to send the constitution straight to the thirteen states, so Giscard d'Estaing asked the heads of government to present the text, unaltered, to their populations. But whereas Washington's request was honoured, Europe's leaders began arguing over the draft. Ratification then ran into the sand, and in 2007 the member states decided to scrap everything in the text that made it resemble a constitution. The European would-be constituent assembly was blocked by the national governments and peoples. The member states, it gradually became clear, were not about to relinquish their say on fundamentals.

This outcome was, of course, not yet known when the Convention began considering future amendments – in other words, the post-constitution constitution. The member states had not discussed the revision rule during earlier changes to the treaty, but the Convention had powerful motives, both concrete and psychological, for tinkering with the text. It regarded transition to revision by majority as a marvellous symbol of a new beginning for Europe. Without official revisory powers for the inner sphere, the fate awaiting future conventions might be the same as that which Giscard's Convention feared for itself: becoming merely a talking shop in the governments' shadow. That was the reason several convention members entered into an energetic and sometimes emotional debate on the issue. An almost desperate plea for self-renewal of the Union, independent of the unanimous states, was only to be expected.

The starting point was the existing revision procedure, with its peculiar division into a prelude (initiative) and three acts (decisions on the whether, what and how of renewal). The convention members came up with creative variations on all these phases. One particularly amusing proposal was produced by a British Conservative: the European Council should henceforth have to decide unanimously on the convening of an intergovernmental conference, in Act I. This attempt to make good the Milanese defeat of his former party leader eighteen years earlier was not given a hearing. In response, it was spelled out, at the request of the Belgians, that the leaders take this decision by ordinary majority. The gate was left unbarred.

A great deal more fuss arose over Act II, about actual control of future renewal, and it was there that the ongoing rivalry between Convention and intergovernmental conference found its natural arena. There was a widespread feeling: This Convention thing works really well and deserves to be repeated; at last we're rid of the secretiveness of the palaces and chancelleries and can speak publicly about the future of Europe. Thus convention members indulged in mutual congratulation. Such enthusiasm was only to be expected from Europarliamentarians and European commissioners, but they were supported by the national parliamentarians, numerically the largest group. They, too, had previously been forced to wait and see what kind of treaty their governments would bring home. Though rather less thrilled themselves, there was little that government representatives could do about this prevailing mood of satisfaction.

Beneath this consensus lurked fundamental differences between convention members. Who, after all, had a real say on renewal – the Convention or the governments? Several convention members wanted to do away with intergovernmental conferences altogether. More subtle were variations that would allow the Convention and the intergovernmental conference onto the stage together, but shift the balance of power in favour of the former (for example by having the governments decide on proposals by weighted majority). This was exactly what opponents of the convention approach feared: a growth in the self-renewal power of the Union. German conservative Joachim Wuermeling wrote that the member states, if they were to remain 'masters of the treaty', would have to decide for themselves about every transfer of sovereignty to the Union. This meant that 'institutions or representatives of the Union must not be involved in decisions on treaty amendments'.[123] The constituted powers must be sidelined.

Most convention members had fewer concerns about constitutional purity. Take Austrian governmental representative Hannes Farnleitner. He was 'fundamentally positive' about the Convention, but he did believe that the member states must remain 'masters of the treaties'. Such conceptual generosity meant that the Praesidium could decide to give its blessing to the experiment of the Convention without violating the privileges of the governments. The draft treaty stated that a future convention would make 'recommendations' to an intergovernmental conference, which would then take the final decision.

The intrinsic tension contained in the Convention – constituent assembly or advisory body? – was deemed irresolvable for the time being: an unorthodox solution, but appropriate in the circumstances. The text, which itself wavered between constitution and treaty, was provided with the appropriate rules of amendment, involving both a constitutional convention and an intergovernmental conference. On that front at least, the tension between renewal and self-renewal resulted in a truce sealed with a treaty. The battle over the power to change the content of the pact, an inevitable consequence of the establishment by the governments of a convention, would be resumed in the next performance of Act II.

In the debate on Act III, future ratification, feelings ran high. The prospect of a breakthrough to ratification by a majority of states served as a constitutional litmus test. Unanimity meant a classic treaty; majority, the breakthrough to a constitution. For that reason, the idea was defended not only by representatives of the inner sphere, but also by the vice-chairman of the Convention, Giuliano Amato, an academic and former Italian prime minister. He had told a colleague that 'the professor of constitutional law in him would commit suicide if unanimity was retained'.[124] (The man to whom he made this confession, Jean-Luc Dehaene, added that the politician in Amato would survive the experience.)

What Amato and the federalists were after was a veiled founding moment. Legally there was something to be said for that: future ratification by majority is easier to defend than its abrupt introduction now. No infringement of existing rules is involved; no leap, but instead a tidy transition, its way paved by unanimous ratification of the treaty at hand – a bridge from the old order to the new.

Yet the advantages of a bridge (as opposed to a leap) had little impact on the debate. The same two camps faced each other. On one side, groups of Europarliamentarians and national parliamentarians produced proposals with thresholds of four-fifths or five-sixths of the states. On the other side, the British, Irish and Swedish governments made known in advance that this was unthinkable. In late April 2003, British representative Peter Hain placed a bomb under any imaginable bridge to majority ratification: he would not sign the treaty if it included a blank cheque. Although amendment by majority was a bridge from a legal point of view, politically it was still a leap. And London did not want to make that leap – not today and not tomorrow.

So the old spectre of a total blockade arose. A way out was found in a new distinction between 'heavier' and 'lighter' ratification procedures. The gradually developing notion of a constitutional treaty that was divided into several parts – Parts I, II and IV for constitutional provisions and Part III for policy – was well suited to the task. Many convention members who insisted on strong ratification for the constitutional elements proved willing to consider making the groundwork for policy change a little less restrictive. This introduced for the first time, after the 'whether' and the 'by whom' of renewal, the fundamental question of 'how easily?'

Having hit the buffers with their majority plans, the federalists threw all their weight behind a lighter procedure for specific parts – by majority, without ratification, anything. As well as representatives of the Parliament and the Commission, this little plan suited some governments, including those of Belgium, the Netherlands and Finland. Life would be easier (they thought) if there was scope for policymaking such that no parliamentary brake could be applied. Via these shortcuts, all kinds of European policy areas had been expanded in the past with the assent of all governments, and they were hardly trivial: energy; the environment; regional, consumer and research policy. There was fundamental opposition from others. German representative Wuermeling argued that there should be no surreptitious circumventing of the ratification rights of national parliaments.

In the hectic final days of the Convention, a broad coalition under Amato's passionate leadership ranged itself behind a complex formula. Ratification by five of the six member states would be sufficient for certain parts, so long as less than a third of the national parliaments objected on the grounds of loss of competencies. 'Good idea, but too late', decided Giscard d'Estaing on 12 June, believing that the governments would reject it.[125] As a gesture of courtesy, the chairman of the Convention forwarded to the incoming chairman of the European Council (Italian Prime Minister Silvio Berlusconi) a letter in which his deputy, Amato, and Europarliamentarians Elmar Brok and Andrew Duff defended the plan.

In Act III, then, the Convention did not get far with self-renewal: no majority ratification and the member states remained in charge. At the final press conference, *il Dottor Sottile* was inconsolable. Asked about his greatest personal disappointment, Amato pointed to the failure to secure a new revision rule. Playing on words (*trattato*, 'treaty', is masculine; *costituzione*, 'constitution', is feminine), he declared that the baby the Convention had produced was, unfortunately, 'a boy'.[126]

The heartbroken Amato and other convention members failed to appreciate the fundamental transition brought about by the Convention: a move towards more self-renewal. This was not limited to the holding of future conventions. All the whining and muttering about the veto had produced two successes, one unforeseen and one unseen.

Unforeseen was the fact that the message in a bottle from the Amato–Brok–Duff trio did arrive in Rome. The idea of a light amendment procedure was taken up by the governments. If treaty change affected only internal policy and did not increase the competencies of the Union, then (the ministers decided in November 2003) it could take place without an intergovernmental conference. A decision by a unanimous European Council would be required instead, followed by ratification in all member states. Does this change anything? Some commentators complained that, once they got together, the governments left the veto in place and scrapped the Convention with its parliamentary overseers.[127] This verdict, however, falls into the same conceptual trap as Thatcher in 1985 ('another conference'). The leaders who gathered would be wearing different hats.

'Revision-lite', which has since come into force, is therefore extremely significant. The intergovernmental conference and the Convention have both disappeared from Act II as constituent powers, and the European Council, an institution, formulates amendments in their stead. Eighteen years after the 'whether' of Milan, the 'what' of renewal has, in part, been drawn into the Union as well.

For anyone still in doubt, in March 2011, less than eighteen months after the Lisbon Treaty came into force, the heads of government used this route to launch a treaty change. Under pressure from the euro crisis – an unforeseen event that struck at the very heart of the club in 2010 – they decided to set up a permanent emergency fund for the eurozone, something that would have been utterly unthinkable a few months before. Two additional sentences were introduced into the treaty to give this rescue fund a sound legal basis. It seemed excessive to mount a classic total negotiation for a targeted amendment: each of the governments would be tempted to make its own demands, hindering ratification and causing further financial unrest. So the leaders decided to take a simplified route, via the European Council. The very first crisis to test the foundations of the Union had shown in concrete terms the vital importance of self-renewal.

Moreover, the dividing up of the shared foundations into elements that could be more or less easily changed signifies a constitutionalising of Europe's political order. 'Light amendment' no longer takes the form of a refoundation. This means that the dual structure of foundation (or refoundation) followed by legislation that pertained in the early days of the Community has formally evolved into a triple structure: foundation (or refoundation), then revision (or 'revision-lite'), then legislation. Legally, the club is slowly creeping out from under its founders.

The unseen success was the change to the revision procedure that the Convention forced through as a consequence of several influential members persistently hammering away at the need for majority decision-making. It introduces the concept of a *passerelle* or footbridge. Many convention members, the parliamentarians in particular, were displeased that their draft treaty did not settle upon the cherished 'Council by majority plus Parliament' formula for every kind of decision or law. But in reality most of the governmental representatives had one veto or another that they did not want to give up. As a compromise, the Praesidium built footbridges at two points in the treaty. One such bridge meant that, in almost all situations in which the member states retained a veto, the European Council could unanimously decide to switch to majority voting. (The exception was on military matters.) The other footbridge opened the way for the European Council to decide unanimously that, in cases where the Council was the only legislator, the Parliament could be made co-legislator. These *passerelles* would in future enable the Union to make the transition from unanimous or special decision-making to ordinary decision-making without amending the treaty, and therefore without national ratifications.

The intergovernmental conference that followed the Convention decided that the *passerelle* was a workable idea. The Italians integrated it into the revision article. Crossing the footbridge was made more difficult in one respect: the European Council has to announce to the national parliaments any intention to cross. They are then given six months to raise an objection. If one parliament objects, the footbridge remains closed. (The British parliament has relinquished its right to approve the use of the *passerelle*, transferring this to a referendum.) This might look like a licence for parliamentary obstruction, yet in comparison to traditional ratifications it strengthens the position of the club. Instead of Europe having to wait for the yes-word like a jilted lover, the parliaments need to take measures in time if they decide to say 'no'. This type of renewal is therefore fully drawn into the Union, all the way from the prelude to Act III. In itself, it contains no surprises: the number of vetoes covered by the clause is finite and knowable. Once the footbridge is ready, the only question that remains – asked and answered by the European Council – is: 'When do we cross?' The joint monopoly on the power of revision held by the founders has been reduced to a guarantee that any formal parliamentary objection will be honoured. This gives individual founders little reason to carry on self-confidently striking up their 'masters of the treaty' chorus. Characteristically, though, even in these situations there is no transition to majority. All the national parliaments retain their right to object.

***

The member states do not want a Europe that can renew itself without them, as a political body with a will of its own. So revision by a majority of members is not in prospect. Such a complete emancipation would indeed be a founding moment for Europe, but it would spell the end for the independent states. And the states are not going away. If the club wanted to provide itself with the political power of historical versatility, then a different path was going to have to be found – as indeed it was.

Europe's power of revision resides permanently with the national governments and parliaments as a whole, in the intermediate sphere of the members.

The trick was, therefore, to make the *pouvoir constituant* into, at one and the same time, a *pouvoir constitué*. This could not be done by simply sidelining the unwilling; everybody had to be drawn into the game one step at a time. The European Council, in which the governments joined together as an institution at the highest level, pointed the way.

This approach was pursued act by act, until all were exposed to the duress of joint renewal. It started in 1985, in Milan, with Craxi's coup in Act I (the 'whether' of renewal). He pushed the heads of government over an invisible threshold and set the renewal mechanism going. Changes in Act II (the 'what' of renewal) were brought about by the Laken summit of 2001 and the treaty negotiations of 2002–04. The governments were forced to move slightly closer together, making space for a convention that has brought – and will continue to bring – on-stage both the national parliaments and the European Parliament (for ordinary revision), while at the same time the governments had to give way to the European Council (for light revision). In Act III (the 'that' of renewal) there was another cautious shift. It lay in the clause that provided for a host on the steps, which was deleted for ratification of the current treaty but retained for future treaty changes. The legal requirement of unanimous ratification, lifeblood for the members, was now accompanied by an acknowledgment of joint political responsibility for any revision that was set in train.

Having arrived at the end of the process, the question is: from what point onwards can the ratifying parliaments, now the last bastions of the member states in the case of light amendments, be regarded individually or jointly as a constituted power? It is an open question, but the footbridge confirms the counterintuitive direction in which Europe is seeking the answer. The successor to unanimous ratification is not majority ratification, but unanimous non-refusal.

The *passerelle* significantly increases the pressure exerted by the club. In military terms, laying down a footbridge means switching the main challenge from attack (members jointly) to defence (members severally). A crossing can perhaps be prevented for a while by one parliament or another standing on the footbridge, but in the end the combined forces will find an appropriate moment to break through. Machiavelli warned that you must never attempt to combat your foe on a mountain pass: 'For the enemy it is easy to come in full force, for his intention is to pass, and not to stop there; whilst on the contrary he who has to await the approach of the enemy cannot possibly keep so large a force there, for the reason that he will have to establish himself for a longer time in those confined and sterile places, not knowing when the enemy may come to make the attempt to pass.'[128]

Lastly, the footbridge is important as a metaphor. It is an image that points to the fact that the club experiences the move as a passage, or more specifically as the crossing of a river or other watercourse – in this case the foundational river. The image also points to Europe's aversion to leaping and its preference for small, secure steps. And it clearly expresses the way Europe makes use of time: We don't dare cross now, but we'll lay down a plank anyway, for when it's needed. Contrast these three elements with the Rubicon that Caesar stood before in 49 BC – or George Washington et al. (in their own view) more than eighteen centuries later: if they had calmly laid down a footbridge, they would never have reached the Capitol.

PART II

VICISSITUDES OF FORTUNE

World history with its great events does not come along at a steady speed like a railway train. No, it moves forward jerkily, albeit with irresistible force. All anyone can do is always to be on the lookout for the Lord striding through world history and then leap at him and cling to his coat-tails, to be carried along by him as far as possible. It is dishonourable foolishness and decrepit statesmanship, as if the aim were to gather up opportunities and introduce murkiness, and then go fishing in that.
Otto von Bismarck[1]

In the River of Time

In a famous passage at the end of *The Prince* (1513), Machiavelli claims that the world is controlled neither by the vagaries of chance alone nor by human free will, concluding instead that 'Fortune is the arbiter of one-half of our actions, but that she still leaves us to direct the other half, or perhaps a little less'. He goes on:

> I compare her to one of those raging rivers, which when in flood overflows the plains, sweeping away trees and buildings, bearing away the soil from place to place; everything flies before it, all yield to its violence, without being able in any way to withstand it; and yet, though its nature be such, it does not follow therefore that men, when the weather becomes fair, shall not make provision, both with defences and barriers, in such a manner that, rising again, the waters may pass away by canal, and their force be neither so unrestrained nor so dangerous.[2]

This insight, expressed by Machiavelli and several of his contemporaries, denoted a break with the past. Medieval Christendom attached little significance to the earthly association between people and princes. What mattered was the salvation of the soul in its relationship with the eternal God. History with its contingencies came second to eschatology. Prophets who detected the hand of God in natural disasters or political events – such as the sack of Rome in 410 – were heretics. The furthest you might go would be to say that divine Providence called down disasters upon people to test their faith. Outside of belief you saw merely the dominion of blind fate, the absurdity of Fortune.

In Renaissance times, wars and calamities ravaged the Italian peninsula. The invasion by the French king in 1494 had upset the balance of power between the Italian states. Machiavelli, from 1498 to 1512 a senior civil servant in the Florentine republic, writes of 'the great changes in affairs which have been seen, and may still be seen, every day, beyond all human conjecture'.[3] In *The Prince* and *The Discourses* he attempts to find ways to keep Fortune at bay by investigating which political courses of action had proved most effective in countless historical and contemporary situations, including dictatorship and republic, war and peace, foundation and legislation. One modern commentator has shown how Machiavelli's conclusions can be systematised into recommendations for dealing with historicity.[4]

Time governs our lives. According to Machiavelli, however, this is not the eschatological time of theology or the regular time of physics, but time as a stream of chance events. History has no plan, no logic. There is only one relationship between things that happen: before and after, antecedent and consequent. A single event can change all those before it by placing them in a new light. Which is why Machiavelli speaks of time as 'the father of all truth'.[5] To him, the magnitude of an event is measured by its consequences.

The difficulty for people and for states is that, far from standing on the bank, they are right out in the current, part of countless chains of events and, at the same time, called upon to direct them this way and that. Machiavelli wants to know how politicians, looking upstream, can anticipate imminent or future events. As in medicine or law, this requires sound judgment, foresight and vigilance. Sometimes events come in constellations that reveal patterns, but there is never any certainty. Only in retrospect will you know whether you have done the right thing.

To Machiavelli, Fortune is not sent by God to try us. Instead she should be treated either as an adversary or as a partner. She resembles a visitor whose arrival brings difficulties, but also creates opportunities. The Wheel of Fortune starts turning more quickly; there is a surge in the tide of events. The capacity to deal with such a visitor is something Machiavelli calls *virtù*. He writes of this 'virtue' as a purely political concept, a combination of intelligence and vigour, stripped of any moral or theological connotations. He distinguishes between three phases in dealing with Fortune: in advance of her coming, on her arrival and after her departure.

Phase one: preparation. Since time flows like a river, you can build dykes and dams beforehand. Army commanders, for instance, need to ensure that their troops are disciplined and well organised: 'Where good discipline prevails there also will good order prevail, and good fortune rarely fails to follow in their train.'[6] In affairs of state, it is important to have a sound constitution that can absorb future shocks. The good politician is capable of sacrificing short-term advantage to long-term planning. He must always be on the lookout, expecting a visit at any moment.

Phase two: Fortune's arrival. The best way to act depends on the situation, so flexibility undoubtedly helps. Essentially there are three options. One is to lie down and do nothing, wait until the guest leaves and then get things under control again. In some cases this will prove a successful strategy, although it is risky to give Fortune free rein and no one will think you a hero. Alternatively, you can try to profit from the situation, to grab events by the tail and turn them to your advantage. This demands a profound understanding of the overall situation, including things that may yet be in prospect. You will therefore do best to play for time, observe events from a distance and act later. The third option is to try to steal a march on your visitor by going on the offensive, by attempting to get a grip on her before she can seize hold of you. It calls for speed, audacity, bravado – hazardous, certainly, but Fortune sometimes succumbs to chutzpah. What you must never do is ignore what is happening or try to swim against the current. The illusion of living outside time invites catastrophe.

Phase three: after Fortune's departure. Here equanimity is the required trait, characteristic both of strong states and of outstanding personalities: 'A truly great man is ever the same under all circumstances; and if his fortune varies, exalting him at one moment and oppressing him at another, he himself never varies, but always preserves a firm courage.'[7] He knows how fickle Fortune is. By contrast, weaker souls are altered by her, becoming insolent when she raises them up, losing heart when she casts them down.

Machiavelli makes clear that, to some degree, we hold our fate in our own hands. To be a good human being or a good politician, each of us must step into the river of time, accept the contingency of events and take responsibility for the open future. This demands foresight, preparedness and an awareness that we can always be surprised: 'Events, dear boy, events.'

From this politico-philosophical perspective, a European political body exists when it is capable of making an impact on history. Part II of this book concerns the question of whether – and if so, how – Europe can step into the flow of time as a single entity. Is there a Europe that matches up to events originating outside it? How does it respond to the visitor's knock at the door? Fortune can assume countless guises: wars, diplomatic crises, the collapse of a currency, floods of refugees, terrorist attacks, environmental disasters. How can we tell whether or not Europe is stepping into this river of events as one political body?

The logical criterion must surely be a joint diplomatic performance in the face of the outside world, in dealing with other political orders. After all, Europe is an association of states, each of which is in charge of its own domestic security. ('National security remains the sole responsibility of each Member State', as the Treaty on European Union makes clear.[8]) Even should this change, it would still be hard to determine when European governments were acting on their own behalf and when jointly. In theory, Europe can implement domestic economic reforms, environmental legislation or anti-terrorism measures under the mantle of the nation state. Inwardly, each state can obfuscate the issue of responsibility – but not outwardly. To an American diplomat, a Chinese negotiator or a Congolese warlord, it clearly does matter whether the person he is talking to is speaking on behalf of all European member states or just one.

This difference between speaking as a nation and speaking 'on behalf of Europe' is precisely the source of Europe's added value. Outward unity is the supreme goal for many politicians. 'Europe must speak with one voice in the world', we have been told for many a long year. For purposes of analysis, it makes more sense to turn this around. Recall Hobbes' insight: 'A multitude of men are made *one* person, when they are by one man, or one person, represented.'[9] It is not a matter of a voiceless Europe developing a single voice. Instead it is in that one voice, so long as it is actually heard, that Europe takes shape as a political body.

The European club entered the current of history not in one step but in two. A single move would have sufficed, but that proved unachievable. Between the first step and the next, it waited and prepared itself. This particular passage therefore came in three stages: the years of foundation (1950–57), the sojourn in the Community (1958–89) and the time since the fall of the Berlin Wall (1989–today).

The opening move took place when six European nations decided that they wanted henceforth, in certain respects, to adopt a joint stance towards the outside world. Three times they established a Community for that purpose: once for coal and steel, once for an army and once for a market. The European army never materialised and from 1957 onwards low politics was practically all that remained. So in a sense the club placed itself outside time. Yet this waiting period had its uses, as developments occurred in the sphere of the member states. (A later observer would compare the Community to a 'cocoon', waiting to become a butterfly without any idea when that would happen.[10]) Not until the fall of the Wall in 1989, which shook the whole of Europe to its core, did the circle of member states find itself unable any longer to shirk history. Since then it has taken a second step, throwing off the Community and entering into the river of time as a Union.

Central to Part II of this book are Europe's transformations in response to events in the outside world. Its relationship with those events has not been inherently coercive – Fortune did not simply bring the European states into line. Sometimes the member states have seen reason to act, outwardly, as a single entity; sometimes one of them has given a particular twist to one of Fortune's visits, for example by pushing through some other plan of its own with particular haste. On occasion, each of the members did as it liked and pandemonium ensued. There is therefore as little sense in disappointedly holding up a federalist ideal as a contrast to every single foreign policy dispute between member states, as there is in claiming beforehand that, in view of the historical burden of the nation states, attempts to take joint action in the world are doomed to failure. The facts defy such preconceptions.

It is possible, though, to regard the past sixty years as the story of four major steps that Europe has taken in its dealings with fate. First of all, geo-political relationships and concerns weighed heavily when the Communities were founded. The main players recognised the primacy of politics over economics, which suggests that at least as much importance was attached to the political significance of the club's existence as to its economic rules. It was a significance located partly in the future, however. The founding pact contained a double *telos* that has worked through to the present. The circle of Six would grow into a political order that would one day encompass the entire continent. Europe was not simply a fact: it was a promise.

Second, the European Community was initially ill-equipped to respond to the vicissitudes of fortune. There was no provision for a foreign policy, since to most member states that seemed neither possible nor desirable, and in any case unnecessary. The European institutions were engaged in low politics, as intended. The job the treaty assigned to them included direct contact with the outside world – in trade policy, for example, or later through development aid – but the lines drawn around those competencies were strictly policed by the members. For high politics, each of the Six individually relied on the American umbrella to shelter them from the storm. (Only France liked to pretend it had no need of such protection and often played a double game.) The threat of another Franco-German war seemed to recede; the Russians were held at bay by the Americans in conjunction with Nato. Little thought was given to the new guises in which Fortune might appear. In fact, there were some in the inner sphere who still hoped it might be possible to step outside the current of time – that a 'new Jerusalem' was at hand.[11] Other politicians chose to wait because they could see no alternative. They played for time.

Then, third, European non-members knocking on the door made the member states realise that, if only because such a door existed, they were a single power bloc as far as the rest of the world was concerned. The Six experienced this first in 1961, when the British knocked. Greater and more unexpected was the shock of the fall of the Berlin Wall (1989), when the somewhat forgotten eastern half of the continent turned up in the waiting room of the Twelve. The relationship between the circle of members and the continent as a whole forced the member states to politicise their association. Some went along reluctantly, but there was no other option.

Fourth, the member states did not transfer their political voice to the institutions of the inner sphere as a way of becoming better able to respond to the demands of the outside world. Instead, after much hesitation and many internal quarrels, they found other routes that might lead to an 'on Europe's behalf'. The heads of government staged a coup, uninvited, and as a result the in-between world of the member states took shape. Here in their own sphere, outside the treaty, they organised summits of heads of state or government (several times from 1961 onwards), institutionalised those summits as a European Council (1974) and – after the fall of the Wall – entrusted this forum with responsibility for foreign policy (1993) within a Union established for the purpose, before giving it a permanent president (2009). So the table of the heads of government became a vehicle for European high politics. Only there can an individual stand up and speak to the White House or the Kremlin on behalf of Europe as a whole.

Finally, a word about the basic political motives of the three most important European states since 1945. France looks to Europe for a reincarnation of itself. Germany seeks (or has sought) redemption from guilt. Britain wants 'a seat at the table' whenever the others meet. True, these motives are familiar, but taken together they have been decisive for the outcome, for the way European politics is distributed across various spheres of action.

France was the initiator. After 1945, its role as a world power was played out, and from then on it used Europe as a lever. It was only because of Europe that it could still be 'free', which to Paris means taking charge of your own destiny, being able to speak and to act, demonstrably shouldering responsibility for your situation – being a player. It could not reconcile itself to becoming a military vassal of Washington, or to living under the monetary yoke of the Bundesbank. These high aspirations were fashioned into concrete and ingenious plans. Paris worked to create a Europe *à la française*, featuring political tenacity, bureaucratic discipline, an eye for the long term, and diplomatic powers of persuasion that its partners (with the possible exception of London) could come nowhere near to matching. The lever worked, since France followed up on a robust initial advocacy of European unity (the

'Schuman moment') with a refusal to be absorbed into that larger whole (the 'de Gaulle moment'). Once the Community existed, Paris succeeded in giving shape to the intermediate sphere of the member states, where history and law, national power and European unity intersect. On the stage where national leaders perform, every French president feels in his element.

In 1945, Germany was a pariah among nations, occupied, guilty and divided. From Konrad Adenauer onwards, the Germans used Europe as a means of securing political and moral redemption. It was both a route back to the concert of free states and a project to create a better world. (As well as by its good behaviour, Germany's guilt was paid off in cash, its contributions filling the European coffers.) From a geopolitical perspective, Bonn needed Washington, but it also needed Paris. Only from America could it expect help against Russia, which had East Germany in its grip – and that meant existential dependence. Meanwhile France alone offered the redemptive framework of 'Europe'. The tension between Washington and Paris, which sometimes made itself felt in Bonn, too, was in part resolved by a preference for the European inner sphere, for Europe as more of an idea than a power bloc. Here the existence of a European parliament suited the (potentially) most populous member state rather well. After German unification was achieved in 1990, the motif of redemption wore thin. Nevertheless, even now, having become the largest and in many ways the most powerful member state, Germany remains reluctant to exert its power too blatantly in its relationships with its partners and neighbours. The memory of Auschwitz lingers.

Post-war Britain, by contrast, had no need of Europe as a screen onto which to project either a passion for freedom or moral preoccupations. In London, the adage remained: 'We have no friends, only interests.' But because of the destruction of the European concert of states and the supremacy of America in the Atlantic world, the country had lost its cherished role of 'European balancer'. Only when a European conference table was in place did the British start to fear that it might result in their interests being damaged if they were not present to defend them. London finds exclusion almost unbearable: its fundamental European motif is 'a seat at the table'. (The recent eurozone crisis has rather called this motif into question, with as yet unpredictable consequences.) Since 1956, Britain has lived in good-tempered obeisance to American authority. It shares with France an unwillingness to see the inner sphere emancipated. Throughout the first four decades of Britain's membership, every governing party has kept a grip on that European chair: only parties in opposition have sometimes wanted to back away into the free outer sphere.

Forward movement on Europe does not usually originate in London. It arises on occasions when France and Germany come together to initiate something. From 1974 onwards, the division of roles was such that Paris continued to shape the intermediate sphere of the members, while Bonn/Berlin also helped to strengthen the inner sphere. Of the big three, therefore, France offered the best preparation for a visit from history. If Europe wants to step into the current of time as a body politic, the intermediate sphere is the place where it needs to show that it can act and take responsibility.

Is the result – a European Council that has become the main vehicle of European politics – the product of a French plot? That would be too simplistic. Ever since de Gaulle, France has repeatedly insisted that Europe must have a voice in the world; but a voice alone would not suffice – certainly not in a Union of twenty-seven. Paris was successful partly because it contributed the best script. The member states eventually realised that their club was not immune to the vicissitudes of Fortune – that bomb attacks, monetary shocks and waves of redundancies could threaten the common fabric. Only time could bring this insight. The governments are aware (more so than their populations) that it is increasingly hard to stand up to fate on your own. Simply put, over a period of sixty years, France has managed to infect the circle with its desire to be a player.

4

Coming Together as Six
(1950–57)

I undoubtedly thought for a moment that the first step towards a European federation would be this union of the two countries [France and Germany] and they alone – and that the others would join later. In the end I added to the original version that evening, by hand, that the Authority would be 'open to the participation of the other countries of Europe'.

Jean Monnet (1976)[12]

Fear of fate knocking on the door was decisive at the time of Europe's founding. For France, Fortune wore the cloak of a recovered and warlike Germany. Neighbours of these two traditional enemies shared the same anxiety. There were even some German leaders who believed that the German people must be protected against their country's own evil genius. (They lived with the terrible possibility of themselves becoming the uninvited guest at the table.) With the Cold War, a second spectre appeared in the shape of Communist Russia, the most terrifying power on the continent. Although under American protection, several Western European leaders felt they needed to be capable of meeting that future threat without Washington's help. They could hope to do so only by working together. This way of thinking was encouraged by the Americans – up to a certain level and until a certain point. European unity would enhance everyone's security in a turbulent world: that of the other five against Germany, and that of the Six jointly against Russia.

It is important to remember that Europe had three distinct founding moments. We will look at them chronologically. Two are famous, because successful, one leading to the Coal and Steel Treaty of Paris in 1951 and the other to the common market Treaty of Rome in 1957. On both occasions, the pressures of the wider world had a greater impact than is suggested by the evangelical stories about Europe's founding fathers that feature in textbooks and Brussels brochures. In a third founding moment, the Six laid out plans for a European army. This third episode – the most radical of all in its aims – ended in dramatic failure in 1954 and has since disappeared from the collective memory. Still, that fiasco explains why the Six did not step into the historical current together in 1958, but felt it safest for the time being to stick to 'low politics'.

SCHUMAN'S VOICE AND ADENAUER'S EAR (BEFORE 10 MAY 1950)

Now, if *you* were to come up with a plan for Germany . . . wrote the American secretary of state to his French colleague in the autumn of 1949. The following spring, the American became more insistent: by their next meeting, at the latest, there must be something on the table. That encounter was planned for Wednesday, 10 May 1950 in London. France had been put on the spot and Schuman knew it. He would have to act.

It was almost five years since the end of the 'Second Thirty Years' War' and Europe's standing in the world had changed. The balance of power between states had been destroyed by Hitler's self-destructive drive for conquest. Only Russia and Britain, on the periphery of the continent, had stood up to Hitler – with the help of America. The other European states (aside from those that remained neutral) had been either occupied by the Nazis or defeated along with them. In Yalta, confident of victory within months, Stalin, Roosevelt and Churchill had redrawn the map of Europe. The leaders of the Big Three moved Poland's borders westwards and divided Germany into three zones of occupation. Given Roosevelt's desire to bring American troops home, Churchill feared that he would be left alone to face the Russians and Germans. And so, at his urging, France was offered a folding chair at the victors' table and was allocated a territory to occupy, trimmed from the British and American zones. A few months later, in July 1945 in Potsdam, the decision was taken that, for the time being, these four powers would govern Germany.

As to what should happen to the defeated enemy, the views of the four diverged. They were undeniably united by a fear of a repeat of 'Versailles', the peace treaty that had given birth to rampant German revanchism. To avoid repeating old mistakes, would they have to be harsher or more generous than in 1919? Broadly speaking, in 1945 France and Russia belonged to the former school, while the British and Americans vacillated. To the extent that no joint decision could be taken, each concentrated on governing its own zone.

In a remarkable speech in the autumn of 1945, French general, war hero and president Charles de Gaulle asked an audience of French officers and men in the Kurhaus in Baden-Baden: 'What are we doing here the day after our victory?'[13] He sketched out a programme that would permanently weaken the traditional enemy. Its two main points sounded familiar: first, a permanent French presence in German territories along the Rhine, specifically the Saar, the Eiffel, the Palatinate, part of Hessen and the city of Cologne – not an 'annexation' at all, said the General, but 'an economic and moral union'; and second, permanent French control of the Ruhrgebiet, the source of the coal needed by Western Europe, and especially France. The area served both as 'collateral' to neutralise the German threat and as a 'resource' that would enable France to become an industrial power. Tellingly, de Gaulle referred to the defeated nation as *les Allemagnes*, 'the German lands'. This plural form had been in use before Bismarck's creation of a unified state in 1870 – the root of all evil in French eyes. De Gaulle regarded 1945 as the perfect moment to destroy Bismarck's legacy at a stroke, while at the same time realising Napoleon's dream and exploiting Hitler's arms foundry. Germany was to be split into pieces, driven back well beyond the Rhine and stripped of its coal.

While Paris under de Gaulle was still acting towards its defeated neighbour on the basis of ancient national causes and fears, Washington and London soon spotted a new visitation from history looming on the horizon. It was that other Western European war hero, Winston Churchill, who, in a speech in March 1946, put the transformation into words:

> From Stettin in the Baltic to Trieste in the Adriatic, an iron curtain has descended across the Continent. Behind that line lie all the capitals of the ancient states of Central and Eastern Europe. Warsaw, Berlin, Prague, Vienna, Budapest, Belgrade, Bucharest and Sofia . . . all are subject in one form or another, not only to Soviet influence but to a very high and, in many cases, increasing measure of control from Moscow.[14]

Churchill's powerful image of a curtain coming down across Europe lodged itself in the global consciousness and was soon being written with capital letters, as a new reality: the Iron Curtain.

The Americans were slower than the British to recognise Moscow's expansionist urge. President Franklin Roosevelt, who died in April 1945, had pinned his hopes for a peaceful world on the United Nations, his brainchild, and he made more concessions to Stalin in Yalta than were militarily necessary – to the annoyance of Churchill, an anti-Communist since 1917. Roosevelt's successor, Harry Truman, was less subject to delusion. After an appeal for help from the Greek government, which feared a Communist takeover, he decided to assume control of the military bases in Greece and Turkey, from which London was having to withdraw for lack of money. It was a significant moment. Of the three great powers at Yalta, only two were left, and they were no longer allies, but enemies in a new, 'cold' war.

The pace of events now increased. In June 1947, an American general, George Marshall, presented a plan that would give extensive financial support to all European states. Washington asked the Europeans to organise its distribution. London and Paris took the lead. Russia forced Poland, Czechoslovakia, Hungary and other states in its sphere of influence to refuse the offer. This meant that Stalin was confirming from his side the political line of demarcation between Russians and Americans, between Eastern Europe and Western Europe, the latter including Greece and Turkey. In centres of government west of this boundary, the last remaining illusions about Soviet intentions vanished with the Communist coup in Prague of February 1948. (Within the Western European intelligentsia, those illusions proved more durable and remarkably resistant to political reality.)

This profound change in post-war European relations placed the German question in a completely new context. France, trampled underfoot by its neighbour three times since Bismarck, had the greatest difficulty in adjusting, but the way in which it eventually did was radical.

Paris failed to attain the goals outlined in de Gaulle's Baden-Baden speech. It could not control the Rhineland because of resistance from the allies. The Saar alone was provisionally brought into an economic union with France; control of the Ruhrgebiet, which lay within the British zone of occupation, remained beyond France's grasp. The need for containment of a potentially centralised German power was recognised in the form of a ban on pan-German political parties, but the fusion in early 1947 of the American and British zones into a 'Bizone' was unhelpful in that respect.

Why such a meagre result? The pressure France could put on Washington was limited. Economically it needed American credits. With the start of the Cold War, its dependence became even more obvious, and after 1947 France found itself in the Western camp, like it or not. At the same time, the Cold War strengthened France's position within its dependent relationship, since in Washington Paris could conjure up the spectre of a Communist takeover of France (the party was already good for a quarter of French votes) unless certain commitments were made. This sometimes produced results.

The first surprise came in May and June 1948, during a conference in London of the three Western occupying powers and the Benelux countries to discuss the future of Germany. Washington made it clear that the German question took second place to the struggle against the Soviet Union. America wanted an end to the dismantling of German industry and the establishment of a constituent assembly for a West German state, which would have to include the French zone. The Americans and British had announced only quite recently that the regional authority in their Bizone would be allowed to exercise economic sovereignty over the Ruhrgebiet. To Paris this was a nightmare scenario: the coal and steel industries back in German hands; a green light for a German state. The French were in too weak a position to walk away from the London conference, but they did not have to capitulate on all points. Although the French government abandoned its opposition to statehood, it managed to ensure that German coal and steel production would be supervised by an 'International Ruhr Authority'. Bowing to pressure from Washington, Paris accepted the creation of a West German state in June 1948, in return for a French say on the Ruhrgebiet.

Although the French government had reason to be satisfied with this deal, the London accords met with fierce opposition back home. So soon after liberation, the French public still saw '*les boches*' as a bigger enemy than 'the reds' in Moscow, and it now realised with a shock that practically nothing was left of France's post-war plans for Germany. The Gaullists, in opposition, accused the foreign minister of treason. The governing coalition tottered, but it steered the accords through parliament by a narrow majority.

Shortly afterwards, on Bastille Day, 14 July 1948, the government issued an astonishing declaration intended to dispel the French population's doubts about Germany. On two major points, the historic destiny of the French was explained to them with rare honesty. First, the reality of those '70 million German people' in the middle of Europe made a return of Germany to the concert of European states inevitable. Second, the radical transformation of relations between the two superpowers, America and Russia, meant that Germany posed only a secondary threat to France – at most that of a small conflict within a larger one. As a result, it became possible to believe that the 'Franco-German duel' was at an end.[15]

The new Ruhr Statute could be read in two different ways. Diplomats saw it as achieving French security goals: permanent guardianship of the German coal and steel industries; legitimisation of rule by the winners over the losers. To other observers it was a transitional solution, the first step towards the granting of equal rights to Germany in a federation of European states. In the autumn of 1948, the *Süddeutsche Zeitung* wrote of an 'interim solution', after which the definitive solution 'will settle the fateful question of whether there will one day be real Europeans in Europe, or still only nations'.[16]

It was Robert Schuman who would tackle the latent contradiction in French Ruhr politics, German politics and European politics. Some could detect a reversal in attitude soon after he took up his post – *Die Zeit* said that under the new minister, France was abandoning the balance-of-power route to opt instead for a European arrangement 'for the first time since Richelieu'[17] – but he did not make his move straight away.

During 1949, the power-politics interpretation given to the Ruhr Statute came under intense scrutiny as a result of two setbacks. First, the French discovered that the Statute gave the Ruhr Authority insufficient control over the German coal and steel industries; the Germans would test the boundaries and bend the rules, and the regulations did not provide the security guarantees France was after. And second, there was growing American pressure on Paris to agree to an increase in German coal and steel production above the maximum level laid down in 1945. The dismantling of heavy industry, which was accompanied by huge job losses, met with mass resistance from the German people. In light of the granting of Marshall Aid to tackle poverty and unemployment, it was beginning to look absurd. The British government could not deal with all the demonstrations staged in the Ruhrgebiet, and in effect it gave up the dismantling process that autumn. This meant that in November, at his six-monthly meeting with his American and British colleagues, Robert Schuman was isolated in his opposition to the German coal and steel industries. His last line of defence was the French vote in the Ruhr Authority. It seemed inevitable that he would soon lose that card as well.

At the same time, from the autumn of 1949 onwards, a trio of crucial developments created room for a French initiative outside the remit of the Ruhr Statute. First, in September 1949, a West German government was formed in Bonn. Chancellor Konrad Adenauer was seeking a way for Germany to shake off its pariah status, the legacy of the Hitler regime. His overwhelming priority was his country's return as a sovereign player in the Concert of Europe. Adenauer seemed prepared to make concessions to achieve this, even with regard to authority over the Ruhr. Indeed, in an interview with an American journalist in March 1950, he contended that 'a union between France and Germany' could bring 'new life and a powerful boost to a critically ill Europe'.[18] He suggested establishing an economic union.

Second, in Washington, Secretary of State Dean Acheson had come to the conclusion that the key to policy on Germany lay in Paris. In a letter to his ambassadors in Europe, he advocated the founding by the Europeans of 'supra-national institutions, operating on a less than unanimity basis for dealing with specific economic, social and perhaps other problems'.[19] A short while later, Acheson wrote to Schuman: 'I believe that our policy in Germany, and the development of a German Government which can take its place in Western Europe, depends on the assumption by your country of leadership in Europe on these problems.'[20] Even before this, French diplomats had realised that their country would lose the respect of Germany if it did nothing but follow America. It had to act on its own initiative. Now it was being given a chance to do just that.

Third, there was little understanding in London for French problems, senior civil servants in Paris concluded in the spring of 1950. Experiences in the Marshall Aid organisation and the Council of Europe (1949) showed that international cooperation with the British would not run deep enough to restrain the Germans. In any case, falling back on a Franco-British entente was an option that inspired little confidence in light of the German invasions of France in 1914 and 1940.

So Bonn lent a willing ear, London remained stubbornly deaf, and Washington encouraged France to write a script of its own. It was impossible to wait any longer. Amid this constellation of freedom and coercion, Schuman found a voice.

Developments from this point on have been described thousands of times in European reference books. In April 1950, Schuman embraced a proposal by senior official Jean Monnet. In the Council of Ministers on Wednesday, 3 May, he mentioned that there was something he wanted to discuss the following week. Since he needed to be in London on that Wednesday for a top-level meeting between France, Britain and the United States, he asked for the next cabinet meeting to be brought forward by one day. On Monday, 8 May, Secretary of State Acheson made a stopover in Paris and expressed his support for the plan. The British were not informed.

That same day, a courier brought Adenauer in Bonn a personal message from Schuman. The chancellor assented to the Frenchman's proposal, on his own authority, by return and 'wholeheartedly'.[21] He under-stood immediately the nature of the opportunity before him. 'This is our breakthrough', he told his advisors.[22] For the first time since the war, Germany would be joining an international organisation on an equal footing with the other members. It meant a return to the Concert of Europe and anchorage in the Western alliance, taking Germany one irreversible step towards regaining its national freedom of action. Adenauer regarded a union between France and Germany 'as the sole means of defending Western Europe against a military advance by the Russians'.[23] Set beside these existen-tial political goals, the sharing of sovereignty over coal and steel seemed a relatively minor matter.

With agreement in principle from Bonn, Schuman presented his proposals to the French cabinet on Tuesday, 9 May, where they were accepted almost without debate. At six o'clock in the evening, he went to his ministry's Salon de l'Horloge. Before the hastily drummed up domestic and foreign press, Schuman delivered, in a flat, faltering voice, his famous declaration:

> [The French government] proposes that Franco-German production of coal and steel as a whole be placed under a common High Authority, within the framework of an organisation open to the participation of the other countries of Europe ... This proposal will lead to the realisation of the first concrete foundation of a European federation indispensable to the preservation of peace.[24]

During the round of questions that followed his speech, Schuman was unable to give answers to all the technical and economic issues that arose. He was also in a hurry to catch his train to London. One astonished journalist asked: 'Is this perhaps a leap in the dark?' 'Yes, that's what it is', the minister answered, sounding solemn now. 'A leap in the dark.'[25] The Schuman Declaration is rightly regarded as the moment of Europe's conception. It was both a cry of despair and a cry of joy.

EUROPE WITHOUT A UNIFORM (AFTER 25 JUNE 1950)

In the early hours of Sunday, 25 June 1950, North Korean troops crossed over the line of demarcation into South Korea. The invasion was instantly interpreted by Washington as a Russian move in the Cold War. Up to that point, political tensions between the two superpowers, during the months-long poker game for control of Berlin for example, had been prevented from escalating into military conflict. This was different. The Communists had taken up arms. Washington had no choice but to strike back.

The repercussions spread across the globe. Did the attack mark the start of a worldwide Communist offensive? Did what had happened to South Korea that night await Western Europe? Disquiet grew.

Following German capitulation, a new system of military alliances had taken shape in Western Europe. In March 1948, France, Britain, Belgium, the Netherlands and Luxembourg had signed the Brussels Pact, which committed them to lending each other military support should any of them be attacked. They had been prompted to move ahead with the plan by the Communist coup in Prague, in February of that year. The five founders had their eyes mainly on Russia, but they saw Germany, too, as a potential invader. They knew their pact would be worth little without the involvement of America, the only Western nation to have the atom bomb. They asked the American government for a security guarantee. In April 1949, in Washington, the North Atlantic Treaty was signed by America, Canada, the Brussels Five, plus another five European states (Iceland, Norway, Denmark, Portugal and Italy). All these countries swore that, in the event of attack, they would help each other. The western half of the old European states system had been replaced by an Atlantic pact.

West Germany was kept out of this alliance. By summer 1950, the young Bonn republic had both a constitution and a government, but still no foreign policy, no diplomatic service and no army. The mere thought of German uniforms was extremely disturbing to neighbouring countries, especially France. But who in the long run would defend 50 million West Germans against an attack from the East? This question was bound to crop up at some point, but after the outbreak of the Korean crisis it demanded an answer.

The American nuclear threat was sufficient (in theory) to keep any aggressor at bay. Military strategy nevertheless demanded a capability to hold out against invading Soviet troops for several weeks, even without the bomb, and as far to the east as possible. Whatever happened, American soldiers would remain in West Germany for as long as there were Russian soldiers in East Germany – so Secretary of State James Byrnes had promised back in 1946. Until 'Korea', the claim of military analysts in Washington that the defence of Western Europe was served by the existence of German divisions had found no willing listeners at all. In fact, only three weeks before 25 June, Secretary of State Acheson had advocated complete German demilitarisation. Four weeks after 25 June, however, the highest-ranking American in West Germany told the press that the Germans must be given the chance to defend themselves. But how? 'The real question,' Acheson wrote later, 'was not whether Germany should be brought into a general European defense system but whether this could be done without . . . giving Germany the key position in the balancing of power in Europe.'[26]

The Americans were after a deal: more American troops for the defence of Europe, conditional upon higher European defence expenditure, an integrated command structure and the admission of West Germany to Nato. None of the European allies were keen on this last point. And to France it remained anathema.

Meanwhile Paris was working on an alternative. Monnet understood immediately that the Korean War jeopardised negotiations on the Schuman plan, which had started five days before the North Korean invasion. As leader of the French delegation, he was quick to realise that once the Germans had regained their military sovereignty through membership of the Western alliance, they would have little reason to relinquish control of their coal and steel industries. And France would not be able to resist American pressure for long. Monnet therefore suggested to his political superiors that they should seize the initiative by setting up a European army, using a treaty modelled on the mining plan. In this way they could avoid, for the time being, the need to give a categorical 'yes' or 'no' to the American request.

On 24 October 1950, Prime Minister René Pleven gave a speech to the French parliament. The government had hoped, he said, to let the idea of a European community sink in before broaching the delicate subject of joint defence. But 'world events leave it no option'. German rearmament, unavoidable in the circumstances, would sooner or later revive German militarism. France had no desire to relearn the cruel lessons of recent history. The solution was 'the creation, for the purposes of common defence, of a European army tied to the political institutions of a united Europe'.[27] All decisions would be taken by a European minister of defence, in consultation with the national defence ministers. Pleven invited Britain and the free nations of continental Europe to come to Paris to discuss the details, as soon as the Schuman plan had been signed.

This French counter-proposal for a European army opened a political show in three acts: first came an Atlantic diplomatic episode, next a European constitutional experiment, and finally a French ideological debate. At the end of Act III, the main character was given the *coup de grâce* and they all found themselves back where they started.

Act I (October 1950–May 1952): the Atlantic episode

Reactions to the Pleven plan were mixed. London decided to wait and see. The Benelux countries were not enthusiastic – at any rate not so long as the British remained aloof. Bonn supported the proposals in principle, but there was fierce criticism of the discriminatory elements: Germany would be the only member not to have its own general staff and defence ministry. Banned from developing an arms industry, it would provide not 'divisions' but small 'fighting units'. Washington saw the scheme as purely a delaying tactic. The American military establishment was in a hurry and it would be months (if not years) before a European army could be battle-ready. The Americans and the French each stuck to their own plans. The impasse lasted until the summer of 1951.

Nonetheless, in February 1951 – still two months before the signing of the Coal and Steel Treaty that emanated from the Schuman plan – the Paris conference on a European army got under way. Only four of the invited guests had responded: Italy, West Germany, Belgium and Luxembourg. The other Nato allies sent observers. Schuman, in the chair, stressed in his opening speech that it was out of the question for the Atlantic defence effort to be delayed or endangered. But, he went on,

> the Atlantic system, even if it can meet demands that are urgent as well as being temporary, offers no solution to the Europe problem. We believe that Europe must organise itself, tear itself free from a fragmentation that has become anachronistic and absurd, and should do so no matter what, irrespective of which intercontinental or global solutions are also adopted.[28]

At a lunch with Monnet in late June, the supreme commander of Nato, future President Dwight Eisenhower, threw his weight behind a European defence system – not as a military ideal, but as psychologically the best route to a stable Europe. Eisenhower then won over President Truman to the notion of European unification. In political (though not military) circles in Washington, there was faith in the possibility of bringing about a fundamental reordering of Western Europe.

Publicly, the Americans were now fully committed to a European defence force. As generous contributors of money and troops, they were able to exert pressure on the five participating states to expedite negotiations. They also compelled the Netherlands to become the sixth member. By analogy with the Coal and Steel Treaty signed by the same six states, people started to talk of a European defence community. The British had no intention of joining. To the disappointment of the Six, this did not change when Churchill won a general election in late 1951. As leader of the opposition, he had made rousing speeches about a united Europe (although not about Britain's place in it), but once back in 10 Downing Street he emphasised above all the power of the nation states. A description of his stance on a state visit to Washington sums up his attitude:

> He pictured a bewildered French drill sergeant sweating over a platoon made up of a few Greeks, Italians, Germans, Turks, and Dutchmen, all in utter confusion over the simplest orders. What he hoped to see were spirited and strong national armies marching together to the defense of freedom singing their national anthems. No one could get up enthusiasm singing, 'March, NATO, march on!'[29]

It took a long series of ministerial meetings on both sides of the Atlantic – in Washington, Ottawa, Rome, Lisbon, Strasbourg, Bonn and Paris – to iron out all the military and political problems. In Paris, in late May 1952, six ministers of foreign affairs signed a treaty establishing a European Defence Community. There was plenty of high-flown rhetoric. American Secretary of State Acheson described it as 'the beginning of the realization of an ancient dream – the unity of the free peoples of Western Europe'.[30]

The flood of developments from the sudden appearance of Fortune in Korea in June 1950 to this response two years later had made great demands on all those involved. The Dutch foreign minister, Dirk Stikker, later described how deeply affected he had been by 'the tremendous pressures of the moment, the inescapability of them and how they dominate twenty-four hours a day'. It had made him realise 'how heavily events on a world scale impinged upon a small European nation's domestic affairs'.[31]

The signed document was a point of anchorage for the governments, and they put it to their six parliaments for ratification. The European defence treaty was far-reaching. Article 1 spoke of a Community that was 'supranational in character'. An attack on one member state was an attack on all – as with Nato, but including West Germany. The Defence Community's institutions were modelled on those of the Coal and Steel Community: a Council of Ministers, a parliamentary Assembly, a Commissariat (the less pretentious name for the High Authority) and a Court of Justice. The member states were allowed to retain national armies for their non-European territories and to protect their heads of state, but all other troops would be transferred to the Community. Soldiers would wear a community uniform. The treaty would be valid for a period of fifty years.

Act II (September 1952–March 1953): a European constitutional experiment

With the signing of the defence treaty, German soldiers were, on paper, put into European uniforms. This created an unprecedented situation. After all, what is an army – as distinct from an armed gang – other than a political instrument, and who formulates policy other than the government of a state? In this case, however, the troops were supplied with their training and equipment by a European bureaucracy and received their orders from the American supreme commander of Nato, while for political authority they looked to national ministers gathered together in a Council. This institutional contrivance circumvented a problem without solving it: the European army was about to be set up ahead of any European political order that could provide it with a commander-in-chief, civilian or military.*

The provisional nature of these arrangements was reflected in the defence treaty itself. The Italian premier, federalist Alcide De Gasperi, intervened to ensure that it charged the future parliamentary Assembly with the drafting of a definitive political framework, a 'federal or confederal structure'.[32] In a sense, this article was a request for a European constitutional convention. Since the summer of 1952, there had been calls in Rome and Paris to implement this clause ahead of the treaty's entry into force, so that political arrangements could catch up with military agreements. The Community's parliamentary Assembly might be deployed for the purpose; the Coal and Steel Treaty had been ratified a month earlier, and the same six states were members. During the first meeting of the Council of Ministers of the Coal and Steel Community in September, all six ministers accepted this plan. (So even at its very first meeting, the Council functioned not just as a committee to deal with mining and steel – and therefore as a community institution – but as a conference table for the circle of member states.) In Strasbourg, there was huge enthusiasm for the task. The Community's Assembly was expanded to include additional members and became a constituent assembly named the Ad Hoc Assembly, chaired by a Belgian, Paul-Henri Spaak. It would set about drawing up a statute for a European political community.

On 9 March 1953 – a few days after Stalin's death – the Strasbourg parliamentarians completed their draft constitution. They had overcome disputes about constitutional classics such as the distribution of seats between countries, the appointment of the executive power and the text of the preamble ('We, the peoples of . . .'). In a lyrical speech to ministers to mark his presentation of the document, Spaak quoted George Washington's address on the occasion of his presentation of the American Constitution in 1787. Council President Georges Bidault, the French minister who had recently replaced Schuman, responded laconically with a quotation from England's Elizabeth I: 'Salut aux chercheurs d'aventures.'[33]

Six months later, an intergovernmental conference was convened in Rome, but by then the eagerness to make progress had evaporated. Negotiations dragged on and became farcical. So long as no one could be certain that a European army was about to come into being, none of the Six felt the need to make any profound decisions about their collective political life. Europe did not emerge ad hoc.

---

* Compare the way that, four decades later, a decision was made to introduce a single European currency with neither a binding economic policy to accompany it nor a political authority to deal with crisis situations.

Act III (January 1953–August 1954): a French ideological debate

After signature of the defence treaty by six governments, it was the turn of the national parliaments to speak. At first they seemed in no hurry. Then, from early 1953, the new Eisenhower administration in America, which was sympathetic to the supranational cause, began to increase the pressure. The Hague was the first to fall into line. Luxembourg (good for one division) preferred to wait for Brussels, which needed to change the Belgian constitution before it could ratify. Bonn faced the same task, as the result of a case brought against the treaty in the German Constitutional Court. Nonetheless, by April 1954, all these four capitals had given their assent, leaving just two to go. Rome was favourably inclined, but waited for Paris. And that is where the problem lay.

In France something remarkable happened: the plan for a European army became the focus of an intense national debate. The issue split parties and families. The country was divided into *cédistes* and *anticédistes* (the French abbreviation for the European Defence Community being CED). To the despair of opinion pollsters, views on the issue expressed in parliament and among the public at large did not coincide with any electoral map. The usual positions and interest-based motivations gave way to deep political emotions, such as patriotism, fear of war and belief in change. One renowned political observer claimed: 'Between January 1953 and August 1954, the biggest politico-ideological quarrel broke out that France has known probably since the Dreyfus affair.'[34]

There was something unreal about the debate. It seemed like a 'religious war' or a 'metaphysical conflict'.[35] Identical arguments could lead to contrasting conclusions. One speaker was convinced that a supranational merging of forces into a European army would make German rearmament impossible; another claimed the opposite, since who could fail to discern a German soldier beneath those European fatigues? Diehards on both sides refused to compromise. Advocates of a European federation acted as if their cause would be doomed without a defence force. Opponents argued that not only would Germany gain an army, but France would lose one. Nobody asked what the political or military alternative might be – or how to deal at all with the risks consequent upon Germany remaining unarmed.

The debate dragged on because no French government – and they came thick and fast – was strong enough to force through parliamentary ratification of the treaty by turning it into a vote of confidence. Schuman and Pleven's Christian Democrat 'European' party found itself in opposition, while the Gaullists were in the governing coalition from 1953 onwards. After Stalin's death and the end of the Korean War, armed conflict in Europe no longer seemed imminent, and France now badly needed its promised divisions in Indochina and Algeria. Britain's refusal to take part was also important. After the catastrophic French defeat by the Vietnamese Communists at Dien Bien Phu in May 1954, a new government came to power. Prime Minister Pierre Mendès France had other priorities and wanted to see the matter of the European army resolved. Both the allies and France itself needed to put an end to this ambiguous situation, he announced on taking up office, adding:

> The fact that at such a moment the nation is torn apart by the passionate controversy that has flared up over the forms, modalities and institutions of this defence community, that a major, painful controversy has held our country in its grip for months and that this quarrel threatens to drag on for years is something no patriot can accept; it is something we must put an end to, in the name of national unity itself.[36]

The outcome was plainly hinted at by these words, even though they were greeted with applause by the *cédistes*.

Attempts by Mendès France to negotiate a compromise formula with the British and his five European partners that summer – the weakening of the supranational character of the Community through the postponement of majority decision-making – came to nothing. The undertakings given by the Five did not go far enough. His efforts also met with fierce criticism from both camps at home; there seemed to be no middle course between undermining French sovereignty and betraying the European idea. (Three Gaullist ministers resigned from the Mendès France government over his endorsement of the supranational principle, while Robert Schuman and André Philip, a Socialist, declared that they regarded violation of that principle as unacceptable.) This was the prevailing ideological mood in France's Assemblée Nationale on 30 August 1954, when it voted on a proposal not to discuss the defence treaty. In favour: 319; against: 264. The Gaullist deputies promptly struck up the 'Marseillaise'.

Four years after the launch of the Pleven plan in that same Assemblée Nationale, the curtain had fallen for the European army.

Epilogue

The British instantly seized the initiative in trying to provide an alternative. Within a month, the six signatories to the abortive defence treaty met in London to discuss with Britain, America and Canada what should be done.

Another month later, on 23 October, three accords were signed in Paris. First the Brussels Pact, agreed in 1948 between France, Britain and the Benelux countries, was expanded to include Italy and Germany, and the resulting seven-signatory treaty was renamed the Western European Union. Then, second, the Western occupying forces recognised the Federal Republic as a sovereign state and agreed to end the regime of occupation. Washington, London and Paris retained a say only on German unification and the defining of Germany's borders; on those questions they would at some point need to sign a final peace treaty in consultation with Moscow. Free West Germany imposed upon itself only a ban on the use of nuclear weapons. Third, the Federal Republic was invited to join the political and military structure of the Atlantic alliance. That invitation came from all Nato members, including France.

These Paris Accords were ratified by the French parliament on 30 December 1954 – a puzzle to those who recalled the passionate debates of four months earlier. It was as if Fortune was being looked in the face only now. The choice was not between a 'yes' and a 'no' to German rearmament, but between having German soldiers in a European army and having them in the Atlantic armed forces.

On 5 May 1955, West Germany joined Nato. The American, British and French occupation was formally at an end.

The Suez Canal and the Château de Val-Duchesse (on and around 6 November 1956)

A few months after a conference in Bandung, Indonesia, at which thirty African and Asian states declared themselves to be the 'Third World', their luminary Gamal Abdel Nasser put into practical effect the notion of a neutral political bloc. In September 1955, the Egyptian president bought weapons from Czechoslovakia. It was the first time Moscow was clearly behind a supply of arms to the Arab world. Meanwhile Nasser was seeking financial support from Washington and London for the building of a huge dam across the Nile, intended to bring the Egyptian people energy and prosperity. In the summer of 1956, the Americans suddenly withdrew their offer of credit. Casting about for an alternative source of investment for his prestige project, Nasser tried his hand at poker. By force of arms he nationalised the Suez Canal on 26 July.

London was deeply offended. The opening of the canal in 1869 had created an important transport link between Britain and its colonies: India, Australia, New Zealand and countries in the Far East. After the British conquest of Egypt, free passage through the canal under British protection was guaranteed by international agreement (1888). As recently as the early 1950s, some 80,000 British soldiers had been garrisoned at Suez. The Canal Company was largely in the hands of British and French financiers, although by this point the significance of the waterway between the Mediterranean and the Red Sea had changed. It was no longer the strategic axis of the British Empire, but a trade route along which two-thirds of Western Europe's oil was imported. Control of it remained vital.

Nasser's move was followed by a summer of fruitless diplomacy. British Prime Minister Anthony Eden and French Premier Guy Mollet regarded Nasser as a new Mussolini; they both compared his writings to Hitler's *Mein Kampf*[37] and saw any concession as appeasement. Britain's exasperation at the blockade of her Mediterranean fleet was matched by French anger at Egypt's military support for Algerian resistance fighters, who had begun a war against the motherland. By contrast, American President Eisenhower appeared to rule out the use of force. He was facing elections on 6 November and had no wish to be identified with waning colonial powers. The diplomatic route offered no means of forcing Egypt to back down. At this point, London and Paris entered into a secret deal with Israel, the only country to see its commercial shipping blockaded by Nasser.

On 29 October, Israeli infantry invaded Egypt. As arranged, Britain and France called on the warring parties to withdraw from the Canal Zone. They were banking on Nasser's refusal, which was duly followed on 31 October by a Franco-British air raid on targets in Egypt, mounted from British bases on Cyprus. One immediate setback was that not only Russia, but also America (in the person of Dwight D. Eisenhower) publicly condemned the attack. The military campaign met with rather more success. Within two days, the Franco-British air force had broken Egyptian resistance. A landing of ground troops had been planned for day seven. For the next four days little happened.

Meanwhile, on the periphery of the Soviet Empire, a popular revolt broke out. The Hungarians launched an uprising. Russian tanks were set alight and a multi-party government was installed. Hungary declared itself neutral, a move that was impossible for Moscow to tolerate. On 4 November, the Red Army marched into Budapest to crush the revolt ruthlessly. America and its allies were powerless. The 'thaw' in the Cold War that many had thought they could detect after Stalin's death was clearly an illusion. A sense of imminent peril crept over Western Europe once more.

The day after this show of force, Russian Premier Nikolai Bulganin sent letters to Eden, Mollet and Eisenhower. The 'predatory' armed attack on Egypt must stop, the Kremlin said. In barely concealed terms, the

Bech, Achille Van Acker and Willem Drees came to the Hôtel Matignon. This gathering in Paris can be seen as the first summit of heads of state or government, and therefore as a forerunner of the European Council. As early as 1957, Paris recognised the advantages of a negotiating forum where each individual state could weigh its own interests against European common interests at the highest level. The deadlock on overseas territories persisted, until finally the host, Mollet, who believed that ratification by the Assemblée Nationale would otherwise fail, took the chancellor by the arm for a walk in the garden. That did the trick. Adenauer, the great European, swallowed the bananas.

On 25 March 1957, on the Capitol in Rome, the treaty establishing an Atomic Energy Community and the treaty establishing an Economic Community were signed. Church bells rang out all over the city. After six parliamentary ratifications, both treaties came into force on 1 January 1958.

5

Community Waiting
(1958–89)

Shall we be caught between a hostile (or at least less and less friendly) America and a boastful, powerful 'Empire of Charlemagne' – now under French but later bound to come under German control? Is this the real reason for 'joining' the Common Market (if we are acceptable) and for abandoning a) the Seven, b) British agriculture, c) the Commonwealth? It's a grim choice.

Harold Macmillan (1960)[44]

For the Six the curtain fell in August 1954. A joint entry into the river of time was no longer in prospect. The French '*non*' to a European army put paid to the idea of a federal Europe. The French population, speaking through the Assemblée Nationale, rejected the option of joint European political or military relations with the outside world. Germany was now a member of the Atlantic alliance, with an army of its own. Ten years after the end of the Second World War, the Six found themselves under the American umbrella of Nato, sheltered from the Russian peril. That particular threatening knock at the door had been averted (in their case, at least).

The curtain that rose in Messina in June 1955, ultimately heralding the Treaty of Rome, revealed a stage that looked very different. In the words of one of the negotiators, for fear of another parliamentary defeat high politics were 'left out of the domain of the treaty'.[45] True, the Atomic Energy Community served French geopolitical ambitions, and the German chancellor was among those who saw in it the germ of a political Europe; but even during negotiations, the centre of gravity shifted towards economic concerns. There lay the interests of the other four, as well as Germany and – especially after all the promises made to it – France. After the treaty came into force, little more was heard of nuclear cooperation. From 1958 onwards, the Six concerned themselves with such prosaic matters as import quotas, product safety standards and agricultural prices.

In this economic arena, the role of the club was essential, although seemingly modest. It was not itself a player: it merely set the stage for the actors in economic life – producers, consumers, employers, employees. The Europe of the Community was a market superintendent, an inspector, a groundsman, with a gradually increasing concern for customer welfare. In an outward direction, it engaged in trade relations with other economic powers; but in the years before 1989, the European inner sphere developed largely at its own pace, making intelligent use of the protection offered by the treaty. Even so, the member states found to their surprise that together they were right out in the historical current, if only because of their anomalous position within a wider Europe.

The dominant theme of this chapter is *waiting*. Waiting begins when a 'no' is interpreted as a 'not yet'. That is exactly how figures like Spaak and Adenauer explained the '*non*' of August 1954. The timeline leading to a European political community, which had been shortened considerably after the outbreak of the Korean War, was again rolled out into a distant future. 'Make haste slowly' was the motto. This new, more patient pact was signed, fittingly, in Rome, the Eternal City. After 1957, political action gave way to preparations and expectations.

Exactly what was expected remained unclear. The ultimate political aim of the European project – as distinct from its economic agreements and objectives – was left vague in Rome. After the trauma of 1954, any thinking in terms of federation or confederation, a political goal or a geographical boundary, was taboo. European finality was left out of the picture, mainly to avoid worrying ordinary citizens.

SELF-MADE TIME

In the tunnel (1958–69)

The Treaty of Rome imposed an ingenious form of temporal discipline. It worked like a tunnel. The six states entered together, were obliged to perform all kinds of tasks along the way, twice had to pass through dividing doors, and then, at the exit, would emerge as a single Community, economically at least. There was no provision for backing out.

Two things made this mechanism work. The tunnel offered time (which gave it its length), but it also demanded an immediate leap (rather like jumping through a hoop). There was no doubting that it would take time to become a Community – the moulding of six economies into one market could not happen overnight. The Six gave themselves twelve years, a time span referred to in the treaty as a 'transitional period'. Businesses needed time to adjust to the more competitive environment of a customs union. Governments needed time to draw up accompanying agreements about how the new competition rules or the market in agricultural products would work. The transitional tunnel was divided into three four-year stages, each conferring specific obligations. By the end of the first stage, impediments to trade would be reduced by 30 per cent. As for the common market in agricultural products, the only requirement was that it must be in place by the end of the transitional period. While the member states fulfilled these tasks as they moved through the tunnel, the rules of the game would change. At the dividing doors and at the exit, the method of voting on specific issues would switch from unanimity to majority.

The required leap, the second element of the time mechanism, was innovative in that, unlike the Coal and Steel Treaty, which was valid for fifty years, the Treaty of Rome would remain in effect indefinitely. In the Château de Val-Duchesse, many lawyers had protested at this, but Spaak stood his ground. At the request of Paris, however, one opportunity for reconsideration was built in. Initially, the French had wanted to be able to block transition from the first to the second stage by using a veto. The other five members objected. On 6 November 1956, the French premier and the German chancellor reached a compromise that would allow an obstructive state to delay the process twice by one year. Should it do so on a third occasion, the matter would be referred to an arbitration board. The transitional period could last no longer than fifteen years in total. More importantly, once the Six had passed through the first dividing door, there was no way back. The option of including a secession clause, though discussed, was rejected.

Given that the founding treaty had set down certain imperatives, while offering only a rough framework for other issues, it was predictable that a great deal of pushing and pulling would be involved as the Six took the hurdles on their way to the tunnel exit. The built-in coercion would have to do its work. They were stuck with each other, and once through the tunnel, their time together stretched on into infinity.

Acceleration – 12 May 1960

Before long, the timetable, negotiated by six governments and ratified by six parliaments, became subject to tampering. To everyone's surprise, participants in economic life turned out to find compliance with the treaty anything but onerous. The Western European economy was flourishing by the late 1950s. The Six had rising industrial production, reasonably stable exchange rates and healthier government coffers. The advantages of operating in a larger market more than made up for the increased competition. Businesspeople were looking forward to completion of the customs union. By the summer of 1959, trade and industry were eager to shorten the transitional period.

The question arose as to how the process could be accelerated. The Belgian minister advocated a reduction in the total amount of time allowed, but his partners foresaw legal complications: the treaty was not a concertina that could be stretched or contracted at will. The French had little desire to be made to swallow majority decision-making sooner than planned. Their counter-proposal was to stick with the twelve-year tunnel, but to reach certain goals ahead of time. Still, if the customs union was to be expedited, why not implement some of the other provisions of the treaty more quickly as well? Every member state brought its own specific wishes to the table. The fiercest conflict was over the accelerated introduction of a common external tariff, advocated by Rome and Paris. In community circles it was argued that this would give the outside world 'tangible proof of European solidarity'.[46] Such a tariff held little appeal for the Germans and the Dutch, however, since for them it meant an increase in customs duties, which would be detrimental to their export industries and make imports more expensive.

On 12 May 1960, an accord was reached. The Commission welcomed the decision to accelerate as 'the fundamental economic and political fact in the history of the Common Market since the signing of the Treaty of Rome'.[47] There was still four-fifths of the tunnel to go.

Clock – 31 December 1961

With the transition from the first to the second stage at the end of four years, the Six would reach the point of no return. The tunnel then became a trap. It would require a unanimous 'transition decision', which offered an opportunity for each member state to put additional demands on the table. Indeed, the stakes were raised ahead of time when French Premier Michel Debré declared in June 1961 that the transition was unthinkable without an accord on agricultural policy. The Germans had repeatedly claimed that this could not go ahead without anti-cartel legislation and competition rules. All these elements came together at the end-of-year deadline.

Various desires were expressed. Paris asked for a protectionist agricultural policy with contributions from every country, much to the displeasure of the German finance minister. Bonn wanted strict agreements on the limits to governmental interference in trade and industry, an attitude that contrasted starkly with France's Colbertist tradition. It was difficult to solve such problems individually, but this dual conflict contained the potential for a political trade-off. All the same, a deal does require simultaneity. Shortly before Christmas, the six ministers signed an accord on competition rules that suited the Germans, but it was held in abeyance – 'supposedly because the text had yet to be prepared in two of the four languages of the Community', as a less than trusting parliamentarian put it[48] – until an agreement on agriculture was reached. Despite celebrated marathon sessions, New Year's Eve came with no such deal in place. A legal vacuum was in prospect. On 1 January 1962, France was due to take over the six-month rotating presidency from Germany; the hurdle would have to be cleared before then.

Shortly before midnight, French Foreign Minister Maurice Couve de Murville thought of a ruse. He proposed continuing to negotiate under German chairmanship until a solution was found. All the members agreed and the clock was stopped. The time needed for the decision to be reached took precedence over the calendar. The extended day lasted for two weeks, and only then was the double pact sealed, with all interests tightly woven together. In the early morning of 14 January, Couve de Murville took over the presidency from his German colleague and made the outcome known to the world. The clock was ticking again.

Exit – 1–2 December 1969

In late 1969, the Six reached the end of their twelve-year-long tunnel. The details of most of the treaty agreements had been worked out over the intervening years with dogged determination. The governments decided that the Community could now take the step to its 'definitive phase'. The only protests came from a few Strasbourg parliamentarians, who wanted a postponement until all the promises in the treaty, including their own direct election, had been fulfilled.

To celebrate the transition and to discuss how to proceed, the six leaders gathered in the Ridderzaal in The Hague on 1 and 2 December. Everyone felt things would get moving now. During their time in the tunnel, relations between the Six had been soured considerably by the repeated use of the veto by French President de Gaulle to prevent Britain's admittance to the circle. His successor, Georges Pompidou, elected in May 1969, was prepared to abandon this resistance, but the French wanted a number of concessions in return. The Germans were happy to listen. In Bonn, too, a new figure had recently taken office, Willy Brandt. In order to gain elbow room for his *Ostpolitik*, Brandt was keen to demonstrate an attachment to the Western European alliance.

The only thing that needed arranging beforehand was the financing of agricultural policy. At the Hague summit, the leaders agreed to allocate the Community its 'own resources' for that purpose. Import duties paid at the external borders would no longer disappear into national coffers, but would instead flow into a shared kitty. This was officially confirmed the following year. It provided the French with a guarantee that the other countries would continue to contribute financial assistance for farmers. To Paris, this was the final element of the negotiations begun in 1955–57. It meant the Community had now been 'accomplished'.

Had the programme of treaties reached its conclusion here, 'Europe' would formally have remained an economic supervisory body, an agriculture and fisheries bureaucracy and a trade bloc. In other words, the club would have been permanently chained to 'low politics' – a far from unwelcome outcome for one member state. But events took a different course. The political *telos* of the founding treaty had not yet worked through in full. In The Hague, the six heads of state or government immediately strode off along untrodden paths. Aside from a European University, the two most spectacular new goals were 'economic and monetary union' and cooperation on foreign policy. Both initiatives were to have far-reaching consequences, although not immediately. They developed step by step, as informal practices outside the treaty. The leaders did make one decision in The Hague that signified an immediate breakthrough: an agreement on the opening of accession negotiations with Britain. After such bitter quarrels on the subject, this new way of dealing with the British indicated a fresh self-awareness on the part of the club.

So the exit of the Six from the tunnel marked a beginning as well as an ending. Their Community now existed. The goal that had seemed unachievable in 1955 had been reached. What next? Outside the tunnel, time stretched away like a limitless void. The task of keeping the common market running did not seem to offer the Six an adequate basis on which to face the future. Gathered at the highest level, they promptly reaffirmed the political foundations of their association. Lines were cast in several directions: youth, a currency, the world. There was motion, but as yet no form.

To the market (1985–'1992')

In the summer of 1984, an authoritative figure was put in charge of the institutional inner sphere of the Community for the first time in years. Jacques Delors, the French finance minister, was appointed president of the Commission by the national leaders. He detected a general desire to break through the prevailing malaise.

The 1970s had taught that the Community could not stand up to stiff headwinds. The oil crisis and economic recession had thrown each member state back on its own resources. The Nine (later Ten) were unable jointly to tackle threats to their prosperity that came from outside. Even agricultural policy, once Europe's showpiece, seemed out of control, to judge by surpluses that defied imagination, such as the butter mountain and the milk and wine lakes.

Ahead of 1 January 1985, when his term officially began, Delors took a tour of the ten capitals to discover which initiatives might have the best chance of success. There were four items on his list: European defence, a European currency, institutional reform and the internal market. The last of these turned out to be the only plan that was guaranteed broad support – from Margaret Thatcher in London, Helmut Kohl in Bonn and François Mitterrand in Paris. So that would have to be the one.

The Ten had long been a 'common market' in name, but businesspeople swapped horror stories about lawnmowers that could not be sold in neighbouring countries, about lorry drivers queuing for days at border crossings, and about mountains of tax paperwork. By 1984, tariffs and quotas no longer stood in the way of trade. They had been forbidden since completion of the customs union. Instead it was the maze of rules. Every member state had its own product norms for reasons of health and safety, or to protect the environment. Although in themselves useful and legitimate, such regulations could easily be deployed to shield a nation's industry against foreign competition. The popular bureaucratic remedy was called 'harmonisation of product standards'. There was intense consultation in Brussels, but in the case of some products it took so long to agree directives that technological advances overtook the process by rendering the clauses at issue obsolete. In 1978, the Court thought of a cleverer method: mutual recognition of product standards – not 'All cucumbers must have the same curve', but 'I'll accept your cucumbers and you'll accept mine'. The Commission realised that a new-style European market could be built upon this Court judgment.

Delors' stroke of genius was to set a deadline. On his autumn tour, he had taken advice from Jean Monnet's former right-hand man, Max Kohnstamm, who reminded him of the success of the customs union a quarter of a century earlier. It had come into being as a result of a twelve-year timetable, made up of three four-year stages. Why not introduce something similar for the market – two four-year stages, for example? This idea appealed to the commissioner for the internal market, a Brit sent from London by Thatcher: 'You don't say, let's start building a factory. You decide when you want it running by.'[49]

The date was agreed at a meeting between Delors and his staff that December. On the table were several proposed deadlines: 1990, 1995 and

2000. All were rejected and eventually 1992 was settled upon. Wild theories later did the rounds to explain the choice: was this Europe's contribution to the 500th anniversary of the discovery of America by Columbus? Delors gave a more prosaic reason: the period up to 31 December 1992 coincided with the term in office of two Commissions – the four years starting in 1985 plus the four years of a second mandate. The decision was driven by the logic of bureaucratic time.

In June 1985, two weeks before an important summit of the leaders in Milan, the commissioner for the internal market presented an exhaustive list of measures, including deadlines. If they wanted a 'Europe without borders', then the member states were going to have to enact some 300 legislative measures. Although non-binding, the White Paper sought the same status as the Treaty of Rome. It concluded with the lines: 'Just as the Customs Union had to precede Economic Integration, so Economic Integration has to precede European unity.'[50] With the internal market, Europe was escaping into low politics again, while longing to engage in high politics.

As its president had hoped, a second Delors-led Commission began work on 1 January 1989. By the autumn of that year, half the measures contained in the White Paper had been accepted by the member states. Surely the deadline could now be met.

Pressing time

At the door

The creation of the Community failed to put an end to power politics between member states. It had been moderated in reciprocal relations, certainly, but the principle of a balance of power between states continued (and continues) to operate in Europe, both among members of the club and beyond. After 1952, each of the Six held on to its place in a wider Europe. Three members – France, Belgium and the Netherlands – were going through the trauma of dismantling their colonial empires. West Germany was preoccupied by its separation from East Germany. Were things the same as ever as far as high politics went?

They were not. The founding pact of 1951 stated that 'any European state' could 'request to accede to the present Treaty'.[51] That possibility, which had found its way into the Schuman Declaration as an afterthought, reinforced the Coal and Steel Community's claim to be the germ of something larger. In the founding treaty of 1957, the Six repeated the invitation, which now read that any European state could 'apply to become a member of the Community'.[52]

This was to have far-reaching consequences, not least for the members themselves. It meant they would have to act in concert – perhaps not towards the outside world on every conceivable occasion, but certainly towards any European non-member state that knocked at the door. It gave Fortune a chance to impact upon the Six as a club.

The door unexpectedly became a focus of European high politics, and it remains so to this day. On the outside, it works as a lure; on the inside, as a force for unity, since otherwise it will remain shut. The members keep having to ask themselves: 'To whom do we want to open up? Which countries want to come in and which don't? Are we in agreement? How long should we make newcomers wait outside?' Crucially, it is not the Community that opens the door, but all the members jointly. In disputes over entry, the six founding states discovered that their association went beyond mining and the market. Even outside the treaty they led a shared political life.

Until 1973, that life was dominated by a single issue: British membership. 'When I look back to my many years in ministerial office,' wrote Dutch Foreign Minister Joseph Luns, involved from 1956 to 1971, 'it strikes me how much of my time and effort I devoted to this one major problem'.[53] According to his French colleague, Maurice Couve de Murville, who dealt with it for a decade, the issue at stake was 'not just that of cohesion but of the actual nature, of the spirit and thus of the destiny of the European Community'.[54] There were two distinct phases. The members had to wait to see whether the most important European non-member wanted to pass through the door (1950–61) and then decide whether or not to let it in (1961–73).

Initially, therefore, the question lay with London. Immediately after the war, Britain was by far the most powerful Western European state. It had not been occupied by the Nazis; it was both victor and liberator; and, despite a slow, visible decline, it was still a world power. Many concluded that in 1945 a leadership role in Europe had been there for the taking, but the British had let the opportunity slip. France, the only country to come anywhere close to matching it in political and military power, seized the day in 1950.

British Foreign Minister Ernest Bevin was unusually morose on the evening of 9 May, immediately after Robert Schuman launched the coal and steel plan. He was personally offended, having not been informed in advance by the Frenchman, whereas (to compound the insult) their American colleague Dean Acheson had been. That was not all. It no doubt struck Bevin straight away that Schuman's proposal would change the balance of power on the continent profoundly. The prospect of federation outlined in it will not have spoilt his mood, since in London no one was particularly excited by that either way, and the proposed mining and steel cartel, although perhaps annoying, was no real threat – the British were producing roughly as much coal and steel as the French and Germans combined. No, the disturbing element was the inversion of alliances. The Schuman Declaration, in the words of one insider, hit London like 'a small atomic bomb'[55] because France had unexpectedly opted to interweave its fortunes with those of the arch enemy Germany in a 'supranational' organisation without the British, rather than entering into a looser organisation along with Britain. This disrupted the entente cordiale and undermined old continental relationships.

London was not kept waiting outside. In 1950 it decided against joining; a year later it refused to participate in the European army; and in 1955, when the Six were keen to establish a common market, it walked away from the negotiating table. Its reluctance was profound. Foreign Secretary Anthony Eden said in the House of Commons: 'This is something we know, in our bones, we cannot do.'[56] European institutions did not fit with British democratic traditions. Political and economic links with the Commonwealth weighed heavily. The British wanted only a European free trade zone, without a common external tariff. The pragmatism of British bureaucratic and governmental circles, for all its advantages, had one ultimate disadvantage: again and again, practically everyone in London decided that European initiatives were merely ineffectual verbal gimmickry. (In the same spirit, many years later, Prime Minister John Major saw in preparations for the euro 'all the quaintness of a rain dance, and about the same potency'.[57])

From early 1957, when the Six were on the point of signing the Treaty of Rome and their project therefore seemed bound to succeed, the British sought support for a European free trade zone, hoping it would suffice to absorb the Six into a greater whole. When that scheme failed, London set up the European Free Trade Association in 1958, with countries including Denmark and Portugal. Its members called themselves 'the Seven'. Around 1960, few British journalists proved able to resist writing that Europe was 'at sixes and sevens'.

Yet the manoeuvre with the Seven was of secondary importance. The problem remained Britain's relationship with the Six. Harold Macmillan felt frustrated at not knowing what was being discussed at a table around which France and Germany were sitting – perhaps it was more than just steel, grain and bananas? There were indeed grounds for unease. In 1959, feelers went out from Paris, Bonn and Rome concerning improved coordination of foreign policy. Fine, said Rome, but then the other three member states must be present. The ministers of the Six agreed to discuss the idea in late 1959. Around that time, Macmillan wrote to his foreign minister, without mincing his words: 'For the first time since the Napoleonic era, the major continental powers are united in a positive economic grouping, with considerable political aspects, which, though not specifically directed against the United Kingdom, may have the effect of excluding us both from European markets and from consultation in European policy.'[58] Exclusion – that was the sentiment. Striking, too, was the insistence of American President John F. Kennedy that London ought to join the Western European bloc. His undersecretary of state said this would 'mean substantial additional weight on the Western side of the world power balance.'[59]

Political motives of this kind prompted Macmillan to change course in the summer of 1961. The economy was a factor as well, of course, 'but the controlling consideration', a contemporary concluded in an exhaustive study, 'was the belief that Britain would have more influence – in Europe, with the United States, and in the world generally – as a member of the European Community than it would alone.'[60] Britain, tired of standing on the sidelines, wanted 'a seat at the table'. So it knocked on the door.

From 1961 onwards, therefore, the question lay with the Six. Ought they to open up? Many would still have liked nothing better than for the British to join their ranks, but there had been a change over the preceding ten years. Britain's absence had allowed France to give shape to the treaty sphere largely as it wished. After de Gaulle's return to power in 1958, his country put itself forward as the natural leader of the Six. If the door was opened to the other major European power, France would have most to lose.

At the same time, French dominance of the Community was the main reason why the other members supported British accession. The Dutch and Belgians, in particular, had high expectations. To them this visit by Fortune was a gift, and they were determined to maximise its advantages. They feared French or Franco-German domination, and had an interest in improving the balance of power on the continent. A game with three big players would suit them far better.

The degree to which this was of vital importance to the smaller countries emerged in talks between the Six about a 'political union', held from 1960 onwards. President de Gaulle, having first secured the assent of Chancellor Adenauer, tried to build political cooperation between the member states outside the economic framework of the Community. France's diplomatic leadership needed a way to express itself. Thoughts turned to the possibility of periodic meetings of the six heads of government. Italian Premier Amintore Fanfani also felt that such gatherings could fill a 'void' in European politics. During the summit in February 1961, the idea met with resistance from the

Dutch, based on the argument that Britain had not been invited to join in political cooperation of this sort. Yet discussions began. A year later – by which time Macmillan had submitted Britain's application – detailed plans for a union were drawn up, under the chairmanship of French diplomat Christian Fouchet.

This time, in addition to the Dutch, the Belgians also put up resistance. They took an interesting approach. On the one hand, Spaak and Luns regarded the proposed cooperation at summit level as unacceptably damaging to the supranational treaty structure. On the other hand, they said they would be able to assent to it after British accession. This was odd, not to say contradictory. It was generally known that London was even less keen on supranational approaches than Paris. For the smaller countries, the European ideal of a Community represented a higher form of national interest, in that it offered them protection against larger nations. The fact that they were prepared to barter this European ideal away for the admission of a party that, if anything, would further undermine it drew attention to their self-interested motives. His torpedoing of the political union earned Luns enduring bitterness on the part of Adenauer. Even the agile Spaak almost forfeited his good relations with Paris. Nevertheless, in community circles there was gratitude for this debacle. For years afterwards, the name 'Fouchet' made the Commission foam at the mouth.

This episode makes clear that all the players were aware of the distinction between spheres of action. In their apparently contradictory desires, the Dutch and the Belgians were expressing precisely what they, as good Europeans, had officially always denied: the Community was more than a legal order based on a treaty. It was a political association that also involved a balance of power based on national interests. Before entering into a political union with de Gaulle, they wanted to safeguard their security and independence, whether by using the provisions of the treaty or by having Britain in the Community as a counterweight. As Spaak noted, 'the French plans denied us both'.[61] The response to their either/or proposal was a double 'no'. The Dutch-Belgian stance had the rare effect of making treaty and membership visible as distinct European organising principles.

This explains why the members understood each other so well during the conflict. De Gaulle was not surprised by Luns' refusal, since he would have done the same in his position.[62] Paris and Bonn wanted to organise the member-states sphere into a political union. The Hague and Brussels rejected the method, but countered with an alternative: no summit talks between leaders, but additional members instead. This, too, meant organising the circle. All members recognised de facto that their relationships could not be reduced to the treaty, but were fundamentally defined by their membership.

The Six would discover more yet about their association, through bitter experience, as they continued to negotiate with London. In the autumn of 1961, the ministerial conference began, held to discuss the conditions under which Britain would be able to comply with the rules of the treaty. The main stumbling block concerned British obligations to its Commonwealth, to the European Free Trade Association and to its own farmers. Underlying the technical debates about tariffs and quotas, however, were political ideas about the kind of Europe the parties were aiming to create. The British did not simply want to join; they first wanted to find out whether they could change various rules of the game (to their own or everyone's advantage) and only then make a decision. In this they had the silent support of some capitals. The Commission and many proponents of the Europe of the Community, by contrast, were after strict compliance with the treaty: until the British committed themselves to the ultimate goal of unification, they must not be allowed to dilute the rules. The French, too, had an interest in strict enforcement of everything the Six had laid down in the treaty. This complex diplomatic dance outside and inside the door went on for fifteen months.

Then General de Gaulle slammed the door shut. On 14 January 1963, in his New Year press conference, the French president expounded in detail on the economic and political differences between the Six and Britain and on the danger of American influence on European politics via its British outpost, before declaring offhandedly: 'It is possible that one day England might manage to transform herself sufficiently to become part of the European community, without restriction, without reserve and preference for anything whatsoever; and in this case the Six would open the door to her and France would raise no obstacle.'[63] One day, but not yet. Suddenly the president was acting as doorkeeper.

There was fury and intense frustration and despair both in London and in the capitals of the Five. Macmillan felt profoundly humiliated. For all their doubts about de Gaulle's good faith, no one in London had imagined he would have the gall to cause a rift. (The British tabloids advised the general: 'Take your dreams of independent power, and stick them up your Eiffel Tower.'[64]) His five partners felt deeply affronted by de Gaulle's approach. After such lengthy joint negotiations, without any announcement beforehand, at a press conference for a home audience, simply to deploy the veto – well, it went against all the Community's rules of etiquette. It was a savage blow to mutual trust. Rome and The Hague were intent on revenge. According to a German negotiator, the French were displaying 'insincerity and lust for power' and an 'aspiration to a leadership role which they were not prepared to share with Great Britain'. To spend fifteen months lecturing the British on the sacrosanct rules of the treaty before themselves acting 'outside of the Treaty rather than through it', was unacceptable.[65] The hope entertained by some that Chancellor Adenauer would be able to persuade President de Gaulle to change his mind (they met in Paris on 22 January to sign the Franco-German Friendship Treaty) proved unfounded. A disillusioned Spaak believed the significance of the slammed door went far beyond the issue of British accession: 'It is the foreign policy of the community countries which has suddenly been altered.'[66] Having been open to its surroundings, the association was abruptly closed.

Not until 29 January did the responsible British minister, Edward Heath hear from the chairman of the divided Six that the talks had been terminated. There followed a number of emotional speeches. Spaak believed the community spirit had been broken. The German minister, less sombre than his colleagues, believed the matter was sure to be resolved one day. Couve de Murville was the last of the Six to speak. The Frenchman put the onus on the British, but he convinced no one. Heath, finally, moved his audience with the assurance: 'We in Britain are not going to turn our backs on the mainland of Europe or the countries of the Community. We are a part of Europe: by geography, tradition, history, culture and civilisation. We shall continue to work with all our friends in Europe for the true unity and strength of this continent.'[67] Even the interpreters were close to tears. Then the Brit was sent home. Or was he?

That same evening, 29 January, a remarkable meeting took place in Spaak's offices in Brussels. Ministers of the five members in favour of accession and representatives of the British government aired their frustration at the French veto. The 'new Six', as they called themselves fraternally that evening, discussed how to prevent the Community and Britain from growing apart. In an atmosphere of anti-Gaullist rhetoric, the Dutch minister even toyed with the idea of a new organisation, excluding France and including Britain. The other members, though no less enraged, were more cautious. Giving up everything that had been achieved in the Community seemed unwise. They had to go on together. One of the Germans there present wrote later, with slight regret: 'When we departed from our hotels the next day, nothing remained of the "new Six" of this emotional night.'[68]

With his lightning bolt of 14 January 1963, de Gaulle had drawn decision-making about the Community into a domestic arena. As a head of state, he was standing guard at the entrance to the Six. The boundary between inside and outside did not lie in the inner sphere of the treaty.

The irony is that the Five discovered this, too, but from the opposite direction. When they flirted with the idea of swapping Paris for non-member London, they quickly realised what a tenuous notion it was. The illusory evening of 29 January 1963 makes clear that the duress of membership is stronger than anything expressed by terms such as 'intergovernmental cooperation'. Had it been a matter of agreements between governments, after de Gaulle's veto the Five could simply have set up a conference table for a gathering that would exclude the French and include the British. But the interests of the members were already so firmly interwoven that a schism would have been enormously costly for all of them. Seen in a positive light, they stayed together out of club feeling, because of their 'community spirit'; viewed more negatively, it was because of the considerable losses attached to withdrawal or expulsion. Either way, affinity or calculation, membership signified a political bond whose coercion was powerful and unique.

Four years later, the skirmish at the door was repeated. The second British application to join arrived in May 1967, de Gaulle expressed his opposition at a press conference in November, and the formal French blockade of negotiations followed in December. The case was still closed.

If there was to be movement, it would have to come from Paris. The wait this time was short. The General survived the strikes and the calls for change of May 1968, but stood down a year later nonetheless. Many a government heaved a sigh of relief. New man Pompidou let it be known that 'in principle' he was not opposed to British accession. This time, though, the Six must form a united front. As for the British, they must stop sowing discord by manipulating Luns one minute, Brandt the next, as if (as Pompidou put it to the British ambassador in Paris) 'the United Kingdom was already in the Community'. He went on: 'If you will allow me a comparison, the Common Market is like a fortified town whose outer walls consist of the Community's external tariff. Anyone who wants to enter must come through the door and not try to open breaches in the wall. Never lose sight of the fact that the Six form a whole.'[69]

At the summit in The Hague in December 1969, the Six decided that the British could join. This time negotiations were to be held 'between the Community on the one hand and the applicant States on the other'.[70] A flaw in the treaty was thereby silently repaired: earlier talks had taken place between individual member states and the candidates, so members could be played off against one another. Furthermore, London and other newcomers would be asked to endorse not just the terms of the treaty, but also the Community's political aims and all decisions accepted since 1958. Anyone wanting to join the club would have to sign up to both the letter and the spirit of the treaty, and observe all the customs and practices that had developed in the meantime.

Six months later, negotiations began, with the Six on one side and on the other side Britain, its neighbour Ireland, and its partners in free trade Denmark and Norway. In January 1972, the ten governments reached an accord. The months that followed saw the assent of the British House of Commons (309 'ayes'; 301 'nays'), the Irish population (83 per cent in favour) and the Danish population (63 per cent for). Only the Norwegians voted against. On New Year's Day 1973, the three new members officially crossed the threshold. The Six were now the Nine. The door had, for the first time, proved itself to be an entryway.

As to why France now agreed to British accession, the answer is threefold. First, pressure from the other five members was becoming increasingly hard to withstand. Permanent obstruction was undermining the benefits of the association. Pompidou wanted to be an 'ordinary' member again. Irritation among the Five over the French veto had reached such heights that a rift between the Six seemed conceivable. Given that France's international standing depended on a leadership role in the Community, a circle that included London was better than none at all. Second, there were now fewer disadvantages to British accession. Disagreements over the financing of agricultural policy had been resolved to French satisfaction by 1970. London would no longer be able to change that.

Third, never mentioned yet fundamental: France, too, needed a balance of power by this point. In 1961–62 the Belgians and Dutch had wanted a British counterweight to Franco-German domination; this time Paris was hoping the arrival of London would provide a counterweight to Bonn. The degree to which West Germany's economic power and political aspirations had grown can have escaped no one, which put France's position as leader of the Six in doubt. It was now relying purely on its military superiority. Monetary relationships crystallised after America's abrupt abandonment of the gold standard on 15 August 1971: the strong Deutschmark became an anchor for the other European currencies, including the French franc. More acute were Pompidou's worries about Brandt's *Ostpolitik*. He believed the chancellor had made 'tremendous concessions' to Moscow by recognising the 1945 borders. Moreover, it was unclear where improved relations between West and East Germany might lead. The entire European geopolitical balance was shifting.

In this situation, France sought support in two ordering principles (just as the Netherlands and Belgium had done a decade earlier). It was best, Pompidou said, to 'fasten Germany to Europe in such a way that it can never detach itself again'.[71] For example, monetary matters could be included in the tightly woven fabric of the European sphere. At a summit of the Nine in Paris in October 1972, at Pompidou's suggestion, a symbolically important step was taken when the member states agreed that over the coming decade they would transform their relationships into a 'political union'.[72] Alongside all this, it could do no harm to prepare for a day when German power had to be countered (just imagine if Fortune were to return in her old guise!) by means of a Franco-British entente.

Ouvrez la porte!

Table arrangement

The accession of Britain in 1973 had one important consequence for the club. The three most powerful countries in Western Europe were now members. Given that the eastern half of the continent was under Soviet rule and therefore out of the picture, this made the member states' pretension to speak 'on behalf of Europe' more credible. Not that the Six had ever shown much reticence in that regard, but a former ambassador later admitted: 'Before the arrival of the British it was rather doubtful whether we had the right to call ourselves "Europe".'[73]

The outside world took note of the metamorphosis. American National Security Advisor Henry Kissinger declared 1973 to be the Year of Europe. He has been quoted as saying that he wanted to know which telephone number would get him Europe on the line. It was a pertinent question. In other respects, too, confrontation with the outside world was cause for self-reflection. In that same year, 1973, the leaders of the Nine published a 'Declaration on European Identity', a quite remarkable attempt at self-definition.

A greater combined weight brought a new self-image and a new sense of responsibility. It was during the summit in The Hague at which the door was opened to London that the leaders decided – not in documents prepared in advance by civil servants, but on the spot – to investigate the potential for cooperation on foreign policy. The conclusion the following year was that they all appreciated having a framework within which they could discuss their positions and their common interests in the wider world. What de Gaulle had failed to achieve in the early 1960s because of mutual distrust and ideological hair-splitting was now within reach. The sphere of the members was cautiously becoming organised.

Although this European Political Cooperation, as it was officially called, had been initiated by the Six back in 1970, it assumed greater seriousness when the Six became the Nine. The members promised to share information and to consult each other before adopting a position in any future political crisis.

Kissinger and the Nine – 1973

For the transatlantic relationship, these early feelers were inadequate. The announcement by Kissinger that 1973 was to be the Year of Europe focused a harsh spotlight on this fact. The White House wanted to establish a 'new Atlantic Charter' in which, after a quarter of a century of the Nato pact, America and Western Europe would solemnly reaffirm their shared political values and aims, projecting them into the future. In his speech in April launching the Charter, Kissinger (still Nixon's security advisor) contrasted America's 'global interests' with the 'regional interests' of its European allies. This touched a nerve with the partners. The American president was being dragged down by Watergate, which further helped to temper enthusiasm among European leaders for photo opportunities in the White House. But one reason why the initiative produced a dialogue of the deaf is attributable purely to Europe.

Who, after all, would speak 'on Europe's behalf'? The question was becoming urgent and all the players were aware of it. The German chancellor was the first in a series of national leaders to visit Washington as part of the Year of Europe. During a dinner at the White House, Brandt tried a sophist's formula: 'None of us meets you any longer solely as the representative of his own country but at the same time already, to a certain degree, as a representative of the European Community as well. So, I, too, am here not as the spokesman *of* Europe, but definitely as a spokesman *for* Europe.'[74] Not 'on behalf of' but at best 'for'. The security advisor found that interesting. But what did it mean in practice? So long as there were no European political institutions, he could see 'no focal point for contact with Europe'. In his memoirs, Kissinger put his finger on Europe's problem: 'Brandt in fact faced us with a Catch-22 dilemma: If every European leader was a spokesman for Europe but could not represent it, and those who represented Europe were civil servants with no authority to negotiate, who then could act authoritatively?'[75] In other words, the 'on behalf of Europe' offered by the Commission (and familiar to Washington from trade relations) was too weak. It did not fall within the member-states sphere.

The problem raised its head again in September 1973. Five months after Kissinger's speech, the Nine had their answer ready. Danish Foreign Minister Knud Børge Andersen, holder of the rotating presidency of the Council, presented their response. He was not empowered to negotiate changes. He would have to consult with his eight colleagues first. Quite apart from the uninspired text the Nine had produced, Kissinger (meanwhile promoted to secretary of state) was annoyed that transatlantic consultations were to take place only between civil servants. Andersen, embarrassed: 'You must understand how difficult it is for the Nine to achieve what we have.' Kissinger: 'Yes, it is a considerable achievement for Europe but not for Atlantic relations.'[76]

Oil summitry – 1973–74

On 6 October 1973, an Arab–Israeli war broke out. In a surprise attack, Egypt seized the Sinai desert, while Syria took the Golan Heights. The Israelis regrouped and within forty-eight hours the tide had been turned. The aggressors then deployed the 'oil weapon'. Starting on 17 October, Arab oil-exporting countries reduced supplies to the West. When Russia threatened to join the armed conflict on the Egyptian side, the Americans forced a ceasefire. Peace talks ensued. The war ended and the oil crisis began.

European silence on the Middle East was followed by a buzz of internal activity. 'In the light of recent events, we are obliged to find that the cease-fire and the efforts towards opening negotiations were prepared and effected with no participation by Europe in any form whatsoever,' declared a slightly surprised French president on 31 October. According to Pompidou, silence would leave the way open for a dangerous confrontation between America and Russia, and would reflect neither Europe's historical ties with, nor its geographical proximity to, the Middle East. The Nine had to find a voice. The French government therefore proposed to its eight partners 'that a decision be taken on the principle, according to precise rules, of regular meetings between only the heads of state or government, with the aim of comparing and harmonizing their outlooks under the concept of political cooperation'.[77] The first of these meetings would need to be held before the end of 1973. Privately the British prime minister and the German chancellor lent their support. They shared the analysis that Europe lacked what Heath called 'a focus of authority'.[78]

Although there was some grumbling – why always the French? – this initiative was taken up by the rotating presidency, held by the Danes. A summit was planned for 14–15 December in Copenhagen. Expectations were high. An American diplomat predicted that Europe would draw up a Declaration of Independence. Washington knew that its own authority in Europe was being eroded by Vietnam, Watergate and the fall of the dollar.

Between October and December, the price of a barrel of oil rose fivefold. The energy crisis caused inflation and threatened to disrupt Western European economies. The Arab oil boycott was a further major test of mutual solidarity. The Netherlands, regarded as a friend of Israel, became the only one of the

Nine to endure a total boycott. France and Britain, 'friends' of the Arabs, received normal deliveries, while the other six were threatened with a phased reduction in oil supplies. The strain proved too much. External pressure could sometimes be overwhelming.

The summit ended in chaos. Quite unexpectedly, four Arab ministers turned up at the Copenhagen conference hall, Bella Centret. This was an appearance by Fortune in one of her more burlesque guises. The Algerian, the Egyptian, the Sudanese and the man from the Emirates wanted to talk to Europe about oil and Israel. It remains unclear whether anyone had invited them. Protocol dictated that the heads of state or government could not receive the four lower-ranking guests, who were therefore referred to the foreign ministers. No proper talks took place, but the Arab presence did lead to national oil-supply deals in the corridors. There was nothing remotely resembling a joint standpoint; each state was thinking purely of its own supplies. In vain did the boycotted Netherlands plead for solidarity from the other eight countries. European energy policy had failed before it was even defined.

Despite (or because of) this embarrassing performance, the nine leaders decided to meet more often, so that Europe could speak 'with one voice in important world affairs'. Meetings would not take place at regular intervals, as Pompidou had proposed, but rather, according to the final communiqué, 'whenever justified by the circumstances and when it appears necessary to provide a stimulus or to lay down further guidelines for the construction of a united Europe . . . and whenever the international situation so requires'.[79]

For the time being, the member-states sphere would wait for fate to knock on the door before organising itself.

There was just one further step to be taken. The members would hold summits whenever the situation so required, but wasn't there always something happening in the world? Couldn't Fortune put in an appearance at any moment?

With perpetually high oil prices, stagnating economies, international monetary instability and uncertainty over the continued presence of American troops on European soil, the Nine's need for a permanent political authority seemed obvious. Such an authority could not arise from the European inner sphere, as even founder Jean Monnet knew. The institutions were not up to it. (In recounting his work behind the scenes to prepare the ground for summit meetings, Monnet later wrote: 'We had to disappoint only those who still believed that . . . the government of Europe would one day emerge fully armed from the institutions of the Economic Community.'[80]) Within a year, the national leaders, some with great reluctance, would once again take the matter in hand.

First came a rapid change of personnel in London, Bonn and Paris. In the spring of 1974, Edward Heath, having lost a general election, gave way to Harold Wilson. Willy Brandt handed the chancellorship to Helmut Schmidt after a spying scandal, and Georges Pompidou died and was succeeded by Valéry Giscard d'Estaing, who quickly came to the same conclusion as his two predecessors: 'The goal I had in mind was that the European heads of government would come together regularly. Once that regularity was established, the scope of the power of the leaders would do the rest and the institution would consolidate of its own accord: a European executive power would begin to take shape.'[81]

In August 1974, Giscard d'Estaing gave a televised speech in which he announced 'initiatives regarding the political organization of Europe'. He told French viewers how he felt about the fact that American President Gerald Ford had not used the word 'Europe' in his recent inaugural speech.[82] In September, he organised an informal lunch (a 'picnic summit') in Paris for the nine heads of government, the rotating presidency having now passed to France. The Frenchman asked his guests for ideas. All showed a personal willingness to shoulder more European responsibility. Chancellor Helmut Schmidt suggested turning their conference into a formal institution, but that was not a particularly popular idea. Dutch Premier Joop den Uyl stressed the need to strengthen the Commission. Danish Prime Minister Poul Hartling, who had only just joined the circle and headed a weak minority cabinet at home, was similarly apprehensive about institutional innovation. A follow-up conference would have to decide.

On 9 and 10 December 1974 they set to work. The French president received the other eight national leaders for a two-day summit in Paris. The host saved the most sensitive issue for the afternoon of the second day. In a salon on the ground floor of the Elysée Palace, with his guests jumbled together informally in easy chairs with coffee or tea and biscuits, the truth came out: 'Wouldn't it be nice to bring a little regularity to these gatherings?' Giscard had already assured himself of Schmidt's support: France and Germany were on the same wavelength. The Italian premier, Aldo Moro, was the first to come across. It seemed a good idea to him. Ever since British accession, the Italians had been fearful of a directorate of the big three, and this was one way to avoid it. British Prime Minister Harold Wilson kept his cards close to his chest. The Dane said nothing. The representatives of the Benelux countries were clearly not keen.

But then Leo Tindemans suddenly had an idea. Where should such meetings take place? The Belgian premier was eager that several should be held in Brussels 'for the sake of the cohesion of the European institutions'. Giscard d'Estaing could barely conceal his delight:

> From the moment we started talking about where to meet, the game was over! Making concessions would suffice. So after long discussion – which from that stage onwards I followed with a delightful feeling, since the main point seemed won – it was decided to convene three meetings a year, and always to hold at least one of the two meetings in the first six months in either Brussels or Luxembourg.[83]

As a result of opposition from Denmark and the Netherlands to any new institution, the Nine agreed that their forum would *not* be called the European Council. Nowhere in the officially published conference conclusions does that term appear. The host was not to be held back by such minutiae, however. With the help of his audience, he created the political fact he was intent upon. How? Giscard d'Estaing opened the concluding press conference with the triumphant words: '*Le Sommet est mort. Vive le Conseil européen!*' ('The summit is dead. Long live the European Council!') This semantic coup succeeded – press telexes were already rattling. The European Council was born.

For the Danish delegation, present at the press conference, Giscard's opening words came 'as a surprise'.[84]

In the official language of the summit's conclusions, the leaders established the European Council because of the need for an 'overall approach to the internal problems involved in achieving European unity and the external problems facing Europe', which meant it was essential to ensure 'overall consistency in the activities of the Communities and in the work on political cooperation'.[85] This duality is fundamental. Only the national leaders, gathered together, have authority both over the inner sphere (where their sectoral ministers serve on their own Council and where they appoint the Commission) and over any political cooperation between member states. Their conference table brought the highest ranks of national representation together: every matter that was passed on up the line would eventually end up there. It was only at this point that the club gave itself an institution of which it was possible to say, in Truman's words, 'the buck stops here'.

It was no coincidence that even the conundrum of representation was resolved at the Paris summit, at least on paper: 'The President-in-Office will be the spokesman for the Nine and will set out their views in international diplomacy.'[86] The president of the European Council spoke not on behalf of the Community, but on behalf of the assembled member states. Except that, as yet, there was little he could say.

6

Acting as a Union
(1989–today)

Now and then the course of history is decided on a single day or even in the space of a few hours. On such extraordinary days history becomes visible and everyone can experience it. Highly complex structural developments are concentrated on one event, on a great shock, and can therefore be experienced, known and understood from the perspective of the moment . . . Contemporaries sense the astonishing drama immediately, since political events are compressed into an otherwise rare emotional intensity. These are days of an epoch-making switch in direction, the start of a new historical era.

Joschka Fischer (2005)[87]

In a memorable 1969 essay, German philosopher Hans-Georg Gadamer investigates the nature of the '*epochemachende Ereignis*' – the epoch-making event that ends an era (from the Greek *epokhē*, 'suspension'). Although the expression is often used idly – 'Many momentous events are announced only on the radio', notes Gadamer – he claims that we know perfectly well what we mean by it. Such events are incisions in time, points that mark off the old from the new. They are not picked out in retrospect by historians; strictly constructivist notions of periodisation are untenable. It is the event itself that decides.[88]

The fall of the Berlin Wall is one such event. It began at a precise moment. On 9 November 1989, at half past nine in the evening, thousands of East Berliners began crossing the border with the West, through the Brandenburg Gate. It was a powerful image, since the gouged wall was fact and symbol combined. It also had an appealing materiality. In the months that followed, thousands of history tourists got their hands on tiny bits of wall, relics of a moment when the *Weltgeist* struck.

Almost twenty-five years later, Europe has still not fully absorbed the earthquake of 1989; in fact, we have barely begun to assess its significance. It thrust Western Europeans into a new role, obliging them to take responsibility for conditions on their entire continent. The Soviet Union quickly fell apart. Suddenly young democracies were clamouring to join the Twelve. There were wars in the Balkans, economic globalisation... It all took some getting used to. The shock of 1989 forced the member states to change their stance. They turned their association into a Union and admitted new members. The borders of institutional Europe crept towards those of geographical Europe.

Everybody immediately understood that the fall of the Wall meant the end of an epoch, but no one knew what new epoch had arrived. For the time being, it was designated the post-Cold War era. Initial optimism about a stable world order under American leadership, summed up in Francis Fukuyama's slogan 'the end of history', was dashed twelve years later by a second epoch-making event that is still referred to by its date: 'September 11' or '9/11'. It was a strike at the heart of America, the only world power, and its consequences were felt all over the globe. Europe had no choice but to turn its attention to Islamist terrorism and to American wars in the Middle East and Central Asia.

Fascinatingly, '2001' taught us something about '1989'. The later event cast fresh light on the earlier, forcing Europeans to recognise that their protector across the ocean was not invulnerable, that the world had grown bigger, that history would never stand still. Shortly after 11 September, this new historical consciousness was distilled into the phrase 'the return of history'. People then started to realise that this 'return' had actually begun for Europe with the fall of the Wall. The 'end' of history seemed a fleeting illusion. Only '2001' made '1989' into the undisputed cut-off point that ended the Community's cosy period of waiting, and forced a joint entry into the river of time.

AFTER THE WALL

The shock came, first of all, in the outer sphere, the realm of the balance of power. The entire concert of European states, from London to Belgrade, trembled on its foundations after the fall of the Berlin Wall, as it had not done since 1945. A new balance would need to be found. The inner sphere of the Community, for its part, regarded the blow as an opportunity. Brussels saw a chance to transform the economic vitality evident since 1985 into a political breakthrough – which indeed took place, but not in the way it had hoped. Lastly, the impact was absorbed in the intermediate sphere of the members. The Twelve saw themselves confronted, like it or not, with a historic task.

They transformed their association into a 'Union', and after long hesitation they allowed more than ten states from beyond the Wall to enter their circle. This was the sphere in which the greatest innovation took place. The club of member states had been woken from its geopolitical slumber.

The abrupt acceleration left many European politicians gasping for breath. One national leader later recalled how history had 'galloped riderless through the night of the Fall of the Wall like a runaway horse'.[89] The talented among them grabbed the reins.

Kohl's acceleration (28 November 1989)

The impact on Europe's geopolitical outer sphere was rapid and dramatic. German unification meant redrawing the map of Europe, creating or confirming boundaries between sovereign states. As far as Germany was concerned, we were back in 1945, at 'Yalta'. The players in the diplomatic game were the two successors to the defeated Third Reich and the four occupying powers of that time – in other words, West and East Germany, their respective protectors America and Russia, plus Britain and France. These six, branded '2+4' by diplomats, would unite the two German states, give back sovereignty to the entire German nation and thereby lay the groundwork for a new European order. Concerned onlookers, such as Poland, Italy and the Netherlands, were excluded.

For two weeks, the situation was vague. The American president had declared six months earlier: 'Let Europe be whole and free.' What he wanted was clear. Bush supported the West Germans in all they did. Reform of the East German state still seemed possible, and its leaders came up with an inconsequential plan for a 'treaty community'. Other scenarios in circulation included a confederation of the two states and a militarily neutral Germany. The British and French were not enthusiastic about unification, as the chancellor noted during a meeting. It seemed unlikely that the Russians would ever agree to it.

On 28 November, Helmut Kohl seized the initiative. 'The Wheel of History was spinning more quickly'[90] – that had been his experience since the *Mauerfall*. Waiting any longer would mean letting an opportunity slip. In a speech in the Bundestag, Kohl set out his ultimate goal: German 'unity' and 'reunification'. This was surprisingly plain language. He also unveiled a detailed ten-step plan, from 'cooperation' via 'confederal structures' to a 'federation'. No timetable was mentioned, but in Bonn people were thinking in terms of several years. The American president was the only foreign leader informed in advance, by telephone. He gave his blessing.

Astonishment and shock predominated in the European capitals after Kohl's speech. An amorphous anxiety had suddenly been made concrete: the resurrection of a powerful and rich nation state in the middle of the continent, with 80 million inhabitants. And why did the chancellor not immediately recognise the Oder–Neisse line as the border between Poland and (East) Germany? In the late 1940s, the 'German problem' had been overshadowed by the Russian threat. Now, with the latter apparently receding, the former re-emerged. Responses articulated in London and Paris stuck to the line taken four decades earlier.

Margaret Thatcher, the Iron Lady, was determined to prevent German unification. She clung to the status quo, both German and European. As her foreign minister, Douglas Hurd, put it – breezily passing over more than 100 million people on the eastern side – a Europe divided by the Iron Curtain was a system 'under which we've lived quite happily for forty years'.[91] Since Thatcher could find no willing hearers for her concerns in Washington, she sought support from François Mitterrand. Only a new Franco-British entente could restore the European balance of power and reassure the smaller countries that they would be protected, the prime minister said. She wrote in her memoirs of a conversation with the French president in December 1989: 'I produced from my handbag a map showing the various configurations of Germany in the past, which were not altogether reassuring about the future.'[92] This image of the German foe, even though few in London fully shared it, determined the British stance for a year – until Thatcher fell.

The French also regarded a strong, united Germany as less than a blessing. No longer roughly the same size as France, it would become a larger neighbour both demographically and economically. For a long time, Paris found this hard to accept. Like Thatcher, President Mitterrand, a former prisoner of the Germans, was haunted by spectres of the past. On a visit to West Berlin in late December 1989, he refused to walk through the Brandenburg Gate at Kohl's side. His private explanation: 'That's a matter for the Germans among themselves. I don't need to take part. Kohl didn't inform me about his ten-point plan; he refuses to recognise the Oder–Neisse line. And then he wants me to come and legitimise his grip on the DDR? That's the limit! . . . And the French press says I don't understand . . . Journalists are always willing to throw themselves at the feet of the victor, just like in 1940!'[93] Publicly, too, the president was extremely sparing with gracious rhetoric. Not until October 1990 did he manage to say reasonably convincingly, '*Bonne chance l'Allemagne!*'

All the same, as in 1950, the French did not believe that an alliance with the British best served their security interests, and once again they opted to try to weave Germany into a European order. Paris was less fixated on the status quo than was London: so long as there was movement, there was something to be gained. In particular, Mitterrand sought German assent to European monetary union, a step seen in Paris as the only way of harnessing the supremacy of the Deutschmark. Plans developed by the twelve central bankers under Delors' chairmanship had been ready since the summer of 1989, but Chancellor Kohl was reluctant to fire the starting pistol. In fact, the day before his speech on German unity he had sent Mitterrand a letter saying that the planned negotiations between the Twelve on monetary union would have to be postponed for a year. The combination of these two announcements – German acceleration and European delay – did not go down well in Paris.

This marked the start of a brief, fascinating period of Franco-German poker-play: Bonn set its sights on the German people's right to self-determination, and everything else could wait; Paris wanted a European currency, with an immediate agreement on it in black and white, as a sign of German attachment to Europe. For some ten days, the two main players didn't blink. On 5 December 1989, Kohl sent a letter to Paris saying he was determined to postpone monetary union. On 6 December, Mitterrand flew to Kiev for a meeting with Mikhail Gorbachev. Was he intending to conspire with the Soviet leader to place some obstacle in the way of German unification, as was whispered in his absence, or merely trying to increase the pressure on Kohl? The poker game ended at the table of the Twelve, at the European Council meeting of 8–9 December in Strasbourg. Kohl made the first move. During lunch, he agreed to monetary union. The atmosphere was icy, and Margaret Thatcher, Ruud Lubbers and Giulio Andreotti made no attempt to disguise their unease, but François Mitterrand, in the chair, came up with the political declaration that Bonn was looking for at the end of day two. The Twelve voted in favour of beginning an intergovernmental conference on monetary union by December 1990 at the latest, and at the same time outlined the framework within which Germany could be united. Although never made explicit, the link was obvious to all those involved. Exactly a month after the fall of the Wall, the historic deal was done: for the Germans, a sovereign, united German state; for the French, a European currency.

This trade-off was the last act in the play that began when Churchill insisted that de Gaulle should be given access to the victors' table at the end of the Second World War. Over the past half-century the French had duly made the most of the say they had on matters of political life and death for their defeated neighbour. In 1951, determined to see his country accepted back into the fold as an equal of other states, Adenauer had assented to the

French plan that turned German coal into European coal (and shortly after-wards to a plan to turn German soldiers into European soldiers). Likewise, in 1989, to reassure France and his other Western European partners, Kohl agreed that the Deutschmark would become a European currency. German unification would have happened even without this concession, given that America supported it, but in an environment of distrust. 'We need friends', the chancellor explained to President Bush. Still, this was the final round. With German unification and the accompanying treaties – after the Russians finally gave up resisting in September 1990 – Paris had played its political trump card as one of the victors of 1945.

Delors' hubris (17 January 1990)

In Brussels, new opportunities were discerned in the autumn of 1989. There was a fondness for comparing the political dynamism of Eastern Europe with the economic dynamism brought about by the goal of '1992': the internal market.

'History is accelerating. We must accelerate too', said Commission President Jacques Delors in October 1989, in a speech in Bruges. 'I have always been an advocate of the politics of small steps . . . but today I distance myself from it a bit, because time has caught up with us. We must make a quantum leap.' Europe's decision-making procedures were inadequate 'to enable us to respond to accelerations of History'.[94] The boss of the inner sphere was still contem-plating how Europe could be better governed.

In the new year, Delors hazarded the leap. On 17 January 1990, he set out his vision in Strasbourg. The theme of his speech to the Parliament was the role of the Community in a turbulent world. Wouldn't it be better if, instead of always being overtaken by events, it were first to 'define more clearly what I call *the essential community interests* of the member states, to light their path rather better'? A European foreign policy was needed, and with it a European executive. Delors fearlessly advocated 'the transformation of the Commission into a real, responsible executive. The logic of the fathers of the Treaty of Rome, as well as the need for effectiveness and the challenges of the outside world, demands that we back this solution'. Naturally, the Commission (as a government) would be responsible 'to the democratic institutions of the future Federation'.[95] That word, too, was out. A week later, on French televi-sion, he even offered a timetable: 'My objective is that before the end of the millennium Europe should have a true federation.'[96]

The idea went down badly in a number of European capitals. In London, Thatcher saw her deepest suspicions about the pretensions of Brussels confirmed. In Paris, Mitterrand, watching television at home, shouted during the Delors interview: 'But that's ridiculous! What's he up to? No one in Europe will ever want that. By playing the extremist, he's going to wreck what's achievable.'[97]

His biographer called it Delors' Icarus moment. Swept along by events, he thought for a moment that he could fly. He survived the fall – Kohl's unflinching support functioned as a safety net. But between February 1990 and November 1991, the Commission president gave no more major speeches about Europe's political future. The tide of history did not lift the Community up to a different level. Instead, everything was down to the Twelve.

'The moment has come' (19 April 1990)

Just nine days after the Fall of the Wall, the French president, current holder of the rotating presidency of the Council of the Twelve, held a dinner for the national leaders in Paris. The subject of the special summit was not German unification – though it preoccupied everyone, this was not the appropriate forum for that issue, and it was kept out of the conversation (although Thatcher could not contain herself and, over dessert, let fly at Kohl). Instead, the subject was the situation in Central and Eastern Europe: aid programmes, significant loans to Poland and Hungary, possibly even a new Marshall Plan. On those matters, the dining companions were of one mind, speaking in terms of European unity and solidarity. Belgian Premier Wilfried Martens, one of the company since 1979, concluded contentedly: 'For the first time, we were sitting around the table discussing a political issue like a cabinet at European level.'[98] It was a remarkable moment. On 18 November 1989, the Twelve accepted, de facto, joint responsibility for the situation after and beyond the Iron Curtain. The precedent this set indicated where responsibility lay: at the table of the assembled heads of state or government.

In the spring of 1990, following the acceleration in German unification that had jangled nerves everywhere, the Twelve resumed their conversation about Europe's future. Monetary union as intended in late 1989 no longer seemed an adequate response to the Fall of the Wall. Gradually the realisation dawned that behind the Iron Curtain lived more than 100 million people who regarded themselves as 'Europeans'. A further 'political' strengthening of Europe seemed essential. The Commission and the Parliament had believed this for some time, but now several national governments began to argue along the same lines.

But what to do? As so often, the decisive factor was a Franco-German initiative. The chancellor wanted to reassure his partners that national unification was taking place within a European framework. Bonn also believed that the European Parliament should be given more power. From February onwards, Kohl pressed Mitterrand to join him in launching institutional reform. The French president hesitated. He did not take 'Strasbourg' seriously and wanted to avoid being sucked along in a federalist direction by Bonn. But better to play a duet than to leave Kohl alone at the piano.

On 19 April 1990, the two men sent a short but forceful letter to their ten fellow government leaders: 'In the light of far-reaching changes in Europe and in view of the completion of the single market and the realisation of economic and monetary union,' the chancellor and the president declared, 'we consider it necessary to accelerate the political construction of the Europe of the Twelve'.[99] Referring to a repeatedly postponed plan, they wrote: 'We believe that it is time "to transform relations as a whole among the member states into a European Union"'.[100] A 'political union' was the elastic term under which the German and French visions could be reconciled. At the Paris summit of 1972, the leaders of the Nine had said that they wanted to form a 'union'. No one knew exactly what that meant, but its vagueness was in some ways an advantage. The leaders had restated their aim several times since, most recently in 1985, without any concrete steps eventuating. Now, according to Kohl and Mitterrand, 'the time had come'. The era of waiting was over.

One important detail: Kohl and Mitterrand did not write 'the Community must become a Union' (as the metamorphosis is generally summarised). Instead, they located the origin of the Union in 'the Europe of the Twelve', in 'relations as a whole among the member states' – in other words, in the intermediate sphere of the members. There is an essential difference between an expansion of the community sphere and a partial formalisation of the members' sphere. Dutch diplomacy neglected this to its own detriment eighteen months later.

How the members ought to give shape to their union was an open question – the Franco-German pointers imposed few constraints. Differences between the two letter-writers were verbally smoothed over or compromised upon. A union, they claimed, required an increase in democratic legitimacy and stronger institutions (Bonn), coordination between economic and monetary policies (both) and a common foreign policy (Paris).

Shortly after the Franco-German letter, the Twelve decided to hold an intergovernmental conference on political union. It was to begin in December 1990, along with the conference on monetary union. The prospect concentrated minds. Each member state began to consider the potential benefits for itself and for the club as a whole. Included on the wish-list: foreign policy and defence (France, Germany, Belgium and Spain); citizenship (Spain, Greece); more power for the Parliament (Germany, Italy and the Benelux countries); more social policy (same again, plus France); stricter environmental policy and more concrete benefits for citizens (Denmark); and more money for poorer regions (the southern member states). Whatever a 'union' might signify, all members were heading for no-holds-barred negotiations, followed by refoundation.

Thatcher was no longer among them. After the Fall of the Wall, she had wanted to preserve the German status quo, but was forced to swallow unification. Similarly, she now wanted to preserve the European status quo, but was having a Union thrust down her throat. Three weeks after German unification, that dispute, too, was settled. At the nerve-wracking Rome summit of 28–29 October 1990, she refused to commit to the goals that the Twelve had drawn up for monetary and political union. It was eleven against one. London's isolation was complete. At home, Thatcher reported on the summit in the House of Commons. Challenged by questions from the opposition, she unexpectedly let rip: 'The President of the Commission, Mr Delors, said at a press conference the other day that he wanted the European Parliament to be the democratic body of the Community, he wanted the Commission to be the Executive and he wanted the Council of Ministers to be the Senate. No! No! No!'[101] She also undermined a British alternative to the single currency, for which her own ministers were trying to garner support. After this furious performance, her ever-loyal former foreign secretary, Geoffrey Howe, resigned as deputy prime minister. His motives were spelled out to a deathly silent House of Commons two weeks later: 'The Prime Minister's perceived attitude towards Europe is running increasingly serious risks for the future of our nation.'[102] A revolt in her party followed. On 28 November 1990, Thatcher walked out of 10 Downing Street for the last time. Even a strong, inflexible politician of her calibre could not keep up the struggle against European history, as unleashed in 1989, for much more than a year.

Black Monday (30 September 1991)

The partial transformation of the intermediate sphere into a Union, which the British could not prevent, also met with resistance from the side of the institutional sphere. During the intergovernmental conference of 1991, supporters of the community model tried to avert the danger of a Union, as they had succeeded in doing in an earlier episode, six years before (see Chapter 3). On Monday, 30 September, ten weeks before the concluding summit in Maastricht, it became clear that their attempt would not work this time around.

The new, underestimated factor was external pressure. The need for the Twelve, after 1989, to be able to address the rest of the world with a single voice determined the outcome of the fascinating tug-of-war over the name and structure of the treaty – an expression of the abstract battle between the political spheres of action – with a Union emerging as the winner. How to speak to the world as the Twelve? Informal foreign policy cooperation as it stood was too weak, as almost everyone acknowledged. It was reactive and declaratory, and it committed the members to little more than an exchange of information ('I'm going to do such-and-such') and consultation ('What would you think of that?'). No one was obliged even to attempt to reach a joint stand-point. At the same time, the exposure of foreign policy to community rules was a highly sensitive matter. The Court in Luxembourg would be able to condemn diplomatic moves, the Parliament would be able to discuss them, and (formally at least) only the Commission would be able to make proposals. This ran counter to the member states' sense of national sovereignty. The dilemma: the informal rules were not coercive enough, while the community corset was too constraining. A compromise was required.

As a response to these sensitivities, Luxembourg, in the chair, presented a draft Union Treaty in April 1991. It included three sets of rules, covering community business (economic, monetary and social), foreign policy, and justice and home affairs. If you put a simple roof on these three 'pillars' you had a temple. The model was completely wrong, said Belgium, the Netherlands, Greece and the Commission: it undermined the Community and closed off the route to a federal future for Europe. They preferred to see a 'tree', with a single trunk bearing (if necessary) several branches. By contrast, Britain, France, Portugal and Denmark supported the notion of separate pillars: the Brussels institutions should have as little grip as possible on foreign policy and home affairs. The other members could live with either. At the Luxembourg summit of late June 1991 – the crisis in Yugoslavia had just erupted – the twelve national leaders decided to accept the pillar proposal as the point of departure for a Union Treaty.

The chair passed to the Dutch in July 1991. In The Hague, then still a bastion of community orthodoxy, there was a belief that the process could yet be reversed. Under the leadership of Dutch Secretary of State for European Affairs Piet Dankert, a former president of the European Parliament, the Luxembourg Union Treaty was rewritten. Commission officials around Delors provided editorial support services. The name for the Twelve reverted from 'Union' to 'Community'. Foreign policy was poured back into the community mould. The objective, said the editing civil servant to his minister, was to 'recast [the pillars] as soundlessly as possible into the structure we have in mind'.[103] Given that a passionate debate on this point had been going on between the Twelve since April, the assumption that such an existential transformation could be slipped in under the radar is remarkable. Nonetheless, thanks to an 'astonishing amount of wishful thinking', The Hague managed to ignore all alarm signals from its own diplomats in Brussels and from its partners.[104]

On Monday, 30 September, the ministers of the Twelve gathered to discuss the Dutch draft for a Community Treaty. The criticism and exasperation were unprecedented. The Danish minister spoke first: unacceptable. Most of the foreign ministers proposed returning to the Luxembourg draft of April. Only the Belgian, Mark Eyskens, supported his Dutch colleague, Hans van den Broek. It was ten against two. The Hague capitulated.

In Dutch diplomatic circles, this fiasco is known as 'Black Monday'. It was significant for Europe as a whole, however, and is seldom properly understood. The episode could be described as an attempt by the inner sphere to encompass the whole of the institutionalised club – on this occasion, in vain. There was to be no 'Single European Act Mark Two', the coded term that expressed the wish among some to prevent a 'Union', just as they had done in 1985.[105] When even the Dutch, in the chair, reconciled themselves to the outcome, the community institutions stood alone. In November 1991, shortly before the Maastricht summit, Delors threatened to oppose the Union Treaty if foreign policy was to remain a matter for the states. The Parliament, too, expressed a wish to reject the treaty.[106] Formally, however, the Commission and Parliament had no say on the treaty: it was up to the Twelve. The fall of the Wall had split open the community cocoon. The Union had manifested itself, and proved irrepressible.

States with an active foreign policy – Britain and France foremost among them – were not going to let anyone take it away from them: it was one thing to produce proposals for a common market, but quite another to decide on war and peace. The feeling in the capitals was that such responsibility could not be borne by Brussels officials and Strasbourg parliamentarians. Behind closed doors, the heads of government spoke in remarkably denigrating terms. Dutch Premier Ruud Lubbers, who had visited the Elysée Palace in the summer of 1991 and had requested a strengthening of the institutions, was told by President Mitterrand: 'But what are you saying now? The Commission is zero, the Parliament is zero, and zero plus zero is zero.'[107] To John Major, Mitterrand said he believed the Parliament would not become legitimate 'for a hundred years'.[108] Even Giulio Andreotti in Italy, whose government had been a zealous advocate of the Parliament for decades, seemed to lament its existence as a 'demagogic' concession to federalist rhetoric.[109]

The national leaders (with the exception of the British) did not say these things openly, but they did act accordingly. In Maastricht, united in the European Council, they took ultimate responsibility for foreign policy. The acceleration of European history from 1989 onwards did not lead to a coronation of the inner sphere. Thatcher's nightmare and Delors' dream did not come to pass. Neither cliché – cooperating sovereign states or a European federal superstate – matched the reality. Something else happened: in order to be able to shoulder responsibility in the world, the Twelve turned their informal circle to some degree into a formal union. Only in the years that followed would it become clear how profound a metamorphosis this was.

The form of the Union

At the Maastricht summit of 9–10 December 1991, the Twelve issued their first serious response to the fall of the Berlin Wall: a treaty establishing a European Union. Its most important innovations were a common currency and a foreign policy. At the same time, the Community was to change. It allowed itself to throw off the adjective 'economic' and take on a broader scope. The distinction between the Union and the Community has been gravely underestimated. It touches upon the place the club occupies in the stream of events. The key word is 'responsibility'. The fundamental reform represented by the creation of a Union is that the member states now formally bear joint responsibility. Herein lies the fundamental politicisation of the association.

This politicisation has had one important consequence that is rarely recognised: it works against the legal fiction of member states' equality. The Community's strength has always been in building a market and setting the stage – or creating a 'level playing field' – for the actors in economic life. These actors are businesses, consumers, employers and employees, but *not* the states themselves. Indeed, European rules operate rather as a constraint on the action of states (for instance, in limiting state subsidies to failing industries). In the Community years, the member states could inhabit the fiction of equality under law: each state enjoyed the same rights, Germany no more than Luxembourg. There was some tension between this and actual power discrepancies, but insofar as European rules governing the member states demanded mainly self-regulation, with the tasks of supervision and control placed in the hands of the European institutions, by and large it worked.

The Union is different: set up to deal jointly with unforeseen circumstances, here the member states themselves perform on stage. They are no longer only impartial umpires or subservient groundsmen in the economic arena brought into being by the Community; they are now also themselves players creating the action and dealing with all kinds of unforeseen disruptions and challenges. Put more bluntly, in the Union each member state has an army, a diplomatic service and a police force; each has power and a history. These can no longer be veiled behind a curtain, in order to maintain the legal fiction of equality. Instead they determine the answer to the question of how much responsibility each member will (or can) bear. And the answer is, for example, that player Germany bears more responsibility than player Luxembourg. The member states of the Union are unequal – large and small, rich and poor, with long or short external borders, with friendly or hostile neighbours inside or outside the Union. This changes the nature of their association profoundly.

Their inequality is powerfully expressed in the way they deal with Fortune. For a start, each member state has its own geographical position. Germany has long been involved in the economies of Central Europe and other developments there. France feels a responsibility towards the far side of the Mediterranean, from North Africa to the Middle East, where it would like to involve other southern member states. Sweden and Poland have worried about Russia in relation to their spheres of influence around the Baltic Sea since the time of Tsar Peter the Great. And whereas for Sweden it matters little whether or not Norway ever joins the circle, Poland is praying that its neighbour Ukraine will one day be allowed in.

As well as a position in space, each has a place in time. National history is among other things a result of the way in which each state has responded to Fortune – or indeed challenged her – in the past. A world summit on racism and the slave trade resonates differently in London than it does in Warsaw; Indonesia has a different significance for the Dutch than for the Cypriots; the accession of Turkey would have a different impact on the population of Vienna than on that of Madrid; Greece has been indignant for years about the use by its newly independent neighbour of the name 'Macedonia' (Alexander the Great of Macedonia was, after all, a Greek).

In comparison to these sometimes centuries-old, largely nebulous and impossible to formalise sensitivities of all stripes, the joint history of the member states as *member* states is rather limited. Counting backwards from 2013: for the Six it spans only sixty years; for all who have since joined, at most forty years, and for half of the latter less than ten. It would therefore be a miracle if the Twenty-Seven, as if by magic, presented a united front to the world, their heartbeats and dealings all keeping time with a treaty-prescribed rhythm. *Virtù* cannot be forced, any more than fate is predictable.

All the more remarkable, therefore, is the politicisation of the club brought about since 1992 by the Union. It can be seen in more detail in the treaty provisions on foreign policy. With 'Maastricht', the Twelve recognised joint interests, a supreme authority and the right to contemplate a common defence.

The first of these three elements is contained in the stated aim of the Union's foreign policy: 'to safeguard the common values, fundamental interests and independence of the Union'.[110] By attributing to itself interests of its own and independence in its dealing with the outside world, the circle emancipated itself from its members. The second element lies in the institutional set-up, whereby the European Council defines basic policy guidelines and takes strategic decisions.[111] The table of heads of state or government, where the major community decisions had been taken de facto for a decade, had now been given treaty-based tasks for the first time. True, for the moment it was exclusively for those new tasks laid down in the Union Treaty, rather than for the old tasks in the Community Treaty, but the member states had now confirmed that the authority required for engagement in high politics could not be derived from the community sphere. As far as the third element goes, the member states declared that foreign policy 'might in time lead to a common defence'.[112] Despite serious doubts in Britain, Denmark and the Netherlands (on account of possible rivalry with Nato), and in Ireland (on account of its neutrality) – not to mention active opposition from the Americans – this provision was adopted. The taboo on thinking about a European army, which had prevailed ever since the failure of the defence community in 1954, had now been set aside.

The cautious entry by the club of member states onto the stage of high politics revived another old issue – that of the geographical boundary. This, too, had been a taboo subject in the Community for years, but since 1989 it had clearly required urgent attention, especially with aspiring members from behind the Iron Curtain waiting at the door. In reality, the boundary issue was conceptually unavoidable for the Union. Europe now wanted to act in the world, to stride the world stage. For the time being these were just words, but the desire alone implied a showdown with other players and a sounding out of the spheres of influence, including geographical boundaries.

There is one legal eccentricity of the Union that cannot pass without mention. At the summit in Maastricht, the Dutch chairman of the European Council, Ruud Lubbers, supported by Commission President Jacques Delors, had prevented the Union from being given 'legal personality'. Coming after the public humiliation of 'Black Monday', this episode was a less noticeable rear-guard action by defenders of the Community against the breakthrough to a Union. The incomprehensible result was that the Union, a new political association announced with a great roll of drums, had no legal existence. According to some lawyers, acts such as the deployment of troops were not performed by the Union but by 'the member states jointly'. Others believed that the Union could nevertheless act, in practice, as a legal entity. In April 2001, the Council signed an accord with the former Yugoslavia 'on behalf of the European Union'.[113] The Union turned out to exist in a twilight zone, in between having and not having the legal capacity to act.

The Union assumed a flexible shape. Just as its founding treaty was a response to the earthquake of 1989, so successors came along to deal with the after-shocks. The most important of these was the arrival of fifteen new members, mainly from beyond the Iron Curtain. By fits and starts, as laid down in a series of treaties, the member states adjusted their footing to suit the new situation. 'Maastricht' (signed in 1992) was followed by 'Amsterdam' (1997) and 'Nice' (2001). After that – while in the meantime there were new shocks to absorb – came the constitutional treaty (2004) and 'Lisbon' (2007).

This continual legal refinement of mutual relationships was accompanied by increasing tension between large and small countries in treaty negotiations. It was generally attributed to the fact that a relatively large number of small countries were joining. The ratio of large to small went from one to one in the early years (France, Germany and Italy versus the three Benelux countries) to six to twenty-one by early 2013. The growth in membership necessitated the adjustment of institutional mechanisms designed for six, which led to a noisy battle over the veto, weighted voting in the Council, seats in the Parliament and the number of Eurocommissioners. It was a source of despair and entertainment, and of countless newspaper columns. But the tension between large and small went deeper. It flowed from the steadily increasing politicisation of the association. The community corset was being stretched. As well as a Community of equals 'on paper', the club was now formally a Union of member states 'of flesh and blood'.

In the Lisbon Treaty (2007), the legal distinction between the Community and the Union was abolished: the Community disappeared, leaving the Union. The institutions remained the same, on the understanding that the European Council of heads of state or government would now make all the strategic decisions, irrespective of the policy field. The gathering of national leaders also chose to give itself a permanent president, who could represent it externally. The existence of such a figure turns the Union into a single political body. This was the loudly trumpeted counterpart to a silent juridical revolution completed elsewhere in the treaty: 'the EU shall have legal personality'.[114]

New members and the boundary

What to do about the other side of the Iron Curtain? Despite all the heart-warming stories about an 'end of the division of Europe', post-1989 discomfort was evident in the Western European capitals, which would have preferred things to stay as they were.

This was duly noted. Czech President Václav Havel wrote: 'Four years after the fall of communism, it can be said without much exaggeration that this momentous historical event has caused the democratic West some major headaches. For all we know, many a Western politician' – and the author had undoubtedly welcomed many of them to tea at Prague Castle – 'may occasionally wonder, in the privacy of his mind, whether it might not have been a mistake to support the struggles for self-liberation within the Soviet bloc (even though that support was mainly verbal and moral).' The former Czech dissident detected in the West a 'nostalgia' for the days of Soviet domination. The world had been pleasingly simple then, with a clear and understandable enemy who generally opted for the status quo and turned internal differences of opinion into mere trivia. 'All that has vanished', Havel said. 'The old order has collapsed, but no one has yet created a new one. Meanwhile, the "post-communist world" is constantly springing new surprises on the West: nations hitherto unheard of are awakening and want countries of their own. Highly improbable people from God knows where are winning elections.'[115] Polish Foreign Minister Bronisław Geremek, when asked whether his country had experienced *solidarność* on the part of the Community in the early 1990s, declared: 'I have to give you an honest, not diplomatic answer. No, we did not have the impression that there was an expression of solidarity from the side of Europe towards the new countries.'[116]

Headache or not, on 9 November 1989 the Twelve knew that the life of the club was going to change. To adopt a metaphor from German Foreign Minister Joschka Fischer, the 'back wall' of the European house had disappeared,[117] leaving a gaping hole. The Soviet Union left behind it a power vacuum that would need to be filled by a new order if the member states were to address the risks posed by disintegrating economies, unemployment, collapsing state authority, criminality, and possibly even civil wars, producing floods of refugees within and out of the eastern half of the continent. These visitations by fate would not all stop neatly at the external border. After several years of hesitation, the heads of government of the Twelve decided in 1993 to open up their circle, in principle, to the young democracies of Central and Eastern Europe. For the Twelve, the decisive factor was not a desire to enlarge the European market by some 100 million consumers, but rather a realisation that their own security would be served by more stability to the east. The Balkan War that began in 1991 showed that nationalistic rivalries could have as disruptive an effect as before 1939. A failed coup in Moscow in the summer of 1991 was a reminder that the benevolence of the Kremlin could not be taken for granted.

Germany at the very least – the only country to have been split in two by the Cold War – felt the need for an all-embracing European order. The partition of Germany and of Europe had been analysed and reflected on there for decades. In the autumn of 1989, Chancellor Kohl issued repeated assurances that German unity and European unification were 'two sides of the same coin'.[118] In the Strasbourg Parliament, he said: 'Europe is not only London, Rome, The Hague, Dublin and Paris, it is also Warsaw and Budapest, Prague and Sofia – and of course also Berlin, Leipzig and Dresden.'[119] It was an ambiguous charm offensive.

The eastward expansion of the circle after 1989 was not merely driven by Germany: it actually started there. On 3 October 1990, with German unification, East Germany was absorbed into the Federal Republic, making its territory part of the Community. This was geopolitical enlargement without accession. The European dimension was recognised by Bonn: Commission President Jacques Delors and the president of the European Parliament, Enrique Barón Crespo, were present as the only foreign guests at the German–German unification festivities. Although the German situation was exceptional, this nonetheless set a precedent: a former member of the Warsaw Pact now belonged to both Nato and the Community.

The second step in post-Wall expansion was the accession of Austria, Sweden and Finland. These three countries, militarily neutral, had lain in the grey zone between the American and Russian spheres of influence throughout the Cold War. Finland had a 1,200-kilometre border with the Soviet Union, and after 1945, in light of Soviet behaviour in Poland and Estonia, it had been happy to have its independence acknowledged by the Russians. Only after the collapse of the Soviet Empire in 1991 did it dare to take foreign policy steps of its own. Sweden, neutral since 1814, had previously judged that, since member states cooperated on foreign policy, it would do best to remain outside the Community. Austria, occupied by the four great powers as a defeated Nazi ally, had agreed to neutrality in 1955 in exchange for a more rapid withdrawal of Russian troops. Now that the Kremlin no longer cast its military shadow so far and the continent was in flux, opportunities opened up. Economically the three had come together with Norway, Iceland and Switzerland to form the European Free Trade Association. After the departure of its founder and driving force Britain, this lighter institutional structure was attractive mainly to those who were unwilling or unable to be members of the Community. Attempts to create an umbrella organisation to encompass both the Twelve and the Six failed, and at that point Vienna, Stockholm and Helsinki switched from the one club to the other. In 1995, the Twelve became the Fifteen.

The third and fourth steps in eastward enlargement involved the states that reappeared from beneath the Soviet ice sheet in 1989. Poland and Hungary were the first to knock at the door of the Twelve. Others followed. A prolonged ritual ensued at the threshold. Negotiations, sometimes bitter, were accompanied by a broad palette of transitional requirements and time scales. By 1993, the outcome was clear nonetheless. The member states recognised that, as they had written in the founding treaty, 'any European state' could in theory come in. The only remaining uncertainty concerned the terms and the timing. The terms drawn up led to an impressive transformation of the candidates. Constitutions were rewritten, statute books adjusted, European market rules introduced, minority rights acknowledged – anything to be allowed over the threshold. The timing led to a kind of dance between clandestine delay (existing members, all at their own tempo) and acceleration driven by expectations (non-members outside). In the background, Washington urged haste. On 1 May 2004, the first eight of those states whose territories had formerly lain within the Russian sphere of influence entered the Union, along with two Mediterranean islands. Poland was by far the largest of the ten. It became the sixth biggest member state at a table that now required twenty-five chairs. Romania and Bulgaria, which had failed along the way to catch up with their neighbours in their economic and constitutional development, followed in 2007.

The disintegration of Yugoslavia in a series of horrific civil wars (1991–99) was the greatest post-war catastrophe on the European continent. Fortune wreaked havoc in a way that no one had thought possible after 1945. A many-headed monster of violent nationalism left more than 100,000 people dead, over a million homeless and exiled, cities and historical treasures destroyed, and civilians massacred in cold blood. It was an appalling tragedy.

The member states talked a great deal about the violence in their backyard, but they were notoriously powerless even to separate the warring factions. In fact, the club's internal divisions only helped to fan the flames. One diplomatic low point was the unilateral recognition by Germany of Slovenia and Croatia just a few weeks after the Maastricht summit that had decided in favour of a common foreign policy. For a while it seemed as if the European fault lines of

1914 had re-emerged, with Bonn and Vienna supporting the Croats, Paris and London the Serbs. In the end, it was American aircraft that forced a ceasefire between Serbian and Bosnian fighters in 1995, flying over the heads of the dumbfounded Europeans. Although Washington regarded the Balkans as a regional – and therefore European – concern, the Fifteen turned out to be incapable of acting. London and Paris in particular experienced this as a profound humiliation.

Only when it started to look as if the same kind of genocide as had been seen in Bosnia was about to take place in Kosovo did the West, this time including Europe, draw a 'line in the sand'.[120] 'The catastrophe in the Balkans shook the European leaders awake and got them moving, not without pressure from public opinion', was the German foreign minister's analysis.[121] France, Britain and Germany took the lead in a final round of diplomacy between Kosovars and Serbs. When this proved fruitless, they supported the Americans in using force. In March 1999, Nato bombed Serbia. Europe had finally shouldered its regional responsibility. 'Certainly', the French minister acknowledged in 1999, 'it was action by the Europeans, rather than by the Union as such and its institutions . . . but that doesn't detract from the display of cohesion'.[122] This observation applies in equal measure to what happened in Libya in 2011 during the Arab Spring, when it became clear that there was a risk of a bloodbath in Benghazi.

Significantly, the Kosovo War marked Germany's first involvement in armed conflict since 1945. Its government demanded a leading role alongside London and Paris, partly based on its status as current holder of the rotating Union presidency. From 1999 onwards, Europe's largest member state allowed itself once more to fulfil a military role on the world stage. The time of penance seemed to be over.

Following the Balkan implosion, each of the seven Yugoslav successor states – and even Albania – could entertain the prospect of crossing the Union's threshold. Slovenia entered in 2004; at the time of writing Croatia is on the verge of doing so; Serbia, Macedonia and Montenegro are in the waiting room; and accords have been signed with Bosnia. Kosovo, too – since 2008 a de facto protectorate of the Union – has a 'European vocation'. That would bring the total to thirty-four states.

This geopolitical shift eastwards, which has not yet found its final endpoint, has forced the Union to think about the taboo subject of its boundary. In any situation it takes great political self-awareness to create a border, and in the context of the European project it was particularly difficult. The notion was inevitably associated with the old days of interstate diplomacy and the

Concert of Europe, and therefore with the geopolitical balance and the wars from which people were trying so hard to escape in 1950.

The difficulty lies in the east. To the north, west and south, Europe finds its continental geographical outline in the North Cape, the Atlantic Ocean and the Mediterranean Sea, but to the east a broad plain stretches for thousands of kilometres, beyond Kiev, beyond Moscow, beyond the Urals... Where to draw the line? Was it permissible to draw one? Part of the standard repertoire of Brussels rhetoric in the early 2000s was that any eastern boundary to the Union would be 'a new Iron Curtain' and therefore in effect a reincarnation of evil. It seemed as if the problem was being avoided by pushing it farther away after the maxim of Tsarina Catherine the Great: 'I have no way to defend my borders but to extend them.'[123] Although any school-child knew that the European *Osterweiterung* could not continue all the way to Japan, no one was allowed to ask where it would stop.

That reticence is now on the wane. Since 2003, the member states have been working on a politics of 'neighbourhood' (to use the official term). When the ten accession states of 2004 were almost into harbour, attention turned to what lay 'beyond' them. The Treaty of Lisbon, which consistently avoids the boundary issue, includes a prominent article about 'neighbour-hood'.[124] This entails a recognition of the existence of neighbours – not neighbours of member states individually (they have always existed), but neighbours of the member states as a whole. It marks a step towards defining a boundary. The clause calls for spatial self-definition and is therefore part of the association's process of political maturation.

For lack of geographical markers, politics will decide where the eastern boundary lies. One new fact was that in 2000, Russia, after a decade on the ropes, began to manifest itself once again as a great power with imperial ambitions. Russian accession to the Union became unlikely. This at least clarified matters. The question now was: Where does the (potential) zone of the European circle of members end and Russia's zone begin? In the space between, the Ukraine, Moldavia and Georgia are among the countries that regard themselves as in some sense European. The accession of these and other former Soviet republics would now no longer be a response to the Soviet implosion of 1989–91; rather, it would be a new move in the geopolitical game between the European-Atlantic structures and the Kremlin, with the 2008 'August War' between Russia and Georgia as its most violent eruption. The boundary question has yet to be resolved.

To the south-east lies the republic of Turkey. This large country – a self-declared bridge between Europe and Asia, and a member of Nato since 1952 – signed an accord of association with the Six in 1963, knocked formally on the door of the Twelve in 1987, has been part of a customs union with the Fifteen since 1995 and was allowed to become a candidate member in 1999. The current negotiations, under way since 2005, might lead to Europe crossing the Bosphorus. Yet most members, including Berlin and Paris, have in mind a permanent intermediate status. Should the door be opened to Turkey? It is one of the most important questions that the European member states need to answer. The strategic, geopolitical dimension and the symbolic, identity dimension are both imponderables. The question can be put off, but not avoided. The next few years will be decisive. The outcome is impossible to predict.

Finally, within the European geographical space, in the far north-west and at the centre, lie non-members Norway, Iceland and Switzerland, the three remaining members of the European Free Trade Association. They could switch clubs, as the government of Iceland, badly hit by the 2008 credit crisis, wants to do; but no one is forcing their hand.

All things considered, a Union of thirty-five is probable, and forty not unthinkable.

These geographical and political shifts have changed the nature of political Europe. The implications for power relationships in the institutional inner sphere have been much discussed. It is also intriguing that the territory of the Union increasingly coincides with that of the European continent as a whole. The select circle of the Six that set itself up as a vanguard for all European states is gradually becoming harder to distinguish from the broader Concert. The *telos* built into it in 1950 has almost run its course; the high calling, which after 1989 became a duty, is almost fulfilled.

This does not mean that the club has simply enlarged its field of operations. German professor Karl Schlögel said on the eve of the main eastward enlargement: 'Europe is in transition, but not from A to B, as many clever people would have us believe, but from an old situation A, that we all know, to a situation we do not know, either in West or East . . . Western Europe, too, has long fallen outside European history, outside the experiential and lived cohesion of Europe. For "EU-Europe" as well there is a kind of "Return to Europe".'[125]

What it does mean is that the Union is no longer taking the venerable name 'Europe' in vain.

AFTER THE TOWERS

On 11 September 2001, the rotating chair of the European Council, the president of the European Commission and Europe's high representative for foreign affairs found themselves in the dacha of late party leader Nikita

Khrushchev in Yalta, an emotionally charged location. Was this a repeat of the famous meeting that redrew the map of Europe in 1945? No. The trio – Guy Verhofstadt, Romano Prodi and Javier Solana – had travelled to the Crimea for the annual summit of the European Union and the Ukraine.

When news of an attack on New York reached them that afternoon, they broke up their meeting. On the flight back to Brussels, they knew that thousands of people had been in the Twin Towers, but not that the buildings had already collapsed. They had seen no pictures. During the flight, a fairly conventional statement was prepared. The surprise came on arrival at Brussels airport in the early evening. An excited crowd of 250 journalists was waiting. 'Suddenly we realised the news was huge.'[126]

No 'Yalta' this time, but the world had changed.

The end of the end of history

The fall of the Berlin Wall made such an impression on contemporaries that after 1989 it was possible to conceive of it as an event that had put an end to History. It was the final act; the rest would be an epilogue. The notion was supplied with philosophical trappings by American intellectual Francis Fukuyama, who launched his thesis about 'the end of history' (an idea borrowed from Hegel) in the summer of 1989. He claimed that, of the two most basic human desires – for equality, and to be the best – the first had been satisfied by liberal democracy and the second by the market economy. The advance guard – North America, Western Europe and Japan – had achieved both and had therefore reached history's final phase. All other countries would follow. A peaceful world was in prospect.

This self-satisfied take on history pleased the Europeans: never again an unexpected visitor at the door. It was simply a matter of guiding the eastern neighbours towards the finishing line and the job would be done. Even better, their law-based constitutional order looked like a praiseworthy historical precedent. American President Bush said in October 1990: 'I see a world building on the emerging new model of European unity, not just Europe but the whole world, whole and free.'[127]

It took a while for people to realise that the 'end of history' was another term – critics would say an ideological smokescreen – for the *pax americana*, the American hegemony of the 1990s. After the end of the Cold War, that country had become the linch-pin of a unipolar world order, militarily and technologically supreme, the guardian and prime beneficiary of supposedly stateless economic 'globalisation'. In Washington, there was a growing imperialist tendency to cast national interest in terms of a universal mission, and to regard power and virtue as identical. America's military power was the central geopolitical fact. If Europe had been living 'after history' since 1989, then it was nevertheless doing so under the American umbrella.

The terrorist attacks of 11 September 2001 brought rapid change to the West's politico-historical consciousness. Within a few days, American writer and journalist Robert Kaplan had characterised the period 1989–2001 as the 'twelve-year truce'.[128] He was referring to the return of conflict, to a focus on power, to the primacy of national security over universal human rights. Commentators summed up this change as 'the return of history'. It was more than the media thrill of the moment. Those in positions of political responsibility were no less aware of the change. Four years later, German Foreign Minister Joschka Fischer published a book with precisely that title: *The Return of History. The world after 11 September and the renewal of the West.*[129] The consciousness of history that crystallised within days proved remarkably durable.

The shock of 11 September was a double one for Europe. There was a fear of Islamist terrorism at home – the attacks experienced in New York and Washington might well be repeated in London, Madrid or Amsterdam, especially since they had (to some degree) been planned and prepared in Europe. At the same time, there was a new consciousness of American vulnerability. This had a different effect in Europe than in the country under attack. The protector's umbrella was leaky, which made it all the more difficult to claim that there was no such thing.

The immediate gut reaction was an unconditional sense of solidarity. The European Nato ministers decided on 12 September that the clause stating that an attack on one of them 'shall be considered an attack against them all' should come into effect. The European newspapers declared 'We are all Americans'. European leaders competed to see who could be first to the White House (the French president won, followed by the British prime minister and the German foreign minister). It was striking that the Union failed to find a role for itself in those first few days. The German chancellor suggested on 12 September that a summit should be convened, but the idea was rejected.[130] Belgian Premier Guy Verhofstadt, holder of the rotating presidency of the Council, had to admit several times at press conferences that he had not yet succeeded in getting President Bush on the phone: the White House staff taking his calls did not know who he was.

Yet a Europarliamentarian was able to claim just over two months later: 'Bin Laden may have done more for European integration than anyone since Jacques Delors.'[131] The Fifteen had come up with a powerful joint response, as far as their internal security was concerned. On 21 September 2001 – so not immediately after the attacks, but within ten days – the European Council gathered for a special session. The leaders declared that the fight against terrorism was a greater priority than ever. The European Council 'instruct[ed]' the justice ministers to have the most important measures drawn up within three months.[132] This was unusually forceful language (confirming, as the philosopher Carl Schmitt once put it, that emergency situations show who is sovereign). In December, the member states settled upon an agreed definition of 'terrorism'. This meant a start could be made on the harmonisation of criminal law – something that had seemed unthinkable just a few months earlier. At the same time, a political accord was reached on a European arrest warrant (another issue on which fruitless talks had been under way for decades). In the case of certain serious crimes, judges could relatively easily ask another member state to extradite suspects – a drastic intervention in national systems of justice.

Only when emotions cooled a little, and there was a need to define the relationship with the wounded protector, America, did the problems start.

The head of the table

The Europeans supported the Americans unreservedly in their initial foreign policy response to the attacks: the overthrow of the Afghan Taliban regime in October 2001. But when it came to the intended second response by Washington – the overthrow of the Iraqi regime of Saddam Hussein (presented to the American public as part of the same War on Terror) – the Europeans were bitterly divided.

The leaders of Britain, Spain, Italy, Denmark and Portugal, along with those of aspiring members Poland, Hungary and the Czech Republic, expressed unconditional support for Washington's plans in an open letter to the *Wall Street Journal*. By contrast, France, Germany, Belgium and others were fiercely opposed to an American invasion of Iraq. European quarrels had no impact at all on decisions by the White House and the Pentagon. On 20 March 2003, American ground forces crossed the Iraqi border and on 9 April Baghdad fell.

In the shadow of the Iraq War, talks on the future of the Union took place in Brussels between representatives of all the member states and the European institutions. The European Convention, established a year earlier, was beset by self-doubt in the spring of 2003. How could one develop a treaty on a constitution while the member states were divided on a matter of war and peace? It would seem surreal. Yet the Iraq Crisis did not interrupt this ongoing European discussion.

In the self-image of the Convention, foreign policy was a prominent feature. A Union that could speak 'with one voice' on the world stage was, for many convention members, the best result achievable. Perhaps a bit of majority decision-making could be introduced, as advocated by a working group in late 2002 after a lively internal debate. Another recommendation was for the appointment of a European 'minister of foreign affairs'. In reality, work on the relevant treaty articles was quietly sidelined during the Iraq crisis. Let a little time pass, was the watchword.

The Convention eventually concluded that the member states lacked the collective will required for foreign policy (that was obvious), that such a political will could not be wrung out of them by a decree or a treaty (this was harder for federalist hardliners to swallow) and that therefore the best they could do was to make preparations for the future. Around these lines of reasoning, the deputy chairman, Jean-Luc Dehaene, managed to achieve a consensus.

Yet to talk in terms of a 'political will' is rather misleading – as if such a thing could be conceived as distinct from the form in which it expresses itself. Two authoritative authors have written, correctly: 'To suggest, as some analysts have, that only "political will" is needed for governments to coordinate their policies internationally is disconcertingly like Molière's suggestion that all that is needed to cure sleeplessness is a "dormitive potion".'[133] A political will needs a place in which to take shape.

In the Union, the European Council is that place. Gathered round their table, the leaders defined the main outlines of European foreign policy. When they were not in agreement, no progress was made; and when they were in agreement it was. But the longer they sat there together, and the more common interests they had (or at least the more those interests converged with all their different national interests), the more often they managed to agree.

Many found this situation unsatisfactory. Disunity at the top table would make Europe mute. Simply put, there are two means of forcing quarrelling table companions to toe the line: rules and authority. The first option, bringing European foreign policy within the sphere of the treaty, was advocated in the Convention by Europarliamentarians, the Commission, national parliamentarians and representatives of the governments of the smaller countries (although not those of aspiring members). It would mean an extension of competencies already held by the Commission, on trade policy and emergency aid to the Third World, for example. But – should anyone have doubted it – between January and March 2003 it became clear that this option was unrealistic. The representatives of the larger countries, London and Paris foremost among them, did not want to have their high politics bound by the rules of the inner sphere. These two member states had the most powerful diplomatic services, as well as nuclear weapons and permanent seats on the Security Council. While it would cost the smaller states nothing to advocate majority voting on European foreign policy in the name of the general interest, both these 'glorious nations' had plenty to lose. At the same time, Paris and London recognised that joint action was desirable in many cases. Which is why they opted for a table with greater authority.

All member states have a geographical and historical place in the world, with or without their treaty. If you want to join forces, then you are well advised not to regard existing positions, relationships and interests as regrettable relics, but to combine them. This works best where they are compatible.

The idea was to give the European Council a permanent president. The six-monthly rotating presidency troubled the bigger member states in particular, especially with enlargement in prospect. The president of the European Council was the worldwide spokesman for the Union. What if an international crisis broke out while the presidency was in the hands of Malta or the Czech Republic? The growth in the number of members increased the chances of that happening. Leaders of the smaller countries would by no means always have the authority to speak to other political powers on Europe's behalf. The fact that Guy Verhofstadt, a Belgian, had been unable to get through to the White House by phone after 11 September 2001, and that Costas Simitis, a Greek, could do nothing to prevent European division over Iraq in the spring of 2003, were portents. The best option would be to appoint someone to the head of the table for a number of years.

In Paris, this idea had been around for some time. Convention Chairman Valéry Giscard d'Estaing – responsible for establishing the European Council in 1974 – regarded its implementation as his personal mission. President Jacques Chirac supported him wholeheartedly. In the course of 2002, Britain and Spain rallied behind the plan in the persons of Tony Blair and José María Aznar. Based on the surnames of this trio of leaders, there was talk of the 'A-B-C' proposal. Missing from the line-up was the D for Deutschland. Berlin, however, was not keen. The Germans would prefer to reinforce the European inner sphere. As had become the custom, Paris and Berlin put together a compromise. It was made public on 15 January 2003, a week before the fortieth anniversary of the Treaty of Franco-German Friendship, sealed by de

Gaulle and Adenauer.[134] Its essence was this: a permanent president of the European Council and election of the Commission president by the Parliament. This Franco-German deal made the momentum unstoppable. There was to be a permanent host at the table.

Anxious small member states felt the proposal represented a power grab by the larger states and an undermining of the Commission. The conflict, however, quickly moved from the principle itself to the competencies of the permanent president of the European Council. Giscard d'Estaing had made these quite extensive in the draft text, so that all his opponents' energy would be absorbed in cutting them back. The person selected would not be given an office or specific tasks. Eventually a consensus emerged around the central assertion that the permanent president would be the chair of the highest table, and not a president of Europe.

Two sentences in the treaty text are important. (Both ended up, via the treaty on a constitution, in the Union Treaty that came into force in late 2009.) First: 'The President of the European Council shall, at his level and in that capacity, ensure the external representation of the Union on issues concerning its common foreign and security policy.'[135] So the permanent president speaks on behalf of Europe at the highest level. The Union had been appointing a high representative for foreign affairs since 1999, but there was no way he could be sent to see an American or Russian president. That void had now been filled.

The second important line ran: 'The President of the European Council shall not hold a national office.'[136] Within that short sentence lies a revolution. At this particular table, the host has no national seat. (The same had always been true of the president of the Commission, who never chaired the European Council, but whose membership of it did ensure a vital link between the member-states sphere and the inner sphere.) Whereas, under the old set-up, presidents of the Council had always worn two hats – Angela Merkel on behalf of Europe and Germany, Fredrik Reinfeldt speaking for both Europe and Sweden – the permanent president wears only one. This means he can represent the Union as a whole more effectively than the national leaders, or the Commission president, or the president of the European Parliament. He does not speak on behalf of a national capital, nor on behalf of 'Brussels' or 'Strasbourg', but on behalf of all the member states combined. Moreover, he speaks in that capacity not just to non-members, but internally, too, addressing the national populations as well as outsiders.

On 1 January 2010, Herman Van Rompuy, a former prime minister of Belgium, took office as the first permanent president of the European Council. This embodiment of the Union derives few competencies from the treaty. Both he and his successors will be reliant to a large extent on their personal qualities – above all the respect they command from the members round the table and their public charisma – and on events that compel Europe to act. In the early years of Van Rompuy's mandate, it was not so much pressure from the outside world as the crisis surrounding the euro that impacted upon the fabric of the club and coloured its relations with the rest of the world. Fortune can also strike from within.

Realising that history is not over, and that diplomatic missives and emergency aid do not exhaust the Union's foreign policy arsenal, Europe has acted in many parts of the world since 2001 without waiting for institutional reform. On one occasion, it demanded the highest sacrifice from a citizen of the Union.

Until recently, this seemed unthinkable. With some irony, a German intellectual wrote in 2004 (with reference to Jürgen Habermas' constitutional patriotism): 'If the real litmus test of European unity is the willingness "to die for Solana", as the British *Times* once put it, then perhaps reasoned patriotism is simply not enough ... There are certainly no large European conscript armies waiting to be mobilized by the idea that "*dulce et decorum est pro Javier mori*".[137]

The Union has no army. This 1954 taboo remains in force. Yet there is a joint security policy, relying, among other things, on ad hoc collaboration between national armies. It takes a huge amount of telephone traffic, but troops and equipment can be assembled. Sometimes, at any rate; sometimes not. The General in charge, in a small office in Brussels, is clearly sensitive to European ironies: he has spoken of a 'permanent non-army'.[138]

Since 2003, the Union has deployed crisis missions – both military and civilian – outside its boundaries, aiming to improve security and create constitutional structures where they are lacking. In early 2013, operations were under way on three continents, involving thousands of people. These included a military and police mission in Bosnia; an extensive police mission in Kosovo; and an observer mission in the Caucasus to monitor the ceasefire after the Russo-Georgian war of 2008. Other missions provide judges, police officers and border guards for the Palestinian territories, Iraq and Afghanistan.

Since 2008, the Union has also been present in the Gulf of Aden to take on Somali pirates who threaten the security of the thousands of ships that travel to or from Europe via the Suez Canal. In 2012, Europe agreed to send 250 military advisors to Mali to bolster the government's effort to deal with Islamist terrorism. Elsewhere in Africa, European soldiers monitor security, for instance at the point where the borders of Chad, Sudan and the Central African Republic meet.

It was not far from that spot, on Monday, 3 March 2008, that Gilles Polin, a sergeant with a tiny European flag on his French uniform, was killed by gunfire from the Sudanese army. His unit was composed of Swedish, Irish, Belgian, Austrian and French troops, led by a French captain, and the operation as a whole was under the command of an Irish lieutenant-general. Sergeant Polin's funeral nine days later was attended by President Sarkozy, the French interior, foreign affairs and defence ministers, and the high representative of the foreign policy of the Union, Javier Solana.

When, in the summer of 2008, Fortune visited the Caucasus and war broke out between Georgia and Russia, Nicolas Sarkozy was president of the European Council. He did justice to the preparatory work of his predecessors, using the table as a springboard for European *virtù*. Only four days after the start of hostilities, on 12 August, he flew to Moscow and Tbilisi with his minister of foreign affairs to arrange a ceasefire. The initiative was flawed in some ways, but at least the Russian army was prevented from taking the Georgian capital, which had been its intention. Less than a month later, the Kremlin withdrew its forces.

This was beginning to look like European high politics. The Union had acted as a mediator in a matter of war and peace, with the member states turning a war in their backyard into a joint responsibility. No one can have taken such an approach for granted. In 1995, it had been the American air force that ended the civil war in Bosnia, flying over the heads of the Europeans as they watched. Now mediation in the Russo-Georgian conflict had been undertaken without – in fact in spite of – the Americans; Georgia had received funding and military training, perhaps even incitement, from Washington.

It might be argued that Sarkozy was taken seriously by the Kremlin only as a Frenchman and not as a European. France has a considerable army and is a permanent member of the United Nations Security Council. The Slovene prime minister, president of the European Council six months earlier, would probably not have come away from Moscow with a ceasefire. But, conversely, Sarkozy would have been on a less firm footing as merely a Frenchman than he was now that he could speak 'on Europe's behalf'.

What did this mean in practice? Beforehand, on 11 August, Sarkozy rang Chancellor Merkel in Berlin and Prime Minister Brown in London; at aide level he made contact with his fellow leaders in Madrid, Rome and Warsaw.[139] A meeting after his return was attended by the twenty-seven foreign ministers, and it was followed later by a special summit. On a second visit to

Moscow and Tbilisi, in September, Sarkozy was accompanied by, among others, European foreign affairs representative Javier Solana and Commission President José Manuel Barroso. The Frenchman was therefore speaking for both the ancient French state and the power bloc of Europe.

Under pressure from inevitable appearances by Fortune, the Union is clambering up into the outer ranges of high politics. In light of the past, this is remarkable. Crisis control involving European soldiers in Central Africa goes far beyond the diplomacy of mere word and gesture, to which the Union seemed confined as recently as the late 1990s. All the same, it is a good deal less ambitious than – imagine! – trying to keep the Ukrainian Crimea out of the clutches of Russia by dispatching European troops or gunboats. As one minister closely involved with European foreign policy summed things up: 'It's quite something compared to the past. Compared to what's needed, it's nothing.' He concluded with a warning: 'We'll pay a high price for that. History is merciless.'[140]

PART III

THE QUEST FOR A PUBLIC

Courts and aristocracies have the great quality which rules the multitude, though philosophers can see nothing in it – visibility.
Walter Bagehot[1]

Winning Applause

Is Europe real, or does it exist only on paper? And how can we determine whether it is real or not?

This question has a subjective dimension: the difference between a 'real' and a 'paper' Europe has to do with what goes on in the hearts and minds of the people. Its political leaders realise that they derive their combined power from something impalpable, something purely psychological, and are perpetually fearful that it will slip their grasp. In a report written in 1975 at the request of his eight European colleagues, Belgian Premier Leo Tindemans expressed their unease: 'The fact that our countries have a common destiny is not enough. This fact must also be seen.'² It seems that, for the heads of government, rather than a paper Europe as distinct from a real-world Europe, there is a political reality (to them indisputable) that is distinct from the way in which that reality is perceived by the population (a big question mark) – as if the way in which people see it has the potential to make the political reality even more 'real'. How can this be?

Here we encounter the classic enigma of the status of social phenomena. In contrast to the natural sciences, the social sciences (including history, law and philosophy) deal with the meanings attributed to phenomena. Money, governments or marriages exist because we believe they exist. Yet these things are 'objective' in the sense that their characteristics are not merely a matter of taste or moral choice. It is useful at this point to consider the distinction made by American philosopher John Searle between 'brute facts' and 'institutional facts'.³ One brute fact is that the sun is 93 million kilometres from the earth. One institutional fact is that Barack Obama is president of the United States. Brute facts require words to define them, but they exist independently of observation or language, whereas institutional facts can exist only within a social reality.

An institutional fact comes into being when the social acceptance of something (a person, object or event) means a role or function is attributed to it that it would not otherwise have (president, gavel, birthday). Searle speaks of a 'status function'. He gives the example of a tribe that has built a good stone wall around its village to keep out intruders. Imagine the wall crumbles over the years into a low row of stones. Imagine further that this tribe and the neighbouring tribes continue to recognise the row of stones, behaving as if it remains impossible to climb over. The row of stones has acquired the status function of a border. An institutional fact is born.

Most institutional facts – a currency, a language, a country – are part of the social world in which we grew up. We take them for granted. In a way, modern societies are held together by a durable interweaving of institutional facts. Turning this around, a social order cannot be constructed from a standing start: time is always required.

There is something magical about the creation of institutional facts, which can sometimes make us doubt their existence. They have no physical basis. Often they rely on a speech act (like a marriage that is validated by a reciprocal 'yes') or on conventions that go back into the distant past. Anyone wanting to know why such a fact is a fact will not find any solid ground, only randomness and chance.

The way money works illustrates this. Long ago, money existed only in the form of gold and silver coins. Then bankers discovered that they could lock away their gold and hand out promissory notes instead. Eventually it turned out that you could forget about the gold – the notes would suffice. The bank issues banknotes and so long as everyone believes that the money represents the stated promissory value, it is valid. If people lose faith in it, a $100 bill turns back into a worthless piece of paper.

The idea of a floating social order that rests only on long-term collective acceptance seems hard to grasp (to the extent that people think about it at all). It also sounds extremely fragile, as if the whole system could simply collapse. It can: the stock market crash of 1929 and the implosion of the Soviet Empire in 1989–91 were two occasions on which the rug, as it were, was suddenly pulled from under an institution. Similarly, in the credit crisis of 2008, the certainty of monetary value evaporated and bankers felt they were sliding towards the abyss.

This makes the unease of national leaders about whether or not Europe is real easier to comprehend. Tindemans' common European destiny exists only when it is experienced as such. Just like any other institutional fact, it vanishes unless people collectively believe in it. This radical groundlessness is particularly conspicuous when we compare Europe to an institutional fact such as, say, France, which has behind it centuries of history in which its existence was self-evident, and which likes to present itself as a brute fact.

Institutional facts, according to Searle, are supported by the notion of 'We accept'. But this does not tell us who the 'we' are or on what such acceptance is based. First a look at the 'we' and then at the acceptance.

Who can express acceptance of an institutional fact? A group? Those present? A country? A language community? The whole world? It depends on the type of institutional fact.

Take the following example. The Council of Ministers decides on certain matters by majority. To see who expresses the corresponding 'We accept', you only have to consult any European treaty. The Treaty of Rome from 1957 begins thus: 'His Majesty the King of the Belgians, the President of the Federal Republic of Germany, the President of the French Republic, the President of the Italian Republic, Her Royal Highness the Grand Duchess of Luxembourg, Her Majesty the Queen of the Netherlands, determined to lay the foundations of an ever closer union among the peoples of Europe . . .' Another seven such 'recitals' lead up to '. . . have decided to create a European Economic Community and to this end have designated as their Plenipotentiaries . . .' Then comes a list of the ministers and other signatories who 'have agreed, as follows', after which the actual treaty text begins. One of the articles states that, in all normal cases, the Council will decide 'by means of a qualified majority vote'.

Europe's founding treaties operate in a world of 'We the states'. Six heads of state expressed acceptance and twelve governmental representatives signed the treaty. The assent of all six parliaments made majority decision-making an institutional fact. Conversely, the moment one state refused any longer to accept the treaty's content, as France did under de Gaulle in 1965, the fact came under severe pressure. Acceptance by the public was not required. Even should an opinion poll show a large majority of one or more of the populations to be opposed to European majority decision-making, it would continue to exist as an institutional fact, based on its acceptance within the official world of politicians, civil servants and judges.

At the same time, Europe's leaders have sought to extend this 'we'. Some would like to see people consider themselves European. To take one example, the declaration compiled by the heads of state or government to celebrate the fiftieth anniversary of the founding treaty, on 25 March 2007 in Berlin, includes the sentence: '*Wir Bürgerinnen und Bürger der Europäischen Union sind zu unserem Glück vereint'* (officially translated as: 'We the citizens of the European Union are happily united').[4] The leaders were thereby attempting to breathe life into a world of 'We the citizens'.

The nature of an institutional fact changes according to the nature of its 'we', as this example shows. If 'we' means the states, then it is a legal fact – or, more specifically, a fact of international law. If 'we' means the citizens or something similar – the best-known example being the 'We the people' of the American Constitution – then it is possible to speak of a political fact. Seen in this way, the transition from an international legal order to a political order would be the same as that from 'We the states' to 'We the citizens'.

The inherent fragility of institutional facts justifies concern about the ground they stand on. But opinions may differ as to the type of grounding required. Some politicians felt it was sufficient for Europe to remain a legal fact, resting on a treaty and sustained by the 'we' of politicians, civil servants and lawyers. Others believed that Europe must become a political fact, the expression of a 'common destiny' (Tindemans) and sustained by a 'we' that emanates from the general public. The latter were plagued by larger worries. In wishing for a political Europe, they created their own unease, to some degree at least. Perhaps that is testament to their sagacity, but in any case it was a matter of choice. The question of which kind of 'we' is needed to sustain the institutional fact that is Europe – the states alone or the citizens, too – was, from the start, precisely the issue at stake in the political battle.

With 'We the states' it is clear who is speaking; but an appeal to 'We the citizens' must provide some further explanation, especially in the case of Europe, where many citizens are completely unaware that anyone is speaking in their name. It raises a dual question: Who expresses this 'we' and whom exactly does it include? In a modern state, these two questions tend to be answered together. Political representation is about establishing and nurturing the 'we' that is the population.

At this point, the politico-philosophical problem of constituent power arises. How can a group of people give itself a form of government when the representatives who could speak in its name cannot be called into being, logically, until the state exists? It is the paradox of a foundational category of political fact, of a 'We accept that We accept'. A well-known example is: 'We accept that the Constituent Assembly speaks on our behalf'. This produces a vicious circle. Who is qualified to express such a founding 'we'?

The classic philosophical answer invokes a 'state of nature' – the hypothesis that a unanimous decision was taken once, long ago, to introduce majority decision-making or to give power to one or more representatives.

Hobbes, Locke and Rousseau circumvented the problem of representation by looking outside time. Every individual had constituent power, but only outside history, or at the point when history began. That was fine in theory, but for a foundation in the here and now, within time, it resolves nothing. In practice, the only way to break the vicious circle (or at any rate the least violent) has been the bluff used by self-appointed representatives – the bluff, for example, of the framers of the American Constitution in 1787 or the French *Assemblée constituante* of 1789. Those gatherings put themselves forward as the voice of the people and were supported in that assertion both by contemporaries and by later experts in constitutional law, making possible a political foundation within time. The unworkable hypothesis of the state of nature was replaced with the workable fiction of the nation.

This solution had its disadvantages. It concealed the need for unanimity. (Rousseau had written that, before they could be one people, all must first assent; but little was heard of this requirement after 1800.) The best scenario is one in which the people decide in a referendum, by majority, on a constitution compiled by their representatives. Yet still the vicious circle remains, since who decides which question will be put to the vote, and who decides who is eligible to take part in the ballot? When lodged within time, the foundational power lies not with individuals any longer, but with the people as a whole. As a consequence, the constituent power (people, *peuple*, *Volk*) self-evidently encompasses a specific group. The question of which individuals are part of the nation and which are not remains unanswered. In practice, when that question arises the initiative lies with the representatives. They propose an answer and then try to find support for it.

The history of the Frankfurt Parliament demonstrates the close connection between the two questions (who expresses the 'we' and whom does it encompass?). That parliament, with its constitutional ambitions for the German lands that sent it their delegates in 1848, the year of revolutions, recognised the primacy of representation. It therefore did not wait for a single German people to emerge, but simply assembled, and only then deliberated the question of upon whose behalf it was speaking. The choice was between 'Greater German' and 'Lesser German' unity – in other words, with or without the multi-ethnic state of Austria. This was a political choice, not one that could be resolved by dialect studies, historical research or an exegesis of Fichte's *Reden an die Deutsche Nation*. On 27 October 1848, the parliament settled on the compromise of a Lesser German solution plus a rump Austria. In doing so, it brushed aside the wishes of the Austrian emperor, who decided not to take part. It also failed, despite the promise of citizenship through universal suffrage, to delegitimise the existing political institutions in the eyes of the public. Both the Prussian king and the Habsburg emperor were able to stand by their claim to speak 'on behalf of the Germans'. King Friedrich Wilhelm IV of Prussia – elected as German emperor in March 1849 by 290 votes to 248 – refused to accept the imperial crown from the hands of a people's assembly. A few months later, the parliament was dissolved by armed troops and the constitutional bluff ended in fiasco. The *Nationalversammlung* had proved unable to find itself a clearly delineated public. The German people would have to wait some time yet to be founded.

Just as political parties fight for the favour of voters within an existing order (within, to use Sieyès' terminology of 1789, the *pouvoir constitué*), so at a meta-level there is competition for the favour of the individuals on whom that order is based (for their *pouvoir constituant*). In modern constitutional law, individuals are seen as having given up their constituent power once and for all at 'primal foundation'. This is odd: in day-to-day politics, appeal is often made to the constituent power of individuals. It happens every time they are asked to recognise a specific political community or form of government. Think of political messages like 'Become a Scot and take power back from Westminster', 'Become Dutch and give up your Moroccan passport', or 'Join the demonstration for a new constitution'. Such appeals are not targeted at a constituted 'we', but are intended to create or to change the nature and composition of a political 'we'. It is at this meta-level, where the rise and fall of states is ultimately decided, that the battle for the favour of Europe's public is fought.

If the European club wants to make the transition from legal fact to political fact (and many of its representatives say they do), then appeal will have to be made to the constituent power, or part of it, held by individual citizens of the nation states. This appeal will be judged successful when Europe's political representatives can claim to speak and decide on behalf of a collective 'we', without for that reason being dispersed by troops, booed off stage by the press, or punished by voters.

Such representative claims always contain an element of bluff, so we should not be surprised to see European politicians balancing on a tightrope between courageous decisions and political rhetoric. This may invite sarcasm, but it is in the nature of the business. Their balancing act has been going on for over sixty years. The 'we' is not yet in prospect.

Now for the other element of the magic formula 'We accept' that is presumed to sustain institutional facts: the acceptance. What is the source of collective acceptance? The two simplest answers are power and habit.

Take a traffic rule. Why do we stop at a red light even when the street is deserted? Hypothesis one: because of the threat of sanctions. Behind every red light stands, potentially, an all-powerful sovereign, in the form of a camera or police officer with the power to impose fines or even to jail you. Acceptance of the law rests on power. This is a simple model of obedience, with a certain explicatory force. Yet something is wrong here, as became clear, for example, during the riots and looting in Los Angeles in 1992. The police, vastly outnumbered, were not in a position to round up looters. Instead a man was arrested for wielding a gun in an attempt to guard his own shop. The harsh lesson for this shopkeeper was that, even for the sovereign, the rules exist only so long as they are obeyed by a majority. It turns out that power does not come exclusively from above.

Hypothesis two: we accept a rule because – well, because we always have done. From the time you learn to ride a bicycle, you stop at red lights. Initially it is drummed into you that cycling through a red is dangerous because of the cars, but you forget that. It becomes natural. Everyone stops at the lights. This explanation of collective acceptance is inadequate as well. The origins of the habit remain unexplained. From what point onwards is a given institution accepted? Where can the beginning be found? Not every institution rests on a predecessor, however much we might like to believe that it does. It has to start somewhere.

So power and habit cannot fully explain the workings of collective acceptance, even if, in combination, they are quite potent. They have no account of their own origins to offer.

British philosopher of law H.L.A. Hart introduced two useful distinctions to aid our understanding of how collective acceptance works: between primary and secondary laws, and between internal and external perspectives on their enforcement.[5] In doing so, he also sharpened the distinction between institutional facts of the legal and the political kind.

Primary rules are rules of behaviour that are binding for individuals, such as: don't talk with your mouth full; stop at the red light. Secondary rules are rules about rules, such as: mother decides what counts as smacking; a police officer can fine you; parliament can change the law. Whereas a system of purely primary rules (the rules of etiquette, for example) is rather arbitrary and static, secondary rules allow us to talk in terms of 'validity', 'jurisprudence' and 'legislation'. It is in the emergence of such a set of meta-rules that Hart locates the transition from a pre-legal order to a legal order. The transition to a political order is a further step along that road.

As for compliance, rather than looking at power or habit, Hart prefers to talk of the external and internal perspectives on a rule. The external perspective is that of the observer at the traffic lights who concludes that when the red light comes on, there is a good chance people will stop. To him the rule is an observable fact, stripped of subjective elements such as fear, morality or belief. The internal perspective is that of participants in the traffic (or most of them), who regard the red light as a reason to stop. If you ask why they have stopped, they will say: Because the light is red. The rule is a norm, which cannot be questioned. Here lies the difference between 'People accept, apparently' (external fact) and 'We accept' (internal norm).

According to Hart, the combination of these two distinctions (primary/ secondary and internal/external) renders the conditions under which a legal order functions. The primary rules must be observed by all citizens. It matters little whether they have internalised them or simply obey them for fear of punishment. But it is a different matter with secondary rules. The civil servants, lawyers and other representatives of the official world need to internalise those. The ultimate meta-rule, which sustains the whole system, must, to them, be a self-evident norm. The threat that makes a hesitant citizen obey the rules at the traffic lights will not help judges to determine which law is officially valid. Who, after all, can ultimately wield their sovereign's service pistol? In Hart's legalistic vision, there is a strict division of labour between obedient citizens on one side and system-endorsing magistrates on the other. This view can be challenged on the grounds that it may be adequate for a legal system, but not for a political one.

Politics needs the population to accept the secondary rules as well, in a general sense. Blind obedience for fear of punishment is insufficient, although the minimum requirement is hard to determine: it is clearly less than knowledge of the entire constitution or the whole penal code, but rather more than a sheepish 'that's the law'. To put it broadly, a majority of the population must have a sense that these are 'our legislators', 'our judges' – and indeed 'our police'. If this feeling is lacking, then the situation will be experienced as political domination by a foreign power.

This sense of 'our' is something with which every political order wrestles, Europe included. Grumbling about 'Brussels overregulation', for instance, conveys a sense that a European law is not recognised as 'ours': What are *they* meddling with now? Given that Europe is not a brute fact, mere explanation is of little use. So long as 'Brussels' is seen as a foreign occupying power, all attempts to inform will reek of propaganda.

How can we grasp this sense of 'we'? Countless political thinkers have tried to capture this internal, intangible emotion, seeing it as the glue that holds a political community together. Depending on their own perspective and on the prevailing intellectual fashion, they speak of 'people', 'culture', 'demos', 'solidarity' or 'national identity' – notions at the root of an immense social science literature. Yet there is a problem here: all these terms point not to a fact, but to an internal norm. The 'we' lies inside us. It is a question of collective self-representation.

An external observer can say little about a norm that lies on the inside. It is none of his business. He would do better to concentrate on the outside. So how does popular acceptance of the secondary rules of a political order show itself in observable facts? A sporting comparison might help here. During a match, the rules that determine how a player can score are hardly ever put into words. Nevertheless they are used – primarily by those applying the rules. The referee who expresses judgments such as 'out' or 'goal' is comparable to the lawyer or civil servant who makes a statement about validity, such as 'That's the law'. Only when put into practice does an invisible internal norm reveal itself as an external fact. The secondary rules are interpreted not only by the official world, but also by the population – in this case the spectators. What do spectators do? They come to watch. They cheer. And before the referee has approved a goal by blowing his whistle, they stand up from their seats and shout 'Gooaal!' This is one of the ways – visible and audible to any observer – in which the public expresses its recognition of a secondary rule.

The essential role of the public is often forgotten. In enforcing the primary rules it is indeed irrelevant. When the lights turn red, the citizens are merely subject to the law, called to account for any transgressions. Secondary rules are a different story. Jurisprudence and legislation are part of a 'meta-game' in which the rules are specified, applied and changed. This meta-game is not generally played by the citizens, but rather by those who officially apply the law (judges, civil servants) or change it (politicians). Yet the citizens are indispensable to these tasks. The fact that every courtroom has a public gallery, for example, is no incidental detail. It indicates that the verdict concerns not merely the offender, but society as a whole.

No other group needs the presence of the public as much as politicians do. Even a court of law can remain in the shadows, but a parliament requires the limelight. This distinction stems from the nature of a politician's job. Whereas, in principle, a court judgment points to underlying rules (precedents; the constitution), for a political judgment, which changes or introduces a law, there are no underlying criteria. This is logical, since otherwise the law would already be in place. Yet a politician does not act arbitrarily. He changes (or claims to be changing) the rules 'in the name of the people', 'with the general interest in mind', or some variation on that theme. The trick is to make this claim credible. The only observable indication of success is public support – not just in a representative democracy (where the public, as an electorate, evaluates and replaces the players), but in general. No political order can exist unless it has a connection with the public: without the stands, no arena.

The public is fickle. Sometimes it waves flags and shouts 'hurrah' as the king passes by. Sometimes it sulks, staging demonstrations, strikes or protests. Lazing on the sofa, it keeps track of the activities of the players in the political arena. It discusses things in newspapers or 'down the pub' and formulates a view: public opinion. From time to time, it stands up and votes. But there are also moments when the public loses interest, thereby abolishing itself and leaving public affairs behind, abandoned.

However capricious and intangible, the public – that polymorphous presence by which the population shows that it accepts the secondary rules of the political order – is an indisputable fact. An external observer can see it, hear it, sometimes even smell or feel it. The immense importance attached to the public is clear from the zealousness of investigations into the ways it manifests itself: the exhaustive analysis of voting behaviour; the compilation of viewing, listening and mouse-clicking figures; the sounding of public opinion to great depths. Everything seems to revolve around the question: What is the public after? What is going on in the mind of someone who hangs out the flag, sends a letter to a newspaper or dumps a heap of dung in front of a minister's office? Again, a researcher will not be able to fasten upon that emotion. The will of the people is expressed through public facts alone. Instead of trying to fathom the mood of the people like a psychoanalyst, we would do better to take a behaviourist approach. After all, as the French expression goes: *Il n'y a pas d'amour, il n'y a que des preuves d'amour.*

'Tokens of love' are precisely what a political order asks for and politicians hunger after. Their performance must convince. Politicians devoid of the press, of public opinion and demonstrators would be civil servants. Vanity is their virtue.

THREE STRATEGIES

A European political arena craves a public of, well, Europeans. But do they actually exist?

As with 'Europe', in the word 'European' we hear a complex of geographical, cultural, historical, legal and political meanings, which cannot be subsumed by one another. Yet we are not entirely bereft. Again the analysis benefits from a distinction between spheres of action. In the geographical and cultural outer sphere, we encounter different people from those found in the institutional inner sphere. In the 'great Europeans' department, the pigeon-hole where Columbus or Goethe belong has little to do with the one for Monnet or Spaak.

Since the interwar period, interesting shifts have taken place in the use of the word 'European'. These reveal something of the member states' passage to Europe. French politician and author Jean-François Deniau wrote in 1977:

> There are no Europeans any longer! ... Fifty years ago it was completely natural to speak of Europeans when you wanted to distinguish the inhabitants of our continent from Africans, Asians and Americans. Today the expression is old-fashioned and has practically fallen into disuse. If people talk about Europeans at all, it is only to refer to 'European milieus', in other words opinion-making circles or groups of experts close to Jean Monnet's action committee or the Brussels institutions. In relation to the classifications in vogue now, Third World and Eastern Bloc, we are referred to as 'Westerners', or possibly as 'whites' or perhaps 'industrialised countries'.[6]

This is a fascinating observation. In terms of the spheres distinguished in this book we could say that, after 1950, the word 'European' moved from the geopolitical and cultural outer sphere, where it naturally kept company with 'American', 'African' and 'Asian', to the institutional inner sphere, where it acquired an ideological charge and coincided with the architects and builders of Europe. As a result, Robert Schuman's political party was regarded in the 1950s and 1960s as 'the European party', and it was the 'Europeans' who worked hard for British accession. Charles de Gaulle, although a Frenchman, was definitely not a European. A curious paradox: in the years when so much was talked about Europe, the corresponding people disappeared. 'Europeans' dwindled conceptually from the inhabitants of a continent to the supporters of a project.

At this point we are faced with a remarkable gap. Are there no Europeans in the intermediate sphere of the member states? It seems as if the concept crossed over from the continental outer sphere to the inner sphere of Brussels without stopping at the sphere of the members. This is precisely the gap that European politics has been trying to fill since the 1970s. The Europeans that organised Europe seeks as a public are the populations of the member states. Nothing more – no reason for the Norwegians, Swiss and Russians on the continent to think this concerns them – but nothing less either: the diplomats, parliamentarians, civil servants and lobbyists of the Brussels inner sphere are not enough. In other words, the task faced by the Nine of 1977 was to remove the word 'European' from the inner chambers and make it part, at least, of the self-definition of the Belgians, Luxembourgers, Dutch, French, Germans, Italians, Britons, Danes and Irish.

But how can such a thing be achieved?

Modern states deploy all kinds of strategies to gain and hold the attention of the public – from flag-waving and military parades through parliaments and ombudsmen to pensions, road works and free education. These may be combined (the more the better), but it remains possible to discern different traditions. There are three basic forms, three notions that can lend credibility to a sense of 'we Europeans'. These are: 'our people', 'to our advantage' and 'our own decisions'. With a nod to history, we might call them the 'German', 'Roman' and 'Greek' strategies. European politics has taken shape by deploying these three strategies by turns.

The 'German' strategy relies on a cultural or historical identity shared by rulers and ruled. They speak the same language, or believe in the same values and holy scriptures, or have the same customs, or ancestors who fought the same wars. The public is supposed to feel that 'they' (the rulers) and 'we' (the ruled) belong to the same people. Around 1800, German thinkers such as Herder, Schlegel and Fichte turned nationalism (which emerged with and in the wake of the French Revolution) into an intellectual narrative. They felt they were part of a single German culture, which regrettably lacked a state. In their work they wanted to arouse a sense of being a nation. State power would follow. This ideological programme found imitators all over Europe. From London to Belgrade and from Paris to Palermo people used the same strategies to make a national identity visible, or indeed to generate one. A national history, a flag and anthem, national holidays, conscription and compulsory education, the codification of an official language, monuments to heroes, the 'invention of traditions' – these are all familiar elements.

The 'Roman' strategy bases its appeal on the benefits that people derive from a functioning political system. Rulers offer protection. They create opportunities or distribute money. The public they have in mind consists of clients. The reference is therefore not to republican Rome but to imperial Rome – to the Rome in which the citizen had no voice and the populace was mollified with 'bread and circuses'. Of all the benefits that imperial Rome offered its people, security was the most fundamental. The *pax romana* – along with more material benefits such as aqueducts or baths – was a trump card for an empire attempting to bind foreign peoples to its authority.

The 'Greek' strategy, finally, rests on periodic appraisal by the population of representatives who take decisions on its behalf. Sometimes this is supplemented by a direct vote by the people on specific matters. The aim is to ensure that rules and decisions are felt to be 'our concern'. To this end, a democracy gives the public a voice. The origins of the majority principle (on which rest both direct democracy and its modern, representative version) lie in ancient Greece. In the 'Greek' strategy, the public is allocated a remarkably powerful role, and in the long run this increases a state's political capacity to respond to an open future.

The club of European member states plucked ideas and elements from all these traditions. Elections were organised, subsidies paid and prizes awarded, a flag and an anthem were introduced, appropriate heroes were sought, as were ways in which citizens could be protected – and much more besides. Sometimes one strategy became bogged down, so it was replaced with another. It is no surprise to discover that the institutions of the inner sphere, especially the Commission and the Parliament, have fervently sought public favour. By contrast, the intermediate sphere was full of ambiguity. The member states acknowledged that a public of Europeans was undoubtedly useful for the club and took the most important decisions aimed at creating it; but at the same time they did not want to lose their own national publics. The battle for a European public therefore developed into a major arena of combat, with the club and the member states on opposing sides.

In Chapters 7–9 we will look in more detail at this quest for a public, conducted passionately in the inner sphere and half-heartedly in the intermediate sphere of the member states. The analysis is not chronological; rather it looks at the German, Roman and Greek strategies in turn. Each of these approaches has brought some successes, but each comes up against problems of its own.

Since Deniau's observation about linguistic usage in 1977, when the only self-declared 'Europeans' seemed to live in Brussels and Strasbourg, things have changed somewhat. The word 'European' has moved out from those inner chambers in the direction of the intermediate sphere. The populations of the member states have become, to a limited degree, European (or so they tell opinion pollsters). So perhaps the strategies for acquiring a public, which were stepped up in the mid-1970s, have been successful to some extent. We shall examine this further. But something else has happened as well – something both impalpable and profound.

The geopolitical shock of 1989 gave a new charge to the word 'Europe'. The continent, so long divided between America and Russia, became aware once more of its unity. Two developments are particularly striking. First, the boundaries of the circle of members moved outwards to coincide with those of the continent as a whole. This made any political appeal to the geographical and cultural significance of 'Europe' more credible. Second, the spread of Western economic values worldwide, urged on after 1989 by America and known as 'globalisation', has led to astonishing shifts in economic and political power. The 1975 division of the globe into West, East and Third World became meaningless. The Communist Eastern Bloc disappeared as a global power, and in doing so called into question the transatlantic solidarity of the West. The Third World, to the extent that it still exists, has shrunk to parts of Africa, while Asia, with its great powers China and India, is showing renewed self-confidence and South America, too, is clamouring for a place on the stage. In other words, should the inhabitants of the old continent, now almost all united in the Union, one day find themselves feeling they are 'Europeans', then world history will have played an important part in bringing them together.

7

The German Strategy:
Creating Companions in Destiny

Europe will not be the fruit of a simple economic or even political transforma-
tion; it does not truly exist unless it adopts a given system of moral and
aesthetic values, unless it practises the exaltation of a certain way of thinking
and feeling, and the stigmatisation of another, the glorification of certain
heroes of history and the demonisation of others . . . It was not the Zollverein
that made Germany, it was Fichte's Reden an die Deutsche Nation, *and the*
professors of ethics it has produced.

Julien Benda (1933)[7]

In the opening lines of the founding treaty of 1957, the six states wrote that
they were seeking an 'ever closer union' among the peoples of Europe, a
formula included in the treaty to this day. The phrase is indeterminate.
Permanent motion is built in, but no ultimate goal defined. As far as the states
are concerned, the open ending has been intensely debated ('federation',
'confederation', 'league of nations'?). But what about the populations? They are
supposed to keep moving closer. And then what? Must they eventually merge
into a larger whole, or are they to remain themselves, despite years of drawing
together? Which is it to be: singular or plural?

The desire to evoke a single European identity is strongest in the institutional inner sphere. It was here that people set about building Europe, here
that the diversity of nations was seen as a problem and the creation of
'Europeans' as its solution. Cultural politics and identity politics arose
as a natural consequence. A British anthropologist has shown in a
fieldwork study that this federal calling is ingrained in the self-image, the
mentality and the organisation of the Commission and the Parliament.[8]
In this sphere, the implicit leading question was: How do we, the many,
become one?

The member states, by contrast, were hesitant about pan-European identity politics – not all of them perhaps, but always some. Even the introduction
of 'Europe Day', the anniversary of the Schuman Declaration of 9 May 1950, a
holiday for European civil servants, risked being regarded as an attempt at
nation-building: You'll see, step by step, Europe is going to abolish our
national holidays. This response should not be dismissed as oversensitive or
childish. Both sides understand that, in their ties with the public, their very
existence is at stake.

Although diversity is the lifeblood of the sphere of the members, there
was no escaping the need to foster a common identity. Yet here the sense
of 'we Europeans', regarded as essential to the club of member states, is quite
different from its sense in the inner sphere. For the circle of members it is not
a matter of becoming one, but simply of being together. (Note the dual difference: a state of affairs rather than a process; a plurality rather than a unified
whole.) The states do not want to abolish themselves, and this limits their
interest in the question of how they can ever become one. All the same,
they continually face the questions: Why are we together? What distinguishes
us from non-members? The answer determines how they present themselves
to the world and to their own populations. Their peoples want to know
what kind of company they find themselves in. The self-definition of the
circle of member states has therefore always been the focus of a political
battle.

How do we become one?

In the case of the 'German' strategy, the sense of 'we Europeans' that is
prescribed as a firm foundation for a political order is an awareness of a
common identity. For today's Europe, this is extraordinarily problematic.

Not that such a thing is impossible in principle. A broad choice of ingre-
dients presents itself: a language, a culture, a religion, an enemy, ordeals
jointly withstood. So it must be possible to come up with something that
binds all Europeans – or at least distinguishes them from their neighbours. A
politician will not get far, however, with any anthropological, linguistic or
historical definition. For politics, the main question is whether those involved
regard themselves as Europeans. A sense of cultural fellowship cannot (these
days at least) be imposed from above. It is an expression of self-representation.
The most anyone can do is entice the public, influencing it through images,
symbols or stories.

The problem, therefore, is more a practical historical one. Since the nineteenth century, the European states have made great efforts to give their

populations a sense of identity. In the famous words of Italian parliamentarian Massimo d'Azeglio, shortly after national unification in 1860: 'We have made Italy. Now we must make Italians.'[9] Depending on the starting point, the emphasis lay either on the historical primacy of a people, which ought to be able to express its will in a state (the dream of German nationalists like Fichte) or on the formative power of the state, which could mould the masses into a community of citizens (as in France or Spain). Generally speaking, in this respect most European states were extremely successful. The introduction of conscription and compulsory education, a national press, national historical narratives and national holidays all contributed to cultural unification within national borders. There was a willingness to use brute force if necessary: minorities were oppressed; regional resistance – to a ban on the use of dialects, for example – was quashed. The aim was to turn 'peasants into Frenchmen', as Eugen Weber's famous study of the French variant is called. Whether we choose to call the process a civilising offensive or cultural assimilation, the European concert of states of 1815 was transformed in a little over a century into a continent of tightly-knit nation states. Those that were best able to enforce internal unity emerged as the most stable. (The multi-ethnic states of the Habsburgs and Ottomans fell apart in 1914.) No wonder the states would not willingly give up this existential grounding, which they had taken such pains to acquire, nor share it with a rival.

This restricts the space for pan-European identity politics considerably. In a reference to the Italian slogan, contemporary politicians sometimes say: 'We have made Europe. Now we must make Europeans.'[10] As an expression of the desire for a public, these are honest words; but as an analogy with the project of nineteenth-century nationalism, they are misleading. Operation Nation State cannot simply be repeated at a different level. For one thing, all the populations involved now have strong cultural identities; they have become literate nations and can no longer imagine any other existence. A German intellectual has rightly asked: 'But where today are the provincial illiterates who, voluntarily or not, need to be "Europeanised"?'[11] And in modern European society, compulsory assimilation is no longer acceptable. Imposing the use of a single official language by force of arms is out of the question; in fact, any state wishing to be counted among the foremost civilised nations must give official recognition to its own minority languages.

The European founders of the 1950s would counter that they had no wish to create a European nation, and that indeed they saw themselves as deliberately moving away from the nineteenth-century nation state. They identified nationalism as a destructive force – you only needed to look at the recent world wars. In the immediate post-war years, the European idea was as popular as the nation state was discredited.

Examination of the founders' goal reveals an underlying tension. Was the uniting of Europe a peace project or a power project? Peace project: abolish the nations, break the sovereignty of the states in order to take, in Europe, the first step towards world peace. Power project: fuse the nations into a larger whole, combine the power of the states in order to get into a better position, as Europe, to defend joint interests in the wider world. These lines of thought coexisted for many years. Generally speaking, in The Hague, Brussels and Jean Monnet's circles the emphasis lay on the former; in Paris and (initially) Bonn, on the latter.

Each vision requires a different public. In the peace project, Europe is 'above all a moral act',[12] demanding idealism and a willingness to be reconciled. In the power project, Europe is a political act, demanding powers of historical judgment and a redefinition of self-interest. In the former, national citizens need to become denationalised world citizens (or depoliticised consumers); in the latter, committed or even proud Europeans. The peace project requires the attenuation of national identities, so that universal values can be promoted; the power project requires the development of a European identity.

It is possible to see 1973 as a tipping point in the relationship between the two. The peace project lost its urgency as a new Franco-German war became less likely. At the same time, the power project gained in importance as the Cold War and decolonisation drew attention to Europe's dwindling power in the world. These two gradual developments intersected when Britain joined in 1973. From that point on, the member states could collectively speak to the rest of the world 'on behalf of Europe'. It is no coincidence that in December of that year, in Copenhagen, the leaders of the Nine discussed who they actually were as a club of countries facing the rest of the world. The result was a 'Declaration on European Identity' – not just another academic treatise written by intellectuals, but an attempt at self-definition at the highest political level.

The extent to which the European heads of state or government set in train the quest for a European public from 1973 onwards, on several fronts, is striking and rarely remarked upon. Their Copenhagen declaration endorsed the 'German' strategy, and the chance to develop a European cultural politics was seized upon with gusto by the inner sphere. A year later, the leaders agreed on direct elections to the European Parliament, which gave a boost to the 'Greek' strategy. Another year on and, based on the Tindemans report of 1975, they discussed policies that would offer visible and tangible advantages to Europe's citizens, thereby explicitly deploying the 'Roman' strategy.

These moves show that the leaders of the Nine had decided, in effect, that their being together – a legal fact since 1952 – must also become a political fact. The political *telos* contained in the founding treaty, initially tucked away near the start in non-binding declarations, began to have factual consequences. This was a fundamental turnaround. To this day, the member states argue over the 'how' question; but the 'whether' question of a European public was settled in the years after 1973. Once their circle, if on tiptoe, had stepped onto the world stage, it could no longer operate without a public of its own.

Cultural politics

For the inner sphere, the declaration by the nine national leaders that Europe possessed an identity had the effect of firing a starting pistol. Now it was possible to develop proposals for bringing that identity into the open, redis-covering and reinforcing it. Almost inevitably, the Commission and the Parliament settled upon the political techniques of nineteenth-century nation-alism: polishing up a European past as a mirror for us all today; mobilising storytellers and image-makers in the hope of permeating the consciousness of the population.

In 1977, the Commission came up with a package of proposals for cultural policy that was aimed at achieving a free exchange of cultural goods and serv-ices. Given that the founding treaty did not provide for competencies in cultural politics, the Commission was forced to operate under an economic cloak. Yet there were several symbolically loaded plans, such as the idea of 'European rooms' in museums, where 'works which form part of the Community's heritage' would be exhibited, or the establishment of commu-nity cultural institutes and a series of 365 television programmes 'each of which will last five minutes and be devoted to a great European of the past or present'.[13] The Council of Ministers refused to discuss the report. Britain and Denmark led the opposition, silently supported by France and Germany. The issue of joint protection of a cultural heritage could certainly be discussed, but European museums and a gallery of heroes? It reeked of nation-building. Surely, the member states felt, that was not what their club was about.

The Commission's plan to give a 'European dimension' to education came up against a wall of opposition as well. It is perfectly understandable that the Brussels education department gave it a try – had the national leaders not themselves said that a European identity existed? Could history and geog-raphy lessons not perform miracles when it came to reinforcing this identity in young people?

The absolute nadir was the production of a book about European history, intended for a broad readership and published in many languages: *Europe. A History of its Peoples* by Jean Baptiste Duroselle. It told the story of the moral triumph of European unity over the evil forces of division – from Zeus' abduction of Europa via the Romans and Charlemagne to the disasters of nationalism and new hope after 1945. The critics were merciless. The British press pointed to parallels with Soviet-bloc historiography, or 'history in the service of an idea'.[14] The Commission withdrew from the project. The fate of an accompanying school textbook was downright comical. Historians from twelve countries each drafted a chapter and then began arguing over specific words: in the chapter on France, the term 'Barbarian Invasions' had to be replaced by 'Germanic Invasions'; the Spanish description of the English maritime hero Sir Francis Drake as a 'pirate' was dropped. It was clearly going to be hard to agree on a neutral, 'European' version of historical events.

These fiascos provided an uncomfortable lesson: attempts to legitimise the European order by generating a sense of 'we Europeans' could boomerang. Accusations of propaganda were never far away. The strategy of cultural politics was risky.

The Brussels institutions nevertheless made courageous attempts to penetrate the citadel of national identity through the mass media and the film industry. Any revolutionary worth his salt knows that these days you seize power by taking control of the television studios. Translated into a (non-binding) resolution by the European Parliament in 1982, the reasoning was as follows: 'European unification will only be achieved if Europeans want it. Europeans will only want it if there is such a thing as a European identity. A European identity will only develop if Europeans are adequately informed. At present, information via the mass media is controlled at national level.'[15] Ergo, a European television channel was needed. Comparable arguments were used in relation to the film industry.

Monopolies of national media were in any case frowned upon by the Commission. Spurred on by the Parliament (albeit on economic grounds), it took steps to break them. After years of negotiation, a directive entitled 'Television Without Frontiers' was adopted in 1989. It obliged member states to allow access to radio and television broadcasts from anywhere in the Community, at the same time harmonising the advertising market, in the hope that from a common market for television programmes, shared imagery and shared stories would emerge. The unintended consequence was the dominance of English-language television shows, mostly from America.

Europe had been hoping to create a sense of 'we Europeans' and instead got *Dallas* with everything.

When the shortest route to the 'self' becomes impassable, the detour of 'not the other' presents itself. American domination of the entertainment market could be seized upon as a motive for protecting Europe's own cultural sector. This was an old French theme, given greatly increased emphasis after the arrival in Brussels of the French Social Democrat Jacques Delors in 1985: the culture industry as the defender of European civilisation; a crusade against intellectual imperialism. But this rhetorical motif was poorly received by the public and by governments of the more Atlantic member states, such as Britain, Denmark and the Netherlands, so it did not serve to galvanise the whole European club. This was a recurring problem: the relationship with America did not define Europe, but instead split it in two.

Then came a third step in the quest for identity. When the 'self' is elusive and the 'other' provides no defining contrast, only one fallback remains: to conceive of the 'self' as a multiplicity. From that starting point, the Commission developed a film and media policy that could count on acquiescence from member states. One tactic was to stop simply subsidising film production in the hope that through cooperation a European style would materialise, and instead to support the distribution of national productions to other member states by, for example, offering subsidies for subtitling services and distribution networks. A comparable shift can be seen in education policy. Unified European lesson content had led to squabbles, whereas exchange programmes for students, internships for language teachers and an insistence on mutual recognition of diplomas met with a favourable response.

From the perspective of the political quest for a single European public, the emphasis on multiplicity was a withdrawal tactic, but the then-prevalent intellectual fashion for diversity and multiculturalism provided a way to beat the retreat with heads held high. The goalposts were blithely moved. Instead of the cultural construction of a self, it was now a matter of becoming acquainted with the European other. That struck the right note. To this day, European cultural policy – with a budget of hundreds of millions of euro a year – still invokes 'cultural diversity' and 'intercultural dialogue'.

This conclusion can be found in the treaty texts. Ironically, although the Commission and Parliament had long devoted themselves to giving cultural policy a basis in the treaty, when they finally achieved that aim in 1992 ('Maastricht') the text avowed that the Union does not have a single culture. The relevant article tends more towards diversity than unity and avoids the term 'European culture', although it does attribute 'culture' to the states and even the regions. One crumb of comfort was the potential for supporting 'artistic and literary creation' – in other words, awarding prizes, doling out subsidies and compiling reports.[16]

Resistance to the notion of a single European culture as the bearer of a single political order was overwhelming. The member states did not want their citizens to see themselves as European only. Because of this refusal, Brussels cultural politics sought an outlet from the late 1980s onwards in practical cultural exchange and the story of diversity. The inner sphere has found a modest, if essential, role for itself: it strengthens the bond between the populations of the member states without transforming them into one nation.

Yet this did not mean the 'German' strategy was played out. The toolbox of nineteenth-century nationalism has more to offer than that. When any particular cultural content runs up against objections, it is possible to bring images or stories into circulation that are based on universal values, on self-reference, or on empty symbolism. The latter option has proved particularly productive.

Flag

On 29 May 1986, Brussels was witness to a peculiar ceremony. Right outside the headquarters of the Commission, the new flag of the Community was solemnly consecrated. Schoolchildren waved miniature paper versions, while a few civil servants watched, passers-by looked round in surprise and Sandra Kim, a teenage Belgian singer of Italian descent, gave a rendition of the song with which she had won the Eurovision Song Contest a few months earlier: 'J'aime la vie'. Then the blue flag with twelve stars was raised for the first time in its new function, while a choir sang the European anthem. There followed speeches from Commission President Jacques Delors and the president of the Parliament, Pierre Pflimlin, who both expressed the hope that the flag would become a symbol of efforts for European peace.

The ceremony was the culmination of years of lobbying by the community institutions. Strictly speaking, what was raised was not a 'flag' but a 'logo' – that was the semantic compromise to which the ambassadors of the member states had eventually felt able to give their assent. The 'logo' could be printed on a variety of materials – a rectangular piece of fabric, for instance.

A flag is a symbol. It means nothing; instead it stands for something else. Not in the way that a map stands for a landscape or a photograph for a person, but by more or less arbitrary convention – the way a letter represents a sound, or an anchor symbolises hope. There does not have to be any intrinsic connection between symbol and symbolised; in devising a symbol, the most important thing to do is to make the public see the connection as self-evident. As Hannah Pitkin writes, it is 'a matter of working on the minds of people who are to accept it rather than of working on the symbol itself. And since there is no rational justification for the symbolic connection, for accepting this symbol rather than that one, symbol-making is not a process of rational persuasion, but of manipulating affective responses and forming habits'.[17] People who solemnly kneel in front of a cross or raise a flag have formed such habits. By their actions they accept the symbol's significance.

The first raising of the European flag therefore marked a breakthrough. The flag makes the club visible. It says nothing about the identity of that which it symbolises. Rather than pointing to that entity's origins or past, it simply demonstrates that it exists. This is the bare minimum required by the German strategy – form without content, a request for attention and nothing more. Conversely, by its visibility the flag enables the public to express acceptance of the entity symbolised. Many democrats with concerns about Europe's legitimacy would perk up considerably, perhaps in spite of themselves, at the sight of a crowd waving blue flags adorned with a ring of stars.

The breakthrough of 1986 was part of a saga that had dragged on for years. The blue flag with twelve stars originally belonged to the Council of Europe in Strasbourg, which had a parliamentary Assembly whose members wanted their own flag after the example of the European Movement – the green 'E' on a white background was popular in the years around 1950, especially in France and Belgium. It took a contest, several studies of heraldry and protocol, as well as tough negotiations before the fifteen member states came to a decision. The blue flag with a circle of twelve stars was officially raised for the first time in December 1955.

It was at the invitation of the Strasbourg Council that the Community adopted the same flag three decades later, along with an anthem, the 'Ode to Joy' from Beethoven's Ninth. The anthem confirmed Europe's universalistic tendency ('*Alle Menschen werden Brüder*'), while the flag meant it was choosing an identity irrespective of how many members it had: the number of stars is and will remain twelve.

The decision to deploy a symbol was a response to the European elections of 1984, with their worryingly low turnout. The public seemed insufficiently aware of the Community's importance. Several weeks later, at the Fontainebleau summit, the national leaders decided to commission a study into how the Community could 'strengthen and promote its identity and its image both for its citizens and for the rest of the world'.[18] The final report duly concluded: 'There is clearly a need, for both practical and symbolic reasons, for a flag and an emblem to be used at national and international events, exhibitions and other occasions where the existence of the Community needs to be brought to public attention.'[19] The heads of state or government endorsed this recommendation at the Milan summit of June 1985.

The presentation of the idea was more tentative. The report vowed that it 'will be used at appropriate places and on suitable occasions, without of course affecting the use of national flags'.[20] Making the Community visible in citizens' everyday lives would surely help enormously in getting decisions taken by the national leaders implemented in practice. Nonetheless, when a forty-page Commission proposal called 'Council Regulation on the Statute of the European Flag' was produced in the autumn of 1985, complete with ceremonial protocols, sanctions for misuse and so forth, some member states were rather shocked. 'You can imagine Margaret's reaction when this document thuds onto the doormat of 10 Downing Street', the British ambassador grumbled to a colleague.[21] Even its proponents preferred to avoid any discussion of sovereignty, if at all possible. They knew a flag would never be introduced if they expressed themselves in nation-building terms. The chairman of the meeting found a tactical solution by arguing that it was all about a house style, a corporate identity. That proved acceptable. The political connotations of a 'flag' were retracted and the Community was given a 'logo'. Such diplomatic subtleties escape ordinary citizens, so Delors et al. had reason to be satisfied with the symbolic coup. No one has ever flown a logo.

A flag has to win ground by displacing other flags. While the institutions of the Community and the Union can use the flag on its own, in the member states it is rarely seen without a national flag fluttering next to it. This makes it a useful indicator of the specific European sphere in which a building exists or a meeting takes place. The flag's use differs in each member state and is continually changing. French President Sarkozy opted for a state portrait with both the European flag and the French tricolour for distribution to all schools and public buildings, a tradition continued by President Hollande. Britain has proved far harder to convince: the British government refused for many years to add the blue logo with twelve stars to the nation's vehicle licence plates.

At a European summit meeting about the credit crisis, in October 2008, the flags reliably indicated the position of each of the participants in the three spheres of action, neatly reflecting protocol. Invitations to the meeting came from the rotating chair of the European Council, Nicolas Sarkozy. Three other heads of government were present: Angela Merkel, Gordon Brown and Silvio Berlusconi, as well as three representatives of European institutions: Commission President José Manuel Barroso, central banker Jean-Claude

Trichet, and the chairman of the eurozone finance ministers, Jean-Claude Juncker. How were their positions conveyed? At the concluding press conference, the first four sat with little national flags plus the European flag in front of them; the latter three with the European flag alone.

The flag and anthem came close to gaining promotion in 2004. As 'symbols of the Union', they were written into the proposed constitution. After the ratification process ground to a halt, they again became the subject of debate. The Hague, London and Prague, in particular, felt that the flag was too reminiscent of nation-building. It made their home publics uneasy. At their urging, the symbols were left out of the Lisbon Treaty. Disgruntled, sixteen other member states declared that the flag and anthem 'will for them continue as symbols to express the sense of community of the people in the European Union and their allegiance to it'.[22]

The European flag retains, for the time being, its indeterminate legal status. On the one hand, this 'empty' symbol of corporate identity offers the club something firm and recognisable for use in its attempts to establish a bond with the public. On the other hand, the fuss in 2007 over its nation-building implications shows once again how a stab at creating legitimacy can be counterproductive. This is a duality inherent in public life: those who expose themselves to the public may invite either plaudits or ridicule.

There is no way back, no return route to invisibility. Over several decades, the symbol and the symbolised have been united so successfully in the public mind that lowering the European flag for fear of criticism would amount to the self-abolition of the club.

Pantheon

A pantheon is a real or symbolic place in which the heroes of a nation are buried. It helps a community generate a shared past. Shortly after the Revolution of 1789, the French government took over the recently completed Eglise Sainte-Geneviève for the purpose and named it the Panthéon. The French nation, the new bearer of sovereignty, required historical legitimacy to enable it to face down centuries-old royal authority over the population. Mirabeau was the first to be buried there, in 1791, soon to be followed by Voltaire and Rousseau. In name a tribute by the 'nation' to its great men, it can also be seen as an act of self-invention by that nation, which climbs onto their shoulders to discover itself. It is all about generating in the intended audience a feeling of: This is my man, my people, my country.

The invitation to identification does get rather more complicated when several political communities proudly project themselves onto one and the same figure. Was Christopher Columbus a Spaniard or a Genoese? Historians debate the point. Was Franz Kafka a Czech or a German? It depends which library you're in. Hitler a German or an Austrian? You can keep that one.

In the battle over the pantheon, nation states brook no competition. That explains why the Brussels proposals for television programmes devoted to great Europeans were swiftly dismissed by the member states. All the more remarkable, then, that several pan-European heroes have emerged. There was no need to inaugurate museum wings or to erect statues; the trick was to use specific historical figures as names.

The man with the strongest claim in this regard is a universal intellectual from Rotterdam: Erasmus. The exchange programme named after him, which has allocated grants to over 2 million students since 1987, is an example of successful branding. The name 'Erasmus' now resonates with European connotations. He is well suited to the role: in the interwar years, the travelling humanist and great reconciler was described by a French intellectual as 'the perfect symbol of the citizen of Europe'.[23]

Encouraged by this success, the Brussels education department went on to name programmes after such figures as Socrates, Da Vinci, Comenius and Grundtvig. These attempts at Euro-pantheonisation were unsuccessful. In with a better chance is a technological prestige project from 2002 that was given the resounding name 'Galileo'. It is building a European navigation satellite intended to break the monopoly of its American counterpart. But until the satellite begins to function, the public will be more likely to associate Galileo with free-fall acceleration at Pisa than with Europe's command of the heavens.

To judge by these efforts, the Brussels inner sphere sees the European pantheon as populated by universal scholars and artists, preferably those that no nation state can claim as its own. Typical is the way Comenius (Komenský) is introduced on the Commission's website. He has no nationality but was 'born in what is today the Czech Republic' and is not merely the founder of modern pedagogy but 'a cosmopolitan and universalist who strove incessantly for human rights, peace between the nations, social peace and the unity of mankind'.[24] A man with the world as his fatherland. A precursor to and hero of the peace project.

This points to another concrete way out of the difficulty of defining a common identity that can counteract the gravitational pull of the nations: namely, to see Europe not as a 'multiplicity', the promoter of diversity and dialogue, but as the enlightened bearer of universal values.

It is practically impossible for Europe to call anything after a statesman or politician. In European history, the pride of one nation is usually the bane of another. Napoleon a great European? He regarded himself, with his European calling, as 'the successor to Charlemagne, not to Louis XIV'.[25] But the hero of Austerlitz is also the tyrant of Madrid. Since not all Europeans see themselves as reflected in his person, he cannot confer all-embracing legitimacy.

The difficulty of finding historical references makes self-reference all the more appealing. Readily available are politicians who have contributed to the founding and construction of the Community and the Union. In Brussels, Strasbourg and Luxembourg, buildings housing the Commission and the Parliament have been named after men like Adenauer, Monnet, Schuman, Spaak and Spinelli. Monnet's name is particularly popular. It has been attached to academic chairs, research centres and foundations, as well as several schools. Instead of opening up a new source of legitimacy, this strategy reinforces an existing identity.

All five politicians fall into the select category of 'founding fathers'. The term is an ideological programme in itself, grafted onto the American Founding Fathers. We might predict that politicians of the late twentieth century, such as Delors, Havel or Kohl, will eventually be summoned to the political wing of the European pantheon, but the hailing of a *père fondateur* has a rhetorical force that none of these later figures can generate as yet. While the Union's sense of its own existence remains uncertain, it is reassuring to have founders.

Money

During the introduction of the euro, the Dutch grumbled about the disappearance of 'our beautiful banknotes', the loss of much-loved designs featuring lighthouses, sunflowers and snipe. But behind the disappointingly dull euro notes lies a dizzying array of choices in identity politics. Nowhere is the drama of the European search for a public so visible as in the battle over those few square centimetres of paper.

Aside from all the practical and financial aspects so intensively commented upon at the time, the introduction of a new currency involved a symbolic operation of the first order. Oddly, this aspect attracted little public attention. Money exists only by dint of trust in it. The person handed a coin or a banknote has to have confidence that it will be accepted at face value – not just that it is real (as opposed to counterfeit) money, but that it is money at all. This confidence has, for centuries, been underwritten by states. If faith in a state falls away, its money loses all value and is reduced to scraps of metal or paper. The state provides a guarantee by giving the money a symbolic mark, which explains why the design of the euro notes and coins was so important. The central concern was: What should our shared confidence-inspiring symbol be?

A name can itself be a basic symbol of surety. Many currency names refer to the weight in precious metal represented by the coin (pound, lira, peso), while others refer to the issuing ruler (crown, real, ducat) or state (franc, florin), making a connection between money and power. When the European leaders decided in Maastricht to introduce a common currency, they had not yet settled on a name. The unit of the existing monetary system was called the 'ecu'. The term was short for European Currency Unit, but it resonated with the name of an ancient French currency, the *écu* – a trick pulled off years before by the then president, Giscard d'Estaing. The problem for the Germans, who had the strongest currency, lay precisely in that resonance: wary of forfeiting the German public's faith in the common currency, they were eager to avoid a French name. The matter had to be resolved at the highest political level. In December 1995, at the Madrid summit, the leaders opted for 'euro', as proposed by German Finance Minister Theodor Waigel. It was historically neutral and audibly close to 'Europe'. Contentment all round.

As for the images on the coins, the ministers decided in 1996 that there would be a 'national side' and a 'common side'.[26] This was intended to ease the public's emotional transition. Countries could fill in the national side however they wished, so long as the twelve stars of the European logo were worked into the design somehow. For the European side, the heads of government opted in 1997 for an image of the shared territory of the member states. The shifting external border meant that the territory could not render up a permanent image, but the identity game is a subtle one. The winning design comes in three variations. The one, two and five cent coins show a globe with Europe uppermost; the ten, twenty and fifty cent coins feature a map on which the member states have slid some distance apart, like jigsaw pieces; the one and two euro coins show the same map, but with the member states joined up. Three images – three representations. Europe appears first as a single entity seen from outside, then as a multiplicity seen from within, and finally as a unity: continent, member states, club.

When it came to the question of the banknotes, the debate was fraught – and instructive. They were to be uniform across the Union and were to come in seven denominations, ranging from five to 500 euro. They, too, needed a symbol that would turn the notes into 'our money'. (To simplify checks on counterfeiting, it was decided to forgo a space for national content.) While coins generally tend to feature a portrait of the ruling sovereign or a national symbol, banknotes often feature historical characters, famous buildings, or plants and animals with which a nation identifies. In fourteen of the fifteen member states, the historical portrait was a recognised genre. Applied to the common currency, this artistic tradition raised a painful question: which seven 'great Europeans' deserved to be portrayed – and which heroes would have to be left out?

Responsibility for the design lay with the governors of the national banks, united in the forerunner to the European Central Bank. In late 1994, they set experts to work. The task of coming up with three possible 'design themes' was given to a team of historians, art historians, psychologists and professional banknote designers.

What kind of picture would be appropriate? First the experts defined the criteria. The theme needed to 'symbolise Europe, carry a message of European unity'. Moreover, the notes, quite apart from technical requirements such as readability and security, had to be 'acceptable to the EU public'. That would not be the case with a note showing (to return to the example chosen) Napoleon. And the advisory team was determined to include the European flag: 'Regardless of its precise meaning as a graphic model, its real value is that it is accepted as a signal of "common identity"'.[27] The crisp new notes might well prove in dire need of such support.

A list of eighteen themes was drawn up, including cities, landscapes, monuments, great poetic works, maps, scientists, and flora and fauna. The great majority of the themes were rejected on grounds of national bias; seven notes could not represent all fifteen states by means of a person, monument or poem. Yet one series of portraits made it into second place, as 'Heritage'. The front would feature pictures of famous men and women, and the reverse side would have European achievements in related disciplines. For example: 'Beethoven and music, Rembrandt and painting, . . . Charlotte Brontë and literature, Marie Curie and medicine.' The disadvantage remained national identification: 'Famous historical figures will always be linked to their home country.'[28]

Even with plants and animals, national appropriation was feared, 'insofar as most of the Member States have an animal or flower as a national symbol'. The fauna option prompted a rather snide remark: 'Newly independent countries in other continents have portrayed animals on their banknotes because, at least in part, they have little else to incorporate into a design.'[29] In this disdain for decolonised fauna, an implicit self-awareness could be discerned: Europe wasn't born yesterday.

Self-reference could work as an antidote to national identifications. Two proposals took this route. First there were portraits of the founding fathers of the European Union, featuring the quintet of Adenauer, De Gasperi, Monnet, Schuman and Spaak. The 'symbolic value' of this 'affirmation of our common history' would be 'strong'. A disadvantage was that these figures were not well known to the general public – undoubtedly a correct appraisal, but for anyone striving for a European pantheon, a case of giving up right at the start: the founders finished in seventeenth place. The other self-referential proposal came fourth: 'Aims, Ideals and Aspirations of the European Union'. Here the values contained in the treaties could be given a place, 'e.g. common citizenship, the value of diversity, enhanced trade'.[30] A disadvantage seemed to be that such ideals were not typically European. Here self-reference fell prey to the problem of universalism.

A radical figurative break might perhaps be a way out of the national identification bind. With notes featuring only futuristic, abstract shapes, all cultural sensitivities could be avoided. This proposal did well, coming third.

The winning theme was 'Ages and Styles of Europe'. The front of the notes would show portraits of ordinary men and women taken from existing paintings, drawings or sketches, anonymous and distributed across genders and historical periods. The reverse sides would present an interpretation of the architectural style of the era in question and 'convey, without specific reference to any given building, a clear message on the architectural richness and unity of Europe'. The advisory group felt the theme fitted Europe's global image perfectly: 'To almost everyone in the world, Europe is noted for fine arts, beautiful paintings, famous sculptures and great architectural styles.' Indeed, 'while American and Japanese tourists may be unable to name European leaders, they usually know the names of Europe's most famous museums'.[31] The ravages of Europe's history would be included in its common identity after all – as a tourist attraction.

The governors of the national banks followed this advice. In June 1995, they eliminated the one proposal in the top three that featured historical personalities – the Beethoven, Rembrandt, Brontë approach. The two that remained were 'Ages and Styles' and the abstract series. The latter caused few headaches, but 'Ages' invited on board all the dilemmas of European cultural politics.

Again experts were set to work. For the reverse sides they chose seven historical architectural styles, one for each banknote: Classical, Romanesque, Gothic, Renaissance, Baroque and Rococo, the Age of Iron and Glass, and Art Nouveau and Modern. A majority thought it would be 'inauthentic' to use an artistic interpretation of architectural styles, as they had been asked to do, and instead favoured 'real buildings'.[32] Two series of existing buildings were chosen: for the Classical five euro note, the Maison Carré in Nîmes and the Pont du Gard near Nîmes; for the Romanesque ten euro note, Lund Cathedral and the abbey of Mont-Saint-Michel; and so on, all the way to Finlandia Hall and the Rietveld Schröder House for the 500 euro note. All these styles were familiar across large parts of Europe, and by using real buildings the Union would be able after all to gain a firm foothold in European cultural heritage.

The anonymous portraits planned for the front presented a more complex challenge. National attributions would remain possible, it was feared, based on stylistic qualities or the location of the artwork. In the hope that artistic merit would be enough to settle the issue, two series of images were chosen: for Classicism the face of an athlete (school of Lysippos) or the Antikythera Ephebe (anonymous) and so on, down to a photograph of a young woman by August Sander or a self-portrait by Joseph Kutter for the twentieth century.

In early 1996, the bank governors invited competition entries. More than forty came in for 'Ages and Styles' and the non-figurative series. Ten were subjected to opinion polling in the participating member states, and in December 1996 the bank governors opted for the notes by Austrian designer Robert Kalina. His designs can now be found in the pockets of more than 300 million Europeans.

The winner allowed himself a degree of artistic licence. He dropped the anonymous portraits and chose to depict architectural elements on both faces of the notes. He also rejected the 'real buildings' and reverted to the original proposal, the artistic interpretation of a style. All the banknotes in his series show a bridge on the front and a window or door on the back. These architectural elements symbolise both 'the European spirit of openness and cooperation' and 'communication between the people of Europe'.[33] In addition to the (obligatory) flag, Europe is represented geographically in Kalina's design by a map on the 'bridge side' of the notes. Boundary problems were avoided by opting for a slice of the globe that overlaps with Asia and Africa.

The convoluted selection process demonstrates how hard it is to define a European identity. From beginning to end, there was obviously a fear that national identifications would prove more powerful than a European identity. This forced a break with the design tradition of practically all member states: portraits of famous historical characters. The option of using anonymous portraits was rejected on the grounds that even anonymous people might divulge their names and nationalities one day. The central bankers took a wise decision by opting for a note that, in violation of the terms of their brief, included no human faces. The idea of anonymous portraits had awkwardly straddled two different notions. In attempting to find something in keeping with a European artistic tradition, it failed to recognise the primary function of that tradition, which is to represent a specific political community. A note showing an anonymous person is a profoundly different thing from one that shows, say, George Washington. An anonymous portrait represents, as was the intention, only a specific period or style, whereas George Washington, in whatever fashion he is depicted, always represents the American nation.

In the case of a building, people are no longer looking in a historical mirror in search of a member of their own political community. Yet the men making the choice regarded even existing buildings as having too many national connotations. What if, as was originally proposed, the Pont du Gard had been depicted on the 'fiver'? The public would be supposed to think: Yes, that's our (European) bridge. The bankers, however, did not dare take the risk that the public would in fact think: No, that's their (French) bridge. Imagine if, for this reason, the note was not accepted as 'our money'. It would not be money at all.

In successive phases of the design process, every possibility of historical identification was eliminated. Was this fear overplayed? On the one hand, national sensitivities and grudges are not to be trifled with – the fires of a politically-motivated consumer boycott are quick to ignite. The central bankers, whose decision it was, felt responsible for the new currency and wanted to avoid all possible risks. On the other hand, Europe is often a matter of mustering the political courage to overcome national sensitivities. The introduction of the common currency is in itself an example. If European politicians had been called upon to choose the design, the 'real buildings' might have made it into everyone's pocket.

The bankers removed all historical references. Yet they did want to hold onto something recognisable, rather than opting for the radical break represented by the non-figurative notes. After successive phases of anonymisation, an essential element remained: the idea of time and of changes in form. Time was given a beginning, too. Europe, the notes said, was born in Antiquity, has a long history, and cherishes her metamorphoses.

Did this create a link between the European currency and power, constantly – with every cash transaction – reminding the public of the political order that stands behind the money? One visual detail introduces an element of doubt. On the notes, Europe, already alluded to by the name (euro) and present as a historical repository, flag and territory, is represented in a fifth sense by the organisation that issues the currency: the European Central Bank features both as an abbreviation (in five linguistic variations) and in the form of its president's signature. This is the mark of surety that needs to convince the public that the seven pieces of paper are banknotes. The European Bank, however, has a somewhat ambiguous status. It is a bank without a state. Given that not all member states use the euro, it cannot be said to belong to the Union as a whole. The political order underpinning it is that of the 'eurozone', a less than appealing entity which, as yet, lacks a public – although the current economic crisis may have begun to change that. The Bank has actually managed to underline this uncertainty, since the series of initials on the notes is preceded by the international copyright symbol, an additional guarantee that is both strange and counterproductive. It suggests that the Bank is a company attempting to protect its intellectual property, whereas currency counterfeiting should be regarded as a far more serious crime (as it has been for centuries). Money becomes real not through the assertion of a copyright on the design, but through its claim to represent a political community. By including the copyright symbol, the Bank is suggesting that such a claim cannot be substantiated. It is a disturbing lapse.

WHY ARE WE TOGETHER?

While the European inner sphere was agonising over the question 'How do we become one?', in the intermediate sphere of the members the question was 'Why are we together?' This question did not really suggest an assignment or mission, so no great thirst for action resulted; but it did prompt self-examination, with immense political consequences.

Self-examination by the member states over the past sixty years is akin to a gathering around a campfire – a circle of equals swapping stories, reminiscing and taking stock of their place in society. The identity of the circle is determined more by the members than by the rules. Again and again, the possible entry of new members interrupts the conversation. The circle expands. Then a new intimacy has to be found and the stories adapted. The self-definition of the ever-widening circle is not just loose talk; the member states take it extremely seriously. With each fundamental redefinition, from Paris 1951 to Lisbon 2007, diplomats battle over words that are intended to give the club a place in history and in the world. Europe has long wrestled with the tension between its continental promise and its arbitrary membership.

This tension emerged at its founding. The Six represented only a small part of the totality of European states. They had no recourse to the cultural values or historical experiences of the continent as a whole, although that was, nonetheless, a temptation.

In the founding treaty of 1951, the Six recognised that their past was one of 'historic rivalries' and 'bloody conflicts'. They wished to draw a line under precisely those aspects of their history. The founding states described themselves as 'resolved ... to establish ... the foundation of a broad and independent community among peoples long divided'.[34] The prospect of a new beginning would be all the more attractive if it applied to other European countries as well, so the founders laid their association open to 'any European state'.[35] The invitation was repeated in the 1957 treaty.

It was a momentous step from the perspective of cultural politics, carrying within it a promise: today, the Six of us; in the distant future, all of Europe. Because of this teleological turn, additional cultural and historical value could be gained by reference to the continent as a whole; the title 'European Community' need not engender embarrassment thanks to the rhetorical device of the *pars pro toto*. At the same time, the open invitation to non-members made the development of an identity for the circle in the here and now more difficult. Suppose credible stories could be found that helped their populations to grow accustomed to the Six. Would they still be valid for the Seven, the Eight, the Nine, the Ten . . .? The member states eventually came to see that their open door set up a dynamic that did more to alienate the public than to win its loyalty. It kept introducing fresh randomness that was hard to turn into a story.

Of the successive memberships, from six to twenty-seven, only the Six found any historical basis. It was not the same basis, however, as it had seemed at first. They were brought together not by an identical heaven, but by a shared earth.

In the early years, a whiff of Catholicism hung around the Community's campfire. The main founders were Christian Democrats: Robert Schuman in France, Konrad Adenauer in Germany, Alcide De Gasperi in Italy. All three politicians attributed great importance to the Christian faith in the moral (and indeed the general) post-war reconstruction of the continent. As a result, some outsiders saw 'Europe' as a Vatican plot. Anti-Catholic prejudice played its part in the decision by the British Labour government not to join the Coal and Steel Community: the junior minister for foreign affairs noted in his diary that its proponent, Robert Schuman, a pious Christian and indeed a bachelor, was acting under the influence of priests, and that his plan could mean 'just a step in the consolidation of the Catholic "black international"'.[36] The Swedish Social Democrat prime minister, Tage Erlander, was also wary of joining a predominantly Catholic Community. The Dutch Social Democrat premier, Willem Drees, was no more enthusiastic, but his country did take part.

Catholicism forged an affinity between several of Europe's founding fathers, and as a universal religion it offered something of an antidote to nationalism, fitting perfectly with the post-war peace motif – the idea of the European Community as a clean slate. Yet there was no common identity here to build upon; one of the members saw itself as a Protestant nation and another had roughly as many Protestant as Catholic inhabitants. However they might feel about the idea, the Six could not be a Catholic club.

The member states unexpectedly found a historical basis elsewhere. The territory of the Six roughly coincided with the medieval empire of Charlemagne, king of the Franks. He held court at Aachen, extended his territory as far as the Pyrenees, subdued the Saxons in the east and forcibly Christianised them, and in 800 had himself crowned emperor in Rome. The fact that he was called *pater Europae* in certain old manuscripts made the coincidence seem like a gift. A heroic ancestor to talk about round the camp-fire had been tossed into the laps of the Six.

The figure of Charlemagne became fashionable in conservative West German circles immediately after the Second World War. The Nazi regime had tainted any appeal to Germanic or Teutonic roots, whereas the early-medieval Frankish empire was seen as the forerunner of both the French and the German nations. Until 1800, all German emperors had been crowned on Charlemagne's marble throne, which can still be seen in Aachen, while a proud equestrian statue of him stands near Notre Dame in Paris. He reigned before the French and Germans separated, before the 'bloody conflicts' under which the Six wanted to draw a line. With the Treaty of Verdun (843), his grandsons divided the Carolingian Empire into three, opening up a theatre of war now symbolised by that same Verdun (1916). This made Charlemagne a fitting symbol of Franco-German reconciliation. He could also be commended to Catholic and conservative circles for having defended the earthly authority of the pope, and indeed for trouncing the heathen barbarians in the eastern part of his empire – distant predecessors to the Communist atheists from Moscow. In December 1949, prominent citizens of Aachen, the ancient capital, established an International Charlemagne Prize for worthy contributions to European unification. This political award has since grown into a '*gesamteuropäischer Ritterschlag*', as the writer Dirk Schümer put it – an 'all-European accolade'. Charlemagne was used as a symbol so demonstratively that the leader of the West German Socialists, an opponent of the Coal and Steel Community, wrote in the early 1950s: 'We do not want the principles of the Carolingian Empire to serve as the basis for the structure of twentieth-century Europe.'[37]

Charlemagne's image weathered internal German polemics. In 1967, when the Council of Ministers inaugurated an office building for itself in Brussels, it chose the name 'Charlemagne'. This was a powerful piece of identity politics by the Six – except that it came rather too late. By the time the governments moved in four years later, they were about to be the Nine, and even the proud knightly emperor had not made it all the way to the shores of Ireland, Britain and Denmark.

So on 1 January 1973, the members once again faced the question of what they had in common. By their arrival, the three newcomers had knocked the Carolingian historical props away from under the club, allowing political contingency to enter. The lack of firm ground did not result in free-fall, but instead gave wings to the European political body.

The member states decided this time to explain themselves. In December, the nine national leaders, meeting in Copenhagen, published their 'Declaration on European Identity' to tell the world and their own populations who they were. Just as they had two decades earlier, they started out from a shared determination to overcome ancient enmities and a conviction that European unity was necessary to ensure 'the survival of the civilisation which they have in common'. Exactly what that civilisation was proved difficult to say. The best they could manage was a 'diversity of cultures within the framework of a common European civilisation', 'common values and principles' and an 'increasing convergence of attitudes to life'. The outside world was reassured that European unity was 'not directed against anyone, nor . . . inspired by a desire for power'.[38] European identity seemed a thin membrane, difficult to capture in words, between plurality on the inside and a mild universalism towards the outside world. In their political interpretation of these generalities, the Nine found a firmer footing. They wanted to make a strong stand for 'the principles of representative democracy, of the rule of law, of social justice – which is the ultimate goal of economic progress – and of respect for human rights'. Another striking element was that the member states regarded 'the construction of a United Europe' as an aspect of their shared identity. The break with the past in 1950 had by this point acquired a history of its own.

Despite the hollow phrases, this exercise in self-definition by the Nine marks a twofold change of tack in cultural politics. First, a discourse on European values, identity and culture was legitimised by the highest political authority. In that respect, the content of the declaration was less important than the fact of its existence. The 'German' strategy had been officially adopted; we have already seen how it was used in community circles from 1973 onwards as the point of departure for European cultural policy. Second, in Copenhagen the member states defined themselves more explicitly than before as a circle of parliamentary democracies. Perhaps the introduction by newcomers Britain and Denmark of their old and proud national parliaments into the sphere of the member states was a factor here.

It was a self-image that endured for twenty years. Seen from the outside, the Nine did indeed have the aura of a democratic circle. This was clearly demonstrated when, from the mid-1970s onwards, Greece, Spain and Portugal made the transition from dictatorship to parliamentary democracy. The young governments knocked at the door of the Nine. They undoubtedly had the advantages of the common market and European subsidies in mind, but the desire to embed themselves in a democratic environment – think of Spain after the failed coup of 1981 – was a prime motive. The European circle grew from nine to twelve without any difficulty.

By chance, Copenhagen was also the location for the next fundamental decision in identity politics, in June 1993. After the Fall of the Wall, the atmosphere was tense. The circle grouped around the campfire – now disturbed by youngsters from the wrong side of the tracks who believed they had a right to join in the conversation – no longer spun historical tales, since that would mean having to budge up and make room sooner than they wished. For more than three years, the Twelve had been at a loss as to what to do with the Central and Eastern European countries that had reappeared from behind the Iron Curtain in 1989, keen to affiliate themselves with their Western neighbours. Up to this point, the member states had made the aspiring members wait in no man's land. The heads of government did not feel much like accepting into their midst ten poor, weakened peoples with capital cities they might until recently have been unable to name. At the same time, they felt they had no other option; after all, it had been promised in their founding treaty (and the Americans were being fairly insistent as well). By the urgency of their request to join, the outsiders confirmed the identity of the existing circle – it was more than ever an object of admiration and desire – but they also forced the members to resume the process of self-examination.

Reluctance and necessity came together in the 'Copenhagen criteria', the three conditions that a country had to meet in order to join the club: stable democratic institutions, a functioning market economy, and the absorption of 80,000 pages of European legislation. With this package of demands, the leaders walked farther down the track they had indicated twenty years previously, abandoning the alternative path.

On the one hand, the Twelve made explicit their political self-image of 1973: 'we are a club of democracies'. The rough summary of democratic principles was replaced by an exhaustive list – homework for aspiring members. The open invitation to 'other European nations which share the same ideals' was thereby made conditional. The 'Europeanness' of a state now apparently depended on a stage of development, which would be subject to official assessments. Since 1993, the European Council has decided who is European and from what precise moment.

On the other hand, the Twelve dispensed with the identity prose of twenty years earlier. The access to European cultural politics that the leaders had offered was shut off again. This undermined the rhetoric about a shared past or a common civilisation, casting aside a potential source of public legitimacy for the Union. In short, the 'German' strategy was blocked. Consequently, European politics now has to be entirely self-sustaining. The shift may well indicate strength and self-confidence – as in God to Moses: 'I am that I am'[39] – yet it is doubtful whether the consequences of this dramatic decision were adequately thought through.

In Copenhagen 1993, the member states looked the random nature of the political order full in the face. To aspiring members – and thereby, accidentally perhaps, to themselves as well – they said: 'Europe is the way we are.'

This did not put an end to efforts to give a floating political system a cultural or historical grounding. Every time the club introduces fundamental changes, the issue naturally arises again.

When the member states drew up a new treaty in 2002–04, there was discussion over the historical and cultural references to be included in the preamble. Should the introductory passage include Christendom, Humanism, colonialism and world wars? The fiercest confrontation was between those states that wanted to include Christian principles, or even a reference to God (Spain, Poland), and states that were eager to emphasise the secular character of European public life (France, Belgium). Was Europe a Christian club, yes or no? Tellingly, the press and public paid more attention to this question than to many of the institutional reforms discussed at the same time. In the end, the member states found a compromise formula. It runs: 'Drawing inspiration from the cultural, religious and humanist inheritance of Europe, from which have developed the universal values of the inviolable and inalienable rights of the human person, freedom, democracy, equality and the rule of law . . .'[40] Christianity, not named, is thereby neutralised to become a religious tradition and permitted to serve purely as a source of inspiration for democratic political values. The sentence was included in the Treaty of Lisbon. It is a survivor of the constitution episode, the distillation of five years of diplomatic tug-of-war. The circle of governments still insists upon it: not a Catholic, not a Christian, not even a post-Christian club, but a club of European parliamentary democracies.

Over the coming years, the membership issue will again determine Europe's self-image. The Islamic democracy of Turkey, offered the prospect of membership in 1963 and officially in the European waiting room since 1999, is currently interrogating Europe's identity. Is there really a desire to be a club of democracies, without any further restriction? Europe is hesitant, just as it was after 1989, when ex-Communist candidates were made to wait for years. This issue impacts upon the public mood – from Austria to the Netherlands and from France to Poland – far more powerfully than the finicky work going on in the institutional inner sphere. The populations want to know in which Europe they are expected to feel at home.

With or without Turkey, the limits have almost been reached. The tension introduced at foundation between the states of a wider Europe and the select circle of member states has been reduced. If at the time of the Six it was, in all honesty, ludicrous to talk of 'Europe', now three-quarters of European states belong to the Union; and of the remaining non-members, half will join within ten years.

Their accession may well give a new twist to the conversation around the campfire. When the select circle coincides with all the states on the continent, and when the last candidate has either come through the door or been refused entry once and for all, the residual randomness can be downplayed. The geographical boundary may then acquire the appearance of historical inevitability, with a good story of a kind unavailable to the member states since the end of the Carolingian Europe of the Six. The political question of who is European and who is not may shift back from the bureaucratic checklist of accession criteria and transition periods to the continent's actual historical and anthropological experiences. The 'German' strategy will then be able to emerge from the shadows again to offer European identity the mirror of a larger space, a longer past.

***

A writer once claimed to be able to tell blindfold whether he was in Europe or somewhere else. Europe can be heard and smelt, he wrote: barking dogs, church bells, children playing outdoors.[41] Another believes that its typical features include the human scale of the landscape, the coffee houses, and the streets and squares named after statesmen, scholars, artists and writers of the past.[42]

A third writer agrees that Europe has 'a unique visual and auditory landscape that is found outside Europe only in areas where Europeans live'.[43] He is thinking of crosses on particular buildings and in graveyards; the layout of cities and the architecture of public buildings; the script, which, although it comes in several varieties, is clearly different from both Chinese characters and Arabic or other alphabets; the many images in public spaces and in ordinary people's homes; the countless depictions of human figures, including nude men and women; and again the bell-ringing.

Europe as a whole is quite different, according to these writers, from its neighbours Africa, the Middle East, Asia and America. Transcontinental tourists recognise this intuitively. Arriving home from Beijing or Los Angeles, they are aware, for a day or two, that they are Europeans. But this feeling is apparently fleeting and ephemeral. It soon fades amid the dazzling array of languages, states, nations and religions that exist on European soil either side by side or mingled together.

A longer historical perspective can help to solve the enigma. Twenty-five centuries of European history can be interpreted as an interplay between forces moving in the direction of political and cultural unity and uniformity (Romanisation, Christianisation, the Enlightenment) and forces creating division and diversity (migrations, religious reforms, nation-building). In modern times, these have interacted in unforeseen ways. The invention of the printing press was accompanied all over Europe by the displacement of Latin by the vernacular. Competition between princes and states brought not just wars and conflict, but also emulation and exchange. If one country gained overseas colonies, another wanted the same; if one prince built an opera house, others quickly followed suit. It is therefore wrong to regard nationalism purely as a divisive force. The assertiveness of its nations has both divided Europe and made it more of a unity.

Europe's shared space and shared time can be discussed around the nocturnal campfire. When there are no longer any non-members outside the circle, and therefore no need for members to look over their shoulders to see who is still seeking a place, they will be able to forget about the passing of the hours as they stare into the fire of the Occident. A passage will have been completed. Only then, and not before, can the member states say jointly, with conviction, to their publics, using words resonant not just with politics, but with geography and history: 'We are Europeans.'

8

The Roman Strategy:
Securing Clients

*– All right, but apart from the sanitation, the medicine, education, wine, public
order, irrigation, roads, a fresh water system, and public health, what have the
Romans ever done for us?*
– Brought peace.
– Oh. Peace? Shut up!

Monty Python's *Life of Brian* (1979)

The 'Roman' strategy relies on the benefits that a political body brings its
population, such as security, opportunities or money. On the one hand,
these must actually eventuate; to use the prevailing term, there must be
'output'. On the other hand, they must also be noticed, so they need to be
visible, or possibly brought to people's attention. If the public fails to
break into spontaneous applause in response to specific political decisions, it
may perhaps be swayed by publicity campaigns and public relations
stratagems.

Security is the most basic benefit that politics has to offer. As political
philosophers Hobbes and Montesquieu knew, the state justifies its existence
by protecting its subjects against enemy soldiers, robber bands and murderers.
So is peace between member states after their 'Thirty Years' War' of 1914–45
the most important benefit that Europe has conferred on its citizens? Since
the founding pact, no member state has fired a shot at a fellow member state,
despite all the quarrels between them and their wars elsewhere in the world.
The most dangerous wolf in the forest appears tamed. And yet the awarding
of the 2012 Nobel Peace Prize to the Union, for helping to 'transform most
of Europe from a continent of war to a continent of peace,'[44] was greeted with
irony.

Why has this *pax europeana* gained the Union so little respect? There are at least three reasons: American and Russian troops, the invisibility of the European table, and time. After 1945, the continent was divided between two superpowers that would not tolerate war in their own zones. Peace in Europe was not of the continent's own making, but was the product of the *pax americana* in the West plus the *pax sovietica* in the East. In the West, the public showed some degree of gratitude towards Washington for the resulting security. In the East, Moscow made its vassals into police states that, until 1989, terrorised their own subjects. Only after the Iron Curtain came down could Europe demonstrate that its peace was more than a frosty ceasefire and its Union an anchor of stability.

As for the invisibility of the European table, although the founding treaty of 1951 was signed partly as the result of a French and German desire for reconciliation and lasting peace, it did not establish a visible authority able to prevent war. That was precisely the key. The founders' hunch was that a step-by-step interweaving of national interests, economies and possibly currencies would make a Franco-German war 'materially impossible'.[45] The mission succeeded, but the method took its toll. The permanent negotiations between governments are invisible to their populations, who are therefore sceptical when politicians use the 'no more wars' argument to recommend, for instance, a change to the treaty. They understand perfectly well that it is not treaty article such-and-such or the Luxembourg Court that prevents Germany, France or any other member state from invading a neighbouring country. They have no direct experience of the coercion that operates at the European table.

Third, and most obviously, there is the passage of time. The last European war (aside from the Balkan conflict) has faded from the collective memory. The suffering has worn off. Peace between European nations has come to seem natural. This particular form of 'Roman' legitimacy gave the founding act a special glow, but it will not be revived unless we pay the ultimate price of another war.

In the mid-1970s, European leaders began to realise that public support for unification was dwindling. Belgian Premier Leo Tindemans voiced these concerns in a report published towards the end of 1975:

> The European idea is partly a victim of its own successes: the reconciliation between formerly hostile countries, the economic prosperity due to the enlarged market, the *détente* which has taken the place of the cold war, thanks particularly to our cohesion, all this seems to have been

achieved and consequently not to require any more effort. Europe today is part of the general run of things; it seems to have lost its air of adventure.[46]

The prospect of lasting peace in Europe no longer worked as a lure. A new message was needed. The Belgian opted for carefully considered pragmatism.

His report can be seen as the beginning of an explicit European quest for a 'Roman' public. Tindemans is the source of the phrase – part of the jargon ever since – that Europe must be 'close to the citizens'. Its benefits need to be of practical relevance to everyday life. The Belgian premier had in mind measures to safeguard rights and to ensure unrestricted travel within the Community, cheaper international phone calls (even back then) and simplified expenses claims for treatment in hospitals in other member states. He also understood the need to communicate. There was little to be gained from European rules no one knew about. So controls on product quality would have to be broadened, but above all explained better: 'European consumers must be made to understand that they are being afforded real protection against the constant possibility of fraud and other real dangers.'[47] The Community must both protect its citizens and be seen as a courageous protector. As his adage went: 'The fact that our countries have a common destiny is not enough. This fact must also be seen.'[48]

RIGHTS AND FREEDOMS

Two thousand years ago, hauled up before the local authorities in Palestine, the apostle Paul defended himself by saying *civis romanus sum* – 'I am a Roman citizen'.[49] This legal locution gave him access to a Roman judge and spared him from torture in jail. It was the pride of a free man to be able to invoke Roman citizenship.

The European order also grants rights. The Coal and Steel Community created a number of rights for certain industrial workers. Later, other individuals became European rights-holders, as students, consumers or patients, and political rights were established, including the right to vote. The 'political' right that enables voters to participate in law-making is fundamentally different, however, from the 'civil' right of being subject to the law (and will therefore be examined further in Chapter 9).

How do people acquire these rights? They are conferred from above as a benefit, rather than exacted from below as a demand. No European civil rights demonstration has ever marched on Brussels, Luxembourg or any of the other capitals. Instead, what is essentially a barter system has been set up between the states, on the principle of 'you do something for my people in your country and I'll do the same for your people in mine'. Most states were less concerned about 'Roman' legitimacy for the European order than about securing advantages for their own populations. But as soon as rights were created, the club used them as a means of reinforcing its bond with the European public as a whole. This sequence was run through twice, once after the Communities were founded (1951/57) and again after the Union came into being (1992).

Rather than their material scope, of more relevance to the legitimacy that these rights are intended to generate is the answer to the question: From whom can they be claimed? Seen in this way, there are three kinds of European rights, residing with the home state, with another member state and with the Union as a whole. The latter two types affect the relationship between Europe and its public. A Belgian political scientist compares them with two types of constitutional system used by the city states of Classical Greece: 'isopolitics' and 'sympolitics'. The former meant that city states entered into horizontal relationships, such as military alliances, and their citizens were granted access to each other's civil rights. The latter meant that city states had used 'federal' institutions to seal an alliance, perhaps most importantly a democratic assembly for all the citizens of participating states.[50]

Both phenomena exist within the European legal order. The ban on discrimination against nationals of other member states, enshrined in the Treaty of Rome, is pre-eminently isopolitical. It is a fundamental norm that obliges every member state to treat citizens from another member state as equal, within the jurisdiction of the treaty, to its own citizens. The right to ask for subsidies from Brussels or to vote for representatives in the European Parliament is sympolitical. The association between the member states therefore expresses itself to its citizens both in the reciprocal opening up of (existing) national rights and in the development of (new) commonly-held rights.

In practice, isopolitics is the more powerful by far. From a citizen's point of view, European law means primarily the right to work, study, set up a business, reside, consume, receive medical treatment and so forth in another member state. Clearly there are not many tangible advantages for those who stay 'at home' – the vast majority of people, given Europe's limited labour mobility. Indeed, stay-at-homes may encounter problems as a result, in the form of more market competition or the proverbial campervan full of Polish builders parked in the street. The European order gives the benefits of equal treatment only to the footloose.

As so often, the founding moment was decisive. While five governments in the Paris negotiations of 1950–51 were concentrating on the institutional set-up, coal prices and steel quotas, the Italian delegation introduced an element of social politics, insisting that the Coal and Steel Treaty should grant rights to miners and steelworkers. Its motives were both idealistic and economic. Out of the Italian Resistance, a federalist movement had arisen that was influential within political parties and trade unions: as far back as 1943, Altiero Spinelli's federalists had advocated a continental citizenship alongside national citizenship. Italy was also struggling with unemployment. In macroeconomic terms, the country had a labour surplus available for export. The Italian government wanted to increase both work opportunities for its population and the rights of Italians who had already emigrated.

The Italian offensive was successful. Germany and the Netherlands, countries that were also suffering unemployment, had no objection to freedom of movement for the production factor known as labour. By contrast, Belgium (where 50,000 Italians worked in the coal mines) and France feared a further influx of Italian workers. For both countries, the success of the Schuman Plan was a political priority, however, so the Italians got what they wanted: skilled miners could work in any member state; immigrants would receive the same pay as native workers and the High Authority would ensure that there were no unjustified wage reductions.

The result of this clash of national interests was a limited European right that applied only to skilled miners and steelworkers. It was a surprising outcome. If the states had stuck to the usual bilateral migration quotas, this quasi-federal right would not have been created. Italian self-interest found a slot in the Paris negotiations because it spoke the language of Europe's founding moment.

When the Common Market was founded in 1957, the Six extended this right to workers in all sectors, skilled or unskilled. In the Spaak Report (1956) experts had argued that not just goods, capital and services, but also labour (whether employed or self-employed) must be able to move freely in the economic space of the Six. During the treaty negotiations, Italy once again put its case for non-discrimination. Several member states wanted to place additional restrictions on workers' freedom of movement, but Rome played hardball. It threatened to block the free movement of capital – and therefore the investment opportunities for capital-rich member states such as Germany and the Netherlands – if people were not allowed to work wherever they chose within the Community. The result was a deal: both freedoms were included in the Treaty of Rome.

When the agreed transition period ended in 1968, freedom of movement for workers became a reality. 'Thanks to Europe', you could no longer simply be refused by the government of another member state if you wanted to go and work there.

This fledgling socio-economic right then evolved. Once the states had laid out the playing field, representatives of the club became involved in the game, with the Court and the other community institutions on one side, the European Council on the other. They were interested in strengthening the bond between the European order and the public, rather than in any advantages for the national populations.

In its famous *Van Gend & Loos* ruling of February 1963, the Court stressed that the Community was a legal order, 'the subjects of which comprise not only the Member States but also their nationals'.[51] Individuals could appeal to community law, although not through the Luxembourg Court – they had to turn to the judicial system of the member state that had violated their rights. In a series of cases brought to it by national judges for clarification, the Court upheld the principle of non-discrimination on grounds of nationality and extended it to employees in other economic categories named in the treaty, such as service providers and the self-employed, as well as family members of any of the above. This narrowed the scope that member states had for curtailing the rights of residents from other member states by appealing to public order, for example, or public health. The judges now looked not just at each case as such, but out of the corner of their eyes at its consequences for Europe. They expanded the stipulations of the treaty by appealing to its 'spirit', but they stayed on the same essentially functional playing field. Equality of treatment was limited to the individual as a participant in the market.

The national leaders, more explicitly than the Court, regarded European rights as a source of legitimacy for the club as a whole. At the Paris summit of 1974, they asked the Commission to investigate what 'special rights' residents of the member states could be given and whether the abolition of passport controls – in other words, a passport union – might be possible. In 1975, the Commission produced a proposal for freedom of travel.

These plans remained on the shelf at the Council of Ministers. Britain and Denmark claimed that the right to freedom of travel (which would also be valid for residents who were not of any European nationality) required some form of immigration policy and therefore revision of the treaty, which both countries wished to avoid. Other member states, too, were loath to grant migration rights to 'foreigners'. They became even more reluctant over the course of the 1970s, as a result of economic recession, high unemployment and the presence in the old member states of a large number of immigrants from aspiring members Greece, Spain and Portugal.

Nevertheless, the arrival of new members changed the playing field. Like Italy in 1950, the three Mediterranean countries could see great advantages for their citizens in European rights. Because of a fear of mass immigration from Spain and Portugal to the richer north, transition periods were imposed on both countries regarding the free movement of labour (a strategy repeated two decades later with Eastern European accession states). It was a humiliation that Madrid was not quick to forget.

In the autumn of 1989, Spain espied fresh chances. After the fall of the Berlin Wall, the Danish and British standpoint that freedom of travel was not feasible because it would require treaty change no longer impressed anyone. Other member states (Belgium, Italy and Greece foremost among them) were also keen to introduce political citizenship, but the Spanish initiative was decisive. In a letter to his fellow leaders in May 1990, Premier Felipe González advocated the introduction of European citizenship. This longstanding desire on the part of Madrid was repackaged. Freedom of movement for any economic actor within the common market would be made a reality as a matter of course, once there was such a thing as political citizenship of Europe. The premier afterwards explained the issue to his own public: 'A total of 623,965 Spaniards live in other EEC countries. A total of 158,243 citizens of the Community live in Spain. These measures are therefore plainly to the advantage of Spanish citizens.'[52] González was directly deploying the 'Roman' strategy. Europe is in your interests, he told his home audience.

The urgings of Mediterranean and federalist member states produced results. By April 1991, a draft treaty article on 'European citizenship' was ready. Germany and France supported the idea. Of its two customary opponents, Britain and Denmark, the British government had other priorities. It was channelling all its diplomatic energies into weakening agreements on foreign policy and avoiding any obligation to adopt the euro – and anyhow, it did not take terribly seriously the symbolic purport of citizenship. For its part, the Danish government was appeased by the appointment of a European ombudsman after the Danish model. Copenhagen had long advocated this injection of Scandinavian constitutional thinking, which was incompatible with any principled resistance to the creation of European citizens. The Danish government was so keen on the introduction of a complaints desk that it went along with a new statute for those eligible to complain.

On Monday, 1 November 1993, when the Treaty of Maastricht came into force, 300 million people became 'citizens of the Union'. Few were aware of the fact.

The change initially meant little of substance. Under the heading 'Citizenship of the Union', the treaty summarises four groups of rights: the right of citizens to move and to reside freely in the territory of the Union; the right of citizens residing in another member state to vote and to stand as candidates in local and European elections; diplomatic and consular protection by other member states for European citizens, should their own country not be represented in a third country where they need it; and the right to petition the European Parliament and the European ombudsman, and to write to them and to other European institutions in the citizen's mother tongue. This package of rights is almost entirely isopolitical. Three of the four elements concern the reciprocal opening up of existing national rights. The right to petition is sympolitical, but it really amounts to a right to claim isopolitical rights on appeal. Only those holding the nationality of a member state would be citizens – a matter determined by the states themselves. No government was in favour of federal civil rights after the American model, granted by a central authority.

The outcome reveals once again the member states' motivations. At the founding conferences of 1950–51 and 1956–57, as well as in 1990–91, the strongest pressure for rights common to all came from governments that were defending the rights of their own emigrants: in the early years Italy, later Spain. Europe offered their populations an opportunity. Rome and Madrid were successful because the issue had a higher priority for them than for their opponents, and because their efforts were well timed, coinciding nicely with attempts to define Europe's goals. Intended as a 'Roman' benefit for a specific national public, emigrants' rights later turned the populations of all member states into a public that might potentially benefit.

So the member states did not create new rights that formed a direct link between the public and the Union, but instead introduced substitute rights for citizens who had emigrated and could not, or could no longer, exercise those rights in their own states. In a kind of trade-off, countries obliged other member states to treat their citizens as they would their own.

Again the laying out of a new playing field was followed by an expansion of the boundaries. Just as the Court had given the principle of non-discrimination on grounds of nationality an increasingly broad application since the 1960s, so the content of European citizenship has expanded since 1993. To that end, the right to residence was linked to the ban on discrimination. In one controversial judgment, a Frenchman was given the right to a subsidised student loan in Britain. In this 2005 case, the lawyers used words of great purport, saying that Union citizenship was 'destined to be the fundamental status of nationals of the Member States'.[53] It is a formula found in several judgments before and since, further extending the principle of equal treatment for all European citizens.

National leaders have likewise enlarged the concept of European citizenship to please their combined populations. One step was the treaty on a constitution, signed in 2004. At the same time, several of them made their doubts known. Did European rights really benefit their own populations? Austrian Chancellor Wolfgang Schüssel complained in late 2005, partly because of the admittance of German students to Austrian universities, that the Court had exceeded its remit. He was supported by his Danish colleague. Such responses illustrate that not all member states benefit equally from every aspect of the deal.

The ambiguous nature of rights concerning freedom of movement places limits on the 'Roman' legitimacy they confer. They create opportunities for individuals outside their own member states: a Polish plumber in France, a French wine merchant in Germany, a German student in Austria, a Portuguese voter in Luxembourg. Yet although in theory they apply to everyone, these rights and freedoms are not seen as a privilege by the European public in general; sometimes quite the reverse.

The 'Roman' strategy of benefits is at odds with itself. Behind advantages lurk disadvantages. The other side of the coin of increased freedom of movement is greater competition for jobs, which certainly does affect those who remain at home: French plumbers in France, Austrian students in Austria, Luxembourger voters in Luxembourg. There are simply a lot more of them. Which is why the deal entered into by the member states for the benefit of their citizens is good news for cosmopolitan elites or for those with nothing to lose, but is not experienced as beneficial by a majority of the public. The reciprocal opening up of national rights is an opportunity for some and a source of concern to many more.

In the case of the market, increased competition was actually the goal. The entry of more companies onto the field of play leads to greater prosperity. This is a concrete benefit that entails, for example, lower prices; but it is not attributable to a benefactor, European or otherwise. There can be no applause for Adam Smith's 'invisible hand'. Or, as Commission President Jacques Delors once said, people do not fall in love with the single market. So what is the public supposed to do with the information that the European market renders up 'more than 500 euro per person' each year and '3 million jobs'?[54] These benefits are intangible.

When it comes to access to hospitals, student grants or other services provided by the welfare states, the boomerang effect is even stronger. This form of equal treatment demands explicit solidarity – between Finns and Greeks or between Belgians and Bulgarians – which cannot be taken for granted. Given that solidarity was precisely the goal of the quest for a public, this turns out to be a vicious circle. The Roman strategy of rights involves generating a 'we', but because of the isopolitical nature of the system, the strategy itself encounters the need for a 'we'. The goal was: Hurrah, 'we Europeans' can work in twenty-seven countries! The public response has in fact been: Polish builders are coming to take 'our jobs', and Brussels is to blame! This has been especially true of the United Kingdom and Ireland, the only countries not to impose a transitional period after eastward enlargement. The negative effects impact upon the very fabric of the club, yet they are vastly underestimated by the inner sphere. The extension of rights is a strategy that may do more to undermine the Union's legitimacy than to reinforce it.

There is little consolation on offer from those experiencing the positive effects. Travelling without being delayed at the border, settling wherever you like in the French countryside, studying in Barcelona for a year, arranging surgery for your mother over the border: even the select public that actually benefited simply took note of its new rights and freedoms. It seems as if these rights are experienced and valued only when collectively felt to have been infringed. The Poles and other Central and Eastern Europeans who were not immediately given access to the Western European labour markets in 2004 said: We're being treated as second-class citizens. Here was a cautiously indignant 'civis europaeus sum'.

The apostle Paul, after invoking his privilege, was handed over by local officials to the Roman authorities, but the judicial password 'I'm a European citizen' will not see you delivered into the hands of a European protector. At best, perhaps after your case has been heard all the way to Luxembourg, you will be treated no worse than the population of your adoptive country.

PROTECTION

Social security

It was the Roman poet Juvenal, born under Emperor Nero, who famously wrote that the people 'that once bestowed commands, consulships, legions, and all else, now concerns itself no more, and longs eagerly for just two things – bread and circuses'.[55] Bread, or the grain distributed among the capital's proletariat, was not conjured out of the pockets of the divine emperors. Most of it came from the outlying provinces of Sicily and Egypt.

Guaranteeing social security is one of the main tasks of states today. The countries of Western Europe have elaborate systems of support for the poor, jobless, sick, elderly and others in need of help. After the Second World War, the rich states in particular developed astonishingly quickly into systems of collective insurance, in which up to a fifth of the national income was redistributed. Levels of provision and financing, and rights of access, differed greatly between the various national welfare states – Denmark and Italy, Ireland and Austria. Public acceptance of the system rests, first, on each taxpayer's awareness that at some point he might well need state support and, second, on an ideology of solidarity. The entire set-up creates a tight financial and psychological bond between the peoples of Europe and their nation-state insurers – something no one foresaw in 1945.

Compared to the manna of the Western European post-war welfare states, the subsidies, bursaries and other forms of 'bread' distributed by the European inner sphere are paltry. The financial bond between citizens and states is so tight that Europe cannot come between them. The financial resources of the Union are equal to roughly 1 per cent of the aggregate of national incomes. Some discern a greater obstacle to Europe's ties with the public in its members' welfare states (its 'Roman' competitors) than in their national identities (its 'German' competitors). The solution: a single European welfare state. Political scientist Philippe Schmitter has come up with a plan for a 'Euro-Stipendium', a monthly allowance for all citizens of the Union whose income is less than a third of the average, financed by the abolition of the agricultural and regional funds.[56] For a variety of reasons, the concept of European benefit payments is not taken seriously either by politicians or by voters. It would have a huge impact on national economies and would disrupt relations between member states and their citizens.

With pressure on uniform, nationwide support systems increasing in many countries (think of regional tensions in Belgium, Italy and Britain), a European welfare state is barely conceivable. Europe can no more take upon itself the role of *patronus*, protector of the hungry, than it can the *pax europeana*. Collective security and individual social welfare are both out of reach as public justifications for its existence.

There is one exception: agricultural policy. The notorious system of import duties, subsidies and support for producers is, in fact, a welfare state at a European level for one sector only: farming. So for decades it has been the farmers who know where to find Brussels – for noisy demonstrations with hordes of tractors. Those in search of a public should not be put off. Their protests may be disruptive, but for farmers Europe does at least exist.

The emergence of this particular European clientele was not an explicit aim of the founders, but rather an unforeseen by-product of negotiations. It later assumed vast proportions. Immediately after the war, the Western European states were concerned about poverty among farmers and farm-workers, who in Austria, Denmark, France, Germany, Ireland and Italy accounted for 25–40 per cent of the labour force. In the interwar years, dissatisfied farmers had rallied around Mussolini and Hitler at an early stage and in large numbers. The experience of wartime hunger pointed to a need for national self-sufficiency in food. After 1945, therefore, democratic governments were worried. They treated their farmers as providers of a public good. Farming organisations had a disproportionate influence on political decision-making, through agriculture ministers and through parliamentarians from agricultural areas.

The states had essentially two ways of protecting farmers: by keeping competitors out (import duties, import quotas) and by guaranteeing their incomes (farm subsidies, price support, state purchase, export subsidies). Both were deployed at a national level. When, from 1955 onwards, there was talk of a common market, agriculture was included. National protection was transferred to a European level. The intention was laid down in the founding treaty, and its implementation began in the early 1960s. In famous marathon sessions, the Council, urged on by Dutch Eurocommissioner Sicco Mansholt, opted for an extremely interventionist system. Every year since then, the European agriculture ministers have decided annually on the production volumes and prices of, for example, grain, chicken, pork, milk, eggs, fruit, vegetables and wine.

Each member state wanted to protect its own farmers and to support their modernisation; but the result was a 'Roman' attachment of one particular clientele to Europe as a whole. This became clear at a crucial moment. In the French presidential elections of December 1965, the farming electorate – almost a fifth of voters – punished the French president for causing the crisis of the empty chair. Fearful of losing their European subsidies, French farmers deprived de Gaulle of a majority in the first round of voting. After this unexpected humiliation, the president found himself forced to resume his seat at the European table. The agricultural clientele had expressed its gratitude to the club.

Yet the policy damages Europe's image. There is a downside to clientelism. As the slaves in Rome's granaries in Egypt and Sicily could have told the proletariat in the capital, one man's benefit is another's cost – there's no such thing as free bread. The downside became more obvious as the proportion of farmers in the electorate shrank without any resulting decline in agricultural subsidies. Public opinion started to associate agricultural policy with absurd surpluses, subsidies for the richest farmers, and disadvantaged farmers in the Third World. It was no longer seen as benefiting the public. Here lies the dilemma. The inner sphere can gain clients by 'Roman' means, but by doing so it risks losing the support of the general public of taxpayers.

It is striking, too, that criticism of the system has not led to any drastic dismantling. It seems agrarian interests are good at defending themselves. In a national context, farmers, who make up a smaller and smaller proportion of the electorate, might quite conceivably have ceased to receive such income support at some point.[57] This tells us something about weaknesses in the European public arena. Sectoral interests, once interwoven, are practically impossible to disentangle. All member states and all institutions would have to assent at one and the same time, which is improbable – both because this interweaving of interests is a symbol of 'project Europe' (and is therefore above criticism) and because of the absence of parliamentary counter-pressure from a general interest that encompasses the entirety of member states.

Redistribution and solidarity

These difficulties become even more obvious when we look at another major European funding stream: regional policy. After farmers, relatively poor regions are the main beneficiaries of European financing. The money does not go to individuals (or to small family businesses) but to sub-national governing bodies: municipal authorities, provinces, regions or federal states. In the period 2007–13, such grants amounted to a third of the total budget of the Union, around 350 billion euro, and the proportion will be roughly the same for 2014–20. As with agriculture, this redistribution mechanism was put in place at the urging of member states, but the institutions of the inner sphere have used it – far more explicitly than agricultural subsidies – to help legiti-mise the European Union.

Regional policy is a direct consequence of British accession. Reliant on cheap food imports since the nineteenth century, the United Kingdom had a far smaller farming population than the Six. If the rules of the game had remained unchanged, it would have received hardly any European funding. Calculating out loud what proportion of its contributions each member state received back in net terms had been taboo in community circles for many years – because the money had become European. But of course everyone took note. With the arrival of London, the idea arose that the Community could also give money to impoverished cities and industrial regions: Britain had a higher proportion of those than its partners. It was not long, incidentally, before Margaret Thatcher, dissatisfied with the settlement, violated the community taboo on calculating net receipts. She wanted, in her famous phrase, 'our money back'. To the other members, the affront lay, naturally, in that 'our', which bluntly struck out the notion of a European 'we'.

As soon as a redistribution mechanism was in place, it began to take on a life of its own. The poorest states defended it fiercely. In 1991, Spain, which stepped forward as their standard-bearer, managed to have 'the strengthening of economic and social cohesion' included in the Union Treaty as an objective.[58] Solidarity between rich and poor member states was thereby anchored in binding articles. Further lobbying for this manoeuvre had come from the Commission and Parliament, which wanted to use it to give Europe a 'social dimension' (Delors). Community institutions also regarded the regions to which the money was allocated as their allies against the nation states, which were perceived as rivals. If money flowed from 'Brussels' to Galicia or Wales, bypassing Madrid or London, it would create new loyalties. In addition to these predominantly strategic considerations, there was something more fundamental here. The concept of European solidarity worked not just in favour of the poor, but also in favour of the club.

Tellingly, the European benefactor, in good Roman tradition, demands visibility. Tourists will have seen the signs along roads in Spain, Portugal or Greece stating how much money has been received from Brussels for specific construction projects. (Of course, such announcements may arouse jealousy rather than gratitude: 'So *that's* where all the money goes.') Precise rules govern these signs. The European flag must fill at least a quarter of the space, along with the name of the fund in question. There is nothing trivial about this. The European commissioner for regional policy said, in philosophical mood: 'Frankly speaking, this is a policy that is sometimes the only proof that Europe *exists*, if you go to regions that are quite far from national capitals.'[59] A Dutch Europarliamentarian visiting the provinces agreed: 'Money makes Europe visible to residents' and is therefore 'a fine way to generate a European consciousness'.[60] The fear of invisibility is profound.

Regional redistribution policy rests on an alliance between the poorer member states and the institutional inner sphere: the former receive the money, the latter the gratitude – for free, since it is the rich member states that pay, grudgingly or otherwise. This makes for an interesting three-way relationship. Of course, there are critics who condemn all redistribution between member states. In the words of one British Eurosceptic: 'Why should our money go to new sewers in Budapest and a new underground in Warsaw when public services in London are crumbling?'[61] But alongside rich contributors and poor beneficiaries there is a third category, as becomes clear from reactions to the rather more subtle position taken by the governments of Germany, the Netherlands, Britain and Sweden, for instance, which – since the collapse of the aforementioned taboo – have been known as 'net contributors'. They describe as inefficient a system whereby they pay the Union money, which then flows not just to regions in the poorer member states but also to some extent back into their own relatively poor regions. Would it not be better if they managed that tax income themselves, instead of having it 'pumped around' via Brussels? They advocate a partial 'renationalisation' of the regional and agricultural funds.

Strictly speaking, such a book-keeping operation would not reduce net support for poor regions in the poorer member states. Yet the idea does touch a nerve. Renationalisation undermines the notion of European solidarity, to the distress of beneficiaries both financial and symbolic. 'No!' the inner sphere cries in unison; regional policy is more than 'a simple instrument of redistribution', it is 'a main element of the visibility and the legitimacy of the Union'.[62] This reaction shows that the flow of funds is not intended merely to serve the poorest: it also aids Europe's quest for a public. As was the case with agricultural policy, the ideological upgrading of regional policy, based on the concept of 'solidarity', makes the inner sphere's interweaving of the relevant interests more thorough than it could ever have become in a game involving only the rich and the poor.

Does this 'Roman' strategy create a sense of solidarity that encompasses the Union as a whole? Scepticism is called for here. Regional redistribution does not set a specific clientele (of farmers and fishermen, for example) against a general public of taxpayers; rather – and for all to see – it sets rich member states against poor. This puts pressure on relationships around the table.

Financial transfers are always a delicate matter. For many years, the dividing line between rich and poor in Europe ran roughly between northern contributors and southern beneficiaries (Italy, Greece, Spain and Portugal, plus Ireland). Tensions remained limited to bad jokes about the work ethic in 'warm countries'. After the accession of Central and Eastern European states in 2004, the Union's internal prosperity-divide roughly coincided with the former Iron Curtain. This has burdened the redistribution policy with a moral and historical layer of injustice and perceived guilt. It is an emotional cocktail: in the East, deep disappointment at Western indifference and selfishness after 1989; in the West, suspicion at being morally blackmailed on the basis of unfathomable suffering. No amount of clever juggling with objective distribution criteria by sharp-witted civil servants can conceal the underlying structure of the resulting negotiations: 'Why aren't you more generous?'; 'Why aren't you more grateful?' (and so on).[63] There is no financial way out of this conversation.

Even within the context of a single nation, redistribution can be agonising, as became clear in Germany after 1989. In the name of German–German solidarity, high transfer payments were made (up to 6 per cent of the gross domestic product of West Germany), yet suspicion and misunderstanding between *Wessis* and *Ossis* remained. Putting aside their economic merits, it is questionable whether West German financial exertions actually did reinforce the sense of 'we Germans'. Christian Democrat politician Kurt Biedenkopf, originally from the West, but in 1990 elected the first *Ministerpräsident* of the new federal state of Saxony in the East, gained first-hand experience of the problems. It made him hesitant about trying to increase cohesion within the Union by appealing to European solidarity. Biedenkopf points to the fact that social cohesion is required if solidarity between states is to work: 'Legally established duties of solidarity do not confer any inner cohesion upon the Community, rather they presuppose it. For this reason, the European Union must deal carefully with the claims of its citizens from the standpoint of European solidarity.'[64] His main concern is not the balance between contributors and recipients, but rather the cohesion of the club. The visibility of the inner sphere is not the key thing. More important for ties with the public is the emerging European sense of a common destiny. We need to be careful not to demand too much of this new feeling.

The recent euro crisis demonstrated even more clearly that solidarity has its limits. When, in the spring of 2010, it seemed that Greece might be unable to pay its debts, the financial stability of the euro was at risk and the other eurozone countries were forced to step into the breach with more than 100 billion euros in loans. The same scenario occurred with Ireland and Portugal. This was compulsory solidarity, rather than anything sincerely felt. The German gutter press called on the Greeks to sell the Acropolis; the Greek papers responded with references to the Nazi regime. Emergency aid to Portugal was a major factor in the Finnish elections of 2011. (Note that the old financial split between north and south has reappeared.) The euro crisis therefore intensifies national sentiments – in this case, animosity between lenders and receivers of emergency funding – whereas the single currency was specifically intended as confirmation of a desire to live together. The de facto solidarity brought about by the monetary and financial interlinking of eurozone countries is not automatically accompanied by a genuine feeling of solidarity. The tensions between member states that result are potentially greater than those arising from arguments over the Union budget, partly because the sums involved are considerably greater (financial support to Greece alone – admittedly in the form of loans – is already four times the amount paid to poorer regions across the entire Union under the heading of solidarity), and partly because these tensions are not, as with the budget, brought together in a seven-yearly trial of strength around the negotiating table, after which the inner sphere manages the money. Instead, at least for as long as national parliaments retain control of payments, they can flare up at any moment. There is the potential for greater tumult yet.

Results

A modest variant of the Roman strategy emphasises that what is being done really is beneficial. This is less ambitious than offering security or social welfare, but it does present an alternative when neither the full Roman strategy nor the Greek or German strategy is available. In 1975, Leo Tindemans called this approach the 'Europe of the people'. Nowadays, politicians usually speak of the 'Europe of results' or 'of projects'. The depoliticisation it brings about has both strengths and weaknesses.

All kinds of things can be described as 'results': a functioning market; good environmental legislation; scholarships; better border controls; employment opportunities; free debit card payments abroad; cross-border bus connections. In their rhetorical zeal, politicians pile different categories up together, latching onto anything concrete and practical. The weighing of costs and benefits is kept out of sight. European rules may cut costs for all (a single European patent to replace a total of twenty-seven, for example), but we are not usually told that a subsidy for one person is paid for by another, that an opportunity for one means the threat of competition for someone else, or that the protection of workers means more red tape for businesses. Each decision is based on a balance of interests, producing winners and losers, as we all know from experience. In the Roman strategy, the public is sometimes underestimated.

There is one member state in which this functionalist legitimisation seems the only conceivable kind. Since Thatcher, all British prime ministers – whether Conservative or Labour – have asked their partners for 'a Europe which delivers'. They are often criticised for this around the table, since wasn't it all about rather more than that? A common destiny? When this limited 'Roman' tune is sung by other states, too, something has gone wrong.

The summer of 2005 was one such moment. The rejection of the constitutional treaty by the populations of France and the Netherlands was a blow to all member governments. The Union seemed shaky. The 'Greek' strategy of democratic blessing via the ballot box had failed miserably. The voters had said 'no'. The 'German' strategy of a joint identity had encountered resistance: for example, Dutch voters took umbrage at the constitutional status of the European flag. In the precarious situation that followed, a decision was made to fall back on the modest claims of 'Roman' results.

The Commission quickly trimmed its sails to the new wind. On 10 May 2006, its president, José Manuel Barroso, launched his response to the constitutional fiasco: 'A citizens' agenda: delivering results for Europe'.[65] One of its main initiatives followed a year later: mobile telephone companies were forced to lower their roaming rates for calls within Europe, benefiting all consumers who travel abroad with their phones. Every possible effort was made to implement the new rules before the summer holidays, when millions of Europeans turn into tourists ringing home from faraway beaches. Clearly, in the full sense of the term, this was public relations.

The European club cannot play the honourable Roman role of protector, since it is not a credible shield against famine and war. It can present itself to the public only as a deliverer of benefits. This leads to unforeseen problems. Even when everyone has a potential advantage, as with market rights and freedoms, the response is not universally positive. When only a specific group benefits, as with the redistribution of financial resources, the result is bureaucratic clientelism in the inner sphere, along with tension in the sphere of the members. The powerful bond with favoured clienteles – farmers, fishermen, poor regions, universities, European migrants – does not automatically offset mistrust among the general, taxpaying, stay-at-home public. So when deploying the Roman strategy, Europe is always a benefactor to some at the expense of others. Having forgotten that its intention was to create a sense of solidarity that would justify this approach, it has allowed the strategy to backfire.

As well as underestimating the practical disadvantages and costs, the strategy of results evinces a discomforting disregard for the symbolic disadvantages, which are quite often felt in far more intensely emotional terms. The practical advantages Europe brings (its Roman benefits) do not always outweigh a loss of national identity (German costs) or democratic sovereignty (Greek costs). The Dutch government declared in a brochure delivered door-to-door shortly before the 2005 referendum: 'Thanks to Europe . . . you can make free debit card withdrawals abroad'.[66] The caustic response of the 'no' campaign: 'Hurrah! Free card payments. I'd give up over four hundred years of sovereignty for that'.[67]

The Roman quest for a public violates a national 'we' – since ultimately 'we' who are from one member state must pay for, make room for, or share with 'them' from the other member states – without ever managing to constitute an all-embracing European 'we'. It is a strategy that relies on the apparatus of the world of offices and the language of the European project, without in itself making everyone in the European circle conscious of a shared political and historical reality. This fundamental weakness is inherent in any approach to the public as a client or beneficiary. In contrast to 'companions in destiny' or 'fellow citizens', 'co-clients' are unlikely to develop a sense of fellowship. They will merely cause an infuriating crush at the checkout.

It feels just like the Monty Python sketch quoted at the start of this chapter. To the members of the People's Front of Judea, despite all the benefits of Roman rule, Rome was still a foreign occupier. They refused to become a Roman public.

Opinion polls

At the peak of his power – in 44 BC, in a turbulent Republic – Julius Caesar attended a religious festival. Vast crowds thronged the streets. The festivities featured naked young men running through the city, among them Marcus Antonius. At a given moment, to approving cheers, he offered Caesar a symbol of kingship. Caesar, to the even greater joy of the crowds, waved it aside. A second and a third time Antonius offered him the laurels, but each time Caesar declined. And on every occasion the cheers from the public that greeted the offer were drowned out by expressions of joy at his refusal.

This event, which Shakespeare used in the background to the opening scenes of *Julius Caesar*, was debated by contemporaries and later by historians. Some believe Marcus Antonius really had offered to make Caesar king and that Caesar shrank from the offer when he heard the public reaction. Others see it as a piece of theatre designed to assuage distrust of Caesar's ambitions, while some believe it was 'a primitive version of an opinion poll. Uncertain whether to make a move toward regal status, Caesar decided to use this experiment at a mass festival to test the people's support'.[68]

How does a political body that derives its legitimacy mainly from the benefits it confers know what its people want? In the 'German' strategy of identity, the problem does not arise; in the 'Greek' strategy of democracy, there is regular use of the ballot box. The 'Roman' approach has to find other ways of knowing what the public is after, such as asking it. Opinion polls are part of the standard toolkit of modern politics.

One department within the Commission is wholly devoted to canvassing opinions. Note that it was established in 1973. It belongs within a larger history: in this respect, too, the year of British accession brought a breakthrough in Europe's quest for a public. But there was a smaller history as well. The arrival of three new member states on 1 January 1973 necessitated adjustments to the civil service apparatus of the Commission that meant one French director-general would have to go. Fate chose Jean-Jacques Rabier, formerly Jean Monnet's *chef de cabinet*. He suggested staying on as a 'special advisor' to the Commission in order to start systematic opinion polling. The result was the Eurobarometer.[69]

Every six months, the Eurobarometer monitors beliefs about integration in the member states. What is Europe's image? How much confidence is there in its institutions? How many people can describe the flag? What should Europe do? The data, collected in interviews by national bureaus, are broken down by member state. In the results for June 2012, we read that trust in the Union had fallen to 31 per cent, just above the level for national political institutions, while 84 per cent of respondents believed that member states will have to work more closely together because of the crisis.[70] An earlier poll, on the consequences of the Fall of the Wall, was described as demonstrating that 'just over a quarter of Europeans' (26 per cent) believed it had benefited them personally, while the accompanying tables showed that a total of 63 per cent thought they were 'not really' or 'not at all' better off as a result.[71]

The Eurobarometer's main significance does not lie in the figures and their always disputable presentation. More fundamentally, it creates European public opinion as an institutional fact, which (strictly speaking) did not exist before 1973. An assertion such as 'A majority of Europeans expect of the Community that . . .' was given meaning only in and through opinion polling. The Commission thereby supplied itself with an excellent instrument for speaking on behalf of Europeans to the member states. It knew what it was doing, of course. In a commemorative essay collection, the legendary Emile Noël, who had been active in the European movement since 1945 and who, as its most senior civil servant (1958–87), gave the Commission its mix of European mission and French bureaucratic culture, wrote: 'For a long time now, the Eurobarometer surveys have helped the community institutions and activists working for the cause of European integration to sustain confidence despite the setbacks, to stay on course through fair weather and foul, and to safeguard existing gains come what may, so as to provide a foundation for survival.'[72] Noël, the conscience of the inner sphere, was acknowledging the political significance of the opinion polls. In a battle over the question of who could speak 'on behalf of Europe', the introduction of the barometer was a brilliant move.

Yet the battle is still undecided. 'Public opinion is the modern form of acclamation', was the analysis of German political theorist Carl Schmitt. 'It is perhaps a diffuse form, and its problem has been solved neither sociologically nor constitutionally. But in the fact that it can be interpreted as an acclamation lies its essence and its political significance.'[73]

9

The Greek Strategy: Seducing the Chorus

To use the word 'political' in the sense of the Greek polis is neither arbitrary nor far-fetched. Not only etymologically and not only for the learned does the very word, which in all European languages still derives from the historically unique organization of the Greek city-state, echo the experiences which first discovered the essence and the realm of the political ... If, then, we understand the political in the sense of the polis, its end or raison d'être *would be to establish and keep in existence a space where freedom as virtuosity can appear. This is the realm where freedom is a worldly reality, tangible in words which can be heard, in deeds which can be seen, and in events which are talked about, remembered, and turned into stories before they are finally incorporated into the great storybook of human history.*

Hannah Arendt (1961)[74]

Rather than a notion of 'our people' ('German' identity) or 'to our advantage' ('Roman' protections and rights), the 'Greek' strategy involves promoting a notion of 'our concern'. This is hard to do. The public will decide for itself whether something is a cause with which it identifies. It discovers itself precisely in those things that are of 'public concern'. It experiences something, sees something, hears something – a deficiency, an event, a wrong – and realises: This matters to us. And then: Something must be done. It therefore raises its voice, demonstrates, writes to the newspapers, votes for different candidates. In short, it becomes a public. But in order to act, it must turn to politics.

This Greek public is both spectator and participant. In its absence, nothing happens. It finds itself on stage, but not as a player in the spotlight. It is more like the chorus in a Greek tragedy. All it apparently does is deliver commentary on the action, but in fact it lies at the root of the events it is commenting on. As Nietzsche wrote: 'Given what we are used to with the role of the chorus on the modern stage, especially the chorus in opera, [we] have been totally unable to grasp how that tragic chorus of the Greeks could be older, more original, in fact, more important than the actual "action" – as tradition tells us so clearly.'[75] The main feature of a chorus is its voice.

This presents two opportunities for a political body in search of a 'Greek' public. First, politics can give the public a voice, a say in decision-making. Second, politics can provide the public with drama, with on-stage action that captivates it. The genius of Athens bound these two aspects together, inventing both democratic freedom and a public arena. They go together. Political acts without a public voice degenerate into empty spectacle; but a public voice without political drama is equally ineffective – it will fall silent, the chorus will disappear from the stage.

In her essay 'What is freedom?', political philosopher Hannah Arendt makes a connection between the political power to deal with the vicissitudes of fortune (Machiavelli's *virtù*) and 'virtuosity', a word that refers to a quality in the performing arts, in theatre, dance or music (as distinct from the 'creative arts of making', such as sculpture). The performance is virtuoso, not the script, choreography or score. Arendt points out that the ancient Greeks liked to compare politics with flute-playing, dancing, healing and seafaring. She believes politics is not an art in the sense of the state or government as a work of art, as a kind of collective masterpiece created in the privacy of the workshop. Rather it is an art in the sense of a performance before an audience, which derives its power and freedom from the moment: 'Political institutions, no matter how well or how badly designed, depend for their continued existence upon acting men.'[76]

UNISON

There is nothing odd about the fact that Europe has made a huge effort to give the population a say in decision-making. In the member states, democracy is regarded as morally superior to other sources of legitimacy. The non-democratic exercise of power became unacceptable between, roughly speaking, 1789 and 1945. Those politicians who saw Europe as a present or future political power were naturally eager to give it a democratic form.

No less importantly, experience shows that a political body whose exercise of power is based on free elections is robust, standing firm in the river of time. As Machiavelli argues in *The Prince*: 'I believe also that he will be successful who directs his actions according to the spirit of the times, and that he whose actions do not accord with the times will not be successful.'[77] In a democracy, this advice, aimed at individual rulers, applies (as it were) to the political class as a whole. The leaders do not need to change their character to suit the circumstances, since, if necessary, they can be replaced quickly and without violence by the public, by means of the ballot box or parliament (as war leader Churchill discovered in July 1945). 'Nothing ... renders a republic more firm and stable, than to organize it in such a way that the excitement of the ill-humors that agitate a state may have a way prescribed by law for venting itself.'[78]

Three preliminary remarks are in order on the special relationship between democracy and time. First, as soon as the public gains a voice in the exercise of power, it becomes able to sound a dissenting note. Once the public has assented to proposed laws and decisions, it is committed and bears responsibility for them, but its 'yes' is worth little if it is never allowed to say 'no'. Democratic unpredictability is the price rulers pay for a robust political order.

Second, the parliament is the mediating agency between the public and its rulers. Parliamentarians move back and forth between the voices of a people and the decrees of a government. They translate the demands, desires, interests and emotions of the street, conveying them to the state. But they also report back to their supporters, as interpreters of the general interest, the long term, the geopolitical situation. A parliament therefore works to subdue political haste. It can fulfil this role because it has its own time ('mandate', 'term in office'), determined by the periodicity of elections.

Third, the basic democratic principle in both direct and representative systems is majority voting. One man, one vote. Since majorities can change with every election, even the outvoted minority should be able to accept the result as valid; the possibility of future defeat tempers the 'tyranny of the majority'. In other words, democratic legitimacy ultimately rests not on the majority principle as such, but on the open future (embodied by parliamentary opposition), and therefore on the continuing existence of the political community through time.

A democracy is a community of voices, featuring assent and dissent, megaphones and mufflers, cheers and jeers, undertones and dissonances. It all holds together because (and only so long as) every word can potentially be followed by a riposte.

The existence of a parliament does not by itself create a stronger bond between the public and politics. To fulfil its mediating function, a parliament must establish a meaningful relationship with both the people and the government. In Europe, both relationships – between parliament and people and between parliament and government – are complicated. Between whom and whom is a European parliament actually supposed to mediate?

The relationship between parliament and people is the subject of much discussion. Many European politicians and theorists have argued that every democracy presumes a pre-existing populace (Gr. *dêmos*). (Or, in the terms used here: no 'Greek' legitimacy without a 'German' grounding of identity.) On this basis, French, British and several other heads of state or government, as well as the German Constitutional Court, have opposed any increase in the power of a European parliament. Others believe that the relationship between a parliament and a people is more open. Can European institutions and elections not themselves contribute to a sense of a common destiny? This politico-philosophical debate is ongoing. Since a European parliament now exists, that institution will itself help to determine which of the two schools is correct.

A second complication lies in the relationship between parliament and government. Is there an obvious decision-making institution? It will need the parliament as its interlocutor. Can elections lead to the opposition taking over from the government? That is generally regarded as the necessary condition for an outvoted minority to accept a decision. In Europe, no clear answer has been given to either of these questions.

Since 1950, attempts have been made to involve the public in the inner sphere of European politics, the ultimate aim being to create a new European public that speaks in unison. Democratisation was imposed from the top down. There were no grass-roots initiatives or people's tribunes demanding participation in European decision-making. It came about because politicians were wavering uncertainly and seeking solid ground. First a parliamentary Assembly was established (1952), which later renamed itself a Parliament (1958/62). Only then was it given its own voters (1979), only then were those voters proclaimed political citizens (1992), and only then came efforts, which proved futile, to ascribe a constituent power to citizens (2004) – as if work began on the roof and progressed downwards to the foundations. To the Brussels mind, this seemed the only way to make good the democratic 'deficit'.

It was all a matter of placing bets on the future, as the word 'deficit' suggests. For decades, no academic article about European democracy has failed to deploy the expression 'democratic deficit' – a term that, although apparently analytical, carries a political programme within it. Coined in 1977 by the Young European Federalists,[79] it gained wider circulation in 1979, the year of the first direct European elections, owing to a book by the Commission civil servant responsible for relations with the European Parliament. He made no secret of his own political aims ('this book is intended to be prescriptive rather than descriptive, a tract rather than a treatise').[80] What effect does this powerful metaphor have? 'Deficit' conjures up an image of a book-keeping state in which the (outgoing) exercise of power exceeds the (incoming) influence of the citizens. Once we accept this model, it almost goes without saying that the deficit must be redressed by giving the Parliament more say. But why should costs always take precedence over benefits? Isn't a reduction in political outgoings (in other words, fewer decisions) an option as well? Can we not get ourselves a democratic income from elsewhere? Such questions were not asked, because the answer had already been given: more power for 'Strasbourg'.

Only later did it become clear that the club would find less support for the inner sphere among this new voting public than had been hoped. It kept having to run to keep up with the deficit. So European politicians increasingly make explicit appeal to the old national voting publics – that is, to democratic structures in the sphere of the member states, and primarily the national parliaments. Their public does not speak in unison; instead it is polyphonic, making what it says harder to grasp.

A 'Parliament'

To judge by the declaration of 9 May 1950, Schuman and Monnet were relying on the usual political and legal safeguards to lend legitimacy to their plans for coal and steel. The treaty would be subjected to parliamentary ratifications, and there would be 'means of appeal against the decisions of the Authority'. They had not conceived of a special parliament.

The governments that took up France's invitation wanted the High Authority to be subjected to clear political control, as their initial reactions show. While the Netherlands and Belgium stressed the role of national governments (thereby paving the way for a Council of Ministers), Germany wanted a role for the national parliaments. Monnet had already assented to this, even before treaty negotiations began, which explains why the parliamentary forum was given a name as early as the second day of the Paris conference, on 21 June 1951: 'Common Assembly'.[81]

There was a precedent, namely the parliamentary Assembly of the recently established Council of Europe for democratic and human rights in Strasbourg. This was seen as the great achievement of the post-war federalist movement. Peoples' representatives of ten (soon fifteen) countries debated European politics. They were hardly minor figures: during the opening session in

August 1949, Winston Churchill, Harold Macmillan, Guy Mollet, Paul-Henri Spaak, Paul Reynaud and Michel Debré were among those who crossed swords.

A similar, indirectly elected parliament was set up for the Europe of the Six. This, too, would consist of national parliamentarians, 'representatives of the peoples of the member States of the Community'.[82] The parliaments of Germany, France and Italy each had a right to send eighteen representatives; Belgium and the Netherlands, ten; Luxembourg, four. Their task was to keep a check on the High Authority of the Coal and Steel Community.

The Assembly met for the first time in September 1952. How could parliamentarians from six countries speak with a single European voice? They immediately decided to sit in the Assembly in alphabetical order, countering an instinctive tendency to group by member state. The representatives of the Six also formed 'supranational' political groupings: Christian Democrats, Social Democrats and Liberals. There were soon efforts within each grouping to reach accords before entering into debate with the other parties in plenary sessions. A European political realm had begun to take shape. 'Without the political groupings,' a study of the fledgling parliament claimed, 'the Assembly would have assumed the character of a council of experts'.[83] Yet because of the technical nature of the subject-matter (coal prices; steel production), it was hard to interest the public. The dilemma for the Assembly was that it felt it was 'anticipating' national opinions. It could have opted to introduce national interests and emotions into its debates, but in general it did not:

> To some extent, the European represented by the Assembly was an abstract being, just like the 'citizen' of the political writings of the eighteenth and nineteenth centuries . . .: a European citizen enlightened by 'reason', freed from narrow national concerns and prejudices and prepared to look at the diverse interests within the Community in terms of their intrinsic merits.[84]

The Strasbourgers spoke on behalf of ideal citizens who did not exist, with an expectation both that such citizens would emerge and that they themselves, as educators, could help achieve this.

The Assembly had a rather more fruitful relationship with the executive, in the form of the High Authority chaired by Jean Monnet. Close cooperation developed between the two institutions. Members of the Authority derived a political calling from parliamentary controls, a status higher than that of mere technocrats. The Assembly found in the Authority a decision-making body that it could measure itself against. It believed its task was to reinforce the still new inner sphere of European politics against threats from the member states: 'The representatives regarded themselves, along with the members of the High Authority, as pioneers of European unity. They were of the opinion that, as far as possible, they must form a common front against any opposition that might be aroused by the realisation of the aims of the Community.' Internal discord would damage the cause: 'The more unanimous the Assembly was . . . the more influence it would have on the politics of the High Authority and the better placed the European executive power would be to offer resistance to the undoubtedly strong traditional particularisms in the six countries.'[85] It is only a slight exaggeration to say that, just as a national parliament in wartime generally stands behind the government to a man, so the Strasbourg Assembly rallied round the Authority. Its prime concern was the existence of the Community as such.

These experiences brought to light a weakness and a strength. The parliament, a mediator between people and decision-makers, was far closer to the latter. Its voice counted in the European inner sphere, but the voices of the populations barely resonated at all. The parliament did not immediately succeed in making Europe a matter of public concern.

The Treaty of Rome (1957) retained the same division of roles and conception of the task. Two changes were made to the parliament, however: a weakening of its actual power and an upgrading of its status as a future vehicle of the European project. The tension between fact and desire increased.

First the actual weakening. The negotiators for the Six realised that a common market went a good deal further than shared control of mining: it required greater political backing in the member states. Under the new scheme, therefore, decisions were no longer taken by an Authority in consultation with the Council of Ministers. It was now the other way around: the Council took the decisions, in response to proposals by the Commission (the new name for the Authority). The ministers' table was now central.

These institutional shifts affected the parliamentary Assembly, which no longer faced the Commission as the body responsible for decisions. Its interlocutor's loss of power reduced the importance of its own responses. The parliamentarians were given little in return. They gained an advisory role in law-making and the right to dismiss the Commission at any time, and they could amend the budget; but they could not call the Council to account if it ignored their advice or amendments. In 1965, an observer concluded: 'Whereas the Common Assembly could ask the High Authority: "Why did you take that decision?", it can only ask the Commission: "Why have you failed to convince the Council?"'[86] This was disappointing.

As a result of the weaknesses of both institutions vis-à-vis the member states, the Commission and the Parliament were extremely friendly towards one another. The secret calling of the former was to grow into a European executive; of the latter, to become Europe's legislator. So long as they were a would-be government and a would-be parliament, it was in the interests of both to help each other and, as it were, to talk each other up. This put in place a parliamentary culture of optimistic consensus. With a bit of goodwill, it was possible to discern a brand new relationship based on parliamentary confidence, a consequence of the Parliament's power to dismiss the Commission. But even convinced federalists recognised that Europe was 'an as yet "underdeveloped" democracy'.[87]

As well as being weakened in practice, the parliament was potentially upgraded by a new provision of the Treaty of Rome: 'The Assembly shall draw up proposals for elections by direct universal suffrage in accordance with a uniform procedure in all Member States.'[88] This initiative signified a symbolic revolution. In federalist logic, the parliament would represent a single electorate, rather than six added together. It was an opportunity to allow a single European voice to be heard. Italy, the Netherlands and Belgium were in favour, France against. In the Château de Val-Duchesse in 1956, Italian Foreign Minister Gaetano Martino and French Secretary of State Maurice Faure had argued – according to one of those present 'for almost a whole morning' – over the question of whether the treaty should include a deadline for the first election. Martino wanted to name a day, preferably within ten years, 'so that we would know precisely when, between now and a specific date, the European people would be called to the ballot box to elect their own parliament'.[89] He came up with all kinds of formulae. Faure, who had firm instructions from Paris, repelled all advances. As so often, a compromise was found in delay. The Council would 'lay down the appropriate provisions' for elections to be organised when agreed upon unanimously, at some point.[90] No election date yet, then, but a confirmation of the promise.

Its symbolic strengthening in the Treaty of Rome gave the parliamentary Assembly the self-confidence to rename itself the Parliament. By doing so, it was acting as if the promise had already been fulfilled. As soon as the internal rules and regulations were finalised, Dutch representative P.J. Kapteyn expressed a view that the official name 'Assembly' (*Vergadering*) did not hold sufficient appeal for the Dutch people. Why not replace it in the Dutch-language version of the rules with the word 'Parliament' (*Parlement*)? This proposal, which sounded entirely innocuous to non-Dutch-speakers, was accepted. A German representative repeated the trick: *Europäisches Parlament*. By contrast, the French and Italian versions stuck to the official designation

(*Assemblée; Assemblea*).[91] A self-declared parliament in just two languages – for the time being – but a major symbolic coup. In March 1958, the Parliament announced that, although it did not yet actually have voters, the promise alone meant it had risen above the category of a gathering of national parliamentarians. A battle over words had begun.

The importance of the name is clear from the fierce and consistent opposition to it. For a long time this came from France, later from Britain. Opponents believed that anyone who spoke of a 'European parliament' was recognising the existence of a 'European people'. Such a people did not exist and should not be allowed to exist (in their criticism, fact and norm overlapped). The circular character of any political foundation – first the state or first the people? – was evident once again. In their fight for European elections, the Italians adhered to their adage from the Risorgimento: 'We have made Italy. Now we must make Italians.' They had no difficulty conceiving of a people that emerged from (among other things) a ballot-box result. For the French and the British, whose past as nations stretched back into the mists of time, this was unthinkable.

President de Gaulle, in power since 1958, steadfastly refused to refer to the Strasbourg Assembly as a parliament. To do so was ridiculous, he declared, and a source of misunderstanding. His outburst came shortly after the Strasbourgers (on 20 March 1962) had renamed themselves a 'parliament' in French and Italian, too. He told the press, with a hint of sarcasm: 'Although we already have six national parliaments, plus the European parliamentary Assembly, plus the parliamentary Assembly of the Council of Europe … we had to elect an extra Parliament on top of that, characterised as European, which will lay down the law to six states.'[92] Naturally, it was this latter aspect that he found hard to take. So long as Strasbourg was merely a talking shop, a pretentious name was no real obstacle. De Gaulle knew, however, as a born politician, that such vanities conceal potential power bids. The Frenchman thought it inconceivable that a national population would subject itself to laws passed by foreign parliamentarians. This line of thinking became part of his ideological legacy; his successor Pompidou continued to speak of an 'Assembly'.

In 1979, when Thatcher took up the baton from de Gaulle, she too consistently referred to the parliament as 'the Assembly'. The British prime minister wanted to make clear to her home audience, according to one of her diplomats, 'that it was not a proper parliament like our own'.[93] (It seems that to Thatcher even direct elections had not made it a real parliament.) Not until 1986 did the assembled states, including Paris and London, give their blessing to the new name, thereby allocating the Strasbourgers, at a stroke, a bigger say in the legislative process. It happened without any fanfare, in a single sentence of a treaty revision: 'In Article 7, second paragraph of the EEC Treaty the terms "after consulting the Assembly" shall be replaced by "in co-operation with the European Parliament".'[94] Thatcher was sporting enough to accept defeat.

With this change, which came into force on 1 July 1987, 'We the states' accepted the existence of a 'European Parliament'.

Elections

The impact of the Rome treaty's promise of direct elections on the Strasbourg assembly, over many years, should not be underestimated. It would be a *choc salutaire* (to use the term chosen by Belgian representative Fernand Dehousse) that might bring fresh air into the stuffy world of the offices and prove the best way to arouse public interest in the European cause. 'It remains certain', as a speaker at a conference in the early 1960s succinctly put it, 'that the European Parliament will not attain to anything near equal status with the Council unless it can rest on the firm foundation of direct elections.'[95] A voters' mandate would give the European inner sphere a base of its own.

In 1960, a parliamentary working group put a plan for elections on the table. There was support in five capitals, but so long as the Gaullists were in power in Paris the idea would come up against an unshakeable French '*non*'. Then in 1974, under new man Giscard d'Estaing, things started to move. He was eager to institutionalise Europe's summits. This French desire had repeatedly met with opposition from the Benelux countries. Giscard forced a deal through at the December 1974 summit. Belgium and the Netherlands supported the establishment of the European Council, and as a concession Paris signed up for direct parliamentary elections. The reciprocal blockade was lifted, and suddenly there was a double breakthrough. In the European quest for a 'Greek' public it was a key moment. The national leaders opened two new lines of communication between the club and the people simultaneously: a direct voice in the inner sphere and a permanent stage with dramatic performances in the intermediate sphere of the members.

The first direct European elections were held in June 1979. Since then, they have taken place every five years. Strasbourg's expectations were fulfilled in one respect, but not in another. Without any change to its competencies, the elected Parliament did indeed strengthen its power and authority in relation to the Council of Ministers. Within months, in December 1979, the parliamentarians had rejected the community budget for 1980 proposed by the Council. As if to prove they existed, they showed no hesitation in throwing the Community into a political and financial crisis. It was a sign of self-awareness: power isn't given, you have to seize it. Since then, the Parliament, as the underdog, has garnered further competencies with every treaty change, thanks to friendly governments and its own increasing, if still primarily obstructive, power. From toothless advisor it has grown into a co-legislator in practically all policy fields. No one in Brussels can any longer afford to ignore it.

Another expectation, however, was not fulfilled. The Parliament has not won favour with its electorate. Voter turnout speaks volumes: this has declined steadily, from 63 per cent in 1979 to 43 per cent in 2009 as an average across all member states. There has, admittedly, been a decline at a national level, too; but the fall in numbers in Europe is relatively larger and comes from a significantly lower starting point. Moreover, research shows that Europeans do not generally vote with European topics in mind: their choice is an extension of national preferences. Political scientists talk of 'second-order elections'.

The paradox is, therefore, that voters have shown less and less interest in the Parliament over the past three decades, while its formal power has increased significantly over the same period. From the point of view of the quest for 'Greek' legitimacy, it is a disappointing result. The way the Parliament affects the power balance between European institutions is now crucial, but it does not provide the democratic foundations that the club was hoping for. It is a player in the inner sphere, but not a channel for a European *vox populi*.

The top-down order in which the Greek quest for legitimacy was undertaken has come up against its limits. The Parliament was given more power in the expectation that voters would at last rush to legitimise it. This was to forget that democratic legitimacy does not arise automatically from formal parliamentary competencies. The electorate must also identify to some extent with the representative body and see it as 'our parliament' – a feeling that cannot be quantified purely in voter numbers. Strasbourg comforts itself with the thought that turnout for the mid-term elections to the American House of Representatives is 'comparable' to that for European elections,[96] ignoring the fact that many more Americans at least know who their Representative is.

The relative fiasco of direct elections (undeniable after the second instalment in 1984) demonstrated that the Parliament could not by itself create a single public voice. The *choc salutaire* did not occur. Perhaps an interlocutor with executive power could foster the notion that Europe is 'our concern'.

There are two candidates for that role: the Commission and the European Council. The Parliament has for many years done its best to 'politicise' the Commission as far as possible. In doing so, it deploys its trump card: the election results. The choice of Commission president ought to be made dependent upon a parliamentary majority, it argues, so that something is clearly at stake at election time – which requires that he or she must be given more influence over the composition of the College of Commissioners and the distribution of posts.

With recent treaty changes, steps have been taken in both these directions. The Treaty of Lisbon states that the Parliament 'elects' the Commission president, although still on the recommendation of the European Council.[97] After the parliamentary elections of 2004 and 2009, the European People's Party, which won the most seats, secured the appointment of a Commission president of its own political hue – the former Portuguese premier, José Manuel Barroso. Although a few were still attached to the ideal of a technical and neutral governing body, most Eurocommissioners applauded this politicisation. Yet it does have its limits, so long as twenty-seven commissioners are nominated by twenty-seven governments that are rarely of the same political persuasion.

The Parliament has the power to dismiss the Commission *en bloc*. It came close to doing so once, in 1999, but President Jacques Santer and his team stood down before that point was reached. The episode is seen as a highpoint in Strasbourg's history. It resulted from accusations of fraud – a failure of the type by which a bureaucracy is judged. By contrast, five years later, when the Barroso Commission took office, the conflict that arose was more political. In response to the inclusion of candidate Eurocommissioner Rocco Buttiglione, controversial for his opinions on marriage and homosexuality, the Parliament threatened to block the investiture of the entire Commission. At that point, the member states backed down and implemented several changes of personnel. In this episode, therefore, the Commission was not the Parliament's main interlocutor; rather it was itself the subject of a political conflict between the Parliament and the club of member states over who has power of appointment. From this clash – which it won – the Parliament drew self-confidence. And it found itself with a different, more political opposite number.

The other candidate as its interlocutor is the European Council. For over a quarter of a century, the national leaders have jointly taken the most important political decisions in the Union. Nonetheless, the Parliament's constitutional committee, its institutional superego, insisted on expressing an aversion to the European Council. It objected to the fact that a course was laid out for the Community 'in a political stratosphere which Parliament could not reach.'[98] It cherished a quite different vision of the future. Ever since the early years of the Community, the idea had been that the Parliament and the Council of Ministers would eventually grow into legislative chambers. According to the federalist model, the former would address the Commission – the executive power – on behalf of the citizens, the latter on behalf of the states. True, this image did not fit the facts, since as well as the Commission, the Council of Ministers had executive powers, not least in economic and foreign affairs; but that could be dismissed as a temporary aberration, according to the old 'not yet' formula. The formula worked far less well, however, when it came to explaining away the European Council. The rise, from 1974 onwards, of this powerful body in the political life of the club undermined the self-image of the Parliament, which could no longer place all its bets on the Commission. It is therefore gradually adjusting its course, leaving the world of offices behind.

Since 1981, the custom has been for the president of the European Council to give a speech in Strasbourg during his or her six-month term, followed by a debate, and to report to the Parliament on European Council meetings. The cooperation of the Parliament gradually became indispensable in making good on the political promises of a Council presidency, which is why the leaders of countries holding the rotating presidency of the Council of Ministers still present their programmes, even though, since 2010, they no longer chair the European Council. To the talented rhetoricians among them from the larger member states, the Parliament offered a platform on which to enhance their stature as European statesmen, a place where they could address Europe's citizens. François Mitterrand (in 1984) and Tony Blair (in 2005) are among those who have thrilled the chamber.

It will be hard for this dialogue to develop into a relationship of parliamentary responsibility. Heads of state or government derive their positions from their national electorates and cannot be voted out in Strasbourg. The Parliament is therefore unable to deploy its trump card, the election result. This remains the case even now that the European Council has its own permanent president; he is appointed by the national leaders, and the only formal demand made of him is to report to the Parliament on Council meetings. The two bodies rely on different constitutional 'lines of representation'. The Parliament speaks on behalf of the citizens in their capacity as Europeans, while the European Council speaks on behalf of the assembled national governments, and therefore in the name of multiple national citizenries. If this results in political deadlock, voters cannot simply decide between the two. Such a conflict ultimately splits voters themselves down the middle.

Reading about all the efforts that the European Parliament has made to get its foot in the door of the European Council makes painfully clear the difference between the two institutions in the degree of public power they command. Successive presidents of the Parliament have sought to occupy a chair at the leaders' conference table, or a seat at the dinner, or indeed a place in the traditional family photo. This fight for inclusion was begun by Henry Plumb, in 1987. Via a friendly Belgian presidency of the Council, it was arranged that Plumb, as president of the Parliament, would be allowed to speak to the leaders briefly at the start of the summit in June 1987. Most member states had no objection. Margaret Thatcher, however, who had not been consulted, was astonished to encounter her fellow party member: 'Well, Henry, what on earth are you doing here?'[99] Plumb was sensible enough to keep his talk short and businesslike: the seat at the table was more important for now than the debate. With varying degrees of success, subsequent holders of his office have extended the exercise into a brief exchange of views with the heads of government. But to this day, the European Council meeting does not formally begin until the president of the Parliament has left – protocol used by the states as a dig at the intruder.

A former senior civil servant in Strasbourg analyses the 'battle to get in the room' as follows:

> Parliament has prosecuted a thirty-year campaign to be 'present', visibly, at the top table in the European Union. Its dogged persistence, and its seeming obsession with the symbols of protocol, has often caused annoyance, particularly among officials of member-states and the other institutions. At times this campaign has come across as excessively self-regarding and pushy. Parliament's Presidents, who have spearheaded the campaign, are after all politicians with the perfectly human desire to be in the room, to be at the dinner, to be seen and to be in the line-up for the photograph. At the same time, this understandable personal ambition has coincided with the institution's need to be visible.[100]

This is a frank and revealing verdict. The Parliament feeds upon the public visibility of others. Since the base provided by the European electorate is not firm enough, it seeks reinforcement from the gathering of national leaders. It is not a people's tribune, challenging those in power with the support of the street; it is more like a court musician, seeking the prince's attention because behind the prince lies the public.

Political citizenship

A third important step in the top-down development of 'Greek' legitimacy, after the parliament and elections, was the introduction of political citizenship in 1993. This is a powerful symbol of a direct political bond between Europe as a whole and its public. Although as far as the substance went, political citizenship seemed no more than a carrying forward of the connection in law between individuals and the European Union, as proclaimed by the Court (and discussed in chapter 8), the conceptual distinction is important. As Joseph Weiler succinctly puts it, referring to the direct effect of the law: 'Long before women or Jews were made citizens, they enjoyed direct effect.'[101] A subject under law remains a subject, whereas a political citizen takes part in decision-making.

This innovation was a response to the revolutions of autumn 1989, accompanied by a partial reshaping of the intermediate sphere of European politics into a Union. Several member states wanted to strengthen the Union's democratic legitimacy. In March 1990, Belgium argued for the abolition of border controls and for the right of citizens who had emigrated to vote in European and local elections. The Italians asked for a 'legal framework' to fit a situation in which 'a European citizen is developing even before actions by States shape Europe'. Greece wanted to cultivate constitutional patriotism by strengthening the sense 'of belonging to one legal community'. In May 1990, the Spanish government introduced the term 'European citizenship'. 'The move towards Political Union', Madrid explained after the summer, 'radically changes the existing situation and requires the creation of an integrated common area in which the European citizen occupies a central and fundamental position.'[102] The Spanish knew there was disagreement between the states about which rights, freedoms and duties any such citizenship would have to comprise. They therefore proposed first creating citizenship, as a symbolic step, and only then talking about its substance, which could evolve over time. (In this diplomatic offensive, Madrid had its eye mainly on the 'Roman' benefits for Spanish emigrants, but it realised that a 'Greek' constitutional argument was essential to its success.)

The idea that a political union needs citizens to make it legitimate sounded, once formulated, so self-evident that there was little resistance. When, in December 1990, the German and French leaders rallied behind citizenship, the dispute was settled. Yet at the end of negotiations on its content, little was left other than the right to take part in European and local elections in another member state. Grand democratic motives had faded from sight. The Treaty of Maastricht said simply: 'Citizenship of the Union is hereby established. Every person holding the nationality of a Member State shall be a citizen of the Union.'[103]

This laconic definition turned out to raise all too many questions in one member state. In June 1992, the Danish people voted against the treaty in a referendum. European citizenship was one of the three elements that caused most unrest, along with the currency union and defence policy.[104] The Danes gave their consent in a second referendum only after their government had unilaterally added certain provisions. The suggestion that European citizenship was comparable to Danish national citizenship was vigorously rebutted by Copenhagen. Other countries, too, saw the benefit of some clarification. Five years later, a sentence was added to the treaty: 'Citizenship of the Union shall complement and not replace national citizenship.'[105]

The calamity of the Danish 'no' was not resolved by these attempts to reassure the populations. The club had seen for the first time how the pursuit of Greek legitimacy could be counterproductive. The public had been given citizenship, but it had come close to rejecting the offer. A crack opened up between two capacities of the democratic public – between the new European citizens and the national citizens as a whole; between motivated supporters of the inner sphere and those who, grumbling and unpredictable, sustained the sphere of the members.

Some observers compared the introduction of citizenship to a marketing gimmick. Given that citizenship was not accompanied by any new rights or political influence, it was a mere pacifier. European law expert Joseph Weiler wrote of the Europe 'product' in 1995: 'Citizenship and the "rights" associated with it are meant to give the product a new image (since it adds very little in substance) and make the product ever more attractive to its consumers, to reestablish their attachment to their favourite brand.' He believed that the national leaders were behaving like 'managers, alarmed by customer dissatisfaction, engaged in brand development'.[106] The criticism is apt, but it ignores the time factor. No one made this analysis before the Danish 'no' of 1992 and before the leaders' bluff had been called, when there was still a chance that the whole exercise would prove to be an act of far-sighted statesmanship. And after the point at which the European Court, in the late 1990s, began to fill the 'empty' mould of citizenship with content, Weiler's analysis lost its relevance. The market reproach hit home when the original intention failed and no new twist had as yet been given to it.

A constitution

The Treaty Establishing a Constitution for Europe, signed in October 2004, never came into force. But the failed attempt to find a public – both the fact that it was tried and the fact that it failed – says a great deal.

The political gesture contained in the name 'constitution' is an important aspect of this episode. A constitution meant replacing the pact between states with a pact between citizens. The club would attain the longed-for solid ground. In late 2001, the national leaders asked a convention to investigate, among other things, whether a simplification of the treaty 'might not lead in the long run to the adoption of a constitutional text'.[107] No wonder the Convention went on to behave like a constitutional convention and some members dreamed of a founding moment à la Philadelphia 1787.

This desire needs to be interpreted in constitutional terms. In the American Constitution, the audacious singular 'We the people' in the preamble created a tipping point from many to one. In Europe, the option of compiling a treaty in the name of 'We the people of Europe' was never seriously considered. The singular use of 'people' is taboo. The Community and the Union were established by the 'plenipotentiaries' – in other words, the signatory states. The Convention likewise observed the taboo against a singular 'people'. An early draft text stuck to 'Led by the will of the peoples and states of Europe . . .' To several member states, this national plural was no less unwelcome. The German, Spanish and Greek governmental representatives were among those who suggested adding the citizens, as a European plurality.[108] Three motives under the same constitutional cloak: Germany, as the most populous member state, had an interest in the power of numbers; Madrid, as a nation's central power, wanted rid of the *pueblos*, a term that in Spain refers to the separate 'peoples' of the Spanish regions; Greece had the rights of its emigrants in mind. In a subsequent version, the Union briefly had three pillars, but after that the 'peoples' disappeared and the final version of the opening article declares that the treaty on a constitution has been inspired by the 'will of the citizens and States of Europe'.[109]

This was a huge step. European citizens were ascribed constituent power. As well as being based on the will of the states (as in all previous treaties), the Union would be based on the will of the citizens. The figure of the citizen would sustain the institutions, having been promoted from decoration on the facade to component of the foundations. More than the much-discussed symbols (the flag and anthem) or the state-like vocabulary ('minister', 'law'), this lent the 2004 pact the features of a constitution – only the features, since the states remained: the citizens did not have the entire constituent realm to themselves.

At several places in the text, the tension between citizens and states was considerable. In a subtle manoeuvre, Giscard d'Estaing had given the draft constitution a motto, a famous line from the eulogy by Pericles to the Athenian form of state: 'Its administration favours the many instead of the few; this is why it is called a democracy.'[110] This classical reference did not survive negotiations between the governments. Finland and Ireland were said to be particularly opposed to it – two small member states, granted, but as rotating chair of the Council during the final negotiations, it was a simple matter for Ireland to have the idea abandoned. Why Helsinki and Dublin rejected the motto is anyone's guess. Too far from Athens geographically? Fear of majority power, which would disadvantage member states with small populations? Or fear of the word *dêmos* contained in it, that unmentionable bedrock? It was a revealing excision. The forum that spoke on behalf of the states, peoples and citizens created a historical opening to the Greek inventors of democracy; the assembled states closed it again at the last moment.

In the spring of 2005, the constitutional treaty came up against a 'no' from two of the four populations asked to ratify it by referendum: the French and the Dutch. While the tenor of the debate in France was that the people wanted a different constitution, one that did not grant so many economic freedoms, in the Netherlands it became clear that people did not want a constitution at all, regarding it as a threat to national identity. The Dutch 'no' vote was nationalistic in nature. The fact that something called a constitution was on offer caused disquiet in several other member states as well. Would their own constitutions disappear? Might they suddenly find themselves part of a European superstate? The politicians advocating the new pact had no convincing response to these questions.

After an uneasy pause for thought, the national leaders decided in June 2007 to discontinue ratification of the constitutional treaty. They retraced their steps: no constitution, but instead a traditional revision of both the existing treaties (Union and Community). The resulting pact would not be given 'a constitutional character'; the state-like terminology would be adjusted; flag and anthem were dropped. The European Council announced starkly: 'The constitutional concept, which consisted in repealing all existing Treaties and replacing them by a single text called "Constitution", is abandoned.'[111] More significant than this textual reorganisation, however, is the fact that the new treaty, like its predecessors, was concluded in the name of the states: the European citizens lost their constituent power. The constitutional experiment was over. The democratic grounding had not been attained. The inner sphere remained floating in the air, attached as if by cables to the member states.

There has been a strong tendency in retrospect, among both commentators and politicians, to regard the fiasco surrounding the name 'Constitution' as a failed public relations exercise. Mischievous voices have attributed the choice of the word to the vanity of Convention Chairman Giscard d'Estaing, suggesting that he wanted to go down in history as a European George Washington. 'We must be frank', wrote American political scientist Andrew Moravcsik in June 2006; 'The draft constitution was, above all, an exercise in *public relations*'.[112] This author had always claimed as much, but after the failed ratification others suddenly gained the same insight. 'It is more obvious now than it had been before', a German legal journal noted just as the heads of government were signing a substitute treaty in Lisbon, 'that the constitutional pomp and glamour served as a public relations strategy'.[113]

This interpretation of the constitution as an advertising blunder is too easy. It ignores the fact that the constitutional episode was the final stage, for the time being, in a sixty-year quest for 'Greek' legitimacy. It also ignores the fact that the parliament, the elections and the citizenship, which did come into being, could equally well be dismissed as semantic showmanship or public relations manoeuvres (as in fact happened in the case of citizenship). More generally, it ignores the fact that every political body, by the nature of things, goes in search of a public with all the means at its disposal. Insofar as this quest is unsuccessful, it is not failed advertising but failed politics. In this case, the fiasco meant that Europe would have to set off in search of a different, more robust electorate.

Polyphonic

The Union is a club of parliamentary democracies. Democracy is not just an external stamp of quality and an entry requirement for aspiring members, but a characteristic of its political life. Without its twenty-seven-voiced national democratic system, Europe would collapse. The Union depends on its agglomeration of national publics.

Awareness of this was lacking for many years. The ideologists of the inner sphere wanted a new electorate and were oblivious to the old electorate, the national voters, who merely stood in the way. The ideologists of the states believed that the national publics were purely at the service of their own member nations – German voters for Germany, Swedish voters for Sweden, and so on.

Both were wrong. European politics as a whole cannot do without the German, the Swedish and all the other national electorates. The totality of national publics carries out vital tasks, either directly or through its national parliaments. It chooses and controls the figures who will sit at the most powerful European table, reaches agreements about the rules of the game and about membership and accession, and judges whether any proposed European policy is necessary.

There is a much-lamented disadvantage to this older public: it is not one but many. The great compensating advantage: it exists. No need to create what is already there. The task for the club is to allow the voices of the national electorates – first the parliaments, then the voters that stand behind them – to be heard in European democracy. This is a far from simple challenge, but the member states do not have a great deal of choice.

The European Council and the Council of Ministers

This underpinning by the national democracies is acknowledged by the governments in the most recent treaty. In a prominent article they declare: 'The functioning of the Union shall be founded on representative democracy. Citizens are directly represented at Union level in the European Parliament. Member States are represented in the European Council by their Heads of State or Government and in the Council by their governments, *themselves democratically accountable either to their national Parliaments, or to their citizens.*'[114]

National elections determine the composition of the European Council. Each electorate sends one person to the European top table, based either on direct presidential elections or on parliamentary elections. Admittedly this is a second-order function, derived from the primary function of national elections, which is to staff national parliaments and governments. Yet with the growing power of the heads of government, the importance of national elections increases. Who will be the new German chancellor? Who will become prime minister of Italy? This is more than a hunger for gossip: the discontinuities brought about by national elections are a vital factor in European political life. After the Franco-Dutch 'no' of 2005, the 'period of reflection' consisted less of reflection than of waiting for a new French president. The upcoming British elections, scheduled for 2015, may have a bigger impact on Europe's political life than the European elections of 2014.

Each national public seems aware that it makes a difference which politician it sends to the highest European table. Anyone who reduces Europe to the institutional inner sphere, to its policy machinery, might conclude that since 1952 only one election has been decided by issues concerning Europe.

European topics are thought too boring or, to use the jargon, not salient enough. (Moravcsik, who adheres to this point of view, believes that the French presidential election of 1965, with its peasants' revolt against de Gaulle, is the single exception.[115]) Anyone, by contrast, who pays attention to the fact that Europe is a circle of member states will notice that many national elections have featured arguments over the place and identity of that member state in the Union.

Take the Polish parliamentary elections of October 2007. The Kaczyński government, regarded as nationalist and xenophobic, was punished for its anti-European attitude. Its defeat was the result of an unexpectedly high turnout among young people, urban residents and emigrant Poles. Some voters said they wanted Poland to become 'a normal European country in a normal Europe'.[116]

In the Spanish parliamentary elections of March 2004, the governing Conservatives unexpectedly lost to the Socialists. Their defeat can be attributed to the lies told by the Conservatives about the bomb attack on a railway station in Madrid three days before the election, when they blamed the Basque separatist movement instead of jihadi terrorists. During the campaign, the Socialists had promised to withdraw Spanish troops from Iraq and to end Spanish opposition to the European constitutional treaty. Given the dramatic situation in the aftermath of the attacks, this move away from America and towards Germany and France satisfied the electorate's desire for security – a salient subject if ever there was one.

A national leader occupies the most important European post in his or her home country. It remains a dual role: that of a head of state or government representing a country in Europe, and that of a member of the European Council representing Europe back home. Take German Chancellor Angela Merkel. Before she travels to meetings with fellow leaders, she consults the Bundestag. There she can explain what the government is going to try to achieve and hear about the wishes or demands of the German parliament. Afterwards she reports back. As a national leader, Merkel takes responsibility for negotiations: on behalf of Germany *I* have fought hard to achieve point X, although for such-and-such reason point Y was lost. As a member of the European Council, she takes responsibility for the result: on behalf of the Union, *we* have decided as follows… The German chancellor thereby commands a parliamentary majority for a Union decision.

This two-way exchange is not a matter of courtesy alone. Once, in 1990, a leader was forced to stand down when action taken on Europe led to parliamentary criticism at home: Margaret Thatcher, no less. The occasion was the

European Council meeting in Rome in October of that year, which decided on a currency union. In the House of Commons, the British prime minister made clear that she would not commit herself to that joint decision ('No! No! No!'). Her former foreign minister and ally of many years, Geoffrey Howe, resigned as deputy prime minister as a consequence. Shortly afterwards he gave a devastating resignation speech to an aghast parliament, reproaching Thatcher for isolating Britain in Europe and saying that her attitude was 'running increasingly serious risks for the future of the nation'.[117] It was the signal for a revolt by the Conservative party. Within two weeks, the Iron Lady had fallen. In 2011, it was Iveta Radičová, prime minister of Slovakia, who was forced to sacrifice her government under pressure from parliamentary opposition. The euro crisis has been a decisive factor in several recent changes of government (Ireland, Portugal, Greece and Italy), but in Slovakia it was a refusal by the majority to support the prime minister in coming to the aid of these countries in their hour of need that shaped subsequent developments. Feeling bound by commitments made at a euro summit of 21 July 2011, Radičová accepted an 'offer' from the opposition to lend her its support in exchange for early elections.

The same line of responsibility runs between national parliaments and the members of the ordinary Council, the sectoral ministers. It was for this reason that in 1950 the Benelux ministers pressed for a role for governments in the European mechanism. They alone bore democratic responsibility towards their populations. The involvement of the national governments would give their parliaments a supervisory function, a right to review the Council's decisions. Here again there is a responsibility on both sides. Ministers, sometimes charged by their parliaments with specific tasks, take part in the decision-making process in the Council with national aims in view. But once a decision has been taken, each minister represents the Union at home. This is precisely the intention. The treaty states: 'The Council shall consist of a representative of each Member State at ministerial level, who may commit the government of the Member State in question.'[118]

Via the governments the parliaments are brought to the European table, and via the parliaments the national publics. This can be seen most clearly of all when majority decisions are taken. Even if personally outvoted, a minister bears responsibility for a European decision vis-à-vis the national parliament – and ultimately, therefore, the home population.

Many national ministers duck this responsibility. There is a great temptation to claim only the successes and to blame 'Brussels' for any failures. Although a national parliament could, in theory, have a minister dismissed for failing to convince, it turns out to be more attractive all round to opt for indignation or to cast doubt on competencies: 'Europe can't decide about that.' In a national parliament, the sought-after 'Greek' legitimacy may veer round into its opposite. Instead of a sense of 'our European decisions', an image emerges of Brussels as a foreign occupying power.

There are huge differences in parliamentary culture between the member states. Some parliaments send ministers to Brussels with a strict mandate. Like errand boys, they are allowed to come home with only one outcome. The Folketing, for example, which generally gives Danish governments little room for manoeuvre, has tried to prevent ministers committing themselves to decisions it dislikes. Such defences, incidentally, do not help a parliament keep its distance from European politics; in fact, it may be sucked in all the more strongly. The spirit of the Folketing hangs over the negotiating table in Brussels where the Danish government sits. This national parliament thereby shows itself to be a consummate European institution.

Referendums and the basis of membership

The position of the assembled national publics is strongest when settling fundamental issues. Without the permission of each of the existing members, no new member can join the circle and the rules of the game cannot be changed. This right to withhold consent is firmly anchored. The treaty says of such weighty decisions that the governments must ratify them 'in accordance with their respective constitutional requirements'. This means that a joint decision is valid only if, in each member state, either the parliament or the population gives its consent.

All 'European' referendums have been national referendums on a European issue. The most commonly heard argument in favour of holding them is that a change to European fundamentals is like a change to a national constitution, which in some member states requires the assent of the people. The holding of a European referendum has, in every case, been forced through by national political players, for example by means of a Supreme Court ruling (Ireland), a presidential decree (France) or a parliamentary majority (the Netherlands).

First of all, there is the question of a country's own membership. Of the twenty-seven current members, fourteen joined after a referendum on entry. One held a referendum shortly after joining on whether or not it would do better to leave again (Britain). One candidate twice held a membership referendum, but on both occasions the public said 'no' (Norway). Fifteen national populations, therefore, have committed themselves to a European existence with their 'yes'. In these referendums on joining or leaving, the 'Geoffrey

Howe issue' is clearly at stake: the future of the nation; its place within the concert of European nations. Each voter is aware of the weighty, historic choice he or she is being asked to make. A 'yes' is a leap, a 'no' throws up a wall that no politician can knock down.

For the existing members, the arrival of a new member is less dramatic. It is usually their parliaments that decide. In one case, a member state did organise a referendum about a newcomer. This was France in 1972, voting on British accession. (President Pompidou thereby enabled voters to dispense with his predecessor de Gaulle's anti-British veto.) This type of referendum is being considered at the moment in several member states on the pending issue of Turkish accession. From a constitutional point of view this makes sense. Just like a change to the treaty, the accession of a new member fundamentally affects the club.

Then there are referendums on new rules of the game. These are less straightforward. A typical 'no' campaign focuses on a multiplicity of individual treaty articles, which it disputes, whereas a typical 'yes' campaign counters these baton charges by enumerating the benefits of the European order as a whole – a shotgun blast, as it were, against the threat of a single bomb. The ambiguity is inherent in the question. The assent of the populations to altered rules serves both as confirmation of those rules and as a reconfirmation of the founding moment, although the reconfirmation is not fully visible. When a national public votes 'no' in a treaty referendum (as has happened five times so far), is it saying 'no' to the new rules or to the Union as such? The voters can hardly be blamed for this ambiguity, since it flows from their lack of opportunities to express themselves as national electorates on specific European issues at an earlier stage.

The governments have until now jointly deployed two strategies for hauling resistant populations on board. The defensive strategy is to ensure parliamentary ratification of the same or a comparable treaty, which is how the partners enabled Paris and The Hague to resolve the post-'no' crisis after 2005. The offensive strategy changes a treaty referendum (implicitly or explicitly) into a membership referendum. For the governments involved, this is awkward, but both Copenhagen (1993) and Dublin (2002 and 2009) have been forced into it by their partners. It may not be 'fair', but it is a sign of the growing power of the club as a whole, as compared to the individual members.

What the constituent power is to the new, European public whose creation is so fervently wished, the membership issue is to the old, national publics. It touches on fundamentals. In a membership referendum, the public has to decide: does it want to continue to support the joint political performance as part of the chorus, or would it prefer to leave the stage? For lack of a shared foundation, Europe's democratic legitimacy rests on each national public's ability to leave the Union.

The new secession clause in the Treaty of Lisbon – 'Any Member State may decide to withdraw from the Union in accordance with its own constitutional requirements'[119] – therefore provides an essential clarification. Its introduction was discussed in 2002–03. The representatives of the founding states, the 'old Six', were anxious about it. They felt that such a provision ran counter to the community spirit, and their reaction was an emotional one: 'Isn't Europe dominated by an *affectatio societatis*? Surely the Union is more than a hotel lobby where you can simply waltz in and out. Won't this give the Eurosceptics a shot at an open goal?'[120] 'On the contrary,' said advocates of the change, 'this clause will not be used lightly – you mustn't underestimate your public.'[121] The second group won the argument. The exit clause was intended for public consumption. International law, as the governments knew, already provides member states with the option of leaving, yet they decided to include the article. The member states were saying to their national publics: You can always step out of the circle.

The doubts and concerns expressed over the secession clause say a great deal about the half-hearted, rather anxious way in which the assent of the public is sought: what if the majority of a national population really did vote to leave Europe? Well, if that is really what they want, then they will have to face the consequences. In deploying the 'Greek' strategy, the club comes up against a hard truth: you cannot give the public a voice and then fall into a swoon when it speaks. Any legitimising 'yes' is worthless if a 'no' is inadmissible.

A senate

Ever since expectations of gaining a firm voter base for the European Parliament were frustrated, the club has been explicitly seeking support from the national electorates. Existing elements – national parliaments as a check on individual members of the European Council and the Council of Ministers, plus referendums for changes to fundamentals – provide some support, but not enough, it would seem.

The two lines of thought that have been pursued lead to two different constitutional forms: 'congress' and 'senate'. A congress would be a forum for periodic meetings between national and European parliamentarians. (The term refers to the overall name for the two legislative chambers in America or France.) Since 1989, there have been meetings twice a year, under the name Cosac, to which the European Parliament and each national parliament send

six representatives. This, however, looks more like an expert meeting for legislative committees than a democratic congress. In the Convention of 2002–03,
Chairman Giscard d'Estaing advocated a European congress, in which
respected national and European parliamentarians would come together
annually to listen to a 'State of the Union' address by the president of the
European Council. There was massive opposition. Perhaps Giscard's congress
seemed too much like a parliamentary applause machine redolent of the Fifth
Republic. The idea was rejected.

The line of thought that leads to a senate would produce a permanent
chamber peopled by national parliamentarians. The emphasis lies not so
much on the legitimising of the executive power as on the organisation of
authoritative dissent. A European senate, representing the national populations, would act as a brake on Brussels centralisation. Key terms in arguments
in its favour are therefore 'scrutiny' and 'democratic checks'. The idea has been
promoted mainly by British politicians, including former minister Michael
Heseltine in 1989 and Prime Minister Tony Blair in 2000, as well as in reports
by the British and French parliaments.

By contrast, the Commission, the Parliament and member states including
Belgium have consistently opposed the creation of a permanent European
forum of national parliaments. They believe that a second legislative chamber
is ready and waiting: the Council of Ministers. In supranational thinking, the
European Parliament represents the citizens, while the Council, as the body
of the states, is destined to grow into a senate (and to lay aside its executive
power in favour of the Commission).

This reasoning ignores the fact that the national publics assembled in the
intermediate sphere do not, by definition, have the same interests, wishes and
fears as those same publics in their capacity as European citizens in the inner
sphere. Should bullfighting be banned? Do we need European rules for
divorce? Yes, that would make rights more equal, hope European citizens. No,
that's a violation of our own civil rights, believe national citizens. Freedom of
choice for hospital patients? Good idea, think wealthy, well-travelled and
multilingual Europeans. But that means they won't have a bed for me at my
local hospital, fear national citizens. The European Parliament cannot articulate all these perspectives, any more than the national governments can –
which is why the viewpoint of the assembled national citizens requires direct
representation at a European level.

Plans for a senate made it into the 2007 Lisbon Treaty in a watered-down
form. The treaty does not actually introduce a new European institution, but
it does involve national parliaments directly in European law-making. They

are allowed to express an opinion on the fundamental question of whether law-making should take place at a European level. When the Commission proposes a new law, national parliaments are given eight weeks to assess whether the measure could instead be introduced at a lower governmental level. If a third of the parliaments protest on these grounds, the Commission must reconsider the proposal. After being shown this 'yellow card' it can withdraw or amend the proposal, or submit it again unchanged. This last possibility displeases those who advocate a 'red card', but in practice it makes little difference, since the Commission will not be able to resist a united democratic front of nine or ten parliaments. This direct line from the national parliaments to European decision-making, without any mediation by the Council of Ministers or the European Council, creates a new link between the public and the club.

Under pressure from public opinion, at least one government has come round to a position in favour of such parliamentary consultation. The Dutch government was initially lukewarm about the idea, complaining that 'it threatens to slow down decision-making'.[122] After the kick in the teeth of the 2005 'no', The Hague became an advocate of the national parliaments. During the June 2007 summit on the successor to the failed constitutional treaty, an unexpectedly fierce argument raged on this point – at three in the morning, after the actual deal had been done – between the Dutch and Belgian prime ministers. Dutchman Jan Peter Balkenende wanted to strengthen the controls available to national parliaments, whereas Belgian Guy Verhofstadt believed that would be a betrayal of the European project. This was no Benelux side-show: it was a battle over the best way to achieve democratic legitimacy.

Crucial to all this is the collective involvement of national parliaments. The fact that a 'no' from a third of the parliaments is sufficient to block accession means that they all bear responsibility if the outcome is a 'yes'. This can be seen as a third step in the involvement of national political systems in the European order. As happened in 1950 with the national ministers (who, after intercession by the Benelux countries, were allowed to take part in decisions 'on condition they act in concert' (Monnet) and therefore became a single European institution) and in 1974 with the national heads of state or government (who jointly threw themselves in at the deep end and together grew to become Europe's highest political institution), so something similar is now happening with the national parliaments. As in the previous two cases, this step will strengthen the club. The parliaments, too, will end up with a dual role.

'Is this a task for Europe?' is the boundary question in the relationship between the voting public and the Union, the threshold the national parliaments jointly police. It is a question that could lead to the politicisation of matters now confined to bureaucratic dossiers. Demonstrations and campaigns might begin to take place in the national capitals, as well as in Brussels or Strasbourg. The voice of the people might be heard in the national parliaments, and from there go direct to the Commission in Brussels, without first being filtered through the government concerned. This represents a crucial underpinning for the Union.

The idea that national parliaments have de facto been given a European role may take some getting used to; but it fits in nicely with the gradual formalisation and increasing independence of the intermediate world of the joint member states. Anyone who looks closely will see that all national constitutional systems change under European pressure. Breakthroughs are sometimes located in small details.

One Dutch example is significant, given the background of long-term resistance by governments to the institutionalisation of the European Council, a constant theme for Dutch ministers from Luns in 1961 ('My "no" to de Gaulle') up to and including Premier Balkenende in 2003 ('No two captains on one ship').[123] The Hague regarded the European Council as a dangerous French game and a threat to the Commission. Moreover, coalition partners pedantically pointed out that a Dutch *minister-president* is not, according to the constitution, actually the overall boss – unlike the French president or the German chancellor – but rather a *primus inter pares*. So what happened in November 2006? Rules governing the structure of the Dutch cabinet were changed. From then on, the Dutch premier could put on the agenda any point he chose. The reason: owing to his role in the European Council, he cannot always wait for a sectoral minister to do this. The result: the *minister-president* of the Netherlands is now formally a cut above the other ministers and, like most of his European colleagues, a head of government.

Such details make beautifully clear how pressure from the European club works all the way through to the governmental structures of the member states.

DRAMA

In the hope that it would start to see Europe as 'our concern', the member states gave the public a say in government in various ways. Citizens acquired a special right to vote in the European inner sphere and saw their national voice become a factor in European politics. Yet doubts about European democracy remain. The blame is often placed on the number of languages involved, which is said to thwart the political game of argument and counter-argument. The public does not understand itself. A more fundamental problem, however, is that European politics fails to excite. There is a lack of action, of events. Summing up both objections in a single phrase, a critic once described the Community as a 'paper Tower of Babel'.[124] The public, many-tongued and easily bored, cannot live by talk (and translations) alone. It demands visible drama.

Its great diversity of languages is one of the chief characteristics of the European public. The six founding states started out in 1957 with four languages: French, German, Italian and Dutch. Each of the accession states brought one further language, with the exception of Austria and Cyprus. The Union now has twenty-three official languages for its twenty-seven member states, making it the biggest translation factory in the world.

The multiplicity of languages is a basic constitutional norm. It is respected on symbolic public occasions – just as the flags of all the member states are flown. Any legislative decision that affects citizens directly is formulated in all the Union's languages. All citizens can write to European institutions in their own language and receive an answer in that language. In public debates, many members of the European Parliament use their own nation's official tongue, as do ministers in the Council, although in their internal meetings judges, parliamentarians and commissioners stick to the 'working languages': English, French and German. The constitutional character of this linguistic diversity is clear from the fact that decisions on the use of languages require unanimity. As a basic norm, it is inviolate.

The number of languages in use obviously impedes the emergence of a 'European public sphere', in the sense of a debating chamber where all European nations or language communities speak at the same time about the same things (as in multilingual democracies like Switzerland or South Africa). Researchers, however, have retreated from the idea that a separate, supranational public sphere – sustained by television broadcaster EuroNews perhaps, or the Brussels newspaper *European Voice*, or European magazines – is an essential precondition for a European debate. The sound of Europe is not purely that of an inner voice. Nowadays studies stress instead the progressive 'Europeanisation' of national public space. Media researchers look at the amount written about the Union in national newspapers, for instance, or the degree of similarity in the way topics are treated. Countless European issues turn out to concern all the member states.

There is another reason why the multiplicity of languages should not be seen as an insurmountable obstacle to a European interplay of voices. Public space requires more than debate alone. It would be more accurate to say, as Arendt does (in contrast to her colleague Habermas), that it is sustained by stories, by events and acts. According to Arendt, public space arose out of the Greek desire for immortality, which is to say a desire by the heroes of the Trojan War, for example, to be remembered for their words and deeds: 'The organization of the *polis* . . . is a kind of organized remembrance. It assures the mortal actor that his passing existence and fleeting greatness will never lack that reality that comes from being seen, being heard, and, generally, appearing before an audience of fellow men.'[125] Only by means of a public arena can a small story, which would be lost with time, be absorbed into a larger story, into history.

But which stories? They are not selected purely by political players who aspire to a leading role. Professional storytellers have just as much influence on the choice. The connection between politics and the public is made by the media. As we know, journalists are not neutral 'mediators', sheets of glass between events and viewers: they are storytellers who select facts and create images. An essential requirement for an effective news story is drama.

One good story, for instance, was the affair surrounding Rocco Buttiglione, the Italian candidate for Eurocommissioner who caused a stir in 2004 with his personal opinions on homosexuality. In the midst of the bickering over the content of what he had said, the national leaders and the Parliament let fly at each other in a dispute about power: who can appoint the Commission? The media lapped it up. The Greek debt crisis of spring 2010 made another good story. Would that country be punished for cooking the books, or would another country help out with financial support? The key lay with the German chancellor, and for weeks everyone wondered when 'Angela' would make her move.

Drama also surrounds flagrant violations of the rules of the game or of European taboos: de Gaulle, who slammed the door in British faces; Thatcher, who transgressed all the codes by demanding 'our money back'; Czech President Klaus, who refused to fly the European flag on his palace in Prague. Are these not heroic deeds, spoken about for years afterwards? Abuses and incongruities, too, are the stuff of legend: Europarliamentarians who do no work, but nevertheless collect their attendance allowance; scandals in officialdom brought to light by whistle-blowers; agricultural subsidies for royal millionaires. Unequal treatment for large and small countries in the budget rules, for example, has been a continual source of public indignation in the smaller member states. Conversely, defiance of 'Brussels' by a small nation such as Denmark or Ireland sometimes arouses sympathy.

Political conflict is an essential element: between member states, between national leaders, between Council, Commission and Parliament, between interests, plans and ideas. Only when an all-or-nothing battle breaks out is the public drawn into the performance as an empathising chorus. Just as no one develops a passion for football by reading the rules, so the law books, procedures and regulations are not interesting in themselves. What thrills us is the game.

Here the fact that European politics is extremely consensus-oriented takes its toll. Ideological and political fault lines between right and left, rich and poor, north and south are tempered by technicalities and compromise. Coalitions between countries shift all the time. Decisions in the Council are rarely taken by majority – the ministers prefer to deliberate until a consensus is reached, which is to say until they all have a story that can be sold at home and told at their own press conferences, in their own languages.

The 'de-dramatisation' of European politics was a merit of the Community that cannot be overstated. In the years 1914–45 Europe had had all too much drama. The flight from history into bureaucracy that Monnet et al. had in mind in 1950 was farsighted in that situation. Their aim was to exchange the unpredictability and pathos of relationships between states for a treaty and a sober interweaving of interests. They worked on this largely out of sight of the public – a conscious choice and, given the nationalistic sentiments they faced, perhaps the only available option. Insofar as any doubt existed on the matter, it was quashed by the lacerating 'religious war' that broke out in French public opinion in 1953–54 over whether there should be a European army.[126] From 1955 onwards, Europe limited itself to the economy and low politics. It was not a player on the stage. Instead it operated mainly in the corridors of law-making and regulatory oversight. There was no need for a public.

The European inner sphere, in particular, struggles with this heritage. Its strength gradually became a weakness. In the 1970s, an image arose of faceless bureaucrats, endless corridors, piles of paper and impenetrable procedures. Public indifference was the least of the resulting evils. An invisible, anonymous power arouses distrust in the public. Freedom demands that power be visible, that individuals, in the limelight, bear clear responsibility for decisions. Only in tyrannical regimes do we encounter rulers who fear to show themselves in public and, like Montesquieu's despot, shut themselves up in palaces or harems.[127] This explains why damning terms have been used to refer to the invisible power of Brussels, such as 'dictatorship of the bureaucracy'. With the deal reached in December 1974 – a European Council of national leaders, plus direct parliamentary elections – Europe was aiming to shed more public light into the offices from two sides. It was no coincidence that it did so at a point when it was eager to try to take action as the Nine on the world stage.

Of all European institutions, the European Council has acquired the most visibility by far. The summits of national leaders are nowadays attended by over 2,000 journalists and covered by up to 100 television stations. The European Council has the protagonists above all to thank for this public success. Almost all citizens know at least one participant: the man or woman who heads their own government. Many will also know the leaders of Britain, France and Germany, and perhaps one or more of their immediate European neighbours. The players are not anonymous bureaucrats, but familiar faces. Summits also have an attractively dramatic plot. The characters come together round a table and are expected to produce a result at a single gathering, before parting for another two or three months. When their meeting ends, they are required to address public opinion by means of a joint statement. The pressure to do so is immense. The main players want to avoid stepping into the lights of the television cameras without any result to announce. But even if a summit fails, the press will still have a good story.

Quarrels are all part of the game. Problems are often solved one or two summits later. But even the press, which ought to know better, prefers to forget that political accords take time; that it is not always possible to squeeze all interests and emotions into a deal at a single sitting; that players must sometimes wait and do business at a later date – because they are facing elections, for example. A British ambassador in Brussels analysed this lack of understanding in a valedictory dispatch sent to his foreign minister in the autumn of 1985: 'How to convince them that the constant clash of views and interests is not a sign of fundamental disunity but rather of the breadth of the front on which European integration is moving and the vitality of the process? Only a static Europe would be calm and united.'[128] Disagreement is a prerequisite of public freedom.

Those involved recognise that the attractions of European politics as drama are minimal. In football, the tiresome passbacks of the ball have been banned. The European political game is likewise using rule changes in an effort to increase its public appeal. For many years, the leaders worked on achieving a more transparent decision-making process. In 2008, for instance, the Parliament decided to raise its threshold for the minimum number of members of a political grouping, the intention being to create a more structured debating chamber. In 2007, after long hesitation, the Council decided that its own legislative meetings, though none of its other gatherings, should be made public (they can be seen on the Internet). The effect of visibility, however, is that negotiations have moved backstage. The need to keep all the member states at the table is more pressing than the need to thrill a European audience. Pressure to compromise trumps the enticements of drama.

Despite the three main strategies for creating a European public – shared identity; protections, freedoms and advantages; political participation and the beginnings of drama – the public still has its doubts. It distrusts Brussels as a self-propelling machine that abuses familiar forms of politics. It will become excited only if it can once again see Europe as a joint response to a great history that affects 'us'.

How can the democratic Greek chorus be both participant and spectator at the same time, both the origin and the audience of Europe's politics? It is down to the order in which public and politics, chorus and actors, acceptance of power and exercise of power come about. In most people's minds, this sequencing issue determines the legitimacy of power. As contemporary democrats, we would like to see populations consent to the founding of a political body before the power it holds is exercised: first the voice of the chorus, then the players to give us the drama. In that sequence lies the modern concept of political legitimacy, which can arise only out of elections and referendums. We might talk of a 'ballot-box sequence'.

It is a sequence that functions excellently within an existing political system. The fact that a ballot box does not always speak unambiguously (think of Bush versus Gore in 2000) usually passes unnoticed. The ballot-box sequence, however, does not enable us to understand how any given democracy, with its elections and parliament, ever took shape. In practice, it turns out that even a democratic founding moment requires representatives who stand up and speak before they are formally appointed as such. A ballot box cannot establish itself.

So, seen historically, the reverse founding sequence is the normal one: first the players, then (if necessary) a chorus. We could come straight out with it and call this second version the 'coup sequence'. Every royal or imperial dynasty starts with a power-grab; every founder is a usurper. Granted, in the years and sometimes centuries that follow, a great deal of political, legal and symbolic energy is invested in the organisation of non-violent intergenerational transfers of power and in the acquisition and sustenance of public goodwill towards the royal family in question; but – as Lady Macbeth's hands remind us – the founding act can never be completely expunged. The monarchy is at best 'modified by time and softened by habit'.[129]

Still, the legitimacy of power is not necessarily adversely affected by the fact that the public appears only afterwards – so long as it does appear. What the ballot-box sequence offers the political players immediately, the coup sequence can provide for them in due course. The appearance of the public indicates that this has occurred. Dynasties gain legitimacy from a sense, which develops over time, that they are facts of nature. Democracies likewise benefit from force of habit. James Madison, one of the men who drafted the American Constitution, spoke of 'that veneration which time bestows on everything, and without which perhaps the wisest and freest governments would not possess the requisite stability'.[130]

That the sequencing issue is less crucial than we tend to assume does not mean that all power is legitimate or becomes so with time. There is, of course, such a thing as illegitimate power. The proposition that political legitimacy depends on publicly expressed acceptance is no tautology; rather it suggests that, conversely, the holder of power or a political order is not legitimate if it has no public. But how do we know when a public is 'truly public'?

The great thing about spectators – whether at a football match, in the theatre or in politics – is that they come and watch of their own accord. This presumes that all are free to enter and that there is something worth seeing. The first condition can be taken for granted. A genuinely free state guarantees its citizens, if nothing else, freedom of expression, of the press, of association, of party politics – in other words all those civic freedoms that enable a public to manifest itself as such, whether through an op-ed in the paper, as a political party, or by watching a parliamentary debate from the public gallery. Illegitimate exercise of power is characterised by the repression of public freedoms. The legitimising effect of the public is demonstrated by the tendency of tyrants to force the populace to appear as an audience. Think of rigged elections or those 'spontaneous' manifestations of support for Communist regimes. A fake public of that kind confers only a Potemkin legitimacy. An unfree public is not a public at all.

A public, once free, will simply turn up whenever it feels excited, because there is something to see: emotion, tension, events, drama. When there is nothing to see, the stadiums, theatres and op-ed pages remain empty.

Yet it is arguable that a 'public' can precede the existence of politics. This third possibility might be called the 'question–answer sequence'. The public poses a question, and politics does (or does not) take it upon itself to provide an answer.

In his *The Public and its Problems* (1927), American philosopher John Dewey claims that the public emerges as a response to things that affect people in general – be they external, natural events or the indirect conse-quences of human actions as they affect third parties. An agreement between two friends to go fishing remains private; an agreement between two conspir-ators or two monopolists can affect other people as well. As soon as such indirect consequences are observed, Dewey says, a public exists. At first, that public is formless, unorganised; but once it organises itself and attempts to combat, boost or mitigate the consequences in question, 'something having the traits of a state comes into existence'.[131] It is therefore the public that, with its eyes on the world, demands political action.

The needs of the public are continually changing, as Dewey was aware. No one can predict them. After all, the public's demands often arise in response to unforeseen events and developments. In any case, managing public affairs has consequences of its own. Mistakes, misjudgments, impractical laws and abuses of power are commonplace. Since the situation changes all the time, the demands of the public change too, which is what public debate is all about. Dewey has a sharp eye for the tension that can arise between a 'new public' (emerging in response to a new historical situation) and established political institutions: 'To form itself, the [new] public has to break existing political forms. This is hard to do because these forms are themselves the regular means of instituting change.'[132] The public can use periodic elections to make its wishes known or to send politics off in a different direction, but it cannot abolish the holding of elections.

The question–answer sequence, the third perspective on the order of appearance of chorus and actors, interprets legitimacy in terms of responsi-bility. A new historical situation poses a question; the public then demands a response, which politicians choose whether or not to give – in other words, they choose whether to take responsibility. It is more than mere wordplay to link the concept of 'responsibility' with 'response'. Its etymology reminds us that responsibility, however much it may be a creative quality, always comes after something, after some kind of demand has been made by reality. (This is experienced most clearly when there is no response to such a demand.)

The Greek chorus is free. When it is able to express itself in an unrestrained clash of opinions, it can allow its political representatives freedom of action. The public expresses its wishes. The actors make promises before stepping on stage, but they cannot actually commit themselves beforehand to everything they are going to do: the unpredictability of the vicissitudes of fortune, which demand a response from them during their allotted time on stage, makes such a commitment impossible. Chorus and actors both know that the real verdict will come later, on the next election day. In their actions, therefore, the players anticipate that retroactive verdict. The chorus, for its part, realises that its 'no' vote is, in essence, more powerful than its 'yes' vote; that its haughty rebuff inspires more respect than its trusting affirmation. It can, however, make its voice heard in the meantime, or even make its power felt.[133]

***

It was the historical situation in 1945, along with the ongoing stream of events, that persuaded the national political players in several European states to develop a shared space for politics. Six states took responsibility for this from 1950 onwards, without the public asking them to do so. Initially their work was protected against the vicissitudes of fortune by the fixed rules of a mainly economic treaty, so it could be kept largely out of sight. New developments – with 1973 as a step up to and 1989 as the crossing of a threshold – convinced national leaders that the European member states also had joint responsibilities to bear in the world around them. Together they sought an active role on the stage. This was no longer a question of competencies that could be based on a treaty, but one of responsibilities towards a joint public.

The Greek chorus, speaking in unison, which was gradually introduced onto the stage by the club of member states as its interlocutor, is not very powerful. It expresses desires and offers pointers, but it is still seeking ways to hold the most important players to account for their acts and omissions. By contrast, the polyphonic performance by national choruses, which have little training in expressing European demands and expectations, does have the capacity to project a forceful 'no'. It cannot change the entire cast in one go, but it can vote individual actors off the stage. Here too, in its verdict on the fundamentals of the circle of members, its 'no' has a greater impact than its 'yes'. In European politics, therefore, we hear an expectant, unified chorus speeding things up and a coercive multiplicity of voices slowing things down.

The connection between all these different voices and speeds is made in the intermediate sphere of the member states. The European Council of heads of state or government, its most eminent expression, hears the call from the inner sphere and above all recognises, under the pressure of events, that joint responsibilities are increasing. At the same time, it is very sensitive to the mood among the separate European populations concerning the desirability or otherwise of joint action. The dual role that all actors in the intermediate sphere must fulfil makes great demands of their political talents. The tension between the coercion of the table, along with the stream of events demanding a response, and the voice of the voters back home can sometimes become unbearable. Virtuosity in European politics is therefore shown by those who succeed in beguiling both the joint public and the separate publics with their performances. The latter challenge is the more difficult. The complaint from the inner sphere about slowness and imperfection (which the actors can ultimately choose to ignore) comes face to face with a multivocal reproach from the intermediate sphere for haste and uniformity (a verdict the actors personally cannot escape). Moreover, sometimes the inner chorus and the polyphonic intermediate chorus seem to contest each other's right to say anything. Speaking 'on behalf of Europe' remains a gamble.

The European political body is not a necessity, not a fact, not a goal in itself. It exists on condition that, in word and deed, it can thrill its manifold public for a moment. Its power, long unimagined, resides in an intermediate status, half-old and half-new, that is gradually coming into its own, making a connection between events originating in the outside world and a joint response to them. It no longer appeals purely to the prospect of a future of unity, but gives shape to itself in multiplicity – in drama, conflict and action – driven by the events of the moment. This transformation required a long journey through time.

European politics is ultimately sustained by a many-headed national public. Although this public has never yet chosen to step out of the European circle, splitting into its component parts, it rarely regards Europe as 'our concern'. Only when members of the chorus, rather than just the actors, individually inhabit their dual role will it be possible to complete the passage to Europe.

Afterword

The human being is a creature in time. Occasionally we might yearn to be animals and to live in and for the moment, with no concept of yesterday, today or tomorrow – *unhistorical*. Nietzsche, who captured this feeling magnificently, feared that too much consciousness of history would see any desire to act swept away in the 'stream of becoming'.[1] He believed that people, like animals, needed forgetfulness, which to him was a sign of robust health. But we are not animals. The human being, says Nietzsche, 'has bred for himself a counter-device, memory, with the help of which forgetfulness can be suspended in certain cases – namely in those cases where a promise is to be made'.[2] This capacity to make promises allows mankind – unlike beasts – to consider the future.

It is man's task to tame the open future, and by doing so to gain a degree of control over the stream of time, both individually and collectively. In its best moments, politics can transform raw reality into new facts. This is no simple matter, but it can be done – with rules, agreements, laws, promises, power. In European politics it has been attempted, since 1950, by means of a treaty that is intended to offer the states some kind of footing, a degree of predictability in their mutual dealings. The treaty was thrown up rather like, as Hannah Arendt wrote in a different context, 'an isolated island of certainty in a sea of uncertainty',[3] in the hope that the island would expand across the entire ocean as time went on. The European wait had begun.

A political body cannot emerge at a single moment: it takes time. Europe's founders understood this and resolved to harness time. They made the long wait bearable by emulating the feat of the apostle Paul: he transformed the present into a time of transition. Unlike the ancient Jewish prophets, who announced His coming at an undetermined moment in the future, Paul talked about something that had already happened: Jesus' resurrection. But he promised that the story of God's direct involvement with man was not yet over. Between the resurrection and the end times lay an extraordinary present, separate from ordinary historical time – a period of waiting for Jesus' return and final Salvation. It was a time of 'already' and of 'not yet', which became the basic framework for the Christian temporal experience. Similarly, Brussels orthodoxy spoke with veneration of Europe's founding, an incontestable fact set down in a treaty, while at the same time announcing that the final goal for Europe still lay ahead. The Europe it envisaged was both 'already' and 'not yet'. Community ideologues drew a Pauline timeline between the first stone and the yet-to-be-completed building. They gave the future a purpose, as the bearer of a promise. People could gaze at the horizon in search of signs of Its coming.

Of course, there is something deceptive about this experience of time. If the promise remains unfulfilled, then the Pauline present brings with it a sense of continual postponement, of existence in anticipation. Tedium lurks. What was meant as a time of transition becomes an adjournment. The ultimate goal slips out of sight. This contradiction is a common feature of revolutions: 'Behold, the dawn is breaking' – but the sun fails to rise.

Each time, great events and crises sunder the closed horizon of waiting, sweeping away the boredom. They thereby disturb the illusion of a future in which the main features were thought to be fixed. But this ought not to surprise us: historical reality is fundamentally unpredictable. Unintended consequences of human acts, unexpected chain reactions, hasty decisions – such things make the future infinitely uncertain. No plan or treaty can predict the full creativity of history, let alone lay down adequate answers in advance. To the retrospective reproach to politicians that before 1989 there had been no plans for German unity lying waiting in civil servants' desk drawers, a German minister replied: 'Be glad nothing was planned! Just imagine the nonsense those plans would have contained!'[4]

The current financial crisis represents a new test for the beginnings of certainty enshrined in the treaty. When a storm becomes too fierce and the wind blows your boat towards the open sea, it is better to have a good compass than an anchor, better to rely on your sense of direction than on rules. So the euro crisis, like others before it, is forcing the circle of member states to politicise itself, to increase its capacity to act and take responsibility. The power of the European *telos* is such that it is revived by every crisis. In the confusion, the hope of redemption gives way to an even more fundamental desire: to face the future together. But this opening up to new experiences demands the abandonment of any notion of returning to a particular port. The common destiny can no longer be understood in terms of 'finality'. No one ever sails on an ocean of certainty.

'Amid the pressure of great events, a general principle gives no help. It is useless to revert to similar circumstances in the Past. The pallid shades of memory struggle in vain with the life and freedom of the Present.'[5] Turmoil of the single currency internally, upheaval in relations between world powers externally: so many shocks that push Europe to continue to invent and reinvent itself.

Notes

Prologue

1. Michel Foucault, *L'Ordre du discours*, Paris, 1971, p. 12.
2. Winston Churchill, 20 February 1944, letter to Stalin, in Martin Gilbert, *Winston S. Churchill*, vol. VII: *Road to Victory, 1941–1945*, London, 1986, p. 687.
3. Walter Hallstein, *United Europe. Challenge and opportunity*, London, 1962, p. 58.
4. Ernst B. Haas, *The Uniting of Europe. Political, social and economic forces 1950–1957*, Stanford, 1958, pp. xix and 4.
5. Haas, *The Uniting*, p. xxiii.
6. Stanley Hoffmann, congress in Bellagio, 12–16 June 1964, in Alan Burr Overstreet, 'The nature and prospects of European institutions: A report on the second Carnegie Endowment Conference on international organization', *Journal of Common Market Studies* 3:2 (1965), pp. 131–2.
7. Alan S. Milward, *The European Rescue of the Nation-State*, London, 1992, p. 18.
8. Andrew Moravcsik, *The Choice for Europe. Social purpose and state power from Messina to Maastricht*, London and New York, 1998, p. 4 (italics in original).
9. Jürgen Habermas, 'Remarks on Dieter Grimm's "Does Europe need a constitution?"', *European Law Journal* 1:3 (1995), p. 306.
10. Larry Siedentop, *Democracy in Europe*, London, 2000, p. 35 (italics in original).
11. Raymond Aron, *Introduction à la philosophie de l'histoire. Essai sur les limites de l'objectivité historique*, Paris, 1948, p. 313.
12. Hendrik Vos and Rob Heirbaut, *Hoe Europa ons leven beïnvloedt*, Antwerp, 2008, p. 13.
13. J.G.A. Pocock, *The Machiavellian Moment. Florentine political thought and the Atlantic republican tradition*, Princeton, 1975, p. 27.
14. Marc Bloch, *Apologie pour l'histoire ou métier d'historien*, Paris, 1952, p. 13.
15. Otto von Bismarck, November 1876, in Timothy Garton Ash, *In Europe's Name. Germany and the divided continent*, London, 1994, p. 387; Bismarck, November 1876, in Manfred Brunner, 'Ein europäisches Volk gibt es nicht', *Die Welt*, 30 June 2000.
16. Marc Fumaroli, in Lucien Bély, *L'art de la paix en Europe. Naissance de la diplomatie moderne XVIe–XVIIIe siècles*, Paris, 2007, p. 21.
17. Talleyrand, in Adam Zamoyski, *Rites of Peace. The fall of Napoleon and the Congress of Vienna*, London, 2007, pp. 270, 290.
18. Bély, *L'Art de la paix*, p. 225.
19. Fikret Adanir, 'Turkey's entry into the Concert of Europe', *European Review* 13:3 (2005), pp. 395–417.
20. De Gaulle, 1 March 1969, in Henry Kissinger, *The White House Years*, London, 1979, p. 110.
21. Robert Schuman, 'Faire l'Europe', *Revue de Paris* (April 1951).

22. Monnet, 1954, speech to the parliamentary Assembly of the European Coal and Steel Community, in Jean Monnet, *Mémoires*, Paris, 1976, p. 460.
23. Preamble to the European Coal and Steel Community Treaty (ECSC).
24. Philippe de Schoutheete on Etienne Davignon, 11 June 2008, conversation with the author.
25. Willy Brandt, *Begegnungen und Einsichten 1960–1975*, Hamburg, 1976, p. 322.
26. André Szász, *The Road to European Monetary Union*, Basingstoke and New York, 1999, p. 48.
27. J.H. Kaiser, 'Die im Rat vereinigten Vertreter der Regierungen der Mitgliedstaaten', in W. Hallstein and H.-J. Schlochauer (eds.), *Zur Integration Europas. Festschrift für Carl Friedrich Ophüls*, Karlsruhe, 1965, pp. 120, 115.
28. Dominique Rousseau, 'Les constitutions possibles pour l'Europe', *Cités* 13 (2003), p. 14.
29. J. Linthorst Homan, in Jan Werts, *The European Council*, London, 2008, p. 17.
30. Peter Ludlow, *The Making of the European Monetary System*, London, 1982, p. 21.
31. Arts. 96 and 98 ECSC; Arts. 236 and 237 of the European Economic Community Treaty (EEC); Arts. 48 and 49 of the EU Treaty (EU).
32. Preamble and Art. 237 EEC.
33. Monnet, 1953, via E.P. Wellenstein, 13 August 2008, conversation with the author.
34. Art. 213 § 2 Treaty Establishing the European Community (EC).
35. Art. 203 EC.
36. Thomas Hobbes, *Leviathan, Parts 1 and II*, revised edition, eds. A.P. Martinich and B. Battiste, Ontario, 2011, p. 151 (I.16) (italics in original).
37. Lord Ralf Dahrendorf, 'From Europe to EUrope: A story of hope, trial and error', in Andrew Moravcsik (ed.), *Europe Without Illusions. The Paul-Henri Spaak Lectures, 1994–1999*, Lanham, 2005, p. 82; Timothy Garton Ash, 'Catching the wrong bus?' in Peter Gowan and Perry Anderson (eds.), *The Question of Europe*, London, 1997, p. 125.
38. Cris Shore, *Building Europe. The cultural politics of European integration*, London, 2000, p. 28.
39. Jacques Le Goff, *The Birth of Purgatory*, trans. Arthur Goldhammer, Chicago, 1984, p. 6.

Part I The Secret of the Table

1. Jean-Jacques Rousseau, *The Social Contract*, trans. Maurice Cranston, London, 1968, p. 59 (I.5).
2. Hobbes, *Leviathan*, p. 152 (I.16).
3. Rousseau, *The Social Contract*, p. 59 (I.5).
4. Jean-Jacques Rousseau, *Considerations on the Government of Poland and on its Proposed Reformation*, completed but not published April 1772, trans. and available at: http://www.constitution.org/jjr/poland.htm (accessed 5 March 2013).
5. Vaclav Klaus, 1994, in Carlos Reijnen, *Op de drempel van Europa. De Tsjechen en Europa in de twintigste eeuw*, Kampen, 2005, p. 15; Gaitskell, 3 October 1962, in Brian MacArthur (ed.), *The Penguin Book of Twentieth-Century Speeches*, London, 1999, p. 321.
6. Bettino Craxi, 29 June 1985, in Jan Werts, *The European Council*, Amsterdam and Atlanta, 1992, p. 281.
7. Spaak, 11 December 1951, in Paul-Henri Spaak, *Combats inachevés. De l'espoir aux déceptions*, Paris, 1969, vol. II, p. 51.
8. A.J.P. Tammes, *Hoofdstukken van internationale organisatie*, The Hague, 1951, p. 7.
9. Robert Schuman, Declaration of 9 May 1950.
10. Clement Attlee, in Paul Van de Meerssche, *De Europese integratie, 1945–1970*, Leuven, 1971, p. 122.
11. Spierenburg to the Dutch Ministry of Foreign Affairs, 29 May 1950, in Dirk Spierenburg and Raymond Poidevin, *Histoire de la Haute Autorité de la Communauté européenne du Charbon et de l'Acier. Une expérience supranationale*, Brussels, 1993, p. 13.
12. Monnet, in "Een sneeuwveld in 1942": Interview with M. Kohnstamm', in A.G. Harryvan et al. (eds.), *Voor Nederland en Europa. Politici en ambtenaren over het Nederlandse Europabeleid en de Europese integratie, 1945–1975*, The Hague, 2001, p. 92.

13. Preamble ECSC.
14. E.P. Wellenstein, 13 August 2008, letter to the author.
15. Jelle Zijlstra, *Per slot van rekening. Memoires*, Amsterdam and Antwerp, 1992, p. 55.
16. Jean Duvieusart, in E.P. Wellenstein, 13 August 2008, letter to the author.
17. Kaiser, 'Die im Rat vereinigten Vertreter' (see Prologue, note 27).
18. Preamble EEC.
19. Robert Marjolin, *Le Travail d'une vie. Mémoires 1911–1986*, Paris, 1987, p. 293.
20. Jean-François Deniau, *L'Europe interdite*, Paris, 1977, p. 67.
21. Jean-Marc Boegner 3 February 1972, available at: www.cvce.eu (accessed 5 March 2013).
22. Boegner, ibid (accessed 5 March 2013).
23. Marinus van der Goes van Naters, *c.* 1962, via Charles Rutten, 29 November 2006, interview available at: www.cvce.eu (accessed 5 March 2013).
24. European Court of Justice, *Van Gend & Loos*, judgment 26/62 of 5 February 1963.
25. Robert Lecourt, *L'Europe des juges*, Brussels, 1977, p. 260.
26. European Court of Justice, *Costa/ENEL*, judgment 6/64 of 15 June 1964.
27. Lecourt, *L'Europe des juges*, p. 284.
28. Hallstein, *United Europe*, p. 23.
29. Ibid., p. x.
30. De Gaulle, press conference of 15 May 1962, in Charles de Gaulle, *Mémoires d'espoir, suivi d'un choix d'allocutions et messages sur la IVe et la Ve Républiques*, Paris, 1994, pp. 792–3.
31. Hallstein, March 1965, in John Newhouse, *Collision in Brussels. The Common Market crisis of 30 June 1965*, London, 1967, pp. 86–7.
32. Marjolin, *Le Travail d'une vie*, p. 343.
33. Maurice Couve de Murville, 30 June 1965, in Newhouse, *Collision in Brussels*, p. 113.
34. Gerhard Schröder, 30 June 1965, in Newhouse, *Collision in Brussels*, p. 117; John Lambert, 'The constitutional crisis 1965–1966', *Journal of Common Market Studies* 4:3 (1966), p. 209.
35. Press communiqué Elysée, 1 July 1965, in *Bulletin of the European Communities* 8-1965.
36. Sicco Mansholt, *c.* 17 July 1966, in Johan van Merriënboer, *Mansholt. Een biografie*, Amsterdam, 2006, p. 327.
37. Charles de Gaulle, 28 July 1965, in Alain Peyrefitte, *C'était de Gaulle*, vol. II, Paris, 1997, p. 296.
38. Couve de Murville, 16 December 1988, in Jean-Marie Palayret, Helen Wallace and Pascaline Winand (eds.), *Visions, Votes and Vetoes. The empty chair crisis and the Luxembourg Compromise forty years on*, Brussels, 2006, p. 58.
39. Ludwig Erhard, 7 July 1965, in Palayret et al., *Visions, Votes and Vetoes*, p. 116.
40. De Gaulle, 9 September 1965, in *Mémoires d'espoir*, pp. 931–2.
41. Ibid.
42. Couve de Murville, 20 October 1965, in Palayret et al., *Visions, Votes and Vetoes*, p. 256.
43. Council of the EEC, in *Bulletin of the European Communities* 12-1965.
44. Pierre Pescatore, 'The "Luxembourg Compromise"' in Palayret et al., *Visions, Votes and Vetoes*, p. 243.
45. J.M.A.H. Luns, quoted in Council Secretariat, 'Compte-rendu de la réunion du Conseil extraordinaire des Communautés, 17–18 janvier 1966 à Luxembourg', p. 3.
46. Spaak, ibid., p. 4.
47. Council Secretariat, 'Compte-rendu de la réunion du Conseil extraordinaire de la CEE et de la C.E.E.A., 17–18 et 28–29 janvier 1966 à Luxembourg', p. 1.
48. Extraordinary Session of the Council, *Bulletin of the European Communities* 3-1966.
49. Luns, in Merriënboer, *Mansholt*, p. 334.
50. De Gaulle, 2 February 1966, in Peyrefitte, *C'était de Gaulle*, II, p. 620.
51. Andreas Donner, 1966, in J. Linthorst Homan, *Wat zijt ghij voor een vent. Levensherinneringen*, Assen, 1974, p. 268.
52. Pescatore, 'The "Luxembourg Compromise"', p. 245.
53. Emile Noël, 1967, in Palayret et al., *Visions, Votes and Vetoes*, p. 251.
54. Paul Taylor, *The Limits of European Integration*, New York, 1983, p. 40.
55. De Gaulle, in Peyrefitte, *C'était de Gaulle*, II, p. 290.

56. Couve de Murville, 13 November 1965, in Palayret et al., *Visions, Votes and Vetoes*, p. 68.
57. De Gaulle, 15 September 1965, in Peyrefitte, *C'était de Gaulle*, II, pp. 299–300.
58. Linthorst Homan, *Wat zijt ghij voor een vent*, p. 266.
59. Marjolin, *Le Travail d'une vie*, p. 349.
60. C.A. Colliard, 'L'irréductible diplomatique', in Claude Berr et al., *Mélanges offerts à Pierre-Henri Teitgen*, Paris, 1984, pp. 109–26.
61. Couve de Murville, *Une Politique étrangère, 1958–1969*, Paris, 1971, p. 298.
62. Walter Bagehot, *The English Constitution*, ed. R.H.S. Crossman, London, 1963, p. 61.
63. Geoffrey Howe, *Conflict of Loyalty*, London, 1995, pp. 407–8.
64. Geoffrey Rippon, *The Times*, May 1982, in Stephen Wall, *A Stranger in Europe. Britain and the EU from Thatcher to Blair*, Oxford, 2008, p. 14.
65. Edith Cresson, 18 May 1982, in Jean-Paul Jacqué, 'L' évolution du triangle institutionnel communautaire depuis l' élection du Parlement européen au suffrage universel direct', in Berr, *Mélanges offerts à Pierre-Henri Teitgen*, p. 188.
66. François Mitterrand, 24 May 1984, speech to the European Parliament in Strasbourg.
67. Howe, *Conflict of Loyalty*, p. 408.
68. Howe, in Anthony L. Teasdale, 'The life and death of the Luxembourg Compromise', *Journal of Common Market Studies* 31:4 (1993), pp. 574–5.
69. Ibid., p. 578.
70. J.H.H. Weiler, *The Constitution of Europe. 'Do the new clothes have an emperor?' and other essays on European integration*, Cambridge, 1999, pp. 71–2.
71. John Major, *The Autobiography*, London, 1999, p. 653.
72. Art. 23, para. 2, EU.
73. Art. 31, para. 2, EU (Lisbon version).
74. 'Centinel' [pseudonym of Samuel Bryan], letter to the *Independent Gazette* (Philadelphia), 5 November 1787, in Michael Lienesch, *New Order of the Ages. Time, the constitution and the making of modern American political thought*, Princeton, 1988, p. 145.
75. Patrick Henry, speech of 4 June 1788 to the Virginia Convention, in Bernard Bailyn, *The Debate on the Constitution*, vol. II, New York, 1993, pp. 595–7.
76. James Iredell, speech of 30 July 1788 to the North Carolina Convention, in Bailyn, *The Debate on the Constitution*, II, p. 916.
77. Madison, in Alexander Hamilton, James Madison and John Jay, *The Federalist Papers* (1788), eds. Charles R. Kesler and Clinton Rossiter, New York, 1999, no. 40, p. 219.
78. Madison, in *The Federalist Papers*, no. 43, p. 247.
79. Ibid.
80. Luther Martin, speech of 8 February 1788 to the parliament of Maryland, in Bailyn, *The Debate on the Constitution*, I, p. 656.
81. Ibid., p. 661.
82. Patrick Henry, speech of 24 June 1788 to the Virginia Convention, in E.C. Biddle (ed.), *American Oratory, or Selections from the Speeches of Eminent Americans*, Philadelphia, 1846, p. 92.
83. 'Centinel', in Lienesch, *New Order of the Ages*, p. 145.
84. G.W.F. Hegel, *Elements of the Philosophy of Right*, Cambridge, 1991, p. 21.
85. Monnet, *Mémoires*, pp. 368–9.
86. Robert Badinter, *Une constitution européenne*, Paris, 2002, pp. 133–4.
87. Romano Prodi, 'Préface' in A. Mattera (ed.), *Pénélope: Projet de Constitution de l'Union européenne*, Clément Juglar, Paris, 2003, p. 8.
88. CONV 647/03 of 2 April 2003, art. G.
89. Andriukaitis, amendment to art. G of CONV 647/03.
90. De Vries and De Bruijn, amendment to art. G of CONV 647/03.
91. Peter Hain, 25 April 2003, plenary session, Convention (verbatim).
92. Hubert Haenel, 25 April 2003, plenary session, Convention (verbatim).
93. *Official Journal of the European Union* 16.12.2004, C 310/464.
94. Conclusions, European Council 21–22 June 2007, Annex A, point 24. 'IGC' stands for intergovernmental conference.
95. Edmund Burke, *Reflections on the Revolution in France*, ed. Conor Cruise O'Brien, London, 1969, p. 106.

96. American Supreme Court, *Marbury vs. Madison* (5 U.S. 137), 24 February 1803.
97. *Constitution de la Cinquième République française*, art. 89 ('De la révision').
98. Emmanuel-Joseph Sieyès, *Qu'est-ce que le Tiers Etat?*, ed. Jean-Denis Bredin, Paris, 1988, p. 128.
99. Art. 236 EEC.
100. Art. 95 ECSC.
101. German Constitutional Court, 12 October 1993, BVerfGE 89, 155, § 112 ('Maastricht-Urteil').
102. Mitterrand, speech to the European Parliament in Strasbourg, 24 May 1984.
103. Ad-hoc Committee for Institutional Affairs, 'Report to the European Council (Brussels, 29–30 March 1985)', p. 13.
104. Thatcher and Andreotti, 28 June 1985, in Charles Rutten, *Aan de wieg van Europa en andere Buitenlandse Zaken. Herinneringen van een diplomaat*, Amsterdam, 2005, p. 167.
105. Draft conclusion, European Council in Milan, 29 June 1985, in *Libération*, 'Les hauts et les bas du sommet européen', 1 July 1985.
106. Poul Schlüter, 29 June 1985, in Jean De Ruyt, *L'Acte unique*, Brussels, 1987, p. 62.
107. Andreas Papandreou, 29 June 1985, in De Ruyt, *L'Acte unique*, p. 62.
108. Bernard Ingham, 29 June 1985, in *The Times*, 'Thatcher incensed by EEC vote', 1 July 1985.
109. 'European leaders split on changes', *New York Times*, 30 June 1985.
110. 'Why it all went wrong: after the EEC Summit', *Financial Times*, 1 July 1985.
111. Jacques Delors, *Mémoires*, Paris, 2004, p. 217.
112. J. Keller-Noëllet, 16 December 2008, conversation with the author.
113. Mitterrand, 4 May 1985, in Jacques Attali, *Verbatim*, Paris, 1993, vol. I, p. 806.
114. German Constitutional Court, 29 May 1974, BVerfGE 37, 271, § 56 ('Solange-I').
115. Art. 235 EEC, later art. 308 EC.
116. Karel Van Miert, *Mijn jaren in Europa. Herinneringen van een eurocommissaris*, Tielt, 2000, p. 34.
117. Weiler, *Constitution of Europe*, pp. 54–5.
118. BVerfGE 89, 155 § 37.
119. Art. F, para. 3, EU.
120. BVerfGE 89, 155 §§ 63 and 90.
121. R. de Lange, 'Het Bundesverfassungsgericht over het Verdrag van Maastricht: een nieuw Solange?', *Sociaal-economische wetgeving* 42 (1994), pp. 418–36.
122. Art. 50 EU (Lisbon version).
123. Joachim Wuermeling, amendment to art. F of CONV 647/03 of 2 April 2003.
124. Jean-Luc Dehaene, 12 June 2003, in Olivier Duhamel, *Pour l'Europe*, Paris, 2003, p. 125.
125. Valéry Giscard d'Estaing, 11 June 2003, in Alain Lamassoure, *Histoire secrète de la Convention européenne*, Paris, 2003, p. 424.
126. Giuliano Amato, 10 July 2003, in Jacques Ziller, *The European Constitution*, Deventer, 2004, p. 29; and Alain Dauvergne, *L'Europe en otage*, Paris, 2004, p. 307.
127. Bruno De Witte, 'Revision', *European Constitutional Law Review* 1 (2005), pp. 136–40.
128. Niccolò Machiavelli, *The Historical, Political, and Diplomatic Writings of Niccolo Machiavelli*, trans. Christian E. Detmold, Boston, 1882, vol. II, I.23.

Part II Vicissitudes of Fortune

1. Bismarck, *c.* 1890, in Thomas Stahl-Kuhlman, 'Der Mantel der Geschichte. Die Karriere eines unmöglichen Zitats', in idem et al. (eds.), *Geschichtsbilder. Festschrift für Michael Salewski zum 65. Geburtstag*, Wiesbaden, 2003, pp. 212–23, 216 (cited in Max Vorberg, 'Otto von Bismarck: Ein Erinnerungsbild', *Kirchliche Monatsschrift* 18 (1899), p. 2).
2. Machiavelli, *The Prince*, trans. W.K. Marriott, 1908, ch. XXV.
3. Ibid.

4. Robert Orr, 'The time motif in Machiavelli', in Martin Fleisher (ed.), *Machiavelli and the Nature of Political Thought*, New York, 1972, pp. 185–208.
5. Machiavelli, *The Discourses*, trans. Christian Detmold, New York, 1940, I.3.
6. Ibid., I.4.
7. Ibid., III.31.
8. Art. 4, para. 2, EU (Lisbon version).
9. Hobbes, *Leviathan*, p. 151 (I.16) (italics in original).
10. Edgar Morin, *Penser l'Europe*, Paris, 1987, p. 251.
11. Stanley Hoffmann, 'Obstinate or obsolete? The fate of the nation-state and the case of Western Europe', *Daedalus* 95:3 (1966), reproduced in Mette Eilstrup-Sangiovanni (ed.), *Debates on European Integration. A reader*, Basingstoke and New York, 2006, p. 135.
12. Monnet, *Mémoires*, p. 350.
13. De Gaulle, 5 October 1945, in Charles de Gaulle, *Lettres, notes et carnets, VI, 1945–1951*, Paris, 1984, pp. 95–8.
14. Churchill, 5 March 1946, in Brian MacArthur (ed.), *The Penguin Book of Twentieth-Century Speeches*, London, 1999, p. 232.
15. French Ministry of Foreign Affairs, 14 July 1948, in Franz Knipping, 'Que faire de l'Allemagne? Die französische Deutschlandpolitik 1945–1950', in Franz Knipping and Ernst Weisenfeld (eds.), *Eine ungewöhnliche Geschichte. Deutschland – Frankreich seit 1870*, Bonn, 1988, pp. 153–4.
16. Gerhard Kreyssig, 'USA im Ruhrgebiet', *Süddeutsche Zeitung*, 16 November 1948.
17. *Die Zeit*, 21 October 1948, in Knipping, 'Que faire de l'Allemagne?', p. 155.
18. Konrad Adenauer, *Erinnerungen*, Stuttgart, 1965, vol. I, p. 300.
19. Acheson, 19 October 1949, in Alan Milward, *The Reconstruction of Western Europe, 1945–1951*, London, 1984, p. 391.
20. Acheson, 30 October 1949, in ibid., pp. 391–2.
21. Adenauer, *Erinnerungen*, I, p. 315; Hanns Jürgen Küsters, 'Die Verhandlungen über das institutionelle System zur Gründung der Europäischen Gemeinschaft für Kohle und Stahl', in Klaus Schwabe (ed.), *Anfänge des Schuman-Plans 1950-51/Beginnings of the Schuman-Plan*, Baden-Baden, 1988, pp. 76–7.
22. Adenauer, 9 May 1950, in Tony Judt, *Postwar. A history of Europe since 1945*, New York, 2005, p. 157.
23. Adenauer, *c.* 31 May 1950, in 'Konrad Adenauer und der Schuman-Plan: Ein Quellenzeugnis', in Schwabe (ed.), *Anfänge des Schuman-Plans*, p. 138.
24. Robert Schuman, Declaration of 9 May 1950.
25. Schuman, 9 May 1950, in Monnet, *Mémoires*, p. 360.
26. Dean Acheson, *Present at the Creation. My years in the State Department*, New York, 1969, p. 567.
27. René Pleven, 24 October 1950, in *Chronique de politique étrangère* 5:5/6 (1952), p. 589.
28. Schuman, 15 February 1951, in ibid., p. 528.
29. Acheson, *Present at the Creation*, p. 765.
30. Acheson, 27 May 1952, in ibid., pp. 825–6.
31. Dirk Stikker, 12 August 1976 (transcript of interview), in William Fursdon, *The European Defence Community. A history*, London, 1980, p. 3.
32. Art. 38 European Defence Community Treaty.
33. Georges Bidault, 9 March 1953, in Richard T. Griffiths, *Europe's First Constitution. The European Political Community, 1952–1954*, London, 2000, p. 93.
34. Raymond Aron, 'Esquisse historique d'une grande querelle idéologique', in Raymond Aron and Daniel Lerner, *La Querelle de la C.E.D. Essai d'analyse sociologique*, Paris, 1956, p. 9.
35. Stanley Hoffmann, 'Les oraison funèbres', in ibid., p. 60; Daniel Lerner, 'La France et l'Europe dans l'arène mondiale', in ibid., p. 182.
36. Pierre Mendès France, 18 June 1954, in Aron and Lerner, *Querelle de la C.E.D.*, p. 52.
37. Anthony Eden, *Full Circle*, London, 1960, pp. 431, 543; Mollet, in Christian Pineau, *1956. Suez*, Paris, 1976, pp. 38–9.

38. Heinrich von Eckardt, in Mathieu Segers, *Tussen verzoening en verval. De nationale stand-puntbepaling van de Bondsrepubliek Duitsland gedurende de beraadslagingen en onderhande-lingen over de Verdragen van Rome*, Nijmegen, 2006, p. 245.
39. J.W. Beyen, *Het spel en de knikkers. Een kroniek van vijftig jaren*, Rotterdam, 1968, p. 234.
40. Russell Bretherton, 7 November 1955, in Hugo Young, *This Blessed Plot. Britain and Europe from Churchill to Blair*, London, 1999, p. 93 (Young doubts that Bretherton would have said anything so grandiloquent).
41. Mollet and Eden, 6 November 1956, in Pineau, *1956. Suez*, pp. 176-7.
42. Adenauer, 6 November 1956, in ibid., p. 177.
43. Anwar Sadat, 19 November 1956, in Henry Kissinger, *Diplomacy*, New York, 1994, p. 547.
44. Harold Macmillan, diary for July 1960, in Young, *This Blessed Plot*, p. 122.
45. Linthorst Homan, *Wat zijt ghij voor een vent*, p. 233.
46. Josef Illerhaus, March 1960, in Leon N. Lindberg, *The Political Dynamics of European Economic Integration*, Stanford, 1963, p. 185.
47. EEC Commission, *General Report 1960*, in Lindberg, *Political Dynamics*, p. 167.
48. Ivo Samkalden, 1962, in Annette Schrauwen, 'De kunst van het pact', in M. Spiering et al. (eds.), *De weerspannigheid van de feiten. Opstellen over geschiedenis, politiek, recht en litera-tuur aangeboden aan W.H. Roobol*, Hilversum, 2000, p. 213.
49. Arthur Cockfield, in Nicholas Colchester and David Buchan, *Europe Relaunched. Truths and illusions on the way to 1992*, London, 1990, p. 29.
50. European Commission, *Completing the Internal Market. White Paper from the Commission to the European Council (Milan, 28 and 29 June 1985)*, COM(85)310, 14 June 1985.
51. Art. 98 ECSC.
52. Art. 237 EEC.
53. J.M.A.H. Luns, *Ik herinner mij*, Leiden, 1971, p. 169.
54. Couve de Murville, *Une Politique étrangère*, p. 398.
55. John McCloy, 16 May 1950, in Adenauer, *Erinnerungen*, I, p. 320.
56. Eden, January 1952, in Judt, *Postwar*, p. 129.
57. John Major, 'Raise your eyes, there is a land beyond', *Economist*, 25 September 1993.
58. Macmillan, December 1959, in Young, *This Blessed Plot*, p. 118.
59. George W. Ball, *The Past Has Another Pattern. Memoirs*, New York and London, 1982, p. 218.
60. Miriam Camps, *Britain and the European Community, 1955-1963*, Princeton, 1964, p. 513.
61. Spaak, *Combats inachevés*, p. 369.
62. De Gaulle, in Luns, *Ik herinner mij*, p. 145.
63. De Gaulle, *Mémoires d'espoir*, p. 839, translation available at: http://aei.pitt.edu/5777/1/5777.pdf (accessed 5 March 2013).
64. In Stephen Wall, *A Stranger in Europe*, p. 1.
65. Rolf Lahr, memo 19 January 1963, in N. Piers Ludlow, *The European Community and the Crises of the 1960s. Negotiating the Gaullist challenge*, London and New York, 2006, p. 12.
66. Spaak, 29 January 1963, in Camps, *Britain and the European Community*, p. 489.
67. Edward Heath, in ibid., p. 492.
68. Alfred Müller-Armack, in Ludlow, *The European Community and the Crises of the 1960s*, p. 13.
69. Georges Pompidou, 10 October 1969, in Eric Roussel, *Georges Pompidou, 1911-1974*, Paris, 2004, p. 335.
70. Conclusions, The Hague summit, 1-2 December 1969, in *Bulletin of the European Communities* 1-1970.
71. Pompidou, autumn 1970, in Roussel, *Georges Pompidou*, p. 394.
72. Conclusions, Paris summit, 19-21 October 1972, in *Bulletin of the European Communities* 10-1972.
73. Philippe de Schoutheete, 11 June 2008, conversation with the author.
74. Brandt, 1 May 1973, in Henry Kissinger, *Years of Upheaval*, London, 1982, p. 157.
75. Ibid., p. 157.
76. Andersen and Kissinger, 25 September 1973, in ibid., p. 704.

77. Pompidou, 31 October 1973, in *Bulletin of the European Communities* 11-1973.
78. Heath, 16 September 1973, in Monnet, *Mémoires*, p. 593.
79. Conclusions, Copenhagen summit, 14–15 December 1973, point 3, in *Bulletin of the European Communities* 12-1973.
80. Monnet, *Mémoires*, pp. 598–9.
81. Valéry Giscard d'Estaing, *Le Pouvoir et la vie*, vol. I, Paris, 1988, p. 119.
82. Giscard d'Estaing, 27 August 1974, in Werts, *The European Council* (1992), pp. 52–3.
83. Giscard d'Estaing, *Le Pouvoir et la vie*, I, pp. 120–1.
84. Erik Holm, 'Denmark's position at the birth of the European Council', unpublished report to the author, 3 February 2009.
85. Conclusions, Paris summit, 9–10 December 1974, point 2, in *Bulletin of the European Communities* 12-1974.
86. Ibid., point 4.
87. Joschka Fischer, *Die Rückkehr der Geschichte. Die Welt nach dem 11. September und die Erneuerung des Westens*, Cologne, 2005, pp. 9–10.
88. Hans-Georg Gadamer, 'Über leere und erfüllte Zeit', in Gadamer, *Gesammelte Werke*, Tübingen, 1987, vol. IV, pp. 148–9.
89. Félipe González, 'Europa am Scheideweg', *Frankfurter Allgemeine Zeitung*, 17 October 2001, in Tilo Schabert, *Wie Weltgeschichte gemacht wird. Frankreich und die Deutsche Einheit*, Stuttgart, 2002, p. 533.
90. Helmut Kohl, *Erinnerungen, 1982–1990*, Munich, 2005, p. 966.
91. Douglas Hurd, 22 December 1989, in Garton Ash, *In Europe's Name*, p. 2.
92. Margaret Thatcher, *The Downing Street Years*, London, 1993, p. 796.
93. Mitterrand, 21 December 1989, in Attali, *Verbatim*, III, p. 381.
94. Delors, 17 October 1989, in Jacques Delors, *Le Nouveau concert européen*, Paris, 1992, p. 336.
95. Delors, 17 January 1990, in ibid., p. 209 (italics in original).
96. Delors, 23 January 1990, in Charles Grant, *Delors. Inside the house that Jacques built*, London, 1994, p. 135.
97. Mitterrand, 23 January 1990, in Attali, *Verbatim*, III, p. 401.
98. Wilfried Martens, in 'Watershed for Europe', *New York Times*, 22 November 1989.
99. Kohl and Mitterrand, letter to the Irish presidency of the EC, 19 April 1990, in Finn Laursen and Sophie Vanhoonacker, *The Intergovernmental Conference on Political Union. Institutional reforms, new policies and international identity of the European Community*, Maastricht, 1992, p. 276.
100. Ibid.
101. Thatcher, in *Hansard*, 30 October 1990, col. 873.
102. Geoffrey Howe, 13 November 1990, in Howe, *Conflict of Loyalty*, p. 702.
103. Just de Visser, 13 August 1991, in Bob van den Bos, *Mirakel en debacle. De Nederlandse besluitvorming over de Politieke Unie in het Verdrag van Maastricht*, Assen, 2008, p. 177.
104. Peter van Walsum, 2001, in ibid., p. 193.
105. Delors, 5 June 1993, in Grant, *Delors*, p. 142.
106. Delors, 20 November 1991, in Laursen and Vanhoonacker, *The Intergovernmental Conference*, p. 20.
107. Mitterrand, 1991, quoted by Ruud Lubbers in *Buitenhof*, Dutch television, 18 March 2007.
108. Mitterrand, 1991, in Major, *The Autobiography*, p. 270.
109. Giulio Andreotti, 17 October 1991, in Hubert Védrine, *Les mondes de François Mitterrand. A l'Elysée, 1981–1995*, Paris, 1996, p. 469.
110. Art. J.1 EU (Maastricht version).
111. Art. J.3 EU (Maastricht version).
112. Art. B and art. J.7(1) EU (Maastricht version).
113. Council of the European Union, Conclusions 8 April 2001, in J.-P. Jacqué, *Droit institutionnel de l'Union européenne*, Paris, 2001, p. 146.
114. Art. 47 EU (Lisbon version).

115. Václav Havel, 'A call for sacrifice: The co-responsibility of the West', *Foreign Affairs* 73:2 (1994), p. 2.
116. Bronisław Geremek, quoted in 'Europe was very far for us', *European Observer*, 22 March 2007.
117. Joschka Fischer, in *Buitenhof*, Dutch television, 22 May 2005.
118. Kohl, *Erinnerungen*, p. 986.
119. Kohl, 22 November 1989, in ibid., p. 985.
120. Joschka Fischer, *Die rot-grünen Jahre. Deutsche Außenpolitik – vom Kosovo bis zum 11. September*, Cologne, 2007, p. 121.
121. Joschka Fischer, 1 October 2007, conversation with the author.
122. Hubert Védrine, 21 June 1999, in Védrine, *Face à l'hyperpuissance. Textes et discours (1995–2003)*, Paris, 2003, p. 152.
123. Catherine the Great, in Robert Cooper, *The Breaking of Nations. Order and chaos in the twenty-first century*, London, 2003, p. 78.
124. Art. 8(1) EU (Lisbon version).
125. Karl Schlögel, *Im Raume lesen wir die Zeit. Über Zivilisationsgeschichte und Geopolitik*, Frankfurt, 2007, pp. 469–70.
126. Peter Moors, 7 August 2008, conversation with the author.
127. George H. Bush, 1 October 1990, speech to the United Nations General Assembly.
128. Robert Kaplan, 'De geschiedenis slaat altijd terug', *NRC Handelsblad*, 15 September 2001.
129. Fischer, *Die Rückkehr der Geschichte*.
130. Peter Moors, 7 August 2008, conversation with the author; Joschka Fischer, 1 October 2007, conversation with the author.
131. Graham Watson, 29 November 2001, in Mareike Kleine, *Die Reaktion der EU auf den 11. September. Zu Kooperation und Nicht-Kooperation in der inneren und äußeren Sicherheit*, Munich, 2004, p. 101.
132. European Council, 'Conclusions et plan d'action du Conseil européen extraordinaire du 21 septembre 2001', point 2.
133. Robert D. Putnam and Nicholas Bayne, *Hanging Together. The seven-power Summits*, London, 1984, p. 3.
134. CONV 489/03, 16 January 2003, annex: 'Contribution franco-allemande à la Convention européenne sur l'architecture institutionnelle de l'Union' (de Villepin and Fischer).
135. Art. 15, para. 6, EU (Lisbon version).
136. Ibid.
137. Jan-Werner Müller, 'Is Euro-patriotism possible?', *Dissent* 52:2, (2004) pp. 13–17, 15.
138. Henri Bentégeat, in *NRC Handelsblad*, 20 November 2008.
139. Nicolas Sarkozy, 12 August 2008, press conference in Moscow.
140. Joschka Fischer, 1 October 2007, conversation with the author.

Part III The Quest for a Public

1. Bagehot, *English Constitution*, p. 61. This quotation dates from 1867.
2. Tindemans, 29 December 1975, 'Report by Mr Leo Tindemans, Prime Minister of Belgium, to the European Council, pt. 4.B', in *Bulletin of the European Communities* 1-1976, 'Supplement', pp. 11–36.
3. John R. Searle, *The Construction of Social Reality*, London, 1995.
4. European Union, 'Berliner Erklärung', 25 March 2007, available at: www.bundesregierung.de (Presse Mitteilung 117/07) (accessed 1 March 2009).
5. H.L.A. Hart, *The Concept of Law*, Oxford, 1997.
6. Deniau, *L'Europe interdite*, pp. 237–8.
7. Julien Benda, *Discours à la nation européenne*, Paris, 1979, pp. 14–15.
8. Shore, *Building Europe*.
9. Massimo d'Azeglio, 1870, in E.J. Hobsbawm, *Nations and Nationalism since 1780. Programme, myth, reality*, Cambridge, 1992, p. 44.
10. Bronisław Geremek, in *Le Monde*, 18 February 2004.

11. Jan-Werner Müller, 'Europäischer Verfassungspatriotismus – eine Europäische Verbindlichkeit?', *Transit* 28 (Winter 2004/05), p. 175.
12. Benda, *Discours*, p. 124.
13. European Commission, 'Community action in the cultural sector. Communication to the Council', 22 November 1977, in Tobias Theiler, *Political Symbolism and European Integration*, Manchester, 2005, p. 58.
14. Adam Zamoyski, in Theiler, *Political Symbolism*, p. 123.
15. European Parliament, Hahn Report (1982), in R. Collins, 'Unity in diversity? The single market in broadcasting and the audiovisual, 1982–92', *Journal of Common Market Studies* 32:1 (1994), p. 95.
16. Art. 151 EC.
17. Hannah F. Pitkin, *The Concept of Representation*, Berkeley, 1972, p. 101.
18. European Council, 'Conclusions du Conseil européen de Fontainebleau (25 et 26 juin 1984)', pt. 6 ('Europe des citoyens'), trans. in *Bulletin of the European Communities* 6-1984, point 1.1.9, subheading 6.
19. Comité-Adoninno, 'Report submitted to the Milan European Council (Milan, 28–29 June 1985)', pt. 9, in *Bulletin of the European Communities* 7-1985, Supplement, pp. 18–30.
20. Ibid.
21. Rutten, *Aan de wieg*, p. 175.
22. Final Act, 13 December 2007, 'Declaration by the Kingdom of Belgium, the Republic of Bulgaria, the Federal Republic of Germany, the Hellenic Republic, the Kingdom of Spain, the Italian Republic, the Republic of Cyprus, the Republic of Lithuania, the Grand-Duchy of Luxembourg, the Republic of Hungary, the Republic of Malta, the Republic of Austria, the Portuguese Republic, Romania, the Republic of Slovenia, and the Slovak Republic on the symbols of the European Union' (Declaration 52), in *Official Journal of the European Union* 17.12.2007, C 306/02.
23. Benda, *Discours*, p. 47.
24. http://ec.europa.eu/education/programmes/llp/comenius/moreabou_en.html (accessed 8 February 2007).
25. Napoleon Bonaparte, in Benda, *Discours*, p. 39.
26. Conclusions of the informal ECOFIN Council meeting in Verona, 12–13 April 1996.
27. Theme Selection Advisory Group, 'Interim report to the European Monetary Institute's Working Group on Printing and Issuing a European Banknote. On the selection of a theme for the European banknote series', May 1995, pp. 3, 4, available at: www.wbrett.com/busn100/euroBankNote_Report.pdf (accessed 5 March 2013).
28. Ibid., pp. 18, 30.
29. Ibid., p. 28.
30. Ibid., pp. 41, 13.
31. Ibid., pp. 16–17.
32. Feature Selection Advisory Group, 'Selection of Design Features. Report to the European Monetary Institute's Working Group on Printing and Issuing a European Banknote', November 1995, p. 7, available at: http://www.ecb.int/euro/pdf/preparation/Feature_report.pdf (accessed 5 March 2013).
33. Nationale Bank van België, 'De eurobiljetten', available at: www.bnb.be (accessed 12 February 2009).
34. Preamble ECSC.
35. Art. 98 ECSC.
36. Kenneth Younger, 14 May 1950, in Young, *This Blessed Plot*, pp. 50–1.
37. Kurt Schumacher, in Dirk Schümer, *Das Gesicht Europas. Ein Kontinent wächst zusammen*, Munich, 2004, p. 64.
38. European Council, Copenhagen, 'Declaration on European Identity', 14 December 1973, in *Bulletin of the European Communities* 12-1973, pp. 127–30.
39. Exodus 3:14.
40. Treaty Establishing a Constitution for Europe, Preamble.
41. Hans Magnus Enzensberger, in Schümer, *Das Gesicht Europas*, p. 306.
42. George Steiner, *De idee Europa*, Tilburg, 2004, pp. 17–30.

43. Krzysztof Pomian, 'De Europese identiteit: een historisch feit en een politiek probleem' in Leonard Ornstein and Lo Breemer (eds.), *Paleis Europa. Grote denkers over Europa*, Amsterdam, 2007, pp. 30-1.
44. Norwegian Nobel Committee, 'Announcement', 12 October 2012, available at: http://nobelpeaceprize.org/en_GB/laureates/laureates-2012/announce-2012/ (accessed 5 March 2013).
45. Schuman, Declaration of 9 May 1950.
46. 'Report by Mr Leo Tindemans, Prime Minister of Belgium, to the European Council', pt. 1.A.
47. Ibid., pt. 4.A.2.
48. Ibid., pt. 4.B.
49. Acts 22:23-9.
50. Paul Magnette, *La Citoyenneté européenne. Droits, politiques, institutions*, Brussels, 1999, pp. 18-19.
51. European Court of Justice, *Van Gend & Loos*, judgment 26/62 of 5 February 1963.
52. Felipe González, 'La Europa que quiere España', *Politica exterior* 6:30 (1992), pp. 7-20.
53. European Court of Justice, case C-184/99 (Grzelczyk) point 31 and case C-209/03 (Bidar) point 31.
54. José Manuel Barroso, quoted in 'Banken Europa moeten overstap vereenvoudigen', *De Volkskrant*, 21 November 2007.
55. Juvenal, *Satires*, 10, ll. 77-81.
56. Philippe C. Schmitter, *How to Democratize the European Union... And Why Bother?*, Lanham, 2000, p. 44.
57. Milward, *The European Rescue*, p. 317.
58. Art. 2 EU (ex art. B).
59. Danuta Hübner, quoted in 'Money-go-round: Why the European Union is spending billions in rich countries', *Economist*, 28 July 2007.
60. Ieke van den Burg, 'Europa is een betere partner voor regio's dan Den Haag', *Eurowerk* 4:2 (2004), p. 5.
61. Nigel Farage, quoted in 'Money-go-round: Why the European Union is spending billions in rich countries', *Economist*, 28 July 2007.
62. Danuta Hübner, 'Future of cohesion policy', speech of 23 November 2007 (COM speech/07/742).
63. Janos Matyas Kovacs, 'Between resentment and indifference. Narratives of solidarity in the enlarging Union', in Krzysztof Michalski (ed.), *What Holds Europe Together? Conditions of European solidarity*, Budapest, 2006, pp. 54-85.
64. Kurt Biedenkopf, 'In Vielfalt geeint. Was hält Europa zusammen?', *Transit* 26 (Winter 2003/04), p. 46.
65. José Manuel Barroso, 'A citizens' agenda: Delivering results for Europe', 10 May 2006, (COM speech/06/286).
66. Brochure distributed by the Dutch government in advance of the referendum on Europe, May 2005.
67. 'Gratis pinnen!', Willem de Zwijger blog, 23 May 2005, available at: http://dezwijger.blogspot.com (accessed 5 March 2013).
68. Mary Beard, 'Cruising with Caesar', *New York Review of Books*, 18 December 2008, p. 48.
69. Jean-Jacques Rabier, 8 February 2002, interview, available at: www.cvce.eu (accessed 5 March 2013).
70. European Commission, *Public Opinion in the European Union. First results*, Eurobarometer 77, available at: http://ec.europa.eu/public_opinion/archives/eb/eb77/eb77_first_en.pdf (accessed 5 March 2013).
71. European Commission, *Public Opinion in the European Union. First results*, Eurobarometer 70, available at: http://ec.europa.eu/public_opinion/archives/eb/eb70/eb70_first_en.pdf (accessed 5 March 2013).
72. Emile Noël, 'The political prospects for Europe in the wake of the Single European Act: a response to public expectations', in Karlheinz Reif and Ronald Inglehart (eds.),

Eurobarometer. The Dynamics of European Public Opinion. Essays in honour of Jacques-René Rabier, Basingstoke, 1991, p. 63.

73. Carl Schmitt, *Verfassungslehre*, Berlin, 1993, pp. 246–7.
74. Hannah Arendt, 'What is freedom?' in Arendt, *Between Past and Future. Eight exercises in political thought*, London, 1993, pp. 154–5.
75. Friedrich Nietzsche, *The Birth of Tragedy. An attempt at self-criticism*, trans. Ian Johnston, Arlington, 2009.
76. Arendt, 'What is freedom?', pp. 152–3.
77. Machiavelli, *The Prince*, ch. XXV.
78. Machiavelli, *The Discourses*, I.7.
79. Written communication from Richard Corbett, former president of the Young European Federalists, to the author (June 2011).
80. David Marquand, *A Parliament for Europe*, London, 1979, pp. vii, 64.
81. Küsters, 'Die Verhandlungen', p. 79; Monnet, *Mémoires*, p. 379.
82. Art. 20 ECSC.
83. P.J.G. Kapteyn, *L'Assemblée commune de la Communauté du Charbon et de l'Acier. Essai de parlementarisme européen*, Leiden, 1962, p. 115.
84. Ibid., p. 117.
85. Ibid., p. 219.
86. H.H. Maas, 'Parlementaire democratie in de Europese Gemeenschappen', *Internationale Spectator* (1965), p. 888, in S. Patijn, *De uitbreiding van de bevoegdheden van het Europees Parlement*, Rotterdam, 1973, p. 22.
87. Walter Hallstein, *Die Europäische Gemeinschaft*, Düsseldorf and Vienna, 1974, p. 73.
88. Art. 138, para. 3, first sentence, EEC (orig.).
89. Martino, 1956, quoted by Ducci, 22 October 1984, in Maria Grazia Melchionni and Roberto Ducci, *La genèse des Traités de Rome. Entretiens inédits avec 18 acteurs et témoins de la négociation*, Paris, 2008, p. 395.
90. Art. 138, para. 3, second sentence, EEC (orig.).
91. *Publicatieblad* 6/1958; Patijn, *De uitbreiding van de bevoegdheden*, p. 177n1.
92. De Gaulle, press conference 15 May 1962, in de Gaulle, *Mémoires d'espoir*, p. 793.
93. Wall, *Stranger in Europe*, p. 69.
94. Single European Act, art. 6, para. 2, in *Official Journal of the Europeon Communities*, 29 June 1987.
95. Hugh Beesley, 'Direct elections to the European Parliament', in Beesley et al., *Limits and Problems of European Integration*, The Hague, 1963, p. 83.
96. R. Corbett, F. Jacobs and M. Shackleton, *The European Parliament*, London, 2011, p. 10.
97. Art. 14, para. 1, EU (Lisbon version).
98. 'Antoniozzi Report. Opinion from the Legal Affairs Committee', in Werts, *The European Council* (1992), p. 154.
99. Thatcher, in Julian Priestley, *Six Battles that Shaped Europe's Parliament*, London, 2008, p. 27.
100. Ibid., p. 44.
101. Weiler, *Constitution of Europe*, p. 337.
102. Memorandum from the Spanish government, 'The road to European citizenship', unpublished Council document SN 3940/90 of 24 September 1990, in Laursen and Vanhoonacker, *The Intergovernmental Conference*, p. 329.
103. Art. 8 EC (Maastricht version).
104. Memorandum from the Danish government, 'Denmark in Europe', 30 October 1992.
105. Art. 17.1 EC (Amsterdam version).
106. Weiler, *Constitution of Europe*, p. 333.
107. European Council, 14/15 December 2001, Annex ('Laken Declaration').
108. CONV 574/03 of 26 February 2003.
109. Art. I-1 Treaty on a Constitution.
110. Thucydides, Pericles' Funeral Oration, *The History of the Peloponnesian War*, trans. Richard Crawley (1874), retrieved via Project Gutenberg.

111. European Council, 21/22 June 2007, Presidency Conclusions, Annex 1, point 1.

112. Andrew Moravcsik, 'What can we learn from the collapse of the European constitutional project?', *Politische Vierteljahresschrift* 47:2 (2006), p. 220 (italics in original).

113. Alexander Somek, 'Postconstitutional treaty', *German Law Journal* 8:12 (2007), p. 1126.

114. Art. 10 EU (Lisbon version) (italics LvM).

115. Moravcsik, 'What can we learn?', p. 223.

116. Krzysztof Bobinski, 'Poland's generational shift', *Open Democracy*, 5 November 2007, available at: www.euractiv.com (accessed 5 March 2013).

117. Howe, speech of 13 November 1990, in Howe, *Conflict of Loyalty*, p. 667.

118. Art. 203 EC.

119. Art. 50 EU (Lisbon version).

120. European Convention, sitting of 25 April 2003, verbatim (speakers Haenel, De Vries, Meyer).

121. European Convention, sitting of 25 April 2003, verbatim (speakers Stuart, Thorning-Schmidt, Einem).

122. Dutch Ministry of Foreign Affairs, 26 September 2002, 'Europa in de steigers. De Nederlandse inbreng in de volgende fase van de Conventie over de toekomst van Europa'.

123. Luns, *Ik herinner mij*, p. 139; Jan Peter Balkenende, 'Europa niet gebaat bij twee stuurlui', *De Volkskrant*, 4 February 2003.

124. Jean-Marie Benoist, *Pavane pour une Europe défunte. L'adieu aux technocrates*, Paris, 1977, p. 27.

125. Hannah Arendt, *The Human Condition*, Chicago and London, 1998, p. 198.

126. Stanley Hoffmann, 'Les Oraisons funèbres', p. 60.

127. Montesquieu, *De l'Esprit des lois*, II.5 and III.9.

128. Sir Michael Butler, in Wall, *A Stranger in Europe*, pp. 65–6.

129. Benjamin Constant, *De l'Esprit de conquête et de l'usurpation* (1814), ed. Ephraïm Harpaz, Paris, 1986, p. 39 (II.2).

130. Madison, in Hamilton et al., *The Federalist Papers*, p. 282 (no. 49).

131. John Dewey, *The Public and its Problems*, Athens, Ohio, 1954, p. 12.

132. Dewey, *The Public*, p. 31.

133. Bernard Manin, *Principes du gouvernement représentatif*, Paris, 1995, p. 223.

Afterword

1. Friedrich Nietzsche, 'On the Use and Abuse of History for Life' in *Untimely Meditations*, trans. R.J. Hollingdale, Cambridge, 1997, p. 62.

2. Friedrich Nietzsche, *On the Genealogy of Morality*, ed. Keith Ansell-Pearson, trans. Carol Diethe, Cambridge, 2006, p. 36.

3. Arendt, *The Human Condition*, p. 244.

4. Wolfgang Schäuble, in Schabert, *Wie Weltgeschichte gemacht wird*, p. 533.

5. G.W.F. Hegel, *The Philosophy of History*, trans. J. Sibree, Kitchener, 2001, p. 20.

COMMENTARY AND BIBLIOGRAPHY

MEMOIRS AND FIRST-HAND ACCOUNTS

First, a brief description of books by and about fourteen politicians who either played a decisive part in European politics or provide exceptional insights into it, in some cases both.

Acheson. Dean Acheson, *Present at the Creation. My years in the State Department*, New York, 1969. Acheson was assistant secretary of state under Roosevelt and undersecretary of state from 1945 under Truman before becoming secretary of state under the latter (1949–53). The jaunty title alone gives a good impression of what many Americans saw as their mission after 1945: to build a new world out of nothing. A worthwhile book, full of Washington office politics but also giving a detailed account of marathon sessions during which Nato and the European Defence Community were founded. It includes several witty portraits of Europe's leading figures.

Adenauer. Konrad Adenauer, *Erinnerungen*, Stuttgart, 1965–68, vols. I–IV, covering the years 1945–53, 1953–55, 1955–59 and 1959–63 respectively. Plain language from a man close to the events and motives of the moment. Every page of the first volume reflects Adenauer's determination as chancellor (1949–63) to win back Germany's freedom of action, along with the hopes he had for the necessary *Westbindung* in Europe. But the old fox is proud of his lesser tricks too. The same volume includes a moving account of his first official foreign trip as chancellor in April 1951, when he travelled to Paris for the final negotiations and signature of the Coal and Steel Treaty.

Beyen. Johan Willem Beyen, *Het spel en de knikkers. Een kroniek van vijftig jaren*, Rotterdam, 1968. An international banker who had represented the Netherlands at the Bretton Woods Conference and served on the board of the World Bank and the IMF, this non-party Dutch minister of foreign affairs (1952–56) had a lively mind. He launched his plan for a European market at precisely the right time, in 1955, but he lacked vanity and the Belgian Paul-Henri Spaak took the credit. See also the biography by W.H. Weenink, *Bankier van de wereld, bouwer van Europa. Johan Willem Beyen, 1897–1976*, Amsterdam, 2005.

De Gaulle. De Gaulle's memoirs from 1958 onwards and his speeches and press conferences of 1946–69 can be found in Charles de Gaulle, *Mémoires d'espoir, suivi d'un choix d'allocutions et messages sur la IVe et la Ve Républiques*, Paris, 1994. He was a master of words, and the *mise-en-scène* of words, and this book is indispensable to anyone wishing to understand the French position since 1958. Useful supplements are the testimonies of his spokesman (and the only person allowed to take notes during cabinet meetings) Alain Peyrefitte, *C'était de Gaulle*, Paris, 1994–97, vols. I–III, and that of de Gaulle's foreign minister for many years, and briefly prime minister, Maurice Couve de Murville, *Une Politique étrangère, 1958–1969*, Paris, 1971. In

Brussels, Couve de Murville was regarded as a faithful servant to the General, presenting the same arguments in less fiery language.

Delors. Jacques Delors, *Mémoires*, Paris, 2004. A book of interviews in which the famous Commission president (1985–95), formerly Mitterrand's finance minister (1981–84), recalls past events. As a Catholic Social Democrat with a trade union background he was at the centre of European politics, halfway between Kohl and Mitterrand. He subtly managed to combine European, French and institutional interests (his greatest success being the preparations for the euro) but in the transformative years 1989–91 he stressed the latter. His speeches of the period can be found in Delors, *Le Nouveau concert européen*, Paris, 1992. A supplementary book with an alternative perspective is the excellent biography by Charles Grant, *Inside the House That Jacques Built*, London, 1994, which offers an insight into Delors' unmatched control of the Brussels machinery while paying due attention to less glorious episodes.

Giscard d'Estaing. Born in Koblenz in the French-occupied Rhineland, the son of an army officer, as French president (1974–81) Valéry Giscard d'Estaing established a connection between the European inner sphere and high politics. He had a strong sense of timing. His early memoirs, *Le Pouvoir et la vie*, Paris, 1988, vol. I, offer a highly readable account but are among the more conceited of the genre. The role of German Chancellor Helmut Schmidt (1974–82) in both Giscard's major European initiatives – the establishment of the European Council (1974) and the European Monetary System (1978) – receives insufficient attention. After losing the 1981 French presidential election Giscard d'Estaing continued as a Europarliamentarian (1989–94) and as chair of the European Convention (2002–03). The early biography is the best: Olivier Todd, *La Marelle de Giscard, 1926–1974*, Paris, 1977.

Kissinger. A European in Washington. As Nixon's security advisor (1969–73) and subsequently as secretary of state under Nixon and Ford (1973–77) he held up a mirror to the uniting Europeans in 1973 that they were not yet ready to look into. His doorstopper memoirs, which cover receptions as well as *realpolitik*, are Henry Kissinger, *The White House Years*, London, 1979, and idem, *Years of Upheaval*, London, 1982. Between the Vietnam War and Watergate he visited and received countless European leaders. As a German Jew who had fled to America with his parents in 1938, he was himself (as he said of de Gaulle) 'the son of a continent covered with ruins testifying to the fallibility of human foresight'.

Kohl. Helmut Kohl, *Erinnerungen, 1982–1990*, Munich, 2005. As a Christian Democrat, a Rhinelander, and the man who completed the return to sovereignty through *Westbindung*, the long-serving German chancellor (1982–98) was a political 'grandson' to Adenauer. Kohl seized the opportunity for German unification in 1989. For more detail on the acceleration of history after the fall of the Berlin Wall, see Kohl's security advisor Horst Teltschik's *329 Tage. Innenansichten der Einigung*, Berlin, 1991, and Kohl himself in *Ich wollte Deutschlands Einheit*, Berlin, 1996.

Marjolin. Robert Marjolin, *Le Travail d'une vie. Mémoires, 1911–1986*, Paris, 1987. A brilliant and hardworking French economist from a humble background who held senior posts in international organisations after 1945: secretary-general of the Organization for European Economic Cooperation (Marshall Aid organisation); involved in negotiating the Treaty of Rome; and vice-president of the Commission (1958–67). Thereafter he acted on a number of occasions as a 'wise man of Europe'. His memoirs are moving in their unparalleled soberness of mind.

Mitterrand. François Mitterrand, president of France (1981–95), did not write comprehensive memoirs – he died not long after leaving office – but we do have the testimony of his special advisor and 'sherpa' Jacques Attali, *Verbatim*, Paris, 1993–95, vols. I–III (resp. 1981–86, 1986–88, 1988–91): enjoyable gossip, but unreliable according to critics. More substantial are the recollections of Mitterrand's diplomatic advisor, who later became foreign minister, Hubert Védrine, *Les Mondes de François Mitterrand. A l'Elysée, 1981–1995*, Paris, 1996 – very informative about Franco-German relations.

Monnet. Essential reading is Jean Monnet, *Mémoires*, London, 1978. A senior French civil servant, first president of the High Authority (1952–55) and famous source of inspiration for Europe's conception on 9 May 1950, Monnet was influential until well into the 1970s, having founded an Action Committee for the United States of Europe after the fiasco of the defence community. His book teems with politicians, civil servants and lawyers. Some works on Monnet – such as the biography by François Duchêne, *Jean Monnet. The first statesman of interdependence*, New York, 1994 – tend towards hagiography. For Monnet's legendary network in Washington, see for example Kennedy's secretary of state George W. Ball, *The Past Has Another Pattern. Memoirs*, New York, 1982.

Spaak. Briefly Belgian prime minister several times, but mainly foreign minister (for almost twenty years between 1936 and 1966), with a Churchillian stance, Spaak injected a parliamentary consciousness into the Council of Europe (1949–51) and the parliamentary Assembly of the mining and steel community (1952–54) as well as being a passionate chairman of negotiations leading up to the Treaty of Rome (1955–57) and secretary-general of Nato (1957–61). His memoirs of the years 1947–66 are Paul-Henri Spaak, *Combats inachevés. De l'espoir aux déceptions*, vol. II, Paris, 1969. For more details see the lengthy biography by Michel Dumoulin, *Spaak*, Brussels, 1999.

Thatcher. The British prime minister (1979–90) tells in Margaret Thatcher, *The Downing Street Years*, London, 1993, of her collisions with fellow government leaders at legendary summits, but she also speaks appreciatively of European solidarity during the Falklands War (1982). Memoirs with rather greater precision were written by Thatcher's long-serving chancellor of the exchequer (1979–83) and foreign minister (1983–89) Geoffrey Howe, *Conflict of Loyalty*, London, 1995. A useful addition, closer to the permanent negotiating tables in Brussels, is British diplomat Stephen Wall's *A Stranger in Europe. Britain and the EU from Thatcher to Blair*, Oxford, 2008.

Van Miert. Karel Van Miert, *Mijn jaren in Europa. Herinneringen van een eurocommissaris*, Tielt, 2000. A highly regarded Belgian commissioner for transport (1989–93) and for competition (1993–99), Van Miert shows the astonishing effects that the economic rules had in practice, as well as the impact of the political pressure on rule-bound decisions. He steered efforts to ensure European rules were applied accommodatingly during the economic restructuring of the German *Neue Länder*.

***

PROLOGUE

Three European discourses

Few analyses of discourse in political philosophy *à la* Michel Foucault or Quentin Skinner are available on the language used in and about Europe. Works in the field of European Studies are often highly specialised, ranging from case studies on individual terms to a social critique of 'Eurospeak'.

The aim of the threefold distinction used in this book between states-confederalism, citizens-federalism and offices-functionalism, is different and essentially introductory: to offer a history of ways of speaking about Europe that goes back to before 1945, to point to silent alliances between the discourses (their academic guise included) and their political or institutional interests, and to discover a shared blind spot. An early variation on the tripartite division can be found in Altiero Spinelli, *The Eurocrats. Conflict and crisis in the European Community*, Baltimore, 1966, pp. 10–25.

States, citizens, offices

The origin of 'the Europe of States'. The confederalist project of Bohemian King Podiebrad in 1462 as well as a plan by Sully that appeared in 1662, are included in the anthology edited by Yves Hersant and Fabienne Durand-Bogaert, *Europes. De l'antiquité au XXe siècle. Anthologie critique et commentée*, Paris, 2000, pp. 68–74 and 90–5. For de Gaulle's confederalism of the war years, see the speeches in Charles de Gaulle, *Discours et messages I. Pendant la Guerre, 1940–1946*, Paris, 1970. For Winston Churchill's thoughts in the same period, see for example Hugo Young, *This Blessed Plot. Britain and Europe from Churchill to Blair*, London, 1999, pp. 11–13.

The origin of 'the Europe of Citizens'. The impact of the 1789 French Revolution on thinking about Europe is documented in J.J.A. Mooij, *Het Europa van de filosofen*, s.l., 2006, and in Pim den Boer, *Europa. De geschiedenis van een idee*, Amsterdam, 2003, while nineteenth-century pleas for federalism by Saint-Simon and Victor Hugo are examined in Pascal Ory (ed.), *L'Europe? L'Europe*, s.l., 1998, pp. 7–61 and 157–207. Influential in the interwar period was Richard Coudenhove-Kalergi, author of *Pan-Europa* (1923) and many other works. For post-war federalism, see Frank Niess, *Die europäische Idee – aus dem Geist des Widerstands*, Frankfurt, 2001; E.H. Carr et al., *Nations ou fédéralisme*, Paris, 1946; and Julien Benda et al., *L'esprit européen. Rencontres internationales de Genève 1946*, Neuchâtel, 1947. Speakers at the Geneva conference included French intellectuals Julien Benda, Georges Bernanos and Maurice Merleau-Ponty, German philosopher Karl Jaspers, British writer Stephen Spender, Swiss writer Denis de Rougemont, Swiss historian Jean Starobinski and Hungarian Marxist Georg Lukács. After the Hague Congress of 1948 this intellectual moment belonged to the past: enter the civil servants.

The origin of 'the Europe of Offices'. See the aforementioned titles by and about Beyen, Marjolin and Monnet.

Disciplinary constraints

Offices thinking. By a man regarded as the founder of functionalism: David Mitrany, *A Working Peace System. Argument for the functional development of international organisations*, London, 1943. The author advocates the setting up of an international technical agency that would take over governmental functions. The territorial scale would be determined by the function: agreements concerning rail travel, for example, were best made by a whole continent; those concerning television, globally.

Ernst Haas applies Mitrany's functionalism – against the latter's wishes – to the establishment of a regional political community in Ernst B. Haas, *The Uniting of Europe. Political, social and economic forces, 1950–1957*, Stanford, 1958. The result, called 'neofunctionalism', has long dominated both theorising and linguistic usage. For testimony on the resonance of Haas' vocabulary in Brussels in the 1960s, see John Gerard Ruggie et al., 'Transformations in world politics: the intellectual contributions of Ernst B. Haas', *Annual Review of Political Science* 8:1 (2005), pp. 271–96. For intellectual relations between Commission President Walter Hallstein and the neofunctionalists – including an account of his dramatic game of bluff poker with de Gaulle in the spring of 1965 – see Jonathan P.J. White, 'Theory guiding practice: the neofunctionalists and the Hallstein EEC Commission', *Journal of European Integration History* 9:1 (2003), pp. 111–31.

One exponent of the resurgence of Offices thinking in the mid-1980s is Giandomenico Majone; see his *Regulating Europe*, London and New York, 1996, and many other publications. More cautious is Fritz W. Scharpf, *Governing in Europe. Effective or democratic?*, Oxford, 1999, but he too believes that legitimacy derived from results can be not only a 'supplement', but even a 'replacement' for legitimacy derived from consultation. Other authors of the governance school are Simon Hix, Gary Marks and Liesbeth Hooghe.

States thinking. Intergovernmentalism, a reaction to neofunctionalism, was explained in the 1960s by American political scientist Stanley Hoffmann, who drew upon Gaullist France. See for example Stanley Hoffmann, 'Europe's identity crisis' (1964), in idem, *The European Sisyphus. Essays on Europe, 1964–1994*, Boulder, 1995, pp. 9–50 and idem, 'Obstinate or obsolete? The fate of the nation-state and the case of Western Europe', *Daedalus* 95:3 (1966), pp. 862–915 (often reprinted since). With time, nuances creep in: the American was forced to recognise in 1982 that the Community had real power and was showing unexpected resilience: idem, 'Reflections on the nation-state in Western Europe today', *Journal of Common Market Studies* 21:1 (1982), pp. 21–38.

American political scientist Andrew Moravcsik reinforced the intergovernmental claim that European cooperation was always at the service of the states. In *The Choice for Europe. Social purpose and state power from Messina to Maastricht*, London and New York, 1998, based on the positions taken in French, German and British diplomacy, Moravcsik convincingly shows that five major European agreements all fit the same pattern: national preferences reflect not only geopolitical but economic interests; the result of negotiations can be explained by the relative power of the states; and the choice of the type of institution can be explained in game theory by the degree of commitment sought. One nuance: Moravcsik bases his thesis on a limited number of 'dramatic' decisions, which, given that the foundations of the club were at stake, were by definition mainly a matter for the member states.

Alan Milward explores intergovernmentalism in two strong studies of economic history, *The Reconstruction of Western Europe, 1945–1951*, London, 1984, and *The European Rescue of the Nation-State*, London, 1992. The author also puts his finger on the teleological tenor of many studies dealing with the early years of the Community. Functionalists and federalists, enthralled by the European ideal, forgot the degree to which Monnet, Spaak or De Gasperi were most concerned with the reconstruction of their own nation states. See the splendid chapter 'The lives and teachings of the European saints' in Milward, *The European Rescue*, pp. 318–44.

Citizens thinking. For the political importance of Europe's legal structure, see the early studies by Joseph Weiler: 'The Community system: the dual character of supranationalism', *Yearbook of European Law* 1:1 (1981), pp. 267–306, and 'Community, Member States and European integration: is the law relevant?', *Journal of Common Market Studies* 21:1 (1982), pp. 39–56. The 'definitive' version of his argument is J.H.H. Weiler, 'The transformation of Europe' (1991) in idem, *The Constitution of Europe. 'Do the new clothes have an emperor?' and other essays on European integration*, Cambridge and New York, 1999, pp. 10–101. This brilliant essay dissects the transformations the club went through between 1950 and 1990. In later work the author exhibits nostalgia for the Community and passes over the politico-judicial eccentricities of the Union.

Two useful overviews of academic schools and theoretical approaches are Ben Rosamond, *Theories of European Integration*, Basingstoke and New York, 2000, and Antje Wiener and Thomas Diez (eds.), *European Integration Theory*, Oxford, 2009.

The tribunal of events

The best studies on the link between historical and political judgment remain the following two classics: Raymond Aron, *Introduction à la philosophie de l'histoire. Essai sur les limites de l'objectivité historique*, Paris, 1948, and J.G.A. Pocock, *The Machiavellian Moment. Florentine political thought and the Atlantic republican tradition*, Princeton, 1975.

Aron divides the blind spots regarding the historicity of politics into three categories. It is irresistibly tempting to connect this threesome with the three European discourses, namely the sociological 'Europe of Offices', the idealistic 'Europe of Citizens' and the (pseudo-) realistic 'Europe of States'. Aron: 'Three illusions prevent us from recognizing the *historicity* of all politics. One is that of the scientists who imagine a science (of society or of morality) that will permit us to establish a rational craft. The second is that of the rationalists who, owing more than they think to the Christian ideal, assume without reservation that practical reason determines not just the ideal of individual conduct but also that of collective life. The last is that of the pseudo-realists, who claim to base their findings on historical experience, fragmented regularities or eternal necessities, and heap contempt on the idealists, without seeing that they are subjecting the future to a past less understood than reconstructed, a shadow of their scepticism, an image of their own resignation.' (*Introduction à la philosophie de l'histoire*, pp. 324–5.)

THREE EUROPEAN SPHERES

The outer sphere

The wider Europe of sovereign states has been the subject of a great deal of modern writing on political history, beginning in 1833 with Leopold von Ranke's *Die grossen Mächte*, an essay on the European balance of power. Two more recent and entertaining studies on diplomacy and peace conferences are Lucien Bély, *L'Art de la paix en Europe. Naissance de la diplomatie moderne, XVIe–XVIIIe siècles*, Paris, 2007, and Adam Zamoyski, *Rites of Peace. The fall of Napoleon and the Congress of Vienna*, London, 2007.

The term 'European common law' became widespread after 1648, while the term 'European public law', which comes from *Du droit public de l'Europe fondé sur les traités conclus jusqu'en l'année 1740*, 1746, by the French writer Gabriel Bonnot de Mably, was prevalent in late eighteenth-century political discourse. The concept was later revived in Latin as *Ius publicum europaeum* by Carl Schmitt in his *Der Nomos der Erde im Völkerrecht des Jus Publicum Europaeum*, Berlin, 1950.

Europe as a shared cultural and historical space has been the subject of many studies. For the 'idea of Europe' see for example the anthologies edited by Rolf Hellmut Foerster, *Die Idee Europa, 1300–1946. Quellen zur Geschichte der politischen Einigung*, Munich, 1963, and by Pascal Ory, *L'Europe? L'Europe*, Paris, 1998 (which includes texts dating back to 1814). In his convincing 'Did Europe exist before 1700?', *History of European Ideas* 1:1 (1980), pp. 21–9, British cultural historian Peter Burke argues that the term 'Europe' – used by the Greeks and occasionally the Romans, as well as in the medieval world – was in the ascendant from the late fifteenth century onwards and was used by all the great authors (Erasmus, Machiavelli, Montaigne, Shakespeare, Vives). Burke connects this early consciousness with three political developments: invasions by external powers, especially the Turks (1453); the discovery of new non-European regions and cultures, and America (1492) in particular; and political conflict within Europe which involved the threat of rule by one man over the entire continent (first the Habsburgs, later Louis XIV).

A remarkable book about the developmental and ordering principles behind the European formation of states and nations is Peter Flora (ed.), *State Formation, Nation-Building, and Mass Politics in Europe. The theory of Stein Rokkan*, Oxford, 1999, especially pp. 97–152. Particularly useful is Rokkan's concept of the border as a human form of organisation, based on his distinction between territorial borders (geographical space) and social borders (membership space). This helps us to grasp the conceptual difficulty represented by the Europe of the outer sphere: it is both a geographical space, the continent, and a membership space, the 'European concert' of states. In its new existence as a Union (since 1992), the circle of members is obliged to think of itself not just as a social space (as in the Community years) but as a geographical space as well, which explains why, inconspicuously, it has come to function as a successor to the ancient 'concert', for instance by defining Europe's external border.

The inner sphere

Countless books have been written about the Community – the institutions, the founders, the treaties, the policies, the budget, the commissioners, the civil servants. From the outset, this book has underlined the importance of the treaties for an understanding of this sphere. For the self-image of the founders and the later inhabitants, we do best to rely upon memoirs and testimony.

In such figures as Schuman, Monnet and Spaak, the desire to break with the logic of the balance of power and national sovereignty, which had twice failed to prevent devastating world wars, is obvious. Take for example the testimony of Spaak's right-hand man in the treaty negotiations, the Belgian Baron Jean-Charles Snoy et d'Oppuers: 'We had absolutely had enough, in the three Benelux countries, of serving as a battlefield between France and Germany, for the sorting out of quarrels that were not our own, each time at the cost of horrendous destruction. As a result we were taken with the idea of a United States of Europe.' (Snoy et d'Oppuers, 25 May 1984, in Maria Grazia Melchionni and Roberto Ducci, *La genèse des Traités de Rome. Entretiens inédits avec 18 acteurs et témoins de la négociation*, Paris, 2008, pp. 159–84, 167.)

On the Commission we can turn to Jean Joana and Andy Smith, *Les commissaires européens. Technocrates, diplomates ou politiques?*, Paris, 2002; the collections edited by Neil Nugent, *At the Heart of the Union. Studies of the European Commission*, London, 2000, and by David Spence, *The European Commission*, London, 2006; and the insider account by Derk Jan Eppink, *Life of a European Mandarin. Inside the Commission*, Tielt, 2007, which tells provocatively yet affectionately of the power machinery and survival strategies deployed by civil servants surrounding a commissioner.

Works about the Court can be found mainly in the bibliography relating to Chapter 1, 'The spirit' and Chapter 3, 'Collisions and shortcuts'; more on the Parliament in Chapter 9.

The inventor of the term 'Community' for what on 9 May 1950, for want of a better idea, was called a 'pool' (for coal and steel), a 'consortium' or an 'organisation', was Professor Carl Ophüls, who represented the German delegation in the group of lawyers negotiating the mining and steel treaty. In German the word had strong connotations of an organic whole and it also fitted with Schuman's vision of a 'fusion of interests'. See C.F. Ophüls, 'Zwischen Völkerrecht und staatlichem Recht. Grundfragen des europäischen Rechts', *Juristen-Jahrbuch* 4 (1963/64), pp. 137–62, 154, confirmed by Walter Hallstein, 'Zu den Grundlagen und Verfassungsprinzipien der Europäischen Gemeinschaften', in Walter Hallstein and H.-J. Schlochauer (eds.), *Zur Integration Europas. Festschrift für Carl Friedrich Ophüls*, Karlsruhe, 1965, pp. 1–18, 1.

The intermediate sphere

Little has been written about the sphere of the members, as conceived here. Its intangibility and contradictory nature, as well as ideological prejudices on both the community side and the intergovernmental side, have impeded observation. Yet the in-between world was visible from day one, to anyone willing to see it, in the Council. An early and astute legal analysis of decisions taken by the Council within the framework of the treaty but external to it is given in J.H. Kaiser, 'Die im Rat vereinigten Vertreter der Regierungen der Mitgliedstaaten', in Hallstein and Schlochauer, *Zur Integration Europas*, pp. 107–24. For the Coal and Steel, Atomic Energy and Economic Communities, from their founding to the time of writing, the author counts a total of sixty-four decisions taken by the 'representatives of the governments of the member states meeting in the Council'. Kaiser also points to the legal particularity of the members' sphere, halfway between international law and community law. One of those decisions, referred to as the speed-up decision of 1960, had already been perceptively described in Leon N. Lindberg, *The Political Dynamics of European Economic Integration*, Stanford, 1963, pp. 167–205, with legal analysis at pp. 182–3. For a detailed examination of a more recent decision in the same category, see T.W.B. Beukers, 'The invisible elephant: Member States' collective involvement in the appointment of the Barroso Commission', *European Constitutional Law Review* 1 (2005), pp. 217–25.

In 1966 Kaiser formulated the notion of the joint member states as Europe's constituent power in the brilliant J.H. Kaiser, 'Das Europarecht in der Krise der Gemeinschaften', *Europarecht* 1:1 (1966), pp. 4–24, with its inexorable conclusion: 'The totality of the member states stands above the Communities' (p. 23).

An early and fine work on European cooperation in foreign policy, the first policy field of the circle of member states outside the treaty, is Philippe de Schoutheete, *La coopération politique européenne*, Brussels, 1980, revised 1986. Studies on the subject include David Allen et al. (eds.), *European Political Cooperation. Towards a foreign policy for Western Europe*, London, 1982, and Alfred Pijpers et al., *European Political Cooperation in the 1980s. A common foreign policy for Western Europe?*, Dordrecht, 1988.

For the member states' other early informal policy field – monetary cooperation in the 1970s and 1980s – see the books by Dutch central banker André Szász, *The Road to European Monetary Union*, Basingstoke and New York, 1999, pp. 15–109, and by contemporary historian Peter Ludlow, *The Making of the European Monetary System. A case study of the politics of the European Community*, London, 1982. Good story-telling on the underlying power politics can be found in a book by another banker: David Marsh, *The Euro. The politics of the new global currency*, London and New Haven, 2009, revised 2011, while the legitimising effects of the early years of the European Council are highlighted in Emmanuel Mourlon-Druol, *A Europe Made of Money. The emergence of the European Monetary System*, Ithaca, 2012.

The summits and the European Council, the highest political expressions of the intermediate sphere, received from the start a good deal of attention from journalists – sensitive to locations of visible public power – but significantly less from academics. Compared to the shelves of books on the Commission, Parliament, Court and even the ordinary Council, the forum where national leaders gather remained neglected despite having grown, in the opinion of many, into the Union's centre of power. As Ludlow states, 'a four-hundred-page book purporting to give a comprehensive account of the political system of the European Union deals with the European Council in two pages. This, however, is one page more than another recent treatise on decision-making in the European Union' (Peter Ludlow, *The Laeken Council*, Brussels, 2002, p. 5). Ludlow became its unrivalled chronicler with an informative series of commentaries and books about specific manifestations of the European Council from the 1990s to today. An early analysis that has stood the test of time remarkably well is 'Premières réflexions sur le Conseil européen' by Emile Noël, the secretary-general of the Commission of many years, in his *Les rouages de l'Europe. Comment fonctionnent les institutions de la Communauté européenne*, Brussels and Paris, 1976, pp. 43–54. From two political scientists a decade later came Simon Bulmer and Wolfgang Wessels, *The European Council. Decision-making in European politics*, Basingstoke and London, 1987. To them its 'evolution into the most politically authoritative institution of the EC' (p. 2) was obvious. An extensive study of the origins and functioning of this body, based partly on journalistic observation since 1970, is the PhD by Jan Werts, *The European Council*, Atlanta and Amsterdam, 1992, reworked under the same title for the general reader, London, 2008. Wolfgang Wessels, another author following his subject over time, is preparing *The European Council* (forthcoming).

With the entry into force of the Lisbon Treaty (2009) making the European Council formally an institution, scholarly interest has picked up. See for instance Frederic Eggermont, *The Changing Role of the European Council in the Institutional Framework of the European Union. Consequences for the integration process*, Cambridge, 2012, or Véronique Charlety and Michel Mangenot, *Le système presidentiel de l'Union européenne après Lisbonne*, Strasbourg, 2012. Another result of this institutionalisation is that all European Council conclusions since the first formal meeting in Dublin in 1975 have been made available at www.european-council.europa.eu/council-meetings/conclusions. One of the few scholarly journals to reflect systematically on current trends in the imbrication of the national and European political systems is *European Constitutional Law Review* (since 2005); see for instance its perceptive editorial 'The European Council and the national executives: Segmentation, consolidation and fragmentation', *EuConst* 8:2 (2012), pp. 165–71.

PART I: THE SECRET OF THE TABLE

THE TRANSITION TO MAJORITY

For the ideas of the classic 'state of nature' thinkers on foundation, veto and majority see especially Thomas Hobbes, *Leviathan*, 1651, chs. 13 and 16–18; John Locke, *Second Treatise of Government*, 1690, chs. 2 and 8; Jean-Jacques Rousseau, *Du contrat social*, 1762, chs. I.5, I.6, II.7 and IV.2; and idem, *Considérations sur le gouvernement de Pologne*, 1771, ch. 9. Both Hobbes and Locke stressed the analogy between the state of nature and the contemporary foreign policy jungle. In the early nineteenth century the parallel was still self-evident, to judge by G.W.F. Hegel, *Elements of the Philosophy of Right*, §333.

The difficulty of leaving the state of nature is expressed by Rousseau as follows: 'It is difficult for the individual, who has no taste for any scheme of government but that which serves his private interest, to appreciate the advantages to be derived from the lasting austerities which good laws impose. For a newly formed people to understand wise principles of politics and to follow the basic rules of statecraft, the effect would have to become the cause; the social spirit which must be the product of social institutions would have to preside over the setting up of those institutions; men would have to have already become before the advent of law that which they become as a result of law.' (Rousseau, *Du contrat social*, II.7, trans. Maurice Cranston). Rousseau believes this vicious circle can be broken only by violence or an appeal to divine power.

The vicious circle between people and state which traps every founding is brilliantly described in Hannah Arendt, *On Revolution*, New York, 1963, pp. 141–214. The great theoretician of the beginning says of the Founding Fathers: 'The very fact that the men of the American Revolution thought of themselves as "founders" indicates the extent to which they must have known that it would be the act of foundation itself, rather than an Immortal Legislator or self-evident truth or any other transcendent, transmundane source, which eventually would become the fountain of authority in the new body politic.' Her conclusion: 'It is futile to search for an absolute to break the vicious circle in which all beginning is inevitably caught, because this "absolute" lies in the very act of beginning itself' (p. 204). It is a useful intellectual exhortation for this history of a European beginning.

1 THE STEP ACROSS

AT THE TABLE

For the negotiation of the first founding treaty in the summer of 1950, see a book by the Dutch negotiator (with his French co-author): Dirk Spierenburg and Raymond Poidevin, *Histoire de la Haute Autorité de la Communauté européenne du Charbon et de l' Acier. Une expérience supranationale*, Brussels, 1993, pp. 7–52. A good and precise analysis is Hanns Jürgen Küsters, 'Die Verhandlungen über das institutionelle System zur Gründung der Europäischen Gemeinschaft für Kohle und Stahl', in Klaus Schwabe (ed.), *Anfänge des Schuman-Plans 1950–51 – The Beginnings of the Schuman-Plan*, Baden-Baden, 1988, pp. 73–102. From other main players, see Monnet, *Mémoires*, pp. 373–92, and Adenauer, *Erinnerungen*, I, pp. 409–26. Adenauer tells the anecdote about the signing of a blank page.

On the creation, place and operation of the committee of ambassadors known as COREPER, see the legal thesis by Jaap de Zwaan, *The Permanent Representatives Committee. Its role in European Union decision-making*, Amsterdam, 1995. Community objections to it in the early years – in the Commission quickly diminishing, in the Parliament of longer duration – are laid out in S. Patijn, *De uitbreiding van de bevoegdheden van het Europees Parlement*, Rotterdam, 1973, pp. 16–18. On the Council more recently: Fiona Hayes-Renshaw and Helen Wallace, *The Council of Ministers*, Basingstoke and New York, 2006, pp. 72–82, and Martin Westlake and David Galloway, *The Council of the European Union*, London, 2006, pp. 201–16.

THE SPIRIT

The account of the coup by the European Court of Justice in 1963–64 is based on judgment 26/62 of 5 February 1963, 'Van Gend & Loos/Netherlands Inland Revenue Administration' and judgment 6/64 of 3 June, 'Costa/ENEL', to be found with conclusions by Advocates-General Römer and Lagrange respectively in *Recueil de la jurisprudence de la Cour des Communautés européennes* 9 (1963), pp. 3–59 and 10 (1964), pp. 1141–99. Every handbook on European law discusses these classic cases, among them the reliable and detailed Anthony Arnull, *The European Union and its Court of Justice*, Oxford, 2006, pp. 159–83. In Damian Chalmers, Gareth Davies and Giorgio Monti, *European Union Law. Cases and materials*, Cambridge, 2010, the first decision is characterised as 'one of the most influential ever given by a court' (p. 14). An early, influential constitutional interpretation is Eric Stein, 'Lawyers, judges and the making of a transnational constitution', *American Journal of International Law* 75:1 (1981), pp. 1–27.

Interpretations of *Van Gend & Loos* as a moment of founding and bluff include W.T. Eijsbouts, *Het verdrag als tekst en als feit*, Amsterdam, 2002, pp. 11–12, and Hans Lindahl, 'Acquiring a Community: the *acquis* and the institution of European legal order', *European Law Journal* 9 (2003), pp. 433–50. The latter says rightly of the Court's use of time: 'The very act which gives rise to a novel and autonomous European legal order transfers the birth of this order, as novel and autonomous, to the past, and then goes ahead to assert that direct effect is but an "implication" of the origin. But as the Member States, when signing the Treaty of Rome, in no way understood themselves to be instituting an autonomous legal order, *Van Gend & Loos* refers back to "a past which never has been a present"' (p. 439).

For the self-image of the Court at the time of its coup, see the view of its president in A.M. Donner, 'The constitutional power of the Court of Justice of the European Communities', *Common Market Law Review* 11:1 (1974), pp. 127–40, and a French member (later president) in Robert Lecourt, *L'Europe des juges*, Brussels, 1976, especially pp. 250–98.

For the acceptance of the principle of the precedence of European law by the highest courts in Belgium (1971), Italy (1973), Germany (1974, with the exception of fundamental rights) and France (1975), see Lecourt, *L'Europe des juges*, pp. 289–98. Later entrants into the Community committed themselves in advance to the endorsement of 'any decision or expression of opinion by the European Court' on the meaning and operation of the treaty, as section 3(2) of the British European Communities Act of 1972 put it. Yet there too the highest courts were called upon to make a declaration about the principle of precedence. On that occasion, in 1974, Master of the Rolls Lord Denning produced a powerful metaphor: 'The Treaty is like an incoming tide. It flows into the estuaries and up the rivers. It cannot be held back'.

The constitutional treaty signed by the Twenty-Five in 2004 states in article I-6: 'The Constitution and law adopted by the institutions of the Union in exercising competences conferred on it shall have primacy over the law of the Member States.' This confirmation of the principle of precedence, a point of concern in London and Copenhagen even during negotiations, was lost along with the constitutional idea itself. For the Lisbon Treaty of 2007 the member states limited themselves to a declaration about the jurisprudence of the Court regarding precedence.

THE EMPTY CHAIR

Crisis and compromise

The factual account of the empty chair crisis up to and including the Luxembourg Accords is based on (1) official documents, (2) reports by contemporaries, (3) historical studies and (4) memoirs and testimony.

Documents: *Bulletin of the European Communities*, 1965 and 1966, includes official declarations and press releases by the Council, Commission and Parliament; the French communiqué of 1 July 1965; the declaration by the Five of 26 October; the text of the accord of 29 January 1966; and brief accounts of the press conferences after Council meetings. The author is also in possession of unpublished copies of the extensive report compiled by the Council Secretariat of the decisive meetings in Luxembourg of 17–18 and 28–29 January 1966.

Contemporary reports include John Lambert, 'The constitutional crisis 1965–66', *Journal of Common Market Studies* 4:3 (1966), pp. 195–228, and John Newhouse, *Collision in Brussels. The Common Market crisis of 30 June 1965*, London, 1967. Both authors draw on journalistic sources; Lambert is at home in Commission circles while Newhouse, an American based in Paris, has a good deal to say about the Paris–Bonn–Washington triangle.

Historical studies include Jean-Marie Palayret et al. (eds.), *Visions, Votes and Vetoes. The empty chair crisis and the Luxembourg Compromise forty years on*, Brussels, 2006. This valuable collection contains among other things reconstructions of events and motives per member state based on diplomatic archives. An analysis of the crisis in the context of the tense years 1963–69 is offered by N. Piers Ludlow, *The European Community and the Crises of the 1960s. Negotiating the Gaullist challenge*, London and New York, 2006.

Then there are the memoirs: Couve de Murville, *Une Politique étrangère*, pp. 329–39; Spaak, *Combats inachevés*, vol. II, pp. 407–14; Marjolin, *Le Travail d'une vie*, pp. 343–53; Peyrefitte, *C'était de Gaulle*, vols. I and II, *passim*; and German Secretary of State Rolf Lahr, 'Die Legende vom "Luxemburger Compromiß"', *Europa-Archiv* 8 (1983), pp. 223–32. Commission President Hallstein did not write memoirs; his vision of European unification and majority can be found in Walter Hallstein, *United Europe. Challenge and opportunity*, Cambridge, MA and London, 1962, and idem, *Die Europäische Gemeinschaft*, Düsseldorf and Vienna, 1974, especially pp. 62–73. See also the purely legal analysis by a lawyer close to Hallstein in C.F. Ophüls, 'Die Mehrheitsbeschlüsse der Räte in den Europäischen Gemeinschaften', *Europarecht* 1:3 (1966), pp. 193–229. Ophüls 'proved' that the veto meant the end of the Community and was, in truth, impossible.

Passage

The term 'constitutional crisis' (or *Verfassungkrise*) was used as early as 1966 by Joseph H. Kaiser, 'Das Europarecht in der Krise der Gemeinschaften', *Europarecht* 1:1 (1966), pp. 4–24, 23, and by Lambert, 'The constitutional crisis'.

For the role of the Commission in the empty chair crisis see Nina Heathcote, 'The crisis of supranationality', *Journal of Common Market Studies* 5:2 (1966), pp. 140–71; Karlheinz

Neureither, 'Transformation of a political role: Reconsidering the case of the Commission of the European Communities', *Journal of Common Market Studies* 10:3 (1972), pp. 233–48; N. Piers Ludlow, 'De-Commissioning the empty chair crisis: the Community institutions and the crisis of 1965–1966', in Palayret, *Visions, Votes and Vetoes*, pp. 79–96. For the secret constitutional oath sworn by the Five in October 1965 see Newhouse, *Collision in Brussels*, pp. 141–2. He quotes a French diplomat as saying: 'This changes everything'.

Interpretations. The disdain for the Luxembourg Compromise as at best an agreement to disagree is part of the standard textbook narrative. The widely used Desmond Dinan, *Ever Closer Union. An introduction to European integration*, Boulder and London, 2010, refers to 'a short declaration … which amounted to an agreement to disagree' (p. 38), while the classic for French and Italian students, Bino Olivi and Alessandro Giacone, *L'Europe difficile. La construction européenne*, Paris, 2007, states: 'rather than a true compromise it was a matter of a juxtaposition of different arguments' (p. 90). Hundreds of comparable observations could be added.

Yet there are also more positive interpretations of the accord. Among legal scholars, the notion of the Luxembourg Compromise as a 'constitutional convention' occurs at an early stage in Kaiser, 'Das Europarecht', p. 24, and is defended at length in Thomas Beukers, 'Law, Practice and Convention in the Constitution of the European Union', PhD thesis, University of Amsterdam, 2011, pp. 159–95. The Compromise as – like the European Council – an eruption of traditional diplomatic practices into the sanctuary of community life can be found in the convincing C.A. Colliard, 'L'irréductible diplomatique', in Claude Berr et al., *Mélanges offerts à Pierre-Henri Teitgen*, Paris, 1984, pp. 109–26, especially pp. 124–6. For endorsement of this view by a political scientist, see Paul Taylor, *The Limits of European Integration*, New York, 1983: 'The Luxemburg Accord proved to be a durable and realistic arrangement' (p. 40). Historians too have shown little surprise at the place and durability of the Compromise.

Effects of the Compromise. For the standard account of the ramifications of the Compromise between 1966 and 1987 – dominance, decline and supposed happy ending in treaty-based purity – see W. Nicoll, 'The Luxembourg Compromise', *Journal of Common Market Studies* 23:1 (1984), pp. 35–43; De Ruyt, *L'Acte unique*, pp. 112–18; Anthony L. Teasdale, 'The life and death of the Luxembourg Compromise', *Journal of Common Market Studies* 31:4 (1993), pp. 567–79; and Hayes-Renshaw and Wallace, *The Council of Ministers*, pp. 259–99. For the mood of 18 May 1982 from the perspective of the outvoted British see Wall, *A Stranger in Europe*, pp. 9–17. A vivid account of the ambiance in Strasbourg during Mitterrand's European confession of faith in May 1984 is *Frankfurter Allgemeine Zeitung*, 26 May 1984, 'Der verblüffende Wandel Präsident Mitterrands: Die Erfinder des Vetos in der Gemeinschaft wollen davon abkommen'.

For the Compromise after 1987 as a ghost hanging over the negotiating table, see Jean-Paul Jacqué, *Droit institutionnel de l'Union européenne*, Paris, 2001, p. 272, and an interview with Jean-Paul Jacqué by the author on 24 July 2008. Jacqué was director of the legal department of the Council secretariat and for many years he sat at the table in that capacity during the gathering of ambassadors.

Details of the Polish sugar beet case of November 2005 to February 2006 are taken from the following: the author's interview with Jacqué, 24 July 2008; information given in writing to the author by Thijs van der Plas (legal advisor to the Dutch ambassador to the Union) on 11 August and 8 September 2008; 'EU strikes landmark deal to reform sugar market', *AP*, 24 November 2005; 'Poland opposes EU sugar market reform', *Polish News Bulletin*, 21 February 2006; and 'Sugar reform legally adopted after Polish "veto" scare', *Agra Europe*, 24 February 2006.

2 THE LEAP

A MAGIC SPELL

The account of the ratification of the American constitution of 1787, including the special significance of article VII, is based on Bernard Bailyn (ed.), *The Debate on the Constitution.*

Federalist and Antifederalist speeches, articles and letters during the struggle over ratification, 2 vols., New York, 1993; Alexander Hamilton, James Madison and John Jay, *The Federalist Papers*, eds. Charles R. Kesler and Charles Rossiter, New York, 1999; Cecelia Kenyon, 'Introduction to "The Antifederalists": the political thought of the Antifederalists', in Stanley Elkins et al. (eds.), *Men of Little Faith. Selected writings of Cecelia Kenyon*, Amherst and Boston, 2002, pp. 68–131; and Forrest McDonald, *E Pluribus Unum. The formation of the American Republic*, Indianapolis, 1979. The latter stresses convincingly that the unity of the American nation in 1787 was not a historical fact but the fortunate outcome of a political battle. See also the foreword to the marvellous Joseph J. Ellis, *Founding Brothers. The revolutionary generation*, New York, 2000.

An excellent study of the function and development of the political concept 'people' from the sixteenth century to the 'We the people' of 1787 is Edmund S. Morgan, *Inventing the People. The rise of sovereignty in England and America*, New York, 1988.

For the astonishment of European diplomats at the speed of the American Revolution, see for example a letter dated 26 November 1787 from the French chargé d'affaires Louis-Guillaume Otto to his minister in Paris (included in Bailyn, *The Debate on the Constitution*, vol. I, pp. 420–2): 'Perhaps one ought to reproach them only for the impatience of anticipating their future grandeur.'

THE HOST ON THE STEPS

The European treaties all include an article governing the conditions under which they enter into force. For example article 99 ECSC, article 247 EEC and article R EU, renumbered in 1997 to become the current article 52 EU. They all sound more or less the same.

The full text of Spinelli's draft treaty of 1984 can be found on many websites (e.g. www. spinellifootsteps.info). More on its origins and influence can be found in Jean-Marie Palayret, 'Entre cellule Carbonara et conseiller des Princes: impulsions et limites de la relance européenne dans le projet Spinelli d'Union politique des années 1980', in Gérard Bossuat and Georges Saunier (eds.), *Inventer l'Europe. Histoire nouvelle des groupes d'influence et des acteurs de l'Union européenne*, Brussels, 2003, pp. 355–82.

Countless publications have been devoted to the European Convention, the intergovernmental conference of 2004 and the treaty on a constitution. For a reconstruction of the debate on its coming into force and revision, use has been made of verbatim transcripts of the convention debates as published on the website of the European Parliament (www.europarl.europa.eu), the official records of the Convention, including interim versions, amendments and individual contributions, as published on the still-accessible website (http://european-convention.eu.int), and the official records of the intergovernmental conference as available on the website of the Council (www.consilium.europa.eu). For deals behind the scenes and anecdotes from the corridors see (1) books by individual convention members, (2) journalistic reconstructions and (3) contributions from the civil servants involved. The first category includes: Valéry Giscard d'Estaing, *La Constitution pour l'Europe*, Paris, 2003; Olivier Duhamel, *Pour l'Europe*, Paris, 2003, with diary and pointed commentary; and Alain Lamassoure's (rather long-winded) *Histoire secrète de la Convention européenne*, Paris, 2003. In the second category belong: chronicler of summits Peter Ludlow, *The Laeken Council*, Brussels, 2002; former *Financial Times* correspondent Peter Norman, *The Accidental Constitution*, Brussels, 2003; and *Le Point* reporter Alain Dauvergne, *L'Europe en otage*, Paris, 2004. In the third category: Guy Milton and Jacques Keller-Noëllet, *The European Constitution. Its origins, negotiation and meaning*, London, 2005 (a firm hand); Jean-Claude Piris, *The Constitution for Europe. A legal analysis*, Cambridge, 2006 (very precise); and the exhaustive, 1,300-page study by Giuliano Amato, Hervé Bribosia and Bruno De Witte (eds.), *Genesis and Destiny of the European Constitution*, Brussels, 2007.

For complete draft constitutions by convention members which would come into force by majority, see: Robert Badinter, *Une constitution européenne*, Paris, 2002, as well as CONV 307/02 of 30 September 2002, art. 84, and Andrew Duff, annex to CONV 234/02 of 8 September 2002, art. 19. The theoretical exercise by the Commission in December 2002 appeared under the codename 'Penelope', republished in A. Mattera (ed.), *'Pénélope'. Projet de Constitution de l'Union européenne*, Paris, 2003, pp. 171–339.

For scenarios in the event of a 'no' vote during ratification, see for example Charles Grant, *What Happens if Britain Votes No? Ten ways out of a constitutional crisis*, London, 2005, and Bruno De Witte, 'The process of ratification and the crisis options: a legal perspective', in Deirdre Curtin, Alfred E. Kellerman and Steven Blockmans, *The EU Constitution. The best way forward?*, The Hague, 2005, pp. 21–38.

3 THE BRIDGE

MASTER OF THE TREATY

The fact that the formal rules for changing a constitution lay bare the nature of a political order is set out clearly in G.F.M. van der Tang, *Grondwetsbegrip en grondwetsidee*, Gouda, 1998, pp. 47–60. On the origins of the distinction between 'constituent power' and 'constituted power' shortly before the American and French Revolutions see Claude Klein, *Théorie et pratique du pouvoir constituant*, Paris, 1996, pp. 7–18.

Political orders that consist of several states likewise need a revision mechanism. In the case of changes to international treaties to which they are party, states can call upon the Vienna Convention on the Law of Treaties of 1969, but the political problem of revision cannot be solved by legal means. An international system that is not in a position to give shape to the historically changing power relations between participant states risks not stagnation but war. For a shrewd analysis of this issue for the European nations after 'Versailles' see Josef L. Kunz, 'The problem of revision in international law', *American Journal of International Law* 33:1 (1939), pp. 33–55. Kunz claimed (in 1939): 'It is hardly an exaggeration to state that the whole post-war history of Europe is made up of the struggle of revisionism against *status quo*' (p. 34). In contrast we see one of the great innovations contained in the new post-war European treaties: the principle of change was positively valued (by locating an ultimate aim in the distant future) and no longer regarded as reprehensible revisionism. This meant that proponents of the Treaty of Rome could fight for its amendment, while the burden of proof that change was not necessary fell upon defenders of the status quo.

The European treaties all had more or less the same strict revision rules. Examples include art. 95 ECSC, art. 236 EEC and art. N EU, renumbered in 1997 to become the current art. 48 EU. Before the turning point of 1985, the revision procedure had already been quietly used a number of times, in the fusion of the separate institutions of the three Communities into a single Council and a single Commission ('Merger Treaty', 1965) as well as in changes to the budgetary and financial regulations (1971 and 1977) and the statute concerning the European Investment Bank (1978). These were technical adjustments that were not experienced as moments of political revision.

COUP IN MILAN

The account of the Milan summit of 28–29 June 1985 is based on (1) official documents, (2) newspaper articles, (3) memoirs and (4) studies. As is usual with this type of negotiation, the different versions contradict each other on certain points. Efforts have been made throughout to select the most credible of them. For the plot this is not difficult; the sources are unanimous concerning the vote and the astonishment it caused.

Official documents, to be found in *Bulletin of the European Communities* of the time, are: 'Conclusions of the European Council in Fontainebleau, 25–26 June 1984'; 'Report of the Ad Hoc Committee for Institutional Affairs to the European Council (Brussels, 29–30 March 1985)'; and 'Conclusions of the European Council in Milan, 28–29 June 1985'.

Newspaper articles, all from 1985: *Financial Times*, 28 June and 1 July; the *Guardian*, 29 June; *The Times*, 29 June, 1 and 4 July; the *Economist*, 6 July; the *New York Times*, 30 June; *Frankfurter Allgemeine Zeitung*, 1 July; *Le Figaro*, 1 July; *Libération*, 1 July; *Le Monde*, 2 July; *Le Soir*, 2 July.

Memoirs: Thatcher, *The Downing Street Years*, pp. 536–59; Howe, *Conflict of Loyalty*, pp. 397–410 and 443–58; Wall, *A Stranger in Europe*, pp. 41–72; Attali, *Verbatim*, vol. I, pp. 787–830; Hans-Dietrich Genscher, *Erinnerungen*, Berlin, 1995, pp. 373–4; Delors, *Mémoires*, pp. 202–28 ('L'Acte unique: mon traité favori'); Charles Rutten, *Aan de wieg van Europa en andere Buitenlandse*

Zaken. Herinneringen van een diplomaat, Amsterdam, 2005, pp. 166–71 (Dutch permanent representative to the Community).

Studies: Jean De Ruyt, *L'Acte unique européen*, Brussels, 1987, pp. 47–91, 106–10; Nicholas Colchester and David Buchan, *Europe Relaunched. Truths and illusions on the way to 1992*, London, 1990, pp. 14–25; Jan Werts, *The European Council*, Amsterdam and Atlanta, 1992, pp. 183–9.

Regarding the underestimation of the vital moment of passage that the vote in Milan signified, the standard work by Hayes-Renshaw and Wallace, *The Council of Ministers*, speaks of the 'occasional oddity' of majority voting in the European Council (p. 55). In Westlake and Galloway, *The Council of the European Union*, the Milan summit is again ranked with two others as a special case: 'The basic ethos of consensuality has broken down on only a few occasions in the life of the European Council to date' (p. 187). Such reference works attempt to explain how it 'normally' goes, forgetting that every decisive turning point in life – for both persons and institutions – is the product of an exceptional moment.

COLLISIONS AND SHORTCUTS

A good politico-juridical exposition of the battle for European revision power is offered by Neil MacCormick, *Questioning Sovereignty. Law, state and nation in the European Commonwealth*, Oxford, 1999, especially chs. 6 and 7. He argues, putting one of his earlier beliefs into perspective, that 'we need not run out of law (and into politics) quite as fast as suggested by radical pluralism. The potential conflicts and collisions that can in principle occur between Community and member-states do not occur in a legal vacuum, but in a space to which international law is also relevant. Indeed, it is decisively relevant, given the origin of the Community in the Treaties and the continuing normative significance of *pacta sunt servanda*, to say nothing of the fact that in respect of their Community membership and otherwise the states owe each other obligations under international law' (p. 120). See also idem, 'Risking constitutional collision in Europe?', *Oxford Journal of Legal Studies* 18:3 (1998), pp. 517–32.

Practically all the general handbooks of European law discuss the 'Solange' and 'Maastricht' judgments by the German Constitutional Court. On the genesis of the European charter of human rights – the eventual solution to the conflict exposed in Solange I – see a book by the French governmental representative to the Convention, Guy Braibant, *La charte des droits fondamentaux de l'Union européenne*, Paris, 2001. A brilliant and controversial commentary on the Maastricht ruling is J.H.H. Weiler, 'Does Europe need a Constitution? Demos, telos and the German Maastricht decision', *European Law Journal* 1:3 (1995), pp. 219–58, with in fn. 2 a reference to the already extensive literature on the subject.

For the use of the 'flexibility clause' (art. 235 EEC; art. 308 EC) to enable the extension of competencies after 1972, see Weiler, *The Constitution of Europe*, pp. 51–6.

FOOTBRIDGE

For the debate on the rules for change in the European Convention and the intergovernmental conference of 2004, see the sources and publications referred to in Chapter 2, 'The host on the steps'.

The actual article on revision appeared in the Convention as Article F in CONV 647/03 of 2 April 2003. The idea of providing for further conventions in the future came from the Working Group on national parliaments; see CONV 353/02 of 22 October 2002, point 36. An interim version of the article, after the debate of 25 April, was CONV 725/03 of 27 May, art. IV-6. A second debate on revision took place on 5 June and a sentence was added to art. IV-6 regarding the role of the European Council in case of ratification problems; see CONV 802/3 of 12 June. At the same time two *passerelles* crop up in art. I-24 of CONV 797/1/03. The second of them, a fervent wish of the Convention, dates from its final day. Compare CONV 847/03 of 8 July, art. IV-6, with CONV 848/03 of 9 July, art. IV-6: it concerns the addition of an *avis conforme* of the Parliament when the European Council decides that the intended treaty change is not far-reaching enough to merit calling a Convention. For the letter (or cry of distress) from Amato, Brok and Duff to Giscard d'Estaing regarding light revision, see CONV 833/03 of 24 July.

Responding to an Italian initiative, an intergovernmental conference in November 2003 decided to rank the *passerelles* from I-24 among the rules for change as art. IV-7bis, and also to add a procedure for light revision as IV-7ter; see annexes 30 and 31 of CIG 52/03 ADD 1 of 25 November 2003 (Rome's proposal) and annexes 35 and 36 of CIG 60/03 ADD 1 of 9 December 2003 (outcome). For this episode, including an Italian attempt to allow the European Council to decide by majority on light change, see the report by the Italian permanent representative Rocco Cangelosi, 'Il progetto di Trattato costituzionale, la Presidenza italiana e la Conferenza intergovernativa: da Roma a Bruxelles: cronaca di un negoziato', *La Comunità internazionale* 58:4 (2003), pp. 533–60, 545–6.

After the failed ratification of the constitutional treaty, the new revision rules ended up in their entirety in the Treaty of Lisbon. The fascinating thing, therefore, is that the European Council, believing it had abandoned the 'constitutional concept' during the summit of June 2007, nevertheless allowed the convention to continue to exist as an institution. (See Conclusions of the European Council, Brussels 21–22 June 2007, annex I, point 1, as well as art. 48 EU, para. 3, as altered by the Lisbon treaty.)

Finally, it is remarkable that the revision procedure settled upon by the Convention has received such a bad press from its academic friends and several of its most prominent members. Typical is the harsh final verdict from one Belgian professor of European law at the EUI in Florence: 'All in all, there is much ground for pessimism about the capacity of the European Union to reform itself after this Constitutional Treaty has come into force. In the years to come, the Convention and the IGC of 2002/4 could be severely blamed for their failure to allow for further evolution of the European Union' (Bruno De Witte, 'Revision', *European Constitutional Law Review* 1 (2005), pp. 136–40, 139). Comparable noises can be heard in the collection mentioned in chapter 2, *Genesis and Destiny of the European Constitution* by Amato, Bribosia and De Witte. Renaud Dehousse (Sciences-Po, Paris) argues that the Union 'will have to cross the Rubicon and break down the barrier of unanimity' (p. 947) and according to Paul Magnette (ULB, Brussels) it is 'imperative' (p. 1079) to change the revision procedure. These authors reason from the inner sphere and in doing so fail to appreciate the club's growing power of self-renewal, the fundamental steps in the shift of power from *pouvoirs constituants* to *pouvoirs constitués* (future conventions, role of European Council in light change, footbridges) – in short, the strengthening of the club vis-à-vis its members.

PART II: VICISSITUDES OF FORTUNE

IN THE RIVER OF TIME

For the way rulers and thinkers dealt politically with 'Fortune' during the Renaissance see – alongside the writings of Machiavelli himself – the aforementioned masterly work by Pocock, *The Machiavellian Moment*.

The distinction between high and low politics comes from the realist school of political science. In discussions about European politics it is used by authors who, in opposition to Monnet and neofunctionalist ideas of a 'spill-over', choose to emphasise the firm boundary between the realm of economic treaties and sovereign foreign policy. Of these authors, American Stanley Hoffmann seeks the distinction in the degree of emotional intensity involved: on the one hand 'quantifiable interests – capable of being calculated, compensated, bargained' and on the other 'those intangible interests of state which . . . involve the passions that are the stuff of tragedy: prestige and hubris, domination and independence', and which 'can hardly be compromised' (Stanley Hoffmann, 'Europe's identity crisis', p. 33). French philosopher Raymond Aron, seeking for his part the distinction in the issue of whether or not a policy field requires a sovereign decision-maker in times of crisis, wrote in 1962: 'if sovereignty is defined as the supreme power to decide in the case of crisis, it remains, entirely, with the nation states' (Raymond Aron, *Paix et guerre entre les nations*, Paris, 1962, pp. 731–2).

Both authors correctly stress the primacy of politics over economics, turning their backs on the illusion of a procedural or technical depoliticisation. Two notes in the margin. Firstly, even apparently economic decisions, such as the establishment of a market or currency, may be taken for 'political' reasons. Secondly, developments do not stand still. The basic assumptions of the realists may with time lead to altered conclusions about European politics, two examples being the development of the European Council as the decision-making body (not least in times of crisis) and of the Parliament as full legislator.

4 COMING TOGETHER AS SIX (1950–57)

SCHUMAN'S VOICE AND ADENAUER'S EAR (BEFORE 10 MAY 1950)

Memoirs of politicians and diplomats: Acheson, *Present at the Creation*, *passim* (meetings with
Bevin and Schuman, 1949–50); Adenauer, *Erinnerungen*, I, pp. 299–304 (proposal for Franco-
German economic union, March 1950) and 314–24 (reaction to the Schuman Plan and the
reception given to Monnet); Monnet, *Mémoires*, pp. 341–56 (prehistory of his own involvement)
and 359–60 (Schuman's press conference).

A telling account of France's post-war politics regarding Germany is Franz Knipping, 'Que
faire de l'Allemagne? Die französische Deutschlandpolitik 1945–1950', in Franz Knipping and
Ernst Weisenfeld (eds.), *Eine ungewöhnliche Geschichte. Deutschland – Frankreich seit 1870*,
Bonn, 1988, pp. 141–55. The French folding chair at the table of the Great Three for the discussion of German questions, from which so much flowed, was defended by Churchill 'like a tiger'
in Yalta in the face of grudging Americans and Russians: 'the French must grow strong again to
help check a revived Germany' (Churchill, February 1945, in Robert H. Lieshout, *The Struggle
for the Organization of Europe. The foundations of the European Union*, Cheltenham, 1999, p. 37).

For the economic and diplomatic background to the Schuman Plan, see Alan Milward, *The
Reconstruction of Western Europe, 1945–1951*, London, 1984, pp. 362–420. See also the essays in
Schwabe, *Anfänge des Schuman-Plans 1950–51*. Plans comparable to Monnet's proposal were
developed in Schuman's ministry from 1948 onwards. See for example the memorandum on the
management of Europe, 13 December 1948, with a plea for a Franco-German steel pool, in Dirk
Spierenburg and Raymond Poidevin, *Histoire de la Haute Autorité de la Communauté Européenne
du Charbon et de l'Acier. Une expérience supranationale*, Brussels, 1993, p. 3. For the role of
Schuman see Raymond Poidevin, *Robert Schuman, homme d'Etat 1886–1963*, Paris, 1988,
pp. 244–63. Relations between French political parties on the subject are set out clearly in Craig
Parsons, *A Certain Idea of Europe*, Ithaca, 2003, pp. 37–66.

For the political and legal starting point of Germany in the years 1945–49, see Lieshout, *The
Struggle for the Organization*, pp. 36–58. The reflections of Adenauer in late May 1950 were
noted by his informal advisor Hans Schäffer in 'Konrad Adenauer und der Schuman-Plan. Ein
Quellenzeugnis', in Schwabe, *Anfänge des Schuman-Plans 1950–51*, pp. 131–40. Particularly
arresting is the speech by Adenauer's secretary of state and negotiator (and later Commission
president) Walter Hallstein, *Probleme des Schuman-Plans. Kieler Vorträge*, Kiel, 1951. Hallstein
emphasised the opportunities for political development inherent in the Schuman Plan: 'an open
door for further steps in . . . the direction of an orderly entry of the Federal Republic into the
world of free peoples' and at the same time 'a breach in the idea of the nation state to bring about
a more comprehensive European federation' (pp. 4, 17).

As early as the summer of 1949, American diplomat George Kennan came to the conclusion
that 'the German problem' could be solved only in a European circle that included the French
but not the British. In his memoirs he quotes a memo he sent to Acheson: 'It could be taken as
axiomatic, I wrote, that no framework of association which included the United Kingdom but
excluded the United States and Canada would be permitted to advance to a stage resembling a
real merger of sovereignty. British reservations and hesitations would thus inevitably constitute
the ceiling beyond which [European] unification would not be able to advance. This ceiling,
I pointed out, would be far too low to allow for any real merging of sovereignties, and thus
too low to be of value as a solution to the German problem' (George F. Kennan, *Memoirs,
1950–1963*, New York, 1972, p. 453).

EUROPE WITHOUT A UNIFORM (AFTER 25 JUNE 1950)

Memoirs of politicians and diplomats: Acheson, *Present at the Creation*, pp. 524–37 (impact of
the Korea crisis); Adenauer, *Erinnerungen*, I, pp. 332–6 (repercussions for Germany of the Korea
crisis); Beyen, *Het spel en de knikkers*, pp. 207–8 (first meeting of the Council of the Coal and
Steel Community) and 231–3 (report on the Brussels conference of August 1954); Sir Anthony
Eden, *Full Circle*, London, 1960, pp. 146–74 (British initiative of September–December 1954);
Linthorst Homan, *Wat zijt ghij voor een vent. Levensherinneringen*, Assen, 1974, pp. 193–205
(failure of the 'revolution' of the Defence Community); Monnet, *Mémoires*, pp. 393–409 (role in

Pleven Plan) and 419–21 (lunch with Eisenhower, June 1951); and Spaak, *Combats inachevés*, vol. II, pp. 57–8 (speech on the presentation of the draft constitution).

Documents concerning the Defence Community from the Pleven Plan to the signing of the treaty – Prelude and Act One – can be found in *Chronique de politique étrangère* 5:5/6 (1952), including the complete text of the *Traité instituant la Communauté Européenne de Défense*, pp. 592–682. An insightful historical reconstruction of the negotiations based on interviews with the politicians, diplomats and military figures involved is provided by William Fursdon, *The European Defence Community. A history*, London, 1980. In the late 1970s an anonymous French interlocutor offered the author an explanation for the paucity of literature on the subject: 'It is no wonder that so little has been written: no one wants in public to remember, still less write about, a failure that had already succeeded in splitting the nation into two.'

Developments surrounding the European Political Community – Act Two – are chronicled in Richard T. Griffiths, *Europe's First Constitution. The European Political Community, 1952–1954*, London, 2000, including the text of the Strasbourg draft constitution (pp. 189–226). The author devotes a great deal of attention to the intergovernmental conference that followed. Although little came of it, it is worth mentioning the proposal for a common market made in September 1952 by Dutch minister Beyen, which perished along with the defence treaty but was revived in the spring of 1955.

Analysis by contemporaries of the French ideological debate – Act Three – is offered in Raymond Aron and Daniel Lerner, *La querelle de la C.E.D. Essai d'analyse sociologique*, Paris, 1956. There is a great deal to be found here, and it is of a high standard: the tenor of the arguments advanced by proponents and opponents; extensive surveys of the parliamentary procedures involved; research into press reporting; institutional shortcomings. A report on the failed conference in Brussels in August 1954, where Mendès France asked for concessions from the Five while the Americans in the corridors urged perseverance, can be found in Fursdon, *The European Defence Community*, pp. 281–91, and Dumoulin, *Spaak*, pp. 473–86. Minister Beyen recalls (*Het spel en de knikkers*, p. 232): 'At a dramatic moment, in the middle of the night, Adenauer made an appeal to the French premier Mendès France, saying: Does the German Chancellor have to beg you not to put him into a position where he will soon have to work on the reestablishment of a German National Army with a German General Staff?'

For a historical perspective on the transition from the European states system to an Atlantic system, see the excellent Hajo Holborn, *The Political Collapse of Europe*, New York, 1962. Holborn, a historian who had fled Nazi Germany to America, warned his American readership of the tendency to take steps in foreign policy that clash with all local historical models, for instance by giving unlimited support to Monnet's agenda in Europe: 'From this unforeseen novelty of the present European situation it has also been inferred that we could forget its history altogether. But such an inference could lead to … serious blunders … Though the self-contained European political system has broken down and Europe finds itself under the shadow of two world rivals, her nations are not dead' (pp. 192–3). His apt exhortation (in 1951) was: 'A constructive treatment of Europe's present-day problems calls for historical thinking, which is something more than mere historical knowledge' (p. xi).

The Suez Canal and the Château de Val-Duchesse
(on and around 6 November 1956)

Memoirs of politicians and diplomats: Adenauer, *Erinnerungen*, III, pp. 215–75, and Eden, *Full Circle*, pp. 417–584. Eden does not mention his telephone conversation with Eisenhower of 6 November, and his call to Mollet merits a single sentence: 'Our allies [France and Israel] accepted our conclusion with understanding loyalty, though they would have liked to see what even a slightly longer period of action might have brought forth' (p. 557). See also French minister Christian Pineau, *1956. Suez*, Paris, 1976, and Pineau and Christiane Rimbaud, *Le grand pari. L'aventure du Traité de Rome*, Paris, 1991, pp. 151–263; Spaak, *Combats inachevés*, II, pp. 61–100.

For the Cold War background to the Suez crisis, see Henry Kissinger, *Diplomacy*, New York, 1994, pp. 522–49. The Mollet–Adenauer summit as a starting point for Franco-German military cooperation is examined in Georges-Henri Soutou, *L'Alliance incertaine. Les rapports politico-stratégiques franco-allemands, 1954–1996*, Paris, 1996, pp. 58–63, and that same summit as the culmination of European treaty negotiations in Mathieu Segers, *Deutschlands Ringen mit der Relance. Die Europapolitik der BRD während der Beratungen und Verhandlungen über die Römischen Verträge*, Frankfurt am Main, 2008, pp. 271–85. Segers' argument follows on from his analysis that the final result of the negotiations can largely be explained by German economic concessions to the French, pushed through by Adenauer against the wishes of his sectoral ministers under the heading of 'the primacy of politics'. The impact of the Suez crisis on the breakthrough in Franco-German relations is also recognised – despite both authors' decidedly economic explanation of the motives for sealing the treaty – in Andrew Moravcsik, *The Choice for Europe. Social purpose and state power from Messina to Maastricht*, London and New York, 1998, p. 144 ('first major breakthrough') and Alan Milward, *The European Rescue of the Nation-State*, London, 1992, p. 312 ('when almost every obstacle fell').

A great deal has been published about the European negotiations of 1955–57. To the memoirs already mentioned can be added: French negotiator and later Eurocommissioner Jean-François Deniau, *L'Europe interdite*, Paris, 1977, pp. 48–76; Mathieu Segers (ed.), *De Europese dagboeken van Max Kohnstamm. Augustus 1953–September 1957*, Amsterdam, 2008, pp. 189–202 (civil service preparations for the Mollet–Adenauer summit); and Marjolin, *Le Travail d'une vie*, pp. 274–303. Full of facts, anecdotes and motives is Melchionni and Ducci, *La genèse des Traités de Rome*, which includes interviews with eighteen participants from all of the Six. The Belgian diplomat Snoy et d'Oppuers heard a colleague who watched it remark on the Matignon walk of Mollet and Adenauer in February 1957: 'Every step Adenauer took cost him hundreds of millions of marks' (p. 173).

5 COMMUNITY WAITING (1958–89)

Self-made time

In the tunnel

The timetable set by the Treaty of Rome was decisive for its success. The twelve-year transition period, with its complex opportunities for appeal at the important point of transition from the first stage to the second in 1962, was laid down in art. 8 EEC (since expired). For Spaak sticking to his guns on the point of the unlimited period of validity of the treaty, see the French negotiator Deniau, *L'Europe interdite*, p. 74n1. Seven years earlier, in the Paris negotiations of 1950–51 it was the Belgian delegation that refused to give the new High Authority a 'blank cheque' for an unlimited period, according to Spierenburg and Poidevin, *Histoire de la Haute Autorité*, pp. 18–19.

Acceleration. A first-rate analysis of the speed-up decision of May 1960, based partly on interviews in Brussels and other capitals, can be found in Leon N. Lindberg, *The Political Dynamics of European Economic Integration*, Stanford, 1963, pp. 167–205. For the decision-making process from the perspective of the most important trading partner of the Six, see Miriam Camps, *Britain and the European Community, 1955–1963*, Princeton, 1964, pp. 253–73.

Clock. The hard-fought transition agreement of 14 January 1962, in which chairman Couve de Murville had the clock stopped on New Year's Eve 1961, is attractively analysed in Annette Schrauwen, 'De kunst van het pact', in M. Spiering et al. (eds.), *De weerspannigheid van de feiten. Opstellen over geschiedenis, politiek, recht en literatuur aangeboden aan W.H. Roobol*, Hilversum, 2000, pp. 209–19. She illuminates the industrial side of the Franco-German trade-off; the agricultural aspect is dealt with in more detail in Lindberg, *Political Dynamics*, pp. 261–82. Plain and factual is Couve de Murville, *Une politique étrangère*, pp. 314–17; careless with dates but written with verve is a book about his role as mediator on the decisive night by Commissioner for Agriculture Sicco Mansholt, *La crise*, Paris, 1974, pp. 110–15. Commission President Hallstein, proud of the Community result, told an American academic public a few months later of the dramatic circumstances in which an accord was reached: 'Forty-five separate meetings, seven of them at night; a total of 137 hours of discussion, with 214 hours in subcommittee; 528,000 pages of documents; three heart attacks – the record is staggering' (Walter Hallstein, *United Europe. Challenge and opportunity*, Cambridge, MA and London, 1962, p. 55).

Exit. Regarding the summit in The Hague of 1–2 December 1969, see *Bulletin of the European Communities* 12-1969, 1-1970 and 2-1970 for the final declaration, speeches by national leaders, Commission memorandum, resolution in Parliament and press conferences. For their interpretation see Ludlow, *The European Community and the Crises of the 1960s*, pp. 175–98. For the breakthrough in monetary and foreign policy cooperation in The Hague see respectively banker André Szász, *The Road to European Monetary Union*, Basingstoke and New York, 1999, pp. 15–29, and Ambassador Philippe de Schoutheete, *La coopération politique européenne*, Brussels, 1980, p. 27. The performance of the French president during and in the run-up to the summit can be found in the biography by Eric Roussel, *Georges Pompidou, 1911–1974*, Paris, 2004, pp. 334–42.

To the market

For the political and economic background, see Nicholas Colchester and David Buchan, *Europe Relaunched. Truths and illusions on the way to 1992*, London, 1990, and for the same background but with a focus on the bureaucratic feats of the Commission, Gilles Grin, 'The Battle of the Single European Market: Achievements and economic thought, 1985–2000', PhD thesis, University of Geneva, 2002. The Commission president himself discusses his autumn tour of 1984 and the chosen deadline of '1992' in Delors, *Mémoires*, pp. 182–92. For Kohnstamm's part in introducing the idea of a deadline, see Anjo G. Harryvan and Jan van der Harst, *Max Kohnstamm. Leven en werk van een Europeaan*, Utrecht, 2008, pp. 221–8. For the years suggested, see Grant, *Delors*, pp. 67–8.

Pressing time

At the door

For relations between Britain and the Six in the early period, there is none better than Camps, *Britain and the European Community*: well documented, carefully considered verdicts. More concise and closer to events is the work of journalist Nora Beloff, *The General Says No. Britain's exclusion from Europe*, London, 1963. Focused on the obstacles and difficult aspects of the negotiating phase is Simon Z. Young, *Terms of Entry. Britain's negotiations with the European Community 1970–1972*, London, 1973. For a masterly account of fifty years of British politics on Europe see Young, *This Blessed Plot*, which is sensitive to political relationships and moods, and is the product of thorough research crafted by a good stylist.

The annoyance felt by British minister Ernest Bevin on 9 May 1950 is recorded by his contrite guest Acheson in *Present at the Creation*, pp. 501–4.

The background of and responses to de Gaulle's veto on British accession in 1963, including the defence aspects, are covered in detail by Camps and Beloff; for the evening of 19 January 1963 see Ludlow, *The European Community and the Crises of the 1960s*, pp. 11–13.

The extremely important episode of the 1961–62 negotiations on political union is covered exhaustively (in more than 500 pages) in Robert Bloes, *Le Plan Fouchet et le problème de l'Europe politique*, Bruges, 1970. See also Adenauer, *Erinnerungen*, IV, *passim*; Couve de Murville, *Une Politique étrangère*, pp. 347–84; J.M.A.H. Luns, *Ik herinner mij*, Leiden, 1971, pp. 139–63; and Spaak, *Combats inachevés*, II, pp. 357–80. Of the two representatives of the Low Countries, Luns is proud of his stubbornness (which he says was commended by de Gaulle) while Spaak aims to refute the French reproach that his position was inconsistent. See also Jeffrey W. Vanke, 'An impossible Union: Dutch objections to the Fouchet Plan, 1959–62', *Cold War History* 2:1 (2001), pp. 95–112.

Table arrangement

The fact that the national leaders themselves decided to investigate foreign policy cooperation in 1969 was mentioned by the then Belgian diplomat Étienne Davignon in an interview on

18 January 2008 at www.cvce.eu. See also the Conclusions of the summit in The Hague of 1–2 December 1969, point 15. This enquiry culminated in the Luxembourg Report or Davignon Report of 1970, followed three years later by the Copenhagen Report; both are included in de Schoutheete, *La coopération politique européenne*, pp. 179–87, 188–98.

For the Nine and the oil crisis of 1973, see the excellently researched Robert J. Lieber, *Oil and the Middle East War. Europe in the energy crisis*, Cambridge, MA, 1976, especially pp. 1–29 and 44–52. The author attributes the confusing arrival of Arab ministers at the Copenhagen summit to a move by London and Paris (p. 18). For the excessively heightened expectations of 'Copenhagen', see *Time Magazine* of 17 December 1973, 'Toward the Summit of truth', as well as reports in the *New York Times*, 15, 16 and 17 December 1973. General context can be found in Daniel Möckli, *European Foreign Policy During the Cold War. Heath, Brandt, Pompidou and the dream of political unity*, London, 2009.

For the birth of the European Council see, as well as the studies mentioned in the Prologue, the Conclusions of the founding summit of Paris, as well as Giscard d'Estaing, *Le Pouvoir et la vie*, I, pp. 117–21, and Monnet, *Mémoires*, pp. 589–605. For Hartling in 1974, see Erik Holm, 'Denmark's position at the birth of the European Council', unpublished report to the author, 3 February 2009.

For the subsequent history it is useful to note that Giscard d'Estaing wrote in 1988: 'Later, when the European Council is confident of its existence, it will be necessary to think about giving it more structure' (p. 119). In these words it is already possible to discern the goal he achieved as chair of the 2002–03 Convention, namely a plan for a permanent president of the European Council.

6 ACTING AS A UNION (1989–TODAY)

AFTER THE WALL

Fall of the Wall up to and including the Union Treaty. Although German unification and the change in Europe's shape after 1989 are obviously interwoven, both developments are part of distinct historiographical traditions.

In the dominant interpretations the fate of Germany is reduced to a game between America and Russia. In the American reading of events, the Soviet Empire caved in because of the statesmanship and moral leadership of – aside from the Pope – Presidents Reagan and Bush. No small contribution to this interpretation was made by the memoirs of the latter and his security advisor: George H. Bush and Brent Scowcroft, *A World Transformed*, New York, 1999, pp. 3–301, as well as a study based on policy documents by two of the staff of Bush's National Security Council, Philip Zelikow and Condoleezza Rice, *Germany Unified and Europe Transformed*, Cambridge, MA and London, 1997 (first edition 1995). Opposing them is the school that looks for the *dramatis personae* among the losers of the Cold War, in the Kremlin – especially Gorbachev, whose reformist policy got out of hand. Concise in this sense is Tony Judt, *Postwar. A history of Europe since 1945*, New York, 2005, pp. 585–633, which exaggerates by speaking of 'Mr Gorbachev's revolution' (p. 633). A corrective to this American-Russian attribution of praise and blame for '1989' is offered by a group of historians in Frédéric Bozo, Marie-Pierre Rey, N. Piers Ludlow and Leopoldo Nuti, *Europe and the End of the Cold War. A reappraisal*, London, 2008. The book brings Europe into the picture, based on archival material from and about countries including Poland, Hungary, Britain, Italy, France and Germany, and the European institutions.

The importance of the geopolitical transformation for the bursting open of the European cocoon is often dealt with sparingly in the community interpretation, where there is a tendency to imagine the breakthrough to a European Union as a logical extension of agreements made according to the old spill-over model. Hadn't the leaders of the Six proposed an 'economic and monetary union' back in 1969? Hadn't they agreed in 1972, 1983 and 1985 to set up a 'political union'? Hadn't they been in possession of a Delors report about a single currency and a single bank since the summer of 1989? Yes, indeed. But only the rupture of 1989 explains both the timing and the outcome.

An exemplary effort to bind together the institutional and geopolitical threads is the aforementioned André Szász, *The Road to European Monetary Union*, Basingstoke and New York,

1999. Szász convincingly demonstrates that there is a parallel between the deal of 1969 (the promise of European monetary union in return for acceptance of German *Ostpolitik*) and that of 1989 (a decision on monetary union in return for an accord on German unification). Both deals were implicit. In a certain sense, therefore, '1989' transforms into political facts both of the perspectives on the future that opened up in 1969.

On the role of France, especially Mitterrand, there is historiographical controversy. In the dominant American interpretation, President Mitterrand is said for a moment to have wanted to prevent German unity, *à la* Thatcher. Reference is made to his meeting with Gorbachev in Kiev on 6 December and with East German leaders in Leipzig on 21 December. Other authors speak of a 'black legend' (Frédéric Bozo), a notion derived not just from the Americans but from the memoirs of Mitterrand's advisor Attali, especially his *Verbatim*, III, which covers the years 1988–91 and appeared in 1995. The president tried in vain to redress the damage in his posthumous *De la France, de l'Allemagne*, Paris, 1996. For this second school, ambiguous statements were belied by consistent, unambiguous acts. From beginning to end, Mitterrand strove for confirmation of the Polish border (balance in the European concert of states) and an interweaving of Germany into the club (reinforcement of the European circle of members). Two books that support this interpretation are Tilo Schabert, *Wie Weltgeschichte gemacht wird. Frankreich und die Deutsche Einheit*, Stuttgart, 2002, and Frédéric Bozo, *Mitterrand, la fin de la guerre froide et l'unification allemande. De Yalta à Maastricht*, Paris, 2005. Mitterrand's diplomatic advisor and Chief of Staff Hubert Védrine, in his *Les mondes de François Mitterrand. A l'Elysée, 1981–1995*, Paris, 1996, pp. 439-57, reflects upon the discrepancy between the words (and silences) of his boss and what he actually did.

For the German memoirs, in addition to the aforementioned books by Chancellor Kohl and his diplomatic advisor Teltschik there is Hans-Dietrich Genscher, *Erinnerungen*, Berlin, 1995. Kohl, the Christian Democrat, used Teltschik from 1982 onwards as his personal representative to maintain independent contacts with foreign leaders. It was the only way he could circumvent his coalition partner Genscher, leader of the liberal FDP and in the same post almost continually since 1974, and pursue his own foreign policy. One of the reasons that Kohl prepared his ten-point plan within an extremely small circle and launched it entirely unexpectedly – without even informing Thatcher and Mitterrand in advance – was that he feared Genscher would get to hear of it and take all the credit (a situation almost inconceivable in 10 Downing Street or the Elysée Palace).

For British memoirs, a stark contrast with the French, see Thatcher, *The Downing Street Years*, pp. 789–807; *Conflict of Loyalty* by Thatcher's foreign secretary Geoffrey Howe (sacked for being too pro-European in July 1989 and back with a vengeance in November 1990); Douglas Hurd, *Memoirs*, pp. 419–29 (he had been in the foreign secretary post for two weeks when the Wall fell); and the diplomat Stephen Wall, *A Stranger in Europe*, pp. 87–134.

An account of the 1991 intergovernmental conference and an interpretation of its outcome can be found in J. Cloos et al., *Le Traité de Maastricht. Genèse, analyse, commentaires*, Brussels, 1994 (authoritative; the four authors were diplomats of the Luxembourg Council presidency). The debate on the treaty structure – tree or temple – is at pp. 81–7, 107–11. Useful for the official documents reproduced within it and for backgrounds to the positions of the Twelve is Finn Laursen and Sophie Vanhoonacker, *The Intergovernmental Conference on Political Union. Institutional reforms, new policies and international identity of the European Community*, Maastricht, 1992. A well-informed report of the 'Black Monday' of Dutch diplomacy is included in the PhD thesis by former parliamentarian Bob van den Bos, *Mirakel en debacle. De Nederlandse besluitvorming over de Politieke Unie in het Verdrag van Maastricht*, Assen, 2008. See also Cloos et al., *Le Traité de Maastricht*, pp. 88–91.

The Union from 1993: 'widening and deepening'. In the 1990s, the Europe debate was couched in terms of 'widening' versus 'deepening'. Should the new Eastern European members first be given access to the 'European house', or was it a good idea to underpin the foundations before building an extension? It was impossible to read any academic or newspaper analysis without finding the two terms cropping up.

In my account the terms 'widening' and 'deepening' are generally avoided. There are two reasons for this. Firstly, the metaphor was politically loaded. It was mainly used by advocates of 'deepening' and therefore by those who believed that widening eastwards would mainly lead to 'fragmentation', 'dilution' and – worst of all – institutional 'stagnation'. The arrival of new members threatened the elasticity of the European project. Commission President Delors was the most influential exponent of this belief. 'In the EU Commission of Jacques Delors there was a view in the early 1990s that in another twenty-five years it might perhaps be possible to start talking seriously about expansion eastwards' – so said Günter Verheugen, the German politician charged, as a Eurocommissioner from 1999 onwards, with the responsibility for widening the Community, in his *Europa in der Krise. Für eine Neubegründung der europäischen Idee*, Cologne, 2005, pp. 72–3. Paris likewise argued that deepening was a necessary prelude to widening – which would give Germany a central position in the Union – as a way of delaying the accession of new members. The asymmetrical impact of the metaphor is also clear from the fact that advocates of faster accession did not speak in terms of 'widening'. (They preferred to sound a note of moral guilt or historical obligation.)

A second reason is that more than once 'widening' and 'deepening' occurred simultaneously. The arrival of London, Copenhagen and Dublin in 1973 gave a vital boost to the life of the club. This applies to European self-awareness in the face of the outside world (foreign policy cooperation; 'European identity', 1973), the expansion of tasks and competencies (regional policy at the request of the British; environmental policy at the request of, among others, the Danes, 1973), institutional change (e.g. the European Council, 1974) and, consequently, the quest for a public. The accession of Spain and Portugal in 1986 more or less coincided with the signing of the Single European Act, which opened the way to an internal market as of 1992. The arrival of both these 'poor' members strengthened the argument that the market must be accompanied by 'social policy' and funds to promote 'solidarity' (as introduced by the next treaty change). Enough has been said about the simultaneity of German unification, which entailed the arrival of the *Neue Länder*, and the further (monetary) interweaving of the member states. Clearly this points to something else.

The supposed contradiction between 'widening' and 'deepening' is based on a mistaken idea of the club. It is pseudo-logic. Europe is not a 'house' with 'foundations' made of rules and 'extensions' made of member states. Rather, Europe is a closed circle of states that have to some degree brought their reciprocal relations into the sphere of a treaty. When the circle opens up to let in a new member, that may be a good reason to bring more relationships into the treaty sphere – in order to secure a new political or financial equilibrium, for example. There is no necessity about this, however, and it is certainly not the case that the treaty sphere must first be strengthened before the circle can open. Reinforcement often comes later.

It is up to the intermediate world of the members to digest the actual event that the arrival of an outsider represents, to absorb it and if necessary to conduct into the inner sphere the forces it releases – not the other way around.

AFTER THE TOWERS

That the fall of the Berlin Wall meant, on closer examination, a return of history is one of the insights in the historical synthesis by Judt, *Postwar*, of 2005. In the spring of 2004, German Foreign Minister Fischer made the switch from a 'constitutional' Europe, as advocated in his Berlin speech of 12 May 2000, to a 'strategic' Europe, a geopolitical player. He says himself that 9/11 was a decisive factor in this. His French counterpart at the time claims never to have been surprised: Hubert Védrine, *Continuer l'Histoire*, Paris, 2007. Nor was veteran American political scientist Calleo, who, in a rewarding book written just before 9/11, warned of the situation following the 'frozen parenthesis' of the Cold War: 'A Europe returning to its normal history is not an altogether reassuring prospect' (David P. Calleo, *Rethinking Europe's Future*, Princeton, 2001, p. 3).

For European political moves on and after 9/11, see the publications by Peter Ludlow about the European Council meetings of September, October and December 2001, as well as Jan Reckmann, *Außenpolitische Reaktionen der Europäische Union auf die Terroranschläge vom 11. September*, Münster, 2004; Mareike Kleine, *Die Reaktion der EU auf den 11. September. Zu Kooperation und Nicht-Kooperation in der inneren und äußeren Sicherheit*, Münster, 2004; and Javier Argomaniz, *The EU and Counter-terrorism. Politics, polity and policies after 9/11*, London, 2011.

For the creation of new treaty articles on foreign policy after 2001, including the appointment of a permanent president of the European Council, see the works named in Chapter 2, 'The host on the steps', on the European Convention and the intergovernmental conference that followed it (2002–04).

PART III: THE QUEST FOR A PUBLIC

WINNING APPLAUSE

A great deal of political philosophy has been focused on the public as the basis of a free political order. Nowadays, in the wake of Jürgen Habermas' influential body of work, this is sometimes reduced to the 'public sphere', which Habermas sees as a place where civil society can articulate its interests, making the public something like the totality of rational participants in public debate. Even if this leads to important research on the sociological and linguistic conditions necessary for the creation of a 'public space' (see several titles in Chapter 9, 'Drama'), the public the politicians deal with consists of more than those rational citizens who send letters to newspapers and vote every few years. The public grumbles and growls, it weeps and applauds, it demonstrates and cheers, it has wishes, gets bored – above all, it is unpredictable. These manifestations have direct or potential political significance.

Three astute twentieth-century political philosophers remind us, each in his or her own way, of the scope and power of this 'public life': Dewey, Arendt and Schmitt. American John Dewey's *The Public and its Problems*, Athens, OH, 1954 (orig. 1927), especially chs. 1–3, is still inspiring. His public emerges in response to events coming from outside, or to the indirect consequences of human action: perpetually changing, it poses questions that politics has to answer. For the German-American philosopher Hannah Arendt, a public space, where people share their words and deeds, is a precondition of human freedom; see her main work *The Human Condition*, Chicago and London, 1998 (orig. 1958), especially chs. 7, 27 and 28. While Dewey and Arendt place the public in a constituent role, for the constitutional expert and dubious Nazi ideologue Carl Schmitt it is above all in a position to react, to acclaim, which is to say to confer or perpetuate power by applauding, or indeed by chastising with its silence, or by jeering. Schmitt, like Arendt, displays a powerful awareness of the living, capricious nature of the public; see for instance Carl Schmitt, *Verfassungslehre*, Berlin, 1993, pp. 243–4.

In view of the clarity of his argument, we look to John R. Searle, *The Construction of Social Reality*, London, 1995, for the status of social phenomena. The basic idea of what Searle calls 'social constructivism' can be defended in other ways.

For the politico-philosophical problem of the acceptance of a rule, we turn to the legal positivism of H.L.A. Hart, *The Concept of Law*, Oxford, 1997. His 1961 theory is not uncontested, but his distinctions between primary and secondary rules, and between the internal and external perspectives on acceptance, offer a good basis for argumentation.

7 THE GERMAN STRATEGY: CREATING COMPANIONS IN DESTINY

National identity and borders. Among the more influential authors in the historical and sociological debate on national identity are Ernest Gellner (*Nations and Nationalism*, Oxford, 1983); E.J. Hobsbawm (*Nations and Nationalism Since 1780. Programme, myth, reality*, Cambridge, 1992); and Anthony D. Smith (for example *National Identity*, London, 1991). Here we find a good deal of material on nineteenth-century nation-building. The underlying debate again turns on the vicious circle of foundation: Which comes first, nation or state? A British historian, Smith distinguishes between 'ethnic' and 'civil' nationalism, but in the end he places the emphasis on a shared ancestry, an ethnic grounding, as a precondition for modern nations. Gellner and Hobsbawm by contrast stress the 'artificial' character of national identity. Hobsbawm writes crisply: 'Nations do not make states and nationalisms, but the other way around' (Hobsbawm, *Nations*, p. 10). Gellner notes with some regret: 'A man must have a nationality as he must have a nose and two ears. All this seems obvious, though, alas, it is not true. But that it should have come to seem so very obvious is indeed an aspect, perhaps the very core, of the problem of nationalism. Having a nation is not an inherent attribute of humanity, but it has now come to appear as such' (Gellner, *Nations*, p. 6).

There are no 'natural' groups; any group that calls itself a people or a nation does so as the result of a self-definition, writes Norwegian anthropologist Barth in his influential introduction to Fredrik Barth (ed.), *Ethnic Groups and Boundaries. The social organization of cultural difference*, Prospect Heights, 1998 (orig. 1969), pp. 9–38. Of course a group may base its self-definition on race, culture, religion or language, but Barth claims that such 'objective' criteria do not explain the origin, function or durability of such groups, nor the fact that individuals can cross ethnic boundaries. He therefore turns the whole issue around: a shared culture is not the cause but the result of ethnic organisation. Self-definition determines which elements we deploy as markers and which are left in the shadows. (During the Yugoslav Civil War, for example, certain differences in pronunciation between 'Serbian' and 'Croatian', which no one any longer noticed, were again made relevant to ethnic identification, causing a single ethnic group to divide into several.) In a seemingly innocuous but radical sentence, Barth states that what we need to investigate is 'the ethnic boundary that defines the group, not the cultural stuff that it encloses' (p. 15). In contemporary society the provision of a collective self-identity and therefore the fixing of a boundary is pre-eminently a function of politics: Who belongs with us, and who doesn't? This inescapable arbitrariness expresses itself in the existence and enforcement of a border.

HOW DO WE BECOME ONE?

Julien Benda and the European nation. At least one author frankly calls for a repeat of nineteenth-century nation-building on a European scale. In the interwar years it was the French intellectual Julien Benda who, with his *Discours à la nation européenne*, Paris, 1979 (orig. 1933), took this view. His pamphlet is an explicit response to Fichte's *Reden an die Deutsche Nation* (1807–08), the source text of the nationalistic programme. Benda faithfully follows the prescription for nineteenth-century nationalism, presenting a gallery of European heroes, for example.

Cultural politics

Two useful and closely-reasoned books about attempts by the institutional inner sphere to awaken a single European identity, both of them critical, are Cris Shore, *Building Europe. The cultural politics of European integration*, London and New York, 2000, and Tobias Theiler, *Political Symbolism and European Integration*, Manchester, 2005. Shore, who is British, tried, as a political anthropologist, to comprehend 'the native's point of view'; he immersed himself in the Commission for ten months to uncover the ways of thinking, motives and self-image of the 'builders of Europe'. Theiler, a Swiss political scientist, carried out research based on documents and interviews into the Commission's initiatives in the fields of culture, media and education since the 1970s. He rightly studies not only the successes, such as student exchange programmes, but also the failures, which are at least as instructive.

Among historians there is a relatively strong awareness of the political, identity-forming side of the stories they write; see various reflections in Attila Pók, Jörn Rüsen and Jutta Scherrer (eds.), *European History. Challenge for a common future*, Hamburg, 2002, and Alain Bergounioux et al., *Faire des Européens? L'Europe dans l'enseignement de l'histoire, de la géographie et de l'éducation civique*, Paris, 2006.

Flag

For the Council of Europe's choice of design for the flag, see Robert Bichet, 'Drapeau', in Yves Hersant and Fabienne Durand-Bogaert, *Europes. De l'Antiquité au XXe siècle. Anthologie critique et commentée*, Paris, 2000, pp. 807–11. For the ceremony of the first raising of the flag by the Community, in 1986, see Theiler, *Political Symbolism*, pp. 1–2. The semantic compromise of calling the flag a 'logo' was the brainwave of the then Dutch ambassador to the Community; see Charles Rutten, *Aan de wieg van Europa en andere Buitenlandse Zaken. Herinneringen van een diplomaat*, Amsterdam, 2005, pp. 175–6.

Money

The account of how the euro banknotes were designed is based on two reports by the expert committees that made proposals for the 'themes' and the 'features'. They are the 'Interim report to the European Monetary Institute's Working Group on Printing and Issuing a European Banknote: On the selection of a theme for the European banknote series' of May 1995, by the Theme Selection Advisory Group and from the almost identically composed Feature Selection Advisory Group the report 'Selection of Design Features: Report of the European Monetary Institute's Working Group on Printing and Issuing a European Banknote', of November 1995. The reports were 'confidential', but in July 2012 both could be found on the website of the European Central Bank (www.ecb.int/euro/pdf/preparation/Theme_report.pdf and www.ecb. int/euro/pdf/preparation/Feature_report.pdf).

WHY ARE WE TOGETHER?

On the joint search by the member states for reasons for being together – as distinct from unification – there is little truly methodical work available. The account here is based on official debates between the member states at specific times as reported in preambles, treaty texts and other decisions: at foundation; following British accession in 1973; regarding the admission of Central and Eastern European states; during the drafting of the constitutional treaty.

For the 'historical basis' provided to the Six in the person of Charlemagne, and its use, especially by the German Christian Democrats, see Dirk Schümer, *Das Gesicht Europas. Ein Kontinent wächst zusammen*, Munich, 2004, pp. 62–6. For a historian's criticism of this particular myth, see Johannes Fried, 'Karl, der grosse Europäer? Ein dunkler Leuchtturm', *Der Spiegel*, 1 March 2002, special 1/2002, pp. 24–33.

The literature on the historical and cultural unity of the continent as a whole, as distinct from its neighbours Africa, Asia and the Middle East, is immense. Several titles are given in the Prologue, 'Three European spheres' ('The outer sphere'). An excellent synthesis of twenty-five centuries of European history, with its moments of unity and of diversity, is provided by Polish-French historian Krzysztof Pomian, *L'Europe et ses nations*, Paris, 1990. Admirably panoramic and rare in its equal stress on the western and eastern halves of the continent is Norman Davies, *Europe. A history*, New York, 1998. An original and acute insight into European identity is given in Rémi Brague, *Europe, la voie romaine*, Paris, 1993, which seeks European unity in 'Latinity'.

8 THE ROMAN STRATEGY: SECURING CLIENTS

The quoted extract from Monty Python ('What have the Romans ever done for us?') was paraphrased in a propaganda film by the European Movement and several other organisations: see www.whathaseuropedone.org. In academic literature, too, comparison has been made between this type of legitimacy and the Roman Empire. A stern Joseph Weiler said on the occasion of the introduction of citizenship in the Union treaty: 'to conceptualize European citizenship around needs . . . and rights is an end-of-millennium version of bread-and-circus politics' (Weiler, *The European Constitution*, p. 335).

RIGHTS AND FREEDOMS

The remarkable PhD thesis by Paul Magnette, *La citoyenneté européenne. Droits, politiques, institutions*, Brussels, 1999, presents among other things the distinction between 'isopolitical' and 'sympolitical' rights.

On the creation of individual rights in the treaties of Paris and Rome, including the role of Italy, see Willem Maas, *Creating European Citizens*, Lanham, 2007, pp. 11–26, as well as his earlier 'The genesis of European rights', *Journal of Common Market Studies* 43:5 (2005) pp. 1009–25.

The role of Spain regarding the adoption of citizenship in the Union treaty is stressed on all sides. See the Spanish government's memorandum 'The road to European citizenship', Council document SN 3940/90 of 24 September 1990, in Laursen and Vanhoonacker, *The Intergovernmental Conference*, pp. 328–32, and the article by Spanish minister for European

Affairs (later Eurocommissioner and finance minister) Solbes in Pedro Solbes Mira, 'La citoyenneté européenne', *Revue du Marché Commun* 345 (1991), pp. 168–70.

The fact that the British had better things to do in Maastricht than to thwart 'citizenship' is clear from a hilarious reconstruction of their last-minute panic over the euro in Kenneth Dyson and Kevin Featherstone, *The Road to Maastricht. Negotiating monetary and economic union*, Oxford, 1999, pp. 659–63. For the supporting role played by Denmark – an accord on condition of a European ombudsman – see Peter Biering, 'The Danish proposal to the Intergovernmental Conference on Political Union', in P. Nikiforos Diamandouros et al., *The European Ombudsman. Origin, establishment, evolution*, Luxembourg, 2005, pp. 38–51. The Danes had introduced their ombudsman plan back in 1985 during negotiations on the Single European Act, but at too late a stage. In 1991 they were on time and received support from Spain.

PROTECTION

For the part played by farmers in the seizures of power both by Mussolini (Po Valley) and by Hitler (Schleswig-Holstein) – and therefore the fear of a repeat after 1945 – see Robert O. Paxton, *The Anatomy of Fascism*, New York and London, 2004, pp. 58–67. For the transition from national to European protection of agriculture in the years 1945–57 see Milward, *The European Rescue*, pp. 224–317. The negotiations between the Six that led to the famous *Nuit du blé* of 15 December 1963, when a European grain price was set for the first time, are covered in N. Piers Ludlow, *The European Community and the Crises of the 1960s. Negotiating the Gaullist challenge*, London and New York, 2006, pp. 32–9. A clear description of the early years from the perspective of the authoritative agriculture commissioner can be found in Johan van Merriënboer, *Mansholt. Een biografie*, Amsterdam, 2006, pp. 236–320.

Studies on European regional policy often suffer from a fascination with 'multi-level governance'. This approach to public administration theory, with buzzwords such as 'networking', 'complexity', 'decentralisation' and 'nested authorities', is the ideal intellectual smokescreen for administrative client politics, by means of which Brussels binds subnational governmental entities to it by allocating them money in ways that bypass the nation states. Until 1988 regional subsidies were paid to the capitals, which were obliged to channel them to the regions. At the urging of Commission President Delors and under pressure from Spain (a member since 1986), the sums increased, direct links were created between the Commission and the regions and regional policy was renamed 'cohesion policy'. In the Treaty of Maastricht (1992), 'social and economic cohesion' was specified as a goal. A short time later, and in close connection with this development, 'multi-level governance theory' made its appearance in political science; see Gary Marks, 'Structural policy and multi-level governance in the EC', in Alan W. Cafruny and Glenda G. Rosenthal (eds.), *The State of the European Community. The Maastricht debate and beyond*, Boulder, 1993, pp. 391–411. In this way of thinking the regions – federal states, provinces, regional authorities, conurbations – were promoted to a 'third level'. See Udo Bullmann (ed.), *Die Politik der dritten Ebene. Regionen im Europa der Union*, Baden-Baden, 1994. Influential were Liesbet Hooghe (ed.), *Cohesion Policy and European Integration. Building multi-level governance*, Oxford, 1996, and, by two of the authors already named, Liesbet Hooghe and Gary Marks, *Multi-Level Governance and European Integration*, Lanham, 2001.

On the concept of solidarity, see the themed issue 'Über Solidarität' of *Transit. Europäische Revue* 32 (Winter 2006/07). An English-language selection from those contributions can be found in Krzysztof Michalski (ed.), *What Holds Europe Together? Conditions of European solidarity*, Budapest, 2006. The more problematic aspects of solidarity are examined in the quoted essay by Kurt Biedenkopf, 'In Vielfalt geeint. Was halt Europa zusammen?' (pp. 13–29; orig. in *Transit* 26 (Winter 2003/04), pp. 29–47), and the very worthwhile Janos Matyas Kovacs, 'Between resentment and indifference: Narratives of solidarity in the enlarging Union' (pp. 54–85; also in *Transit* 32 Winter 2006/07, pp. 42–66). Kovacs dissects views about solidarity articulated in the 'West' and 'East', which took shape in the battle over regional funding.

For the strategy of results, as pursued by the Barroso Commission after the blow of the referendum results, see for example David Howarth, 'Internal policies: the Commission defends the EU consumer', *Journal of Common Market Studies* 46 (2008), pp. 91–107.

9 THE GREEK STRATEGY: SEDUCING THE CHORUS

The claim that 'Greek' legitimacy presumes the basis of a shared 'German' identity is known in the literature as the 'no demos thesis'. The term comes from J.H.H. Weiler, 'Does Europe need a Constitution? Demos, telos and the German Maastricht decision', *European Law Journal* 1:3 (1995), pp. 219–58. The idea is of course older – French president de Gaulle was its most consistent political exponent – but see also, for example, Spanish intellectual and diplomat Salvador de Madariaga in 1960: 'An Assembly elected by universal suffrage presupposes a nation. Europe is not and will never be a nation. It is a cluster of nations. Its Assembly must therefore be elected by the national parliaments' (Salvador de Madariaga, 'Critique de l'Europe', *European Yearbook V*, in Hugh Beesley, 'Direct elections to the European Parliament', in idem et al., *Limits and Problems of European Integration*, The Hague, 1963, p. 89).

The position of the German Constitutional Court is characterised by Weiler as the 'soft' version of the no demos thesis, or 'the "Not Yet" version: Although there is no demos now the possibility for the future is not precluded a priori'. He contrasts it with the 'hard' version, which 'does not only dismiss that possibility as objectively unrealistic but also as undesirable' (Weiler, 'Does Europe need a constitution?', pp. 229–30). This debate cannot be settled theoretically. The creation of a directly elected European parliament signified de facto a political defeat for the hard version of the no demos thesis, with the result that European democracy is living in a time of 'not yet'.

Unison

Two classic politico-legal theses have been written about the European Parliament and its predecessor: P.J.G. Kapteyn, *L'Assemblée commune de la Communauté du Charbon et de l'Acier. Essai de parlementarisme européen*, Leiden, 1962, and S. Patijn, *De uitbreiding van de bevoegdheden van het Europees Parlement*, Rotterdam, 1973. Both display excellent knowledge of the Parliament from the inside. Useful for the stage the debate had reached at the time, and written with great feeling for the subject, are Hugh Beesley, 'Direct elections to the European Parliament', in idem et al., *Limits and Problems of European Integration*, The Hague, 1963, and David Marquand, *A Parliament for Europe*, London, 1979.

Today's most commonly used reference work, written by a former British Europarliamentarian with co-authors, mainly focusing on internal organisation and functioning and now in its eighth edition, is Richard Corbett, Francis Jacobs and Michael Shackleton, *The European Parliament*, London, 2011, which includes a treasure trove of factual information. A rare combination of political analysis and historical anecdote from 1979 onwards comes from a former secretary-general of the Parliament Julian Priestly, *Six Battles that Shaped Europe's Parliament*, London, 2008. It reports, for example (pp. 6–22), on the budgetary crisis of 1979–80, during which Priestly was a colleague of the instigator Piet Dankert. No less lively, by the same author and Stephen Clark, is *Europe's Parliament. People, places, politics*, London, 2012.

For political citizenship, see the titles given in Chapter 8, 'Rights and freedoms'.

For the constitutional treaty, see the titles given in Chapter 2, 'The host on the steps'.

That the Greek Pericles' motto succumbed to Finnish and Irish resistance is mentioned by Guy Milton (Council Secretariat) in a written message to the author dated 27 October 2008.

Polyphonic

Over the past two decades, the body of literature on the role of national parliaments has grown rapidly. See for instance: Andreas Maurer and Wolfgang Wessels (eds.), *National Parliaments on their Ways to Europe. Losers or late-comers?*, Baden-Baden, 2001; John O'Brennan and Tapio Raunio, *National Parliaments Within the Enlarged European Union. From 'victims' of integration to competitive actors*, London, 2007; and Olaf Tans, Carla Zoethout and Jit Peters, *National Parliaments and European Democracy. A bottom-up approach*, Groningen, 2007. In recent years both the coming into force of the Lisbon Treaty and parliamentary scrutiny in the Eurozone crisis have drawn further attention to the issue; see for instance Ian Cooper, 'A "virtual third chamber" for the European Union: National parliaments after the Treaty of

Lisbon', *West European Politics* 35:3 (2012), pp. 441–65, and Timm Beichelt, 'Recovering space lost: the German Bundestag's new potential in European politics', *German Politics* 21:2 (2012), pp. 143–60.

A much discussed argument for a European Senate composed of national parliamentarians can be found in Larry Siedentop, *Democracy in Europe*, London, 2000, pp. 147–9. See also a book by a British expert on Europe, Charles Grant, *EU2010. An optimistic vision for the future*, London, 2000, which inspired a speech delivered by British premier Tony Blair in Warsaw (6 October 2000).

On the nine accession referendums of 2003, see a special journal issue compiled by Aleks Szczerbiak and Paul Taggart in *West European Politics* 27:4 (2004), pp. 557–777. The most important lesson is contained in the title of Szczerbiak's contribution about Poland: 'History trumps government unpopularity' (p. 671). See also Sara Binzer Hobolt, *Europe in Question. Referendums on European integration*, Oxford, 2009. A multifaceted monograph about a pan-European referendum is Andreas Auer and Jean-François Flauss (eds.), *Le référendum européen. Actes du colloque international de Strasbourg, 21–22 février 1997*, Brussels, 1997. Such a pan-European referendum was indeed proposed by de Gaulle way back in the 1940s, but never held.

DRAMA

The multilingual nature of Europe is analysed in Abram de Swaan, *Words of the World. The global language system*, Amsterdam, 2001, ch. 8. See also Philippe Van Parijs, 'Europe's linguistic challenge', *Archives européennes de sociologie* 45:1 (2004), pp. 113–54, and Dominik Hanf, Klaus Malacek and Elise Muir (eds.), *Langues et construction européenne*, Brussels, 2010.

A great deal of research has been carried out into the creation of a 'European public space'. See the large research project, covering seven countries, 'The transformation of political mobilisation and communication in European public spheres', with results at www.europub.wzb.de, and in Ruud Koopmans and Paul Statham (eds.), *The Making of a European Public Sphere. Media discourse and political contention*, Cambridge, 2010. Other recent studies in the field include: Thomas Risse, *A Community of Europeans? Transnational identities and public spheres*, Cornell, 2010; Patrick Bijsmans, *Debating Europe. Reflections on EU affairs in the public sphere*, Maastricht, 2011; and Paul Statham and Hans-Jörg Trenz, *The Politicization of Europe. Contesting the constitution in the mass media*, London, 2013. A useful distinction is that between the 'public sphere' and the 'public policy sphere', in other words between a general public and a professional public of specific interests and experts (such as are undoubtedly present in Brussels); see Jos de Beus, 'The European Union as a community: An argument about the public sphere in international society and politics', in Paul van Seters, *Communitarianism and Law*, Lanham, 2006.

The stimulating collection Kalypso Nicolaïdes and Justine Lacroix (eds.), *European Stories. Intellectual debates on Europe in national contexts*, Oxford, 2010, offers many examples of how 'Europe' means different things to different people across the continent. An underestimated effect of the Europeanisation of national political spheres is examined in Cécile Leconte, *Understanding Euroscepticism*, London, 2010.

An inspiring book is Bernard Manin, *Principes du gouvernement représentatif*, Paris, 1995, a historical and philosophical investigation of the relationship between political representatives and those represented. Manin demonstrates a strong grasp of the temporal effects of elections, of the political game as the anticipation of a retroactive verdict. He introduces the term 'audience democracy' (*démocratie du public*) for the contemporary form of democracy, following 'parliamentarism' (*c.* 1780–1880) and 'party democracy' (*c.* 1880–1980). The concept captures the impact of today's mass media, but should not make us forget that the public is constituent for every form of democracy, or indeed politics.

Acknowledgments

A book such as this is the fruit not only of study and ideas, but of unexpected encounters and friendships. I should like to thank first of all those who shared their experience of European politics with me while I started researching it, in particular former foreign ministers Jozias van Aartsen and Joschka Fischer; former senior Council civil servants Jean-Paul Jacqué and Jacques Keller-Noëllet; P.J.G. Kapteyn, who served as a judge at the European Court; former Belgian ambassador Philippe de Schoutheete and Belgian diplomat Peter Moors; former Dutch central banker André Szász; and E.P. ('Mom') Wellenstein, who, as young diplomat, was present at the 1950 Paris treaty negotiations and among many other things became secretary-general of the High Authority of the Coal and Steel Community that emerged as a result. During my first stay in Brussels a decade ago, I had the good fortune to learn much from Commissioner Frits Bolkestein and my colleagues Claire Bury, Hans Kribbe, Joshua Livestro and Ben Smulders, as well as from Maryem van den Heuvel and Tom Eijsbouts. Before that, my academic teachers Frank Ankersmit (University of Groningen) and Marcel Gauchet (EHESS, Paris) had encouraged me, directly and by example, not to eschew the big questions of our time. When I at last went into writing mode, I found a dream-team of first readers in Ton Nijhuis at the University of Amsterdam and Patrick Everard, my publisher at Historische Uitgeverij, as well as in Coen Simon, Sipko de Boer and Maarten Brands. Among all those who commented on the Dutch or French editions, I should like in particular to thank – in order of appearance – Christophe de Voogd, Pieter van den Blink, Rob Danz, Daniel Cunin, Olivier Vanwersch-Cot, Jim Cloos, Christine Roger, Larry Siedentop, Philippe Van Parijs and Richard Corbett. For their comments on drafts of the new Preface, thanks are due to Hugo Brady, Sir Colin Budd and Guy Milton. This updated English edition exists as a result of the confidence of Yale's

Robert Baldock and Rachael Lonsdale and the unrivalled dedication of translator Liz Waters. But this book would never have been written in the first place were it not for the constant and vital presence of my wife, Manon de Boer.

Over the past three years as part of the team surrounding European Council President Herman Van Rompuy, it has been a pleasure to share with colleagues such as Frans van Daele, Didier Seeuws, Sarah Nelen, Alice Richard and many others from across the Union, a direct experience of the event-driven nature of European politics.

Index

see also Treaty of Franco-German
    Friendship
Frankfurt Parliament (1848) 216–17
Franklin, Benjamin 82
free trade zone 154, 167, 173
freedom 3, 14, 32, 273, 274, 303, 306, 312
    of movement 254, 256–61
freedoms 254–61, 269, 287, 290, 305, 306
    four freedoms 259
    see also rights
French Revolution 3, 223, 236
Friedrich Wilhelm IV, King of Prussia 217
Friendship Treaty *see* Treaty of
    Franco-German Friendship
Fukuyama, Francis, *The End of History*
    182, 202
functionalism 2, 5, 330–1

Gadamer, Hans-Georg 181
Gaitskell, Hugh 39
Galilei, Galileo 237
Galileo satellite project 237
Gemeinschaft and *Gesellschaft* 16
Genscher, Hans-Dietrich 102, 103, 347
geopolitics 33, 37, 132, 134, 158, 197
    after fall of Berlin Wall 224, 346
    geopolitical balance 173, 200
    shift eastwards 197–9
    see also enlargement
    see also outer sphere
Georgia (country) 200, 208, 209
Geremek, Bronisław 196
'German strategy' 223, 226–51, 268, 269,
    270, 273, 349–50
Germany
    Bundesrat 115
    Bundestag 58, 59, 101, 102, 108, 115,
        133, 183, 293
    and Coal and Steel Treaty 42–3
    Constitutional Court
        (*Bundesverfassungsgericht*) 99, 100,
        112–13, 114–17, 149, 276
    and Council of Ministers debate (1965)
        57–8
    cultural/historical identity 223
    German question 139–43
        see also 'German strategy'
    national election 54, 59, 60
    Nazi regime 3, 137, 166, 183, 197, 246,
        267
    pariah status 134, 141
    partition and occupation of 137–8
    political motives 134–5

rearmament 145, 149, 151
    and redistribution 267
    and 1985 treaty change 102
    unification 134, 151, 183–9, 197, 346
    see also Berlin Wall, fall of; East
        Germany; Franco-German
        relations; Treaty of Franco-German
        Friendship; West Germany
Gibraltar 15
Giscard d'Estaing, Valéry 58, 239, 329
    as Convention chairman 95, 118–19,
        122, 206–7, 290, 291, 298, 346
    and European Council 23, 178–9,
        206–7, 282, 346
globalisation 225
Golan Heights 176
González, Felipe 258
Gorbachev, Mikhail 185, 346
Gore, Al 305
governance 7
government (as term) 10
Greece
    Arendt on 302
    and citizenship 287
    city states 255
    debt crisis (2010) 302
    and democracy 248
    financial support of 267–8
    joins Community (1981) 74
    and Luxembourg Compromise 77
    and Macedonia 193
    and Soviet Union 138–9
    and treaty change 102, 104, 105
    'Greek strategy' 223–4, 229, 268, 269, 270,
        273–309, 353–4
Grundtvig, N.F.S. 237
Guizot, François 3

Haas, Ernst, *The Uniting of Europe* 6–7,
    10, 330
Habermas, Jürgen 8, 208, 302
Habsburg dynasty 228
The Hague, summit (1969) 162–3, 172,
    174, 224, 345
Hain, Peter 121
Hallstein, Walter 4, 55, 56–7, 58, 60,
    64–5, 70, 79, 80, 330, 336,
    342, 345
Hamilton, Alexander 82, 84
Hart, H.L.A. 218–19, 349
Hartling, Poul 178
Havel, Václav 196, 238
Heath, Edward 171, 178